Current Issues in

Marriage and
the Family

Current Issues in *Marriage and the Family*

Fourth Edition

J. Gipson Wells

MISSISSIPPI STATE UNIVERSITY

Macmillan Publishing Company

NEW YORK

Macmillan Publishing Company
866 Third Avenue, New York, New York 10022

Collier Macmillan Canada, Inc.

Library of Congress Cataloging-in-Publication Data

Wells, J. Gipson.
Current issues in marriage and the family.

    Includes bibliographical references.
    1. Marriage—United States. 2. Family—United
States. 3. Divorce—United States. 4. Parenthood.
I. Title.
HQ536.C88 1988   306.8   87-10246
ISBN 0-02-425490-8

Printing: 1 2 3 4 5 6 7   Year: 8 9 0 1 2 3 4

ISBN 0-02-425490-8

Preface

to the Fourth Edition

It is difficult enough to anticipate and predict new issues prior to their emergence, and they are not always recognized when they first appear. However it is even more difficult to predict when an issue will decline and cease to be of great concern to enough people to still rate being referred to as an issue. Social scientists tend to believe, after they have spent considerable time and effort studying and analyzing a particular issue, that it then should be subject to solution and thereafter cease to be an issue. Unfortunately, the public does not always readily accept the solutions offered by social science, and consequently, issues have a way of staying around much longer than seems necessary.

Take, for example, the abortion controversy. When the first edition of this book was published in 1975, I thought that the section on abortion might be out of date already, owing to the relatively recent (1973) U. S. Supreme Court decision that effectively nullified most state laws which had forbidden elective abortions. It appeared that the controversy was settled at last and that the issue simply would disappear. But this has not been the case, because the various sides in this controversy still are battling as strongly as ever. The focus of the anti-abortion forces now is on gaining acceptance of a constitutional amendment to ban abortions, which would thus override the Supreme Court's decision. On the other hand, the major arguments used by both sides differ very little from the arguments used prior to the Court's decision. Thus, this new edition retains the section on the abortion controversy with only minor changes.

Several of the issues that were newly emergent with the earlier editions have been brought now into sharper focus and thus have been treated a

v

little differently in this revision. For example, the issue of having children continues to receive a great deal of attention. Also, most states now have passed new and somewhat reformed divorce laws, so that the emphasis in that section (Part Seven) now reflects those changes along with the increased concern over child custody practices, single parenthood, and remarriage.

One major issue that has exploded on the scene quite suddenly relates to all of the problems surrounding Acquired Immune Deficiency Syndrome (AIDS). That AIDS is a social problem (as well as a health problem) and also a social issue is beyond question. Except for the problem of stymatization, it is not at all clear to what extent it may become an issue closely related to marriage and family, other than in the manner that any other catastrophic illness might have an impact upon the families of those involved. Therefore, no effort has been made to include that topic in the new edition, and it remains to be seen whether this or any other new issue will emerge for later consideration.

I would like to thank those who have found this reader to be beneficial to their students over the years since the first edition. It is my hope that they will find this new edition to their liking as well. More specifically, I would like to thank Pam Davis, Karla Fisher, Susan Laughlin, Letitia Owens, Evelyn Sebren, Frances Walker, and Pat Woolington, all of whom worked on portions of the manuscript in its various stages. I would also like to thank my wife Mildred for her invaluable and timely editorial assistance in preparing the final version of the manuscript.

J.G.W.

Contents

x

Current Issues in

Marriage and

the Family

Introduction

J. Gipson Wells

Many of the crucial social issues currently confronting American society are issues that also are of central importance to the American family system as a basic social institution. In addition, these issues are important to individuals and the families to which most people belong. The society and the family face many common issues because the threads of family life in our culture have been so thoroughly interwoven with the general fabric of the society as to be almost of one cloth. The family always has been seen as the backbone of the nation, and there always has been a strong belief that "as the family goes, so goes the nation." Of course, this has been true to some extent of almost every nation, from an historical as well as a cross-cultural standpoint.

Although the continual fears and predictions that the undermining of the family will lead to the ultimate crumbling of the nation certainly are overblown, one can hardly deny that there is a close relationship between certain problems and issues of national significance and those problems and issues that confront the family. Obviously, one reason for this close relationship is the fact that the family is one of the most basic institutions of any society, and this certainly is no less true in American society.

Almost any current social issue is also a family issue: the question of the efficacy of marriage itself; the question of whether or not to have children, and if so, how many to have; questions related to what the nature of men's and women's roles should be; questions concerning reforms in the areas of divorce, abortion, child custody, child care, and other policy matters; and finally, questions concerning the future of marriage and the family. The purpose of the articles in this book is to take a brief and objective look at each of these problems or issues, viewing them mainly from the perspective of the sociology of marriage and the family rather than as general social problems. That is, the issues will be approached primarily as concerns of marriage and family, both institutionally and individually, and secondarily as they might be related to the larger society. It is certainly no coincidence that many of these issues are direct outgrowths of major social changes or movements that have occurred in our society in recent years, particularly the "sexual revolution" and the Women's Movement.

Essentially, the plan of the book is to deal with specific issues that have emerged, and where possible, to look at each from contrasting viewpoints. Within some of the book's first nine sections, which represent what are believed to be the major issues facing marriage and the family today, there will be several articles that present specific, often opposing, points of view on a given issue. Other sections deal with issues that are less well defined, and thus, specific or opposing viewpoints give way to more general presentations of the issues. The editor's commentaries, accompanying each section, also are designed to increase the reader's overall knowledge and understanding of the issues and to aid in maintaining an objective stance as the reader approaches each issue. The final section (Part Ten) presents commentary along with two articles that aptly deal with the future outlook for marriage and the family institution based on the current trends in some of the issues under scrutiny.

The thirty articles in this collection were gathered from diverse sources, such as widely distributed popular magazines, the more esoteric professional journals, and a few lesser-known national periodicals and reports. They present a broad range of viewpoints, and studying the variety of arguments surrounding each issue, will hopefully provide readers with the information necessary to make more informed judgments about these major questions confronting the family today.

SOME BASIC CONCEPTS

The terms *marriage* and *family* will appear dozens of times throughout this book, and certainly everyone has a pretty good idea what they mean. For most, however, the meanings are far too general, so that it probably is worthwhile to explore these terms for the purpose of giving them more depth and precision. To better our understanding of marriage and family in American society, it should be helpful to use more universal cross-cultural definitions of these concepts as points of departure. In his book, *The Family in Cross-Cultural Perspective*, William Stephens presents relatively universal definitions of both these terms. He defines marriage as "a socially legitimate sexual union, begun with a public announcement and undertaken with some idea of permanence; it is assumed with a more or less explicit marriage contract, which spells out the reciprocal rights and obligations between spouses, and between the spouses and their future children."[1] According to this definition, then there are four basic components that go together to create a marriage: social legitimation, public acknowledgment, an assumption of permanence, and reciprocal rights and obligations. Marriages in almost every culture of the world, both preliterate and modern, appear to have most of these basic components.

Marriage is also a "rite of passage," that is, a status-changing event through which all who wish to create a family unit ordinarily go. As everyone knows, the marriage event is an integral part of families in particular and of the family institution in general. Thus, Stephens bases his definition of family upon his prior definition of marriage. He defines family as "a social arrangement based upon marriage and the marriage contract, including recognition of the rights and duties of parenthood, common residence for husband, wife, and children, and reciprocal economic obligations between husband and wife."[2] This definition of family applies essentially to the family unit as a special social grouping, thus necessitating a conceptual differentiation between the family as a *conjugal* unit and family as an *institution*. However, some aspects of this definition might apply to the family as a basic social institution in the same sense that business, government, schools, and churches are basic social institutions.

Basic social institutions usually are defined in terms of the common functions that they perform for most societies. The family also might be defined in this manner. In most societies the family is the institution given the responsibility of bearing and rearing children, for the purpose of maintaining the population. Childbearing usually requires and allows the legitimation of sexual activity. Providing a legitimate means of sexual satisfaction unrelated to childbearing is also a major institutional function of marriage. In addition, there is a wide range of economic functions assigned to the family, such as providing food, clothing, and shelter for its members. Therefore, the family as an institution might be seen as something far more complex and comprehensive than the conjugal family as a small group. Nevertheless, it is the individual family groups of a society that in turn embody the broader social institution.

THEORETICAL VIEWPOINTS

A number of theoretical or conceptual frameworks have proved useful in analysis of marriage and family issues. Although some of the articles in this collection are journalistic in nature and thus do not reflect any particular theoretical orientation of sociology, the articles from the more scholarly sources do reflect one or more of the sociological frames of reference employed in family analysis. Additionally, the editor's commentaries, which accompany each section, often will rely upon one or a combination of these conceptual frameworks, although in most cases the frameworks will be implied rather than explicitly pointed out. In any event, the reader should be aware, at least in a superficial way, of the various theoretical points of view upon which the articles and commentary rest.

Four such theoretical viewpoints or conceptual frameworks will be delineated here. The first usually is referred to as the *institutional* approach because it deals with marriage and family as a basic institution of any society. One of the definitions of family presented above dealt with it as an institution among other social institutions, and this type of definition coincides very well with the institutional approach. This viewpoint is reflected particularly in those parts of the book in which the issues of concern arise from the relationship between the family and such other institutions as government, the economy, and religion. For example, the family is required to relate to the government with respect to such issues as the control and registration of marriage, the legal aspects of abortion, divorce, and child custody, and a number of other policy matters. The family institution and the religious institution encounter one another on such topics as the form and structure of marriage, whether or not to have children, abortions, and divorce reform. And finally, the relationship between family and the economy is of importance to such topics as marriage versus nonmarriage, men's and women's roles, having children, and to some extent, divorce. Obviously, any analysis of the family and the various issues and problems that confront it must concern itself also with the other social institutions with which the family is integrally involved.

The second conceptual framework might be referred to very generally as the *functional* approach, and as used here, it is not precisely equivalent to structural-functionalism as found in general sociological theory. However, it does retain a few important aspects of structural-functional theory. Under this approach, marriage and the family are defined in terms of their functions, that is, what they do in and for the larger society and its members. The assumption is made that all societal entities have certain functions to perform, and that when these functions are performed properly, society will operate in a reasonably well-organized fashion. Of course, this is an oversimplistic view of social organization based upon questionable assumptions about the nature of people and society, but it does serve as a useful analytical tool when dealing with the family, as well as with other social organizations and institutions.

Under this approach, one would define the family as the social grouping or organization that performs those functions or tasks that traditionally have been accepted as belonging to families. The circular nature of this definition is obvious at once, but the more complete discussion would go on to point out the particular functions that marriage and the family are expected to perform, such as the bearing and rearing of children to maintain the population and to give continuity and support to the culture, the provision of the basic physical necessities for its members, providing a center of affection and companionship for the individual, and providing a means for legitimate sexual satisfaction. There is a close relationship between the functional approach and the institutional approach, and it is made evident by the fact that institutions also were defined to some extent by their functions.

Using the functional approach, family-related issues or problems might be seen as occurring when something interferes with the organization or structure of the family so as to cause it to be unable to perform its functions properly. Furthermore, issues and controversies might arise when other institutions or organizations attempt to take away some of the family's functions, and in some cases, other institutions might try to force new functions upon it. This functional viewpoint might be utilized more specifically with such issues as abortion reform, in which there has been a move toward making such decisions an individual or family matter rather than a legal one. Also, certain issues concerned with the legitimation of sex outside of marriage, for example, might be viewed within this framework as an erosion of a traditional family function.

The third conceptual framework that might be of use here are the basic elements of *role theory*. They are useful to analyze behavior—in this case male-female interaction—in terms of the manner in which people relate to each other through the various roles they enact. Social roles are the behavior that is expected of individuals as they move from one social situation to another, playing a slightly different but related role in each particular situation. The family unit might very well be analyzed and understood as a system or network of social roles, with each family member enacting one or more social roles both within and outside of the family. *Sex roles*—the concept of most importance here—refers to those roles that are defined or differentiated on the basis of the sex of the person attempting to enact the role. In the most basic sense, female children are taught to act as females "ought to act," and male children are taught "masculine" behavior. The result is that most children are raised to play only the sexually appropriate roles, and most social roles have built into them connotations as to which sex should be playing them. There is also a great deal of pressure placed upon members of society to play only sexually appropriate roles. Thus, the effeminate male is disdained, as is sometimes the female who attempts to hold a traditionally male occupation.

This application of role theory will be developed further in Part Three, which deals with marital and family roles and also will be applied indirectly in those sections dealing with divorce, child custody, and child care.

Of increasing significance in the study of marital and family behavior is the theoretical framework referred to as *social exchange theory*. The basic idea behind this approach was borrowed from economic market theories, but it also bears a strong kinship to both functional theory and role theory. Exchange theory views social behavior as being motivated, in varying degrees, by the individuals' perceptions of the possible gains, losses, profits, and costs that might accrue in any given social situation. Social interaction is seen as operating within a market arena where persons attempt to maximize their profits and gains, while minimizing their costs and losses. Granted, this approach tends to cast society as a "dog eat dog" situation wherein everyone is out to get what he or she wants at the expense of others, but it is, nevertheless, a very useful approach to understanding behavior and has proven to have considerable analytical value.

The purpose of this very brief discussion of theoretical viewpoints is simply to alert the reader to the fact that many of the articles and most of the commentary rely upon one or a combination of them. However, these viewpoints are not always readily recognizable, and the reader's prior awareness of them should aid in the understanding of the material.

SOCIAL PROBLEMS AND SOCIAL ISSUES

The concerns of this book might become even more evident through a demonstration of what is meant by the concept of *social issues*. In defining this term, it should be useful also to differentiate between social issues on the one hand and the widely used concept of *social problems* on the other. To begin with the latter term, a social problem might be defined as a social condition or situation that either directly affects or is thought to have some effect upon a significant number of people in ways that are thought by many to be undesirable or detrimental, either to those affected by the situation or to the society in general; furthermore, it generally is thought that something can and/or ought to be done to alleviate the condition through societal action.

There are at least two significant aspects to this definition. First, there are some conditions that have an actual or direct effect upon individuals or segments of the population, whereas other conditions are only thought or perceived to be detrimental. Thus, one type might be referred to as real social problems and the other might be termed *pseudo*problems. For example, segments of most large cities have high rates of street crime, which certainly affects large numbers of people in an undoubtedly significant and direct way. Street crime would be considered a real social problem. On the other hand, many people believe that the sale and distribution of pornography is a serious social problem, when in fact almost all research evidence and professional opinion support the view that pornography essentially is harmless in most cases and might even be helpful to persons with certain kinds of sexual problems. This is an example of a pseudoproblem. However, whether problems are real or not, they nevertheless have an impact upon the society through their effects on public opinion, which in turn affects public policy.

The second significant aspect of the definition of social problems has to do with the number of people involved. There are, broadly speaking, two categories of people related to any social problem: those who are involved directly in creating or receiving its ill effects and those who simply are aware of or concerned about the problem from a distance. In some cases, for example, the former group might be relatively small with the latter segment of concerned citizens quite large and their concern quite strong. Such might be the case with heroin addiction, which directly affects a comparatively small number of people, but about which there is great and widespread concern.

The opposite type of social problem would be the situation in which large numbers are affected directly, but about which there is comparatively little public concern. Such is the case with alcoholism and alcohol abuse, which is estimated to affect more than ten million people, but about which the general public fails to express anything near the degree of concern so often heard regarding other drugs.

The concepts of social problems and social issues are in some ways related, but a social issue is somewhat different in that it is a situation or condition that generates at least two conflicting points of view, both of which may be competing for public acceptance and support. In addition, the competing sides in the issue might be attempting to either bring about or impede change through legislation, court action, or other means. Some examples of social issues are divorce reform, abortion, and cohabitation, which, among others, are considered in this book. In many cases, the same condition might be a social problem as well as a social issue, but there are many situations that are clearly one but not the other.

There are some additional ways in which social problems and social issues might be related. First, some social problems result in the creation of social issues, and this can occur in a number of ways. For example, the *issue* of marijuana legalization is a direct outgrowth of the *problem* of the abuse of marijuana and other drugs. From a conceptual standpoint, the problem and the issue might be seen as being separate from one another, although they do have a special relationship. Social problems also create social issues when heated differences of opinion arise among segments of the public, and perhaps among involved professional experts, over the manner of treatment or resolution of particular problems. An example would be the differences of opinion that exist with regard to the best manner of dealing with various kinds of crime and criminals. Crime is the social problem, and how to deal with it becomes the social issue.

One final way in which social problems and social issues are related is that there is rarely ever complete agreement, either public or professional, over which conditions are social problems and which are social issues. Furthermore, many define as problems some conditions that others might define as issues, and still others might think that a particular condition is neither a problem nor an issue.

CURRENT ISSUES IN MARRIAGE AND FAMILY

The concern of this book is with certain social issues that have a direct bearing upon marriage and family in American society. Some of the issues considered here are related to social problems in one or more of the ways mentioned earlier, whereas others have developed as issues somewhat independently of any specific problems. Most of the issues dealt with throughout the book already have been referred to in this introduction, but they will be more specifically delineated and organized in the book in the following manner:

1. ***To marry or not?***—This issue revolves basically around two questions. One has to do with whether an individual should choose marriage or the single life, and the other has to do with the viability of marriage as a major aspect of the family institution.

2. ***Marriage versus cohabitation***—With the increase in both the number of and the publicity given to couples living together without being married, the topic of cohabitation as it relates to marriage continues to be an issue in its own right.

3. ***Changing marital and family roles***—This issue began with a focus mainly on the roles and statuses of women. Then, the emphasis began to shift, giving more attention to the situation of men because their roles had begun to change primarily as a response to changes in women's roles. Increasingly now, the emphasis is being placed upon creating and maintaining an equitable, workable balance in the roles of both women and men.

4. ***Having children***—During the 1970s, concern over the question of whether or not to have children was generated mainly by public awareness and concern over such problems as resource depletion, pollution, and overpopulation. More recently, however, the basis of this concern over children has shifted to personal and family financial considerations, as well as to greater interest in the particular values of children themselves.

5. ***Childbearing alternatives***—The publicity given to radically different means for families to acquire children, alternative to the more traditional means of normal childbearing and adoption, has caused this whole topic to become a new issue. In addition, rapidly developing technology in this area has introduced new possibilities for which the society has yet to develop a set of norms and values.

6. ***The abortion controversy***—Although the major focus of this issue still is on the moral, religious, and legal aspects of abortion, recent activities have begun to make this whole issue an increasingly political one.

7. ***Divorce and remarriage***—Because most of the states now have some form of no-fault divorce procedures, there is less concern with changing divorce laws, the emphasis moving to problems of judicial application of the new laws. Also, there is concern for more fairness and equity in matters of child custody and support. The new articles in this section reflect the shift in concern about what happens after divorce.

8. ***Child care***—Finding adequate child care facilities is an increasingly difficult problem for dual-worker and single parent families. The issue, however, arises over who is to be responsible for providing that care—the government, employers, or parents.

9. ***Family policy***—To what extent should the society, through its government, involve itself in marital and family matters? Should government specifically implement policies designed to aid families or should it

be concerned only with individuals or with broader segments of the population? There is increasing controversy over the role and scope of government in family matters.

The final section of the book (Part Ten) is less issue oriented and includes two articles that are concerned with the future outlook for marriage and family in American society.

More detailed development of the various positions and shades of opinion on these issues will be found in the editor's commentary preceding the group of articles related to each issue.

NOTES

1 William Stephens, *The Family in Cross-Cultural Perspective* (New York: Holt, 1963), p. 5.

2 Ibid., p. 8.

Part

One

To Marry

or Not?

A basic assumption underlying most of the articles throughout this book is that most people will marry at least once during their lifetimes. Nevertheless, people in our society are increasingly questioning their own feelings and motivations with regard to getting married, whether entering upon a first marriage or moving into a second (or subsequent) marriage after divorce. Thus, it seems logical to begin with this most basic question with regard to marriage and family—whether or not one should marry. This issue, along with questions as to what form or structure intimate relationships should take, which is dealt with in Part Two, has been raised in recent years not only by young people, but with increasing frequency by older generations as well.

The question of marriage versus nonmarriage can be approached from at least two perspectives: from the standpoint of whether marriage is desirable or not for the society in general and from the standpoint of individual choice. On the one hand, the question might be raised as to the viability of continuing the institution of marriage in this or any other society; on the other hand, the issue might be viewed as dealing with the choice that each marriageable person faces as to whether or not he or she will choose marriage for himself or herself. Because marriage is currently and will be, for the foreseeable future, the overwhelming choice of most persons in our society, it is likely to remain an important institution, if not a totally viable one.

When questions concerning the viability of marriage first arose as a public issue (in the late 1960s), discussion was focused mainly upon such then-current social concerns as over-population and environmental pollution, along with increasing concern over the rising divorce rate and the "new" issue of sexual equality. Thus, the view emerged in an abstract sense that perhaps more people should relinquish marriage as a way of controlling population, pollution, and the possible negative consequences of divorce. The emerging feminists at that time were also beginning to present the more radical view that marriage was the major oppressor of women, limiting their freedom and personal development. These points-of-view were the focus of some attention in the first edition of this book (1973), and were reflected in the articles chosen to illustrate the marriage/singlehood issue.

Since that time, there has been a shift away from social concerns to the more personal point-of-view on marriage. Young people seem to be far less concerned about how one's marriage might affect the society in the abstract, as how it will most surely affect their own private and personal lives. Some see this shift as representing more self-centeredness, and it is certainly more pragmatic. On the other hand, it may also represent a recognition that marriage, as an institution, is probably not going to disappear after all, and that a change in marriage rates will not likely have much effect upon major societal problems. Thus, the question becomes a more personal one, as it probably should be.

The question of whether or not to marry, from the individual perspective, also has two sides; that is, does one choose the single life in the sense that he or she wishes to live alone or with someone of the same sex or perhaps remain with one's family of orientation (one's parents); or does one simply wish to avoid the legal and social bonds of matrimony while in fact living in a quasi-married state usually referred to as cohabitation? The basic issue here is whether cohabitation is a total rejection of marriage or rather an attempt to alter its traditional form. Part Two of this book deals with the question of marriage versus cohabitation, but the fourth article in this section also is concerned in part with the questions of cohabitation and the form of marriage.

As stated earlier, the vast majority of people in this country, as well as in other countries, choose marriage over the single life. In the United States, over 95 per cent of all people will marry at least once during their lifetimes. As long as records have been kept and statistics compiled on marriage, the rates of marriage have remained relatively high. Beginning in the 1860s, the marriage rate fluctuated between 8.5 and 9 per 1,000 population, with a slight but steady increase in the rate. This slow increase continued until 1920, when the rate reached 12.0. A sharp decline then occurred, with the rate reaching its lowest recorded point in 1932, at 7.9. Several rapid rises and falls followed, with the highest historical rate of 16.4 occurring in 1946, which, incidentally, was also the year of the highest divorce rate in American history until recent years.[1] The marriage rate declined to 8.4 for the year 1958 but generally was on the rise again until more fluctuations appeared in the 1970s.[2]

Marriage and Divorce Rates: United States, 1935-1985

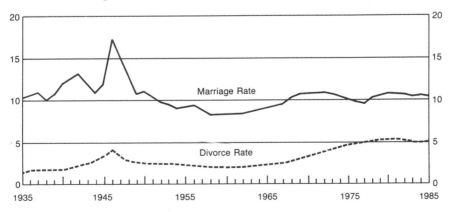

Source: National Center for Health Statistics, U.S. Department of Health and Human Services.

The decline in the marriage rate from 1972 through 1976 was thought by many to indicate a general decline in marriages that would become a major trend.[3] However, the most recent data show another increase in the rate.[4] Thus, there is presently no clear trend and no clear interpretation of recent data to indicate that marriage is on the decline. Most experts are now of the opinion that marriage rates will remain high, although there will be occasional minor fluctuations.

These changes in marriage rates result from a number of unknown elements as well as from some that are clearly understood. One element that clearly influences the marriage rate is the average age at which people marry. Young people, particularly those entering their first marriage, are doing so at a later average age than in previous years. Around 1955, the trend toward increasingly younger ages of first marriage reversed, and for the last thirty years there has been a steady rise in the age of first marriage. In the last ten years the rise has been more rapid, with the median age at first marriage in 1985 being 23.3 for females and 25.5 for males.[5] But this trend has been in effect much longer than the recently declining marriage rate and probably has had only a slight effect on the marriage rate.

Another demographic change that probably has had some effect upon the marriage rate is the declining proportion of young people of marriageable age in the total population. There also are indications that more divorced people are choosing not to remarry.[6] Any changes in the marriage rate are likely the result of the combination of numerous factors, many of which are unaccounted for. The important point is that in our society most people still do marry, as is the case with the members of every society around the world. Although fluctuations do occur, the marriage rate is still quite high.

Some years ago John Sirjamaki stated that in American society marriage was a dominating life goal. His implication was that Americans are unusually concerned with the development and maintenance of man-woman relationships that are within the context of marriage or at least have the potential for marriage.[7] This idea also is basic to Bernard Farber's model of "universal, permanent availability," which he used to describe dating, courtship, and marriage behavior in our culture. In short, Farber said that people were always in the marriage market, even those who were currently married.[8]

Additional evidence of our preoccupation with marriage can be seen in the high rate of second, third, and subsequent marriages found in American culture. About 36 per cent of marriages currently taking place are second or subsequent marriages involving either widowed or divorced persons.[9]

Americans traditionally have desired the married state and continue to do so, even to the point of looking with doubt or suspicion upon the unmarried or never-married members of society. Bachelors and spinsters once were thought either to have some idiosyncrasy that made them unmarriageable or to be homosexual. Single people still are seen as being somehow different or strange, although the stigma attached to the single state has lost strength among younger, especially college-educated, people. Although it is more common today to hear people expressing the desire to remain single, when such opinions do emerge, those holding them continue to find it difficult to enact that view because of a number of very strong social pressures.

The pressures against the single life and in favor of marriage come not only from our cultural traditions but also in a much more direct and personal form from one's family and friends. Most parents of marriageable young people hold with many of the traditional views toward marriage, and more specifically, they have a strong desire for grandchildren. Moreover, in most cases one's own friends are themselves probably married already or are getting married. From the married couple's point of view, continuing friendships with single people present a number of problems that are related mainly to a divergence of interests, but also are related to the feeling that the single person might represent a threat to the member of the couple of the same sex or to the marital relationship itself. Additionally, most entertainment in our culture is based upon couple participation or interaction, and this tends to put the single person in the position of being somewhat out of place.

Even in spite of the pressures upon persons to be married, the single state has increased in acceptability in recent years. It is certainly ironic, then, that the national media rather suddenly in 1986 began to give considerable attention to what one news magazine called "The Marriage Crunch." The reference is to the fact that as women grow older, their chances of getting married drop quite rapidly (for example, according to this source, a woman still single at 35 has only a 5 per cent chance of marrying).[10] During this same period, television and magazines also produced stories wherein women in their thirties who were not married lamented the shortage of eligible men. Many of these same stories included singles, along with some who had married but deferred childbearing, also lamenting the fact that they did not have children and that their "biological clocks" were running down. The media have also publicized a small trend among some single women of going ahead and having children on their own, either through artificial insemination or through the more natural means. Thus, it is difficult for the social scientist to determine just what consistent trends will emerge. Will people reject the recent legitimation of singlehood and begin to revalue marriage? Or, will these early moves toward institutionalizing singlehood, to include single-parenthood, become even more acceptable? Obviously, the current situation is in a state of flux, and future directions are unclear. The one thing that is clear is that people do have increasingly open options and choices in these areas.

Because of the complexity of this whole issue of marriage, which includes not only questions of the viability of the marital institution, but also questions of individual choice that have lifelong consequences, this section will include four articles that speak to many of the questions that have been raised. The articles approach the question of marriage versus singlehood from several points of view, allowing a variety of possible conclusions. The first focuses specifically upon singlehood, the second upon some of the problems of finding a suitable mate, while the third and fourth articles are more concerned with marriage.

In order to make an informed choice about marriage, one needs to understand as much as possible about the alternatives available, and in the first article Peter Stein seeks to overcome the narrow stereotype of the single person by demonstrating the wide variety of types of single persons actually existing. There are, in fact, numerous types of individuals of all ages and walks of life who occupy both temporary and permanent categories of singlehood. Stein offers a useful typology for the further study and understanding of singlehood and suggests that the traditional "life cycle" approach, often used to study marriage, probably is not appropriate to the study of single persons. His alternative is the "life spiral" approach, which allows a more accurate conceptualization of the "pluralistic universe of adult life styles and structures."

The second article in this section, "Marriage: It's Back in Style!" speaks to the "renewed" popularity of marriage in our society. Of course, data introduced earlier indicated that the marriage rate had dropped only slightly in recent years, so that there may be some question as to whether the actual popularity of marriage ever really declined. Nevertheless, the article reflects the fact that in the recent past more questions were raised concerning the viability of marriage, particularly among career oriented people, and how, after putting off marriage immediately after college, these people are beginning to marry in greater numbers. Presumably, this is reflective of a renewed interest in marriage, and the marriage rate is gradually returning to its more normal higher levels. More significantly, the article looks at some of the emerging forms that marriages are taking as this institution adapts to the changing world.

Article number three in this section represents one of the recent mass media revelations of the problems that single people encounter while trying to locate suitable marriage partners. (Incidentally, social scientists have known about this problem for years.) It focuses upon the statistical availability of eligible men and women, particularly in the major urban areas of the United States. The major problem, of course, is that the "marriage squeeze" which for a number of years created a shortage of marriageable men, continues to have a serious impact upon women's marriage chances and choices. The problem is particularly acute as women get older, that is, into their thirties and later. It is interesting to note how various areas of the country differ with regard to the ratios of marriageable women to potential husbands.

The final article in this section, "Marriage: The Traditional Alternative," could have been placed just as easily in Part Two, because it is concerned not only with the question of whether or not to marry, but also addresses the issue of cohabitation as well as the various forms that marriages might take. The authors of this article look at several of the arguments used in opposition to marriage and give particular attention to the importance and the nature of commitment.

NOTES

1 Ruth S. Cavan, *The American Family* (New York: Crowell, 1969), pp. 539-541.

2 National Center for Health Statistics, *Monthly Vital Statistics Report*, Vol. 33, No. 13, " Annual Summary of Births, Marriages, Divorces, and Deaths: United States, 1984." U.S. Department of Health and Human Services, 1985.

3 National Center for Health Statistics, *Monthly Vital Statistics Report*, "Annual Summary for the U.S., 1976," U.S. Department of Health, Education and Welfare, 1977, p. 1.

4 Ibid.

5 U.S. Bureau of Census, *Current Population Reports*, Series P-20, No. 402, "Households, Families, Marital Status, and Living Arrangements: March 1985 (Advance Report)." October 1986, p. 1.

6 Paul C. Glick and Arthur J. Norton, "Marrying, Divorcing, and Living Together in the U.S. Today," *Population Bulletin*, Vol. 32 (Population Reference Bureau, 1977), pp. 8-9.

7 John Sirjamaki, "Cultural Configurations in the American Family," *American Journal of Sociology* 53(1947-48): p. 464.

8 Bernard Farber, *Family: Organization and Interaction* (San Francisco: Chandler, 1964), pp. 103-134.

9 National Center for Health Statistics, *Monthly Vital Statistics Report (Supplement)*, Vol 35, No. 1, "Advance Report of Final Marriage Statistics," U. S. Department of Health and Human Services, 1986.

10 *Newsweek*, "Too Late for Prince Charming?" June 2, 1986, pp. 54-58, 61.

1.

Understanding Single Adulthood

Peter J. Stein

Until quite recently it was assumed that all single persons wanted to marry, they were all waiting for the "right" person to come along, they were relatively unhappy, and that all singles were very much alike. Recent research by social scientists indicates that there is in fact great diversity among single adults, that there are several distinct single life styles, and that singles face very different life chances depending on their education, income, occupation, health, race and ethnicity, age, residence, and parental status.

Some singles are older, others younger, some have already been married and others never will; some would prefer marriage if only the "right" person came along, while others enjoy their single state. Some are well educated, earn good incomes and enjoy comfortable lives, while others are struggling economically, supporting aging parents and have a limited social life. Some live alone, others with roommates or parents; most are heterosexual in their preferences, others prefer same sex partners; some are parents, others prefer to remain childless. (Adams, 1976; Austrom, 1984; Barkas, 1980; Cargan and Melko, 1982; Hass, 1983; Peterson, 1982; Shostak (1986); Simenauer and Carroll, 1982; Staples, 1981; Stein, 1981.)

Yet all singles, as do all marrieds, face certain key issues of adulthood requiring decisions and actions—education; work and careers; living arrangements; friendships, intimacy, and sexuality; emotional and physical health; relations with parents; aging; and whether or not to become parents themselves. But the social context within which they deal with these issues is different from the situation of marrieds. Singles typically have no significant other with whom to make such decisions and they alone must bear

Revised and updated for this volume from an article originally appearing in *Single Life* edited by the author.

the consequences of their decisions. Singles have to rely more on their own resources in dealing with iss .es of adulthood so that some develop great resourcefulness and personal strength while others are subject to more stresses and strains unrelieved by social supports.

The normative strength of marriage in the United States is reflected in the fact that singles are seen as a residual category. An adult is someone who's married; to remain single is to be less than adult. This cultural stereotype is supported and spread by the major social institutions and the mass media. It shapes how marrieds respond to singles and influences how singles themselves see each other and how they interpret their own experiences. This article seeks to present a more accurate portrait of single adults.

A BRIEF DEMOGRAPHIC OVERVIEW

More than 62 million American adults over the age of eighteen are unmarried. (U.S. Bureau of the Census, 1985). As indicated in Table 1, this represents 34.1 per cent of American men and 39.2 per cent of American women. The largest proportion of singles are the never-marrieds. The increasing tendency for young adults to delay marriage is reflected in the median age at first marriage; the 1984 figure was 25.4 for men and 23.0 for women. The corresponding ages in 1980 were 24.7 and 22.0; in 1970 they were 23.2 and 20.8. The proportion of never-marrieds has almost doubled since 1970 for women and men in their late twenties and early

TABLE 1. The Marital Status of the U.S. Population, age 18 and over, 1984

	Total	Married	Never Married	Divorced	Widowed
	Number (in thousands)				
Men	80,546	53,032	20,549	4,892	2,073
Women	88,926	54,074	16,357	7,416	11,079
	Percent				
Men	100	65.9	25.5	6.0	2.6
Women	100	60.8	18.4	8.3	12.5

Source: U.S. Bureau of the Census, "Marital Status and Living Arrangements: March 1984," *Current Population Reports*, Series P-20, No. 399, 1985.

thirties. While a majority of Americans continue to value marriage and 90 per cent still expect to marry and have lasting marriages, future projections suggest that the proportion of Americans who never marry will increase from 5 per cent to 8 or even 10 per cent (Thornton and Freedman, 1983). As more and more women and men postpone marriage and experience single life, some find it sufficiently satisfying and rewarding to remain single. Others who remain single, particularly women, find the number of eligible men depleting, and remain single not so much by choice as by circumstance. Both groups, joined by those who are single again after divorce or death of a spouse, swell the ranks of single adults.

A TYPOLOGY OF SINGLE ADULTS

Recent research has led to a more accurate portrait of single adults summarized in the following typology (Table 2) which is based on whether being single is voluntary or involuntary and temporary or stable. The typology provides a way to identify different groups of single adults and to determine their probable commitment to a single life over time. Of course, people's preferences and satisfactions change, so that membership in these categories is no more permanent than is marriage itself. The population of singles is being continually resupplied with new generations of high school and college graduates, divorced women and men, widows and widowers.

TABLE 2. *Typology of Single Adults*

	Voluntary	Involuntary
Temporary	Never-marrieds and formerly marrieds who are postponing marriage by not currently seeking mates, but who are not opposed to the idea of marriage	Those who have been actively seeking mates for shorter or longer periods of time, but have not yet succeeded Those who were not interested in marriage or remarriage for some period of time but are now actively seeking mates
Stable	Those choosing to be single, both never-marrieds and formerly marrieds Those who for various reasons oppose the idea of marriage Religionaries	Never-marrieds and formerly marrieds who wanted to marry or remarry, have not found a mate and have more or less accepted being single as a probable life state

Voluntary Temporary Singles. Among those who have chosen to be single on a temporary basis are the younger never-marrieds and the divorced who are postponing marriage or remarriage for some finite period of time. They are open to the possibility of marriage, but the search for a mate has a lower priority than other activities such as education, work, career, politics, self-development, and so forth. It also includes men and women who have lived together in order to try out marriagelike arrangements. However, not all of the voluntary temporary singles will marry "on time," since some will not find appropriate mates and others will marry at a time later than desired.

Voluntary Stable Singles. Among those who have chosen to be single as a stable condition are those who have never married and are satisfied with that choice; those who have been married but do not want to remarry; cohabitors who do not intend to marry; and those whose life styles preclude the possibility of marriage, for example, priests and nuns. Also included are single parents, both never married and formerly married, who are not seeking mates and who are raising their children alone or with the help of relatives or friends.

Involuntary Temporary Singles. This category consists of singles who would like to be married and expect to do so within some finite period of time. It also includes younger never-marrieds who do not want to be single and are actively seeking mates, as well as somewhat older men and women who previously had not been interested in marriage but are now actively seeking mates. It includes the widowed and divorced seeking remarriage, and single parents seeking mates. These are men and women who believe in marriage and would like to be married.

Involuntary Stable Singles. This category consists primarily of older divorced, widowed, and never-married people who wanted to marry or to remarry, have not found a mate, and have come to accept being single as a probable life-long situation. It also includes those singles who suffer from physical or psychological impairment which prevents them from being successful in the marriage market.

It is important to note that placement in a particular category of the typology may vary according to one's life course. For example, in time, some younger never-marrieds who viewed single life as a temporary situation, may marry. Others, unable to find an appropriate mate, remain single involuntarily and become increasingly concerned about the possibility that they will never find a mate. Others may enjoy their single state and begin to see it as a stable rather than a temporary condition. The same person can identify singlehood as a voluntary temporary status before marriage, then marry and divorce and become single again. This person may over time be a voluntary stable, involuntary stable, or involuntary temporary single, depending on his or her experiences and preferences and also one's particular stage of the life course.

THE LIFE COURSE OF SINGLE ADULTS

The concepts of *life cycle* and *life course*, initially proposed by Erik Erikson (1959), add a dynamic aspect to our typology. The stage of the life cycle is also related to issues of life style and life chances and the need and availability of social support systems.

Levinson (1978, 1986) has suggested a model for the various stages of adult life. He compares these stages to seasons of a year and suggests that development occurs in predictable segments which follow each other in chronological order. His model, developed from studies of married men, is useful when applied to the lives of single people, but it is limited.

The stage model assumes that development is hierarchical, sequenced in time, and cumulative. The implications of life stages are that (1) every "normal" adult must pass through the stages; (2) each stage has distinctive qualities which are tasks that must be accomplished during that stage; (3) an individual is more or less successful in negotiating these crises; (4) successful resolution of a prior stage is necessary for the successful resolution of subsequent stages; and (5) each stage is tied to chronological age (Brim, 1977). According to Levinson, "although important changes go on within it, each season or era has its own distinctive and unifying qualities, which have to do with the character of living" (Levinson et al., 1978, p. 18).

Etzkowitz and Stein (1978) suggest that life has many seasons and that a spiral more accurately represents life's configuration. Development is not necessarily related to chronological age, and themes of development may be resolved at one age only to need reevaluation later on. Developmental stages may overlap; one may never resolve certain issues. Life is an ongoing process with themes and patterns which repeat. It is less like the seasons of a single year than like a panorama of seasons.

These two contrasting models may be seen as representing a continuum. For adults whose lives follow traditional patterns of development, the cycle, with its stages, may accurately represent their lives. Less traditional lives may be more accurately described by the spiral model. There may be changes over the span of one's life: the spiral may be more accurate at one period, the cycle more accurate at another. First will be considered the cycle model, and then the spiral model of single adulthood.

The Young Never-Marrieds. We can identify various stages of the adult life cycle. The years from the early twenties to about twenty-eight are the period of "getting into the adult world," a time when the focus of one's life shifts from the "family of origin to a new home base in an effort to form an adult life of one's own" (Levinson et al., 1974, p. 246). It is a time of exploratory searching and provisional choices and a time for assessing the correctness of initial choices and increasing the commitment to choices.

The period since 1970 has seen a dramatic increase in the proportion of men and women who have remained single (Table 3). There has been about a 20 per cent increase for the 20-24 year age group; a 15-18 per cent increase for the 25-29 age group and a 7-11 per cent increase for the 30-34 age group. The median age at first marriage has increased to 25.4 for men and 23.0 for women; for women this is the highest since 1890 and for men it is approaching the historic high of 1900.

TABLE 3. Per cent Women and Men Remaining Single (1970-1984)

	1970	1980	1984	Change from 1970-1984
		Women		
Ages 20-24	35.8	50.2	56.9	+21.1
25-29	10.5	20.9	25.9	+15.4
30-34	6.2	9.5	13.3	+ 7.1
35-39	5.4	6.2	7.5	+ 2.1
40-44	4.9	4.8	5.4	+ 0.5
		Men		
Ages 20-24	54.7	68.8	74.8	+20.1
25-29	19.1	33.1	37.8	+18.7
30-34	9.4	15.9	20.9	+11.5
35-39	7.2	7.8	11.6	+ 4.4
40-44	6.3	7.1	6.9	+ 0.6

Source: U.S. Bureau of the Census, "Marital Status and Living Arrangements: March 1984," *Current Population Reports*, Series P-20, No. 399, 1985.

With the increase of young adults who remain single has come the tendency to establish their own households. However, the patterns of the 1970s have been changing in the 1980s. While the number of persons under age 35 who were living alone tripled between 1970 and 1980, increasing from 1.4 to 4.8 million, recently there has been a decline among the youngest singles who live alone. By 1984, 62 per cent of men and 47 per cent of women between the ages of 18 and 24 were living with their parents. However, in the 25-34 age group, 77 per cent of men and 86 per cent of women maintained or shared their own households, though even in this age group more lived with their parents than was the case in 1970. Overall, men are more likely to live with their parents than are women.

The background factors related to the tendency to remain with parents include the postponement of first marriage, divorce, greater emphasis on college and post-college education, employment problems, and the higher costs of housing. Singles who do establish their own households are more likely to live in urban areas and big cities. These singles are concerned with finding meaningful employment, satisfying living arrangements, congenial friends and an entertaining social life. Large cities provide the occupational and social structures to satisfy these concerns. Adjustment to the world of work and patterns of forming friendships provide crucial connections and supportive social structures.

The Age Thirty Transition. Levinson's research indicates that the men he interviewed in this stage experienced considerable turmoil and confusion, and struggled with societal pressures, with their families, and with themselves during their late 20s and early 30s. For others these years involved quieter re-evaluation of goals and values and an intensification of efforts to achieve such goals. Similarly, many men and women who remain single into their thirties also report that the middle to late 20s and early 30s was a period of great difficulty (Stein, 1981). The proportion of adults who remain single into their early thirties decreases dramatically. There is about a 50 per cent decrease in the proportion of women and men who remain single into their early 30s and another approximately 50 per cent decline among those who stay single into their late 30s.

These men and women experienced intense social and parental pressures to marry, and at that time of their lives, some of them worked hard at finding a prospective spouse. Yet many derived little intrinsic satisfaction from the search for a mate, and some reported negative experiences and a decline in self-esteem.

A major source of difficulty during the age 30 transition was work-related. This transitional period marked a deeper commitment to an occupation for some, but for others it involved a rejection of earlier occupational choices as too constricting and not meeting initial expectations of satisfaction. More women than men lacked clear occupational goals upon graduation from college, and viewed their occupations as temporary, unsatisfactory, and noninvolving. Similarly, living arrangements were seen as temporary, often with a same-sex roommate, to be changed with marriage. "As these singles approached 30, many became critical of those patterns and began to re-evaluate their lives. . . [recognizing] the possibility that they might never marry and that they themselves had the responsibility for designing meaningful lives" (Schwartz, 1976). They re-examined earlier occupational decisions, weighed possibilities of starting or returning to graduate or professional schools, re-evaluated living situations and improved living places, developed new interests, started new activities, and expanded and reinforced circles of friends.

The Middle Years: His and Hers Single Life. The number of never-marrieds continues to decline in the middle-years of the life course so that, in 1984, for the 40-44 year old group, only 5 per cent of women and about 7 per cent of men, had not married. (In the 45-54 age group about 6 per cent of men and almost 5 per cent of women had not married.)

What are the experiences of these single men and women? In a summary of many studies of the state of marriage, Bernard (1982) concluded that while "his" marriage is physically, socially, and psychologically good, "her" marriage is filled with frustration, dissatisfaction, negative feelings, unhappiness, and other problems. The situation with respect of singlehood is quite the opposite—long term singlehood tends to be experienced as a more positive state for women and a more negative state for men. This is particularly true of the older never-married singles.

Bernard reports that women who have completed college and postgraduate education, who are in one of the professions, and who earn high incomes are more likely to remain single than women with less education and lower incomes. Doudna and McBride (1981) have asked, "Where are the men for the women on the top?" and found that the men are either already married, playing the field, intimidated by very successful women, or otherwise absent. Studies indicate that many of the women who remain single are "superior" to single men in terms of education, occupation and income. Moreover, the demographics of big cities indicate a dramatic shortage of single men.

In contrast to single women, older never-married men are likely to show mental health problems, including depression, neurotic symptoms, fears, and general passivity. In summarizing a number of studies, Bernard (1982) reported that among the unmarried, men have mental health problems more often than women. We do not know whether the experience of single life is more stressful for men than women or whether the men who remain single have more interpersonal problems to begin with. Bernard does suggest that single women tend to represent the "top" of the marriage market while single men are more likely to be at the "bottom" of the market—not a good fit for either group.

CONTEMPORARY ADULTHOOD: LIFE CYCLE OR LIFE SPIRAL?

The social changes influencing the lives of adult men and women in contemporary society calls into question the usefulness of the life cycle model cited earlier in this article. Etzkowitz and Stein (1978) have suggested that a *life spiral* model more accurately reflects the changes and variations in adulthood by incorporating traditional roles and patterns with alternative and non-traditional ones. The life spiral enables us to see single men and women, not as deviants, which is their definition under the life cycle or stage theory, but as men and women choosing alternate paths of adulthood. The life spiral model identifies the full range of contemporary adulthood—traditional patterns and roles, the emergence of new patterns and roles, and alternative sequences of roles and patterns.

The Life Spiral Study of Single Adults. The life spiral model developed from research with single adults. I conducted interviews with a sample of sixty middle-class men and women between the ages of twenty-five and forty-five (Stein, 1981).

At the time of the interviews, most had completed their formal education and were pursuing professional careers. With respect to both intimacy and work roles, the lives of these men and women followed a mixed pattern. About 30 per cent of the men and women had initially followed the traditional pattern of early marriage (between the ages of eighteen and twenty-two). The average duration of these marriages was three and a half years. Another 20 per cent of the sample had cohabited for an average of two years. For the remaining 50 per cent, singlehood included several important intimate relationships, sexual and nonsexual. Some of these relationships were relatively short-term; others lasted several years. Almost all of the thirty singles were or had been in at least one stable intimate relationship lasting more than two years.

Without marriage and a spouse, the single men and women I interviewed spoke of the importance of substitute networks of human relationships that met their needs for intimacy, sharing, and continuity. For all the adults, major sources of intimacy were opposite and same-sex friendships (Stein, 1986). Friends and support networks such as women's and men's groups, political groups, social groups, therapy groups, and organizations formed around specialized interests helped validate the single lifestyle and the decision not to marry. Although these groups were not restricted to singles, they were cited as helpful in legitimizing new roles and patterns and provided support during critical life events.

With respect to work, the adult life course of these men and women involved experimenting with job and career possibilities, exploring vocational and avocational activities between the completion of school and full-time entry into the labor force, and for some, a return to schooling in the middle and late twenties.

For some of the women and men in our sample, the rejection of earlier, more tentative occupational choices did not crystallize until their late twenties and early or middle thirties. About 40 per cent postponed "entry into the adult world" because they were in graduate school or professional school. About 20 per cent were unable to break economic and psychological ties with their families of origin until their early thirties; their lives fit a pattern typified by experimenting with different life styles, searching for career orientations, and wanting to keep options open.

For these men and women issues of intimacy and work did not surface "on time" but appeared earlier or later than suggested by Levinson's cycle model. Moreover, even when issues were resolved during the expected age period, they might reappear at later times and in different settings. While Levinson's model of adulthood indicates that specific issues are dealt with in stages and transitions, our data suggest that issues of adulthood are not symbiotically linked to age stages.

My study of voluntary singles reveals the complex factors that enter into the decision to remain single, to live with a lover, to marry, or to separate. These factors can be seen as a series of pushes and pulls and are so presented in Table 4.

TABLE 4. Pushes and Pulls Toward Marriage or Singlehood

Marriage	
Pushes (negatives in present situations)	Pulls (attractions in potential situations)
Pressure from parents	Love, emotional attachment
Desire to leave home	Approval of parents
Fear of independence	Desire for children and own family
Loneliness and isolation	Example of peers
No knowledge or perception of alternatives	Romanticization of marriage
	Physical attraction
Cultural and social discrimination against singles	Security, social status, social prestige
	Legitimation of sexual experiences
	Socialization
	Job availability, wage structure, and promotions
	Social policies favoring the married and the responses of social institutions

Singlehood	
Pushes (to leave permanent relationships)	Pulls (to remain or return to singlehood)
Lack of friends, isolation, loneliness	Career opportunities and development
Restricted availability of new experiences	Availability of sexual experiences
Suffocating one-to-one relationship, feeling trapped	Exciting life style, variety of experiences, freedom to change
Obstacles to self-development	Psychological and social autonomy, self-sufficiency
Boredom, unhappiness, and anger	
Poor communication with mate	Support structures: sustaining friendships, women's and
Sexual frustration	men's groups, political groups, therapeutic groups, collegial groups

Pushes represent negative factors in a situation; *pulls* represent attractions toward a potential situation. The strengths of these pushes and pulls vary according to a number of other variables, including sexual identification, extent of involvement with parents and family, availability of friends and peers, and one's perception of choices. For some, dating patterns, pressures from parents, and acceptance of the cultural script led to early marriage. At a later time in their lives, these same people found greater pulls toward satisfying careers, work colleagues and developing friendships, all of which seemed more possible outside of marriage.

Others never married and found the single state satisfying. These men and women offered many positive reasons, or pulls, for remaining single. They spoke of freedom, enjoyment, career opportunities, developing friendships, economic self-sufficiency, enjoyable sexual experiences, and personal development. They experienced the factors Adams (1976) cites as making singlehood a viable life style: economic independence, social and psychological autonomy, and a clear intent to remain single by preference.

The interview data suggest that single life can contribute to a fully developed personality. Singles are highly adaptive. Without the clarity of role models or the support of society as a whole, they shape their lives by taking risks and forging into uncharted territory. Without the support of a marriage partner and with varying social and cultural support, adults who choose singlehood can be understood as pioneers of an emergent cultural life style.

REFERENCES

Adams, M. (1976) *Single Blessedness*. New York: Basic.

Austrom D. (1984) *The Consequences of Being Single*. New York: Long.

Barkas, J.L. (1980) *Single in America*. New York: Atheneum.

Bernard, J. (1982) *The Future of Marriage*. New Haven: Yale.

Brim, O. (1977) "Remarks on Life Span Development," American Institute on Research, mimeographed.

Cargan, L. and M. Melko (1982) *Singles: Myths and Realities*. Beverly Hills: Sage.

Doudna, C. and F. McBride (1981) "Where are the Men for the Women at the Top?" in P. J. Stein (ed.) *Single Life*. New York: St. Martin's, pp. 21-34.

Erikson, E. (1959) *Identity and the Life Cycle*. New York: International Universities.

Etzkowitz, H. and P. Stein (1978) "The Life Spiral: Human Needs and Adult Roles" *Alternative Lifestyles*, Vol. 1, No. 4, pp. 434-446.

Hass, A. (1983) *Love, Sex and the Single Man*. New York: Franklin Watts.

Levinson, D. (1986) "A Conception of Adult Development" *American Psychologist*, Vol. 41, No. 1, pp. 3-13.

Levinson, D. et al. (1978) *Seasons of a Man's Life*. New York: Knopf.

Levinson, D. et al. (1974) "The Psychosocial Development of Men in Early Adulthood and the Mid-life Transition" in Ricks, Thomas, and Roff (eds.) *Life History Research in Psychopathology*. Minneapolis: Univ. of Minnesota Press.

Peterson, N.L. (1982) *The Ever Single Woman*. New York: Quill.

Schwartz, M.A. (1976) "The Career Strategies of the Never Married" paper presented at the Annual Meeting of the American Sociological Association.

Shostak, A. (1986) "Singlehood: The Lives of Never-Married Employed Americans" in S. Steinmetz and M. Sussman (eds.) *Handbook of Marriage and the Family.*

Simenauer, J. and D. Carroll (1982) *Singles: The New Americans.* New York: Simon & Schuster.

Staples R. (1981) *The World of Black Singles: Changing Patterns of Male/Female Relations.* Westport, CT: Greenwood.

Stein, P.J. (1986) "Men and Their Friendships" in R. Lewis and R. Salt (eds.) *Men in Families.* Beverly Hills: Sage.

Stein, P.J. (ed.) (1981) *Single Life: Unmarried Adults in Social Context.* New York: St. Martin's.

Thornton, A. and D. Freedman (1983) *The Changing American Family.* Washington: Population Reference Bureau.

U.S. Bureau of the Census (1985), *Current Population Reports.* "Marital Status and Living Arrangements: March 1984" Series P-20, No. 399.

2.

Marriage: It's Back in Style!

Alvin P. Sanoff

Wedding bells are ringing far and wide in this peak month for tying the knot, and everywhere the trappings that go with this happiest of ceremonies create the aura of an earlier, more innocent time.

Clearly, marriage is back in style after two decades during which men and women dabbled at alternative lifestyles. Last year, a record 2.5 million couples marched down the aisle, their ranks swelled by the large population in the prime marrying years of 18 to 26. With the economy improving, there could be even more weddings this year.

Many couples—even those marrying a second time—are staging old-fashioned, large weddings, the type of gatherings that lost favor in the late 1960s and 1970s when the counterculture reached its heyday. Says Joan Kaner, fashion director of Bergdorf Goodman in New York: "The younger generation is much more traditionally oriented, both in their work styles and lifestyles, and this is showing up in the way they choose to be married."

Something Old, Something New. While people are flocking to the altar again, the unions being forged today are a far cry from those of the past. With social barriers crumbling and women gaining more economic independence, matrimony is taking on a whole new look.

The traditional marriage in which the man works and the woman stays home to tend to youngsters is fast giving way to busy, dual-career alliances. Unions between people of similar backgrounds and values are being replaced increasingly by interfaith and interracial marriages. And many couples still experiment with living together before exchanging vows—a vestige of the sexual revolution.

People today wait longer to marry and expect far more of the marital relationship than their parents did. They demand more and put up with less. At the same time, many couples live far from family, old friends and others who might provide emotional support in trying times.

Such changes help explain why half of all new marriages are expected to end in divorce, a situation that is prompting an array of counseling programs to prepare couples for matrimony and to help them iron out difficulties later on. "Marriage is the single most complex entity short of nuclear fusion — and nuclear fusion may be less complicated," observes Tom Clark, president of the American Association for Marriage and Family Therapy.

Despite the risks, Americans remain the marrying kind. Eventually, more than 90 per cent of the population will marry. Even those who have endured the trauma of divorce usually make at least one more attempt to achieve wedded bliss. Says sociologist Jerry Talley of Stanford University: "People may be disappointed in a marriage partner, but they are not disappointed in marriage in general."

Indeed, a recent study by the National Opinion Research Center found that married people are happier than those without partners. Still, the road to self-fulfillment through marriage has grown far more confusing and treacherous as couples devise new methods to meet the uncertainties and demands of modern life.

CAREERS AND COUPLES: THE NEW MIX

No change has had more impact on married life than the flood of women into the workplace. As women moved away from the homemaker pattern, the number of dual-earner families increased by 500,000 a year during the 1970s. Today, they account for 52 per cent of U.S. married couples.

David Mace, who helped establish the marriage-counseling profession over 40 years ago, sees matrimony changing from a one-vote system in which men made the decisions to a system in which couples sort out choices jointly.

Typical are John and Donna Williams of Manhattan, who have been married nearly five years and share household chores. Donna, a model and actress, normally does the grocery shopping and cooking, while John, manager of a press-relations firm, does the pots and pans. But when she has had a hard day, he cooks, too. "She has no obligation to make dinner," he says.

Problems usually revolve around scheduling. Says John: "I may want to take a vacation and she can't because she's got a big job coming up. You learn to live with that."

For two-career couples with children, time demands can be even more intense. Jeff Justice and Jane Lynk, both 31-year-old lawyers, have few extra hours. "Our fathers could come home from work, have a drink and enjoy the children," says Jane. "But usually when we get home, we're starting dinner and taking care of Luke."

Ever since the child was born two years ago, the Sherman, Ill., couple has split child-care duties. Jane stayed home with the baby during his first two months, and Jeff did the honors in the third month so his wife could go back to work. They take turns picking Luke up from a sitter. Whoever gets home first cooks, and the other cleans up.

Any stresses that arise in the 9-year-old marriage are outweighed by the freedom and financial security that come from having two paychecks, but the couple agrees that juggling careers and family makes it necessary to have more certainty in other parts of their life. Says Jane: "Both of us are pretty committed to staying in one location for our sense of stability and Luke's."

The Commuters. Other dual-career couples have been forced into long-distance marriages so that each can find job satisfaction. Joseph Duffey, 50, and Anne Wexler, 53, who both held top posts in the Carter administration, ended up in a commuting relationship last year after Duffey became Chancellor of the University of Massachusetts at Amherst. Says Wexler, who runs a political-consulting firm in Washington, D.C.: "We don't view this as the ideal way to live, but we have to if we want to pursue our careers."

Wexler travels to Massachusetts most weekends because her husband's commitments and social functions demand that he stay near the campus. Part of her routine is to scan the college newspaper just before seeing her husband so she'll be familiar with issues that he has been grappling with all week. Duffey adds that the couple, married for eight years before becoming commuters, must spend a good deal of Friday evening "just getting back on the same wavelength."

Whatever the problems, dual-career marriages, which now number nearly 30 million, often bring more satisfaction than traditional relationships. A survey by the National Opinion Research Center found that men with working wives are somewhat happier than other husbands. Adds sociologist Frank Furstenberg, Jr., of the University of Pennsylvania: "We as a culture are gradually rethinking what we want and expect of marriage."

CASTING CONVENTION TO THE WINDS

The two-career relationship is by no means the only shift in marriage style. Education and increased mobility have greatly expanded the social circles of most people. "There is a greater mix in marriages as the religious and ethnic barriers come down," says Herbert Glieberman, a Chicago attorney and author of books on marriage and divorce.

For Heidi and Manbir Singh of Mar Vista, Calif., marriage means grappling with differences in religious rites and cultural practices. Heidi, 29, is a Roman Catholic. Manbir, 37, a native of India, is a Sikh, a member of a Hindu sect that also believes in one God and rejects the Indian caste system.

Heidi recalls that the gap in culture created problems, especially at the start of their 12-year marriage: "I was very young, very emotional, from a volatile Irish Catholic home. He was from a serene Indian family and couldn't understand why I cried and had tantrums." For Manbir, who teaches nuclear medicine at the University of Southern California School of Medicine, marriage meant getting used to American ways, including overt displays of affection and saying, "I love you." But the two have adjusted, while still practicing their different religions.

Adjustment is even tougher for couples who must overcome racial barriers, yet the number of interracial marriages in the U.S. climbed from an estimated 65,000 in 1970 to about 165,000 a decade later.

Walt Higginbotham, a white, 34-year-old sales representative in Houston, says that when he married a black schoolteacher two years ago "we were making no social statement. We just cared a lot about each other." But as news of the wedding became public, he adds, "I found out who my real friends were, fast."

Since there is still strong objection to such marriages in some parts of the country, many interracial couples refuse to talk about their experiences publicly, fearing that they will be singled out by "cranks or kooks." Some are concerned, too, about how their children will fare. Says a white computer scientist in Virginia who married a black woman seven years ago: "Our daughter maybe wonders, 'Why couldn't you have married a white lady?' and perhaps asks herself, 'Should I be black or white?' "

Less controversial is divorce and remarriage, which even a generation ago often put men and women on the outs with family and friends. Now, about 75 to 80 per cent of those who divorce eventually marry again, and about 45 per cent of weddings involve at least one person who has been married before. Public attitudes have changed so much that a divorced and remarried man now occupies the White House.

Jeannie and Bruce Anderson of Dallas both had previous experience with marriage when they were wed eight years ago. Jeannie had three youngsters from her first marriage, and Bruce had a stepson with whom he kept close contact. The couple has since added a child of their own.

This "blended family" arrangement, which is becoming more common every day, can create all sorts of tensions. "It is hard to put a new person into a family," says Jeannie. "Sometimes the children resented my new husband. Sometimes he resented how much attention I paid to them. I was always in the middle and still am." But, she adds, most difficulties have been ironed out. "We still have our fusses and problems," she explains, "but basically we get along fairly well."

The couple planned their wedding with the children in mind and took two honeymoons, one without the youngsters and one with them. Says Jeannie: "It is a family marriage."

Also benefiting from the freer atmosphere of the 1980s: senior citizens. Worried about "what the children would think," many older people lived out their lives alone after their spouses died. Now, they feel more comfortable about marrying again. Frequently spared the worries over children and finances that preoccupy young couples, people who marry during their "golden years" often are remarkably content. "It's like starting to live all over again," says Marcia Ballin of Houston, who married her husband Jack two years ago after both had lost their first spouses. "Marriage is a wonderful solution to a lonely life."

MARCHING TO A DIFFERENT DRUMMER

The new flexibility in marriage also makes it possible for more men and women to swap traditional roles. Nino and Tina Nannarone of Brooklyn are doing just that, with him staying home to care for their two young daughters while Tina, 34, works as an auto mechanic for the Port Authority of New York and New Jersey.

At first, Nino, 38, a community organizer, was reluctant to make the switch. "It was a double whammy because she was going into a nontraditional job," he recalls. "Being a man and taking care of my kids at home, I also worried about what friends would say." But for now, the couple seems happy with the arrangement, which has helped Tina succeed in her job. "I have a perfect attendance record because I don't have to worry about the kids," she says.

Others buck old mores by living together out of wedlock—in effect testing their compatibility before tying the knot. The Census Bureau estimates that the number of couples involved in such relationships soared from 523,000 in 1970 to 1.9 million last year.

Many of these couples eventually marry, and Bob Turgeon and Donna Riedinger of Denver, who have shared an apartment for almost five years, are grappling with just that decision right now. When they first got together, Bob, now 28, was on the road a lot selling encyclopedias. "Every time I came back I wanted to see Donna, so I decided we might as well live together," he says.

The relationship has worked, despite concerns about tensions in Donna's family, because each has retained a sense of independence. But now Donna, 34, who is a nurse, wants to make the arrangement formal and has given Bob until August to make up his mind. "I feel that at this point it's more or less a technicality that we ought to take care of," she says. "We're not married, but we're sure not single after five years. We're in limbo."

IN THE OLD-FASHIONED WAY

Despite such changes, about one fourth of all married couples still opt for the old-style marriage in which the wife stays home to raise children while the husband works.

Susan Puckett, 40, of Rock Hill, Missouri, has been a homemaker and mother to three daughters for the better part of her married life. Susan was only 16 years old when she met her husband Gary. "We worked together in a dime store in St. Louis," she recalls. "He was a stock boy and I was a salesclerk."

They married five years later, after he got out of the military, and today Gary is a salesman for an oil company. Says Susan of her marriage: "I didn't want a career. I like the idea of having someone more or less take care of me."

Another throwback to an earlier time—teen marriages—also persists, even though most people today wait longer to wed. The median age for women at first marriage rose from 20.3 years in 1960 to 22.5 in 1982. Still, in 1979, the most recent year for which figures are available, nearly a third of women marrying for the first time were teenagers.

When Sandee and Eric Khloscz of San Francisco became husband and wife last August, it was against the wishes of their parents. But the 18-year-old couple, who began dating when they were 15, reasoned that love would see them through. "Why wait if you know it's right?" asks Eric, who works at a gas station.

So far, they describe married life as "wonderful" despite financial problems that have forced then to sell Sandee's car and pare spending to the bone. "If anything, the money problem has brought us closer together," says Sandee, who will soon leave her job with a real-estate broker to have a baby. "We'll really have to scramble then," says Eric. Their parents, meanwhile, remain cool to the union. "The more they tell us we made a mistake," asserts Eric, "the more determined we are to prove them wrong."

BIG DEMANDS, BIG PROBLEMS

No matter what type of marriage a couple has, they expect a great deal from it. Unlike in the past, men and women rarely join hands merely to have children and the necessities of life. Now, couples marry less for practical reasons than for emotional ones as they hunt for companionship and love. Lenore J. Weitzman, a sociologist at Stanford University, says that today "the marriage partner is supposed to be the be-all and end-all, an intellectual and sexual companion, a conversationalist and a good tennis player, but it is hard for one person to fulfill all these needs."

Analysts say that "the myth of romantic love" fosters unrealistic expectations. "That myth sells a lot of goods and merchandise, but it is not a particularly good criterion on which to select a partner," contends therapist Tom Clark of Winston-Salem, North Carolina. Experts warn that couples who put all their eggs in the basket of romance are likely to find their marriages cracking.

Sociologists also trace breakups to the rise in marriages between people who have different backgrounds. "You have got to minimize potential areas of conflict, and that means similar social class, education, race, religion and the like," argues Clifton Barber, Associate Professor of Human Development and Family Studies at Colorado State University. Others note the lack of commitment in many marriages. "As a society, we have come to embrace the obsolescence theory not only in material things, but in human relationships," observes Chicago attorney Glieberman.

Less stringent divorce laws aid couples in splitting up, and greater financial independence of working women keeps them from being locked into a bad marriage. "As the economic ability of women increases and their dependence decreases, they have a choice," says sociologist M.A. Najmi of the University of Colorado.

Yet many experts insist that the increase in failed marriages is not necessarily bad. They say that couples may be happier than in the past because those who stay together do so by choice, not necessity. "It is preferable to terminate an unhappy marriage than to live in holy deadlock," says Graham Spanier, a sociologist at the State University of New York at Stony Brook.

Still, there's enough concern about marital strains to generate an explosion in the field of marriage therapy. The American Association for Marriage and Family Therapy has increased tenfold over the past decade and today has a membership of 1,000 people who hold advanced degrees in such areas as sociology, social work and psychology.

Besides individual counseling, couples are signing up for marriage encounters, which bring husbands and wives together for a weekend and a series of subsequent meetings to discuss common concerns. An estimated 1 million couples have taken part in the program, which originated in the Roman Catholic Church but has spread to many denominations.

To get their unions off to a good start, more couples are taking marriage-preparation courses. Over 60 per cent of the nation's Catholic dioceses require prospective newlyweds to participate in such programs, which often take the form of workshops dealing with such topics as sexuality and values. The approach also is attracting interest outside the church. The Denver Center for Marital and Family Studies offers a five session course to increase awareness of potential problems and enhance communication.

Programs like this are viewed as long overdue. "There is nothing we do a worse job of than preparing kids for marriage," says Ray Fowler, a marriage and family counselor in Claremont, Calif. "If kids graduating from high school knew a hundredth as much about marital interaction as they do about computers, marriage would be a lot more satisfactory experience."

Marriage experts say that the bedrock of a healthy union is compatibility, respect, intellectual curiosity and shared goals. "Balance of power" in a relationship also is important, say analysts, who warn against one partner becoming too dominant.

Veteran counselor David Mace offers this three-part prescription for achieving marital success: Both husband and wife must be committed to growth and change, have a system for regular communication and accept conflict as normal and inevitable and learn to use it creatively.

MARRIAGE—IT'S HERE TO STAY

Where does all of this leave marriage? Some experts say the institution is in trouble, that more people are waiting longer to marry and spending large parts of their lives in single and divorced states. They point out that the proportion of young women between ages 20 and 24 who remained unwed climbed from 36 per cent in 1970 to 53 per cent last year, reflecting society's growing acceptance of the singles lifestyle. "History shows us that when marriages are postponed they tend to be forgone," says James Weed, a Census Bureau specialist on marriage.

Still, most Americans believe strongly in marriage and regard it as an anchor in turbulent times. A study by the Institute of Social Research at the University of Michigan found that only 3 per cent of 18-year-olds questioned in 1980 thought they would not marry. "The vast majority of Americans marry and will continue to do so," says the University of Pennsylvania's Furstenberg.

Indeed, even homosexual couples are seeking a degree of permanence to their relationships, although such unions are not legally recognized. Says one California man who had his union with another blessed by a sympathetic minister three years ago: "We consider ourselves married even though the law does not."

On a Steady Course. Sociologist Andrew Cherlin of Johns Hopkins University notes that the United States is in a period of stability in marriage after the great roller-coaster changes of recent years. But the divorce rate will remain high through this decade because of the huge number of people in the prime age group for divorce—25-39. Even so, most of these people are expected to marry again, adding to the growing complexity in family relationships and making stepparents and stepchildren as much the norm as the exception.

Through all these changes, there remains the age-old search for self-fulfillment and a yearning for happiness that most people believe can still be found more easily by sharing one's life with another. Explains New Yorker John Williams of his marriage: "I like the feeling that we're growing together. It's exciting in every facet—emotionally, sexually and intellectually."

3.

Figuring the Odds in the Marriage Market

Charles F. Westoff and Noreen Goldman

Whatever our differences, all of us stand equal before the laws of supply and demand. Yet the scarcity that affects Toni Valley, a 37-year-old public relations executive from Los Angeles, is not of money or other economic goods; it's of men. For every 100 unmarried Los Angeles women aged 37, the city has only 65 eligible men.

Like many modern women, of course, Toni doesn't require a man to make her feel happy, secure or fulfilled. She's accomplished in her own right. She owns a profitable public relations firm, which grosses $80,000 to $90,000 a year, and she lives in a spacious one-bedroom apartment in Beverly Hills. Still, Valley wouldn't mind making friends more often than she does with companionable, eligible men. She's not husband hunting, mind you, but she wouldn't object to success in the marriage market either. Says she: "If you're in a relationship and it leads to marriage, that's wonderful."

For the unmarried women of Los Angeles, there is some good news of a sort: things could be worse if they lived in Minneapolis, say, or St. Louis. For every 100 unmarried 37-year-old women in Minneapolis, there are 46 eligible men; in St. Louis, a dismal 45.

Such is the nature of the U.S. marriage market. It is one where the forces of supply and demand work in many of the same inexorable ways as they do in determining the prices of stocks or bonds or widgets. It is one where, at younger ages especially, there are more singles than ever before: since 1960, the proportions of men and women in their twenties and thirties who have never married have increased dramatically. Even more notably, it is one where, at all ages over 25 and in most metropolitan areas, the number of unmarried women exceeds the supply of eligible men. And what constitutes eligibility? We define eligibles as people whom the U.S. Census Bureau identifies as single, divorced, separated or widowed, with a statistical adjustment made by us for people such as homosexuals and confirmed singles–individuals, in short, who are unlikely to marry.

Unmarried men, of course, are as interested in seeking partners as are single women. But because the numerical imbalance of eligible women and men in the U.S. marriage market becomes so unfavorable to women as they age, it is the plight of females that has attracted greater attention. That interest has been evidenced by a spate of 1980s articles and books–under such titles as *Too Many Women* and *The Great American Man Shortage*. And it prompted us to take a statistical look at the marriage market from the woman's point of view.

We've done so city by city and age group by age group for each of the 38 largest metropolitan areas in the U.S. The detailed results of findings, based on marriage statistics and 1980 U.S. Census data, are shown in the tables that accompany this article. Marriage-minded men can get a fairly accurate view of their prospects by reversing the ratios published here.

TABLE 1. Where the Men Are—and Aren't

Ratios of eligible men available for each 100 women between 20 and 59 years of age, living in these metropolitan areas:

San Diego	75.1	Dallas	60.4
Houston	73.5	Milwaukee	60.0
San Francisco	73.2	Atlanta	59.5
New Orleans	70.2	Miami	59.4
Los Angeles	69.9	Boston	58.6
San Jose	68.2	Sacramento	58.2
Fort Lauderdale	66.7	Kansas City	57.9
Washington, D.C.	66.5	Detroit	57.7
Denver	65.6	Philadelphia	57.5
Seattle	64.7	Cincinnati	56.5
Anaheim	63.5	Minneapolis-St. Paul	56.5
New York City	63.1	Newark	55.6
Baltimore	63.0	Indianapolis	55.4
Tampa-St. Petersburg	62.6	San Antonio	54.5
Riverside, CA	62.5	St. Louis	54.2
Portland, OR	61.9	Buffalo	54.1
Chicago	61.5	Columbus	52.5
Cleveland	60.7	Pittsburgh	52.2
Phoenix	60.6	Nassau-Suffolk ctys., N.Y.	49.2

As both tables reveal, the disparities in the relative numbers of eligible men and women can be great, depending on the metropolitan area you live in and, especially, on your age. This is particularly surprising in light of one overarching fact: the total number of unmarried men between 16 and 64 is nearly the same as that of unmarried women. In fact, in the U.S. as a whole, eligible women under 25 enjoy a surplus on the supply side. But from then on the picture gets bleak. Single women aged 25 to 29 face a man shortage of almost 25 per cent—that is, there are just 77 eligible men for every 100 available women. For females aged 35 to 39, the ratio drops to 48 eligible men per 100 unattached women; there are only 38 available men for every 100 eligible women aged 45 to 49.

Why? The answer has three parts. First, studies of marriage patterns demonstrate that men typically marry women younger than they are. Clearly, the statistics confirm an oft-observed cultural phenomenon: in marriage, women tend to favor men older than they are and men typically prefer younger women. Indeed, the older a man gets, the larger the typical age difference between him and the woman he marries. On average, a man at 25 chooses a mate two years younger than he; a 50-year-old man, a woman eight years younger.

Second, women outlive men. According to 1980 census figures, women live an average eight years longer then men, a difference that has increased steadily from a two-year gap in 1920. From the moment of birth, death rates of males exceed those of females. This is largely because of the relatively greater numbers of deaths among men from accidents and from cardiovascular and respiratory diseases. One result is that there are roughly 7 per cent more female 50-year-olds than male and about 32 per cent more female 70-year-olds.

Third, of course, there is an increasingly visible element of the single population that is not a part of the marriage market. Some are confirmed singles, others are precluded from finding a mate for physical or emotional reasons, and a large but unknown number are homosexual. While the U.S. Census provides no direct way of counting this population, we have used an illuminating statistic to help us estimate it: if a person has not married by the age of 45, the chances of marriage thereafter are almost nil—about 1 in 100. Thus, in our calculations we eliminate from the marriage pool never-married men and women who are 45 and older. And under the assumption that similar proportions of would-be lifelong singles exist at all younger ages, we have reduced the total marriage pool at all ages commensurately. The effect of this refinement is a greater reduction in the number of eligible men than in that of available women—a partial confirmation, perhaps, of the widely held view that male homosexuals outnumber female homosexuals.

Almost all the figures presented so far—and all of those that follow—are based on a measure we created called the availability ratio. It relates the pool of eligible marriage partners, whether never married, divorced, separated or widowed, with the competition for that pool. We remove from the pool of available men and women not only those whom we define as ineligible, but also people who say on census forms that they're unmarried but live with a person of the opposite sex. About 7 per cent of single people

TABLE 2. Potential Partners for Given Age Categories of Women

The number of suitably aged, eligible men for every 100 single women in each age
bracket:

Cities	Age Categories							
	20-24	*25-29*	*30-34*	*35-39*	*40-44*	*45-49*	*50-54*	*55-59*
Anaheim	135	93	75	57	46	39	34	29
Atlanta	131	91	74	54	41	33	28	24
Baltimore	133	84	70	55	48	42	38	34
Boston	123	81	62	47	42	40	38	36
Buffalo	117	70	54	43	40	38	37	34
Chicago	129	85	68	52	44	42	38	34
Cincinnati	122	77	61	48	42	37	33	32
Cleveland	128	86	68	51	44	39	36	34
Columbus	122	72	55	42	37	33	30	29
Dallas	128	87	72	54	43	37	33	29
Denver	137	95	79	59	46	40	36	33
Detroit	119	78	63	50	43	40	36	33
Fort Lauderdale	135	97	82	64	50	40	35	31
Houston	149	111	90	68	53	45	37	35
Indianapolis	116	73	60	48	40	38	36	32
Kansas City	119	80	66	51	44	39	34	30
Los Angeles	135	97	82	65	54	46	42	37
Miami	117	78	68	56	47	40	36	33
Milwaukee	120	78	62	50	47	45	41	37
Minneapolis-St.Paul	121	78	62	46	39	37	35	34
Nassau-Suffolk, N.Y.	113	66	49	37	34	33	31	31
Newark	119	77	59	44	39	37	36	34
New Orleans	141	97	83	64	53	46	41	37
New York City	125	90	75	57	47	42	36	33
Philadelphia	125	78	60	48	43	39	35	32
Phoenix	128	84	69	54	45	39	35	31
Pittsburgh	117	70	54	41	36	35	33	32
Portland, OR	126	86	71	55	44	39	38	36
Riverside, CA	130	83	68	53	46	42	40	38
Sacramento	118	75	62	49	43	40	40	39
San Antonio	123	70	56	44	38	37	35	33
San Diego	179	110	83	62	49	44	39	35
San Francisco	136	104	91	73	58	47	41	36
San Jose	142	100	81	63	51	42	36	31
Seattle	131	90	74	57	46	42	40	38
St. Louis	119	73	58	45	39	36	33	31
Tampa-St.Petersburg	127	82	70	57	49	42	38	36
Washington, D.C.	130	97	82	62	48	42	38	33

described themselves this way in 1980. (Unfortunately, to maintain the
accuracy of our data, we have had to restrict our calculations to whites.
The reason is the undercount of young black men in the U.S. Census. This
poorly understood phenomenon, which results in an estimated 7.5 per cent

undercount of black men nationally, has not been adjusted for in census figures for metropolitan areas.)

Here's how the availability ratio works. Take a 30-year-old unmarried woman. The pool from which she's likely to choose consists of eligible men between 23 and 49 years of age. We derive this age range by analyzing U.S. marriage statistics from the late 1970s and eliminating all very infrequent age pairings between grooms and 30-year-old brides. (We use the same method to define age limits of likely eligibles for unmarried men and women at all ages between 16 and 74.) However, that 30-year-old woman has a lot of competition for these men from other women. For example, according to marriage statistics, the 23-year-old that our single woman, aged 30, might marry could, statistically speaking, choose to marry a woman between 16 and 30; her 49-year-old potential spouse presumably would select from a pool of women between 30 and 58.

The availability ratio incorporates these age constraints in defining both the marriage pool and the competition for it. A ratio of 100 would indicate that the market of potential partners is in balance, whereas ratios larger than 100 indicate a surplus of men. The availability ratio for our imaginary 30-year-old single woman: 68—that is, there are 68 potential partners for every 100 women her age.

That figure is a national average. But mate matching, of course, is predominantly a local phenomenon. Business travel and jet-age vacations notwithstanding, most pairings between men and women take place in the communities in which they both live. Each of the 38 metropolitan areas we analyzed presents a unique profile. Yet many common traits appear. The first is that age is the inescapable factor that no city can override. The older women grow, the less likely the marriage market will work in their favor. At older ages, moving to a different metropolitan area can exert only a marginal impact on one's odds in the marriage market.

A second common characteristic is that areas that are good markets for one age group tend to be good for other ages as well. The converse is also true. Nassau and Suffolk counties in New York, which the Census Bureau now separates from the New York City metropolitan area and which are known locally as Long Island, constitute the worst or close to the worst marriage markets for women at any age. Many of the best cities for women are in the West. By and large, they are also the economically expanding cities that experienced a large in-migration, presumably of young men especially, during the 1970s. Such metropolitan areas as Houston, Los Angeles, San Diego and San Jose are at or near the top of most age groups.

The San Francisco metropolitan area ranks relatively high as a marriage market for women. That may come as a surprise, because of the city's reputation as a center of the national gay community. Yet San Francisco's robust economy, pleasant climate and historically unbridled life style unquestionably have attracted significant numbers of heterosexual single men as well as homosexuals. Then too, the San Francisco metropolitan area includes Oakland, Marin County and Berkeley, which are not regarded as extremely heavily populated by gays.

Nevertheless, the proportion of men we define as ineligible in San Francisco proper is extraordinarily high. For example, fully 56 per cent of the central city's unmarried men aged 45 to 59 have never married and therefore are very unlikely to do so. Since the city has attracted a large number of young gay men in recent years, and since our estimate of ineligibles is derived from studying recent marriage patterns for middle-aged and older people, we have almost certainly overestimated the availability of men in San Francisco.

Like San Francisco, New York City has a high proportion (58 per cent) of never-marrieds among its population of unmarried men 45 to 49 years old. Possible explanations for this similarity: New York City also has a large gay population, the city is a haven for confirmed bachelors, or a little of both. Even so, in our rankings New York City, like San Francisco, appears to be a better-than-average marriage market overall for women. Here again however, our measures may have underestimated the number of ineligible men.

Which metropolitan areas have the least attractive possibilities for women, aside from Long Island? Atlanta, for one, is a relatively attractive market for single women under 35. But the city sinks rapidly to the bottom for older women. Other cities, such as Buffalo, Columbus, Newark, Pittsburgh, San Antonio and St. Louis, tend to be consistently bad marriage markets for women of all ages. Except for San Antonio and Columbus, each of these cities has been hit hard in recent years by economic slowdown and realignment. This often brings about the departure of a small but significant number of single men, who typically are more mobile than other segments of the population.

Despite a reputation as a bad marriage market for women, metropolitan Washington, D.C. fares very well indeed in our study when compared with most other cities. As with San Francisco and New York, however, this relatively rosy view from a woman's perspective may partly reflect an underestimate of ineligible men. Like those two cities, Washington has a significant gay population.

Other factors besides age, eligibility and residence affect the odds in the marriage market. Most societies, including the U.S., have pressures that urge females to marry men of equal or higher social class. Studies of U.S. marriage patterns bear this out. For example, among women with four or more years of college, about a third marry men with less education, but among men with four or more years of college, about one-half marry less-well-educated women.

To get a glimpse of the influence of education on the marriage market, we did some further analysis, which is not reflected in the tables. Marriage statistics tell us that marriages between the educational extremes—that is, between those who went to college and people who didn't complete high school—are uncommon. Thus, because college-educated women tend to restrict themselves to partners of equal or greater educational attainment, the marriage market for college-educated women is tighter than that for women whose education ended after high school. Compared with women who discontinued their education after high school, college-educated women suffer an additional market disadvantage of around 25 per cent. (By the same token, men who did not graduate from high school face a disadvantage in the marriage market relative to other men.)

Are the best marriage markets for women in general also the best for college-educated women? The answer is clearly yes, although there are a few exceptions. Both New York City and Washington rank more favorably as marriage markets for college-educated women than for women in general.

Our availability ratios measure relative numbers of potential partners, but they say little about the likelihood of marriage. The odds of that taking place relate to many personal, social and economic considerations that numbers alone cannot capture. Even so, supply and demand undoubtedly exert an influence. And with the supply of eligible men so often out of balance with the number of available women, it's no wonder why for some women finding eligible men is like a real-life game of musical chairs.

4.

Marriage: The Traditional Alternative

Don Sloan and Lillian Africano

Marriage traditionally has been the most binding ritual involving men and women, and there was a time when neither a man nor a woman was considered "complete" without it. Now all that is changing, and "till death us do part" is translated into "as long as we both shall love" or "as long as it's no hassle." Couples often choose the latter description, thinking it's the freest and easiest kind of relationship—and then find themselves falling into an emotionally expensive trap. They might buy the myth that marriage is "just a piece of paper" and then find themselves coping with all the problems of marriage without its social, legal, and emotional safeguards. For despite its difficulties and limitations, marriage has proven itself to be a uniquely productive, protective, and enduring framework for a stable, committed relationship.

WHY NOT MARRY?

When you consider a living-together arrangement, you should be careful to make the decision on the basis of your own values and on a realistic assessment of your wants and needs. Quite often, women today reject marriage because it is tied up in their minds with an old, unliberated stereotype: the perfect wife who bakes bread, raises perfect children, and caters to her husband's every whim (and who, if abandoned, falls apart, with no life or identity of her own).

Instead, women choose a life style on the basis of a new stereotype: the independent career woman who relates to men the same exploitative way the "macho" male relates to women. And in doing so, women exchange one limiting role for another and overlook the fact that real equality between the sexes comes from mutual trust and sharing. Knowing that you can make love and walk out doesn't automatically liberate you sexually or psychologically. In fact, it might trap you. Today's woman doesn't need to follow any one pattern; she can be an independent individual without rejecting the human need for belonging, for experiencing commitment.

But because sex without marriage is so much in vogue, many women are afraid it's not sophisticated or contemporary to admit that they want to be married, even when they know that they do. It's easier, particularly if the men they're involved with say they're "not ready" for matrimony, to let the relationship drift.

In the past, mating rituals followed a more or less predictable progression: a period of dating, with kissing and various kinds of sex play, and with intercourse restricted to "serious" or married couples. Presumably, the degree of commitment grew naturally as a couple took each step; by the time they had reached the point of sharing a roof, they were deeply committed to each other.

Today, with an accelerated pace of living and a desire for "instant togetherness," a couple might opt for living together as a form of engagement: "We'll get married if this works out." They also might say nothing at all but mean, "I love you, I want to be with you, but I honestly don't know where we go from here" or "I don't like living alone, so I might as well move in with you until something better comes along."

PROBLEMS

Let's say however, that a couple begins living together because they're in love and they want their relationship to be free, completely voluntary. They still are going to come up against many of the problems that arise in marriage. Problems involving money (who pays for what) will surface and might well be touchier in an unmarried set-up because the feeling of "mine" and "yours" tends to be stronger than the concept of "ours." There might be "in-law" problems with families who disapprove of the life style. The pains of jealousy also are common, especially when the couple, having chosen "freedom" rather than commitment, think they don't have the right to verbalize their feelings and to ask for the reassurance and security they would have in a marriage.

And sooner or later, what happens in many "just-living-together" arrangements is that one of the pair wants to get married and the other doesn't. This can lead to a tug of war that is draining and demoralizing to both. The one who wants "more" might become tense, worried, and preoccupied with strategies to persuade the other. Whatever insecurities exist probably will become exaggerated, because the basic question is: "Why doesn't he/she want me in the same way I want him/her?" And the answer can be: "He/she doesn't care enough," or worse yet, "I'm not good enough, smart enough, attractive enough, etc." Meanwhile, the reluctant partner starts to feel worried and guilty, and the "easy" part of the relationship evaporates. In fact, the relationship itself probably will fall apart, but not before it causes pain and emotional damage to both.

Of the reasons couples give for not getting married, only one is sound— genuine contentment with the situation. Most couples give other excuses: "Sex is easier." "It's simpler if we keep our lives (and checking accounts) separate." "There's an ex-spouse in the picture and I don't feel like taking on any more responsibilities." "It's easier to split if things don't work out." All of these are the worst kinds of reasons not to make a commitment because they are mechanical rather than human. In addition, most of them aren't even true.

SEXUAL DYSFUNCTION

Take the concept of "easier sex." Lack of commitment actually can inhibit sexual response instead of improving it. For among couples seeking sex therapy, about twice as many unmarried women report orgasmic difficulties as married women.

Psychological orgasmic problems among women often are partly the result of our still male-dominated culture. Traditionally, women have been powerless and dependent, and they respond to this situation negatively, with hostility. They might throw dishes or shoot their lovers, but most often these angry feelings surface during sex and result in a lack of orgasm. In the living-together arrangement, these underlying pressures combine with the uncertainties of noncommitment.

And the woman usually is aware, on some level, that she is taking the greater risk. For example, if a couple start living together in their thirties and then split up in their forties, the man is in a better position to find a new partner. He still is considered extremely eligible, a bachelor with the added attraction of not paying alimony or child support. A woman in her forties, unfair as it might be, has her choice narrowed by custom and prejudice.

But men also have sexual problems caused in part by casual, noncom- mitment living situations. The most typical occurs when the man wants to get married and the woman doesn't. He might want her to agree to com- mitment, as he defines it, because he wants the security of a permanent relationship. When she won't, he can become fearful of rejection. He might experience feelings of sexual inadequacy, a "fear of performance" in bed that can cause episodes of impotence and other problems. He even might worry that his partner wants other sexual experiences. Ultimately, he might not trust her emotionally any more, and when this subtle trust breaks down, it can lead to a vicious circle of sexual dysfunction: His sense of rejection leads to impotence, causing her to have a negative reaction, which rein- forces his feelings of inadequacy.

Although both sets of problems can be treated, the sex therapist relies on commitment as a critical factor for success.

Another variation on the sexual theme is the theory that sex is better, more exciting, in an unmarried relationship. "Why spoil it?" the reasoning goes. "Why risk sexual boredom by getting married?" One case that at first glance seems to support this premise concerns a couple who reported that sex had been satisfactory until they married, at which point the husband became impotent. He then began an affair with his secretary, which started out on a fairly intense level sexually, but after a while he became impotent again. The man tried still another partner, and the problem recurred after just a few encounters. His was a problem caused not by marriage or commitment but by the machismo concept of "scoring." Once the conquest was made, he lost interest sexually.

And it's almost as common to see a woman, whose active sex life is all tied up with role-playing, suddenly lose interest in sex after marriage. She has achieved the "reward" she was after, and the role-playing no longer is necessary.

Cases like these coexist with others in which sex remains the same or even improves after marriage. Because sexual dysfunction is a defense, a way of hiding, it is caused not by a married or committed situation per se but by the underlying problems of the people involved.

VULNERABILITY

As for the standard argument that it's easier to break up when you're not married, this is true only in a legal sense. When any emotionally involved couple thinks of splitting up, there's a lot of negative energy aroused in feelings of guilt, insecurity, anxiety. "What's going to happen to me?" "Will I ever find someone else?" "Can I take the chance of ending up alone?" When the break-up is handled through the institutionalized channels of divorce, many of these negative feelings can be dissipated through rituals, in the mechanics of dealing with papers and judges and lawyers. There's time to sort through anger and hurt and start to heal. But when there is no marriage, "good-by" can be as quick and simple as packing a bag—and as overwhelming as a death in the family. When it's all over in a day, there is no transition, no ritual for dealing with the pain.

There is, finally, one other important reason why couples choose not to marry, and that is fear of vulnerability. Being vulnerable is an integral part of commitment, and crossing the line into a socially structured way of life makes you legally, economically, and emotionally vulnerable. In choosing commitment, you put yourself in a position where someone really can get at you. Becoming so emotionally exposed is frightening, but it offers enormous rewards. To take that step means that you trust each other, and as a wise man once said, "To be trusted is a greater compliment than to be loved."

ARE YOU COMMITTED?

The dictionary defines commitment as "the act of pledging or engaging oneself," but the actual ingredients that bind a relationship can vary. They can be economic ("two can live as cheaply as one"), social ("what would we tell our friends if we broke up?"), emotional ("we're in love and we want to be together").

Whatever your particular motivation is, you might sometime find yourself at a critical point at which your relationship must either move to a new stage or end. When this happens, a few guidelines might help chart a direction.

Ask yourself what attracted you to your partner, what made you agree to each step you've taken thus far. Now consider your answers (whether they be "intelligence," "kindness," "nice smile," "good sense of humor," "nice face," "great body") and ask yourself: "How do I feel about all those characteristics now?"

If the points of appeal still are strong, you're off to a good start toward developing a deeper level of commitment.

> Step 1: Check your level of determination. Unless you both agree to devote a certain amount of energy to making your relationship one that satisfies your needs, it will deteriorate and fall apart.

> Step 2: Examine your expectations, asking if they are realistic. For example, if you have been uncommitted because you want to live in the city and he wants to put down roots in the country, is it possible for one of you to compromise?

> Step 3: And this is crucial! Establish good communications so that the messages from steps 1 and 2 can be given and received in an ongoing way. If a commitment is to grow and survive, you both must maintain verbal, nonverbal, and sexual contact to keep in close touch with each other's feelings and needs.

Part

Two

Marriage

Versus

Cohabitation

At least two issues are involved in most discussions of the relationship between marriage and cohabitation. One is the issue of personal and social morality, and the other is the issue of the meaning of cohabitation in the sociological sense. From the standpoint of the former, there is concern over the rightness or wrongness of nonmarital sexual relationships and over the propriety of such relationships being practiced with some degree of openness. These questions are reflective of a general societal concern.

The major issue from the standpoint of social science is reflected in such questions as the part played by cohabitation in either facilitating or inhibiting marriage, and where cohabitation fits into the dating-courtship-mate selection process. More particularly, those studying this behavior would like to know whether or not cohabitation is simply a new phase or stage being added to the courtship process or if it is becoming, in reality, a substitute for marriage itself.

Although some aspects of cohabitation are recent social phenomena, in one form or another this practice has been around for some time. In fact, the term *cohabitation* was commonly used, until just a few decades ago, to refer to common-law marriage. But recent popular usage has brought a new meaning to the term, now indicating that the couple living together is *not* married in any form, common-law or otherwise. For some there is even an open declaration that marriage is purposely being avoided and that cohabitation is one means of avoiding it. Even with this change in meaning, the type of behavior under scrutiny is still not so new. For example, divorced people who were considering remarriage often lived together (albeit discreetly) for a period of time to see if they could get along. This was likely a result of their not wanting to remarry too hastily with the possibility of making another mistake. As of March 1985, in about 34 per cent of all unmarried couple households, either one or both of the pair currently were divorced.[1] Cohabitation also has been practiced among older and retired persons who have been widowed or divorced but who desire not to jeopardize their retirement income or inheritance arrangement by entering another legal marriage. In about 8 per cent of unmarried couple households, either one or both members of the couple are widowed.[2]

In recent years, there have been at least two new aspects added to cohabitation. One is the increased number of persons involved in such arrangements. Since 1970, that number has quadrupled to almost 2 million, although at the present time, unmarried couple households make up 2.3 per cent of all households in the country, and less than 4 per cent of all couple households. Of particular significance, however, may be the fact that the number of cohabiting couples declined by 5,000 from 1984 to 1985.[3] Whether or not this is a real trend will not be known for several years.

The other new aspect of cohabitation is its emergence among never-married college students as an alternative type of couple relationship and housing arrangement. Popular opinion, of course, would have one believe that a very large proportion of college students currently are living with someone of the other sex. However, census data indicate that those persons likely to be college students (never married, under 25, having no children) account for less than 7 per cent of all unmarried couple households. On the other hand, much of that increase since 1970 has occurred among persons under 25 years of age, some part of them being college students.[4]

The practice of cohabitation among college students and other young people arose as a consequence of several significant changes in the living arrangements of students, with a simultaneous change in the general atmosphere of more openness in sexual relationships and other sexual matters. Specifically, the abolition of dormitory curfews for women, greater freedom in living arrangements on campus (coed dormitories), and the sudden increase in apartment living by students, along with the increase in sexual freedom of recent years, facilitated the development of the alternative of cohabitation as a desirable living arrangement for some students.

A typical pattern has been for a couple to drift into a cohabitation arrangement, located at the living quarters of the male, with the female still maintaining a dormitory room for the sake of appearances.[5] As the couple spend more and more time together at the male's apartment, it's easy to fall into the pattern of simply not returning to the dormitory at night or for the entire weekend, because dormitory rules of the past no longer exist. The reverse process also occurs, with the male spending more and more time at the female's apartment, but males are more likely to live off campus than are females.

The problem that most concerns marriage and family professionals lies in determining just what cohabitation is. That is, what precisely does cohabitation mean to the people involved and to the courtship and marriage institutions? There are a number of possible answers to this question, each of which might have relevance for particular relationships.

Is Cohabitation a Trial Marriage? For some it might be. In the case of young and middle-aged divorced persons who live together for a time, many want to try a marriage-like relationship before they remarry. For these individuals, cohabitation certainly would have to be considered a trial marriage. The picture, however, is less clear with college students. An early study of cohabitation in the late 1960s indicated that most of the couples surveyed intended to get married to each other at some later date.[6] However, later studies have shown less of a relationship between cohabitation and marriage, with most of those questioned, particularly the males, indicating that they had not entered the cohabitation arrangement with marriage in mind.[7] Also, there was a high rate of "breaking-up" for many of the cohabiting couples.

Is Cohabitation a Substitution for Marriage? In the more recent studies, living together seems to be more a matter of convenience and practicality than a marriage-type arrangement.[8] This is not to indicate that these relationships are not based on strong emotional attachments, because most of them are. Sharing a living situation does have certain practical advantages, which often are recognized by the participants. Some liaisons were begun with the knowledge and understanding that they would be temporary in nature, such as the sharing of quarters while traveling on an extended tour of Europe, the United States, or on a vacation during the holidays. Because most couples who live together do not present themselves to the public as being married, cohabitation cannot be considered the same as common-law marriage. Reiss states that because most cohabiting couples make every effort to avoid pregnancy and plan to resort to abortion if pregnancy occurs, these relationships, therefore, lack most of the legal requirements that would define a relationship as a marriage.[9]

Is Cohabitation Another Form of Exploitation? There is some evidence that whereas one member of a cohabiting couple is entering what is perceived to be a "meaningful relationship," the other member might be exploiting the relationship very much in terms of the traditional double standard. One study found, for example, that many of the female partners expressed a desire for, and a high prospect of, getting married, whereas the male partners expressed no such desire.[10] Another study indicated that the female ultimately did most of the household chores, such as cooking and cleaning, following the traditional division of labor found in many marriages.[11] It appears that some males are taking advantage of the new ideology of "meaningful relationships without the necessity of marriage" to further exercise the sexual double standard to their advantage, with little investment by way of long-term commitment on their part.

Is Cohabitation a New Form of Courtship? It should be clear at this point that cohabitation serves different functions and purposes that vary not only from one couple to the next, but also by sex. In our view this new and limited practice represents, for most young people who engage in it, an additional development in the more ordinary courtship process. In the past it was not unusual for some couples to engage in sex prior to marriage, and in many cases without consideration of marriage. The only thing now different about cohabitation might be that it is done more openly, with more interaction being compressed into a briefer time frame. Just as some premarital sexual relationships in the past led to marriage, while others did not, the same is true of cohabitation relationships. They also might be viewed as a more serious or concentrated form of going steady, with a more openly acknowledged sexual element.

Although the cohabitation phenomenon has received a great deal of media attention, especially in the popular magazines, it is nevertheless a pattern of behavior that involves only a small minority of people, and an even smaller minority among young people attending colleges and universities. Cohabitation probably is more widely practiced among those who are not involved in higher education or who are beyond that age group.

Cohabitation has been recognized and studied as a significant practice for over fifteen years now, but as an open lifestyle, the phenomenon of cohabitation is still relatively new. There continues to be widespread public disapproval of this practice. From the public morality point of view, the sides of the issue are fairly clear-cut, there being those favoring and those against such behavior, along with a large proportion of the public who are just tolerant. But from the standpoint of family social scientists, apart from their own moral viewpoints, there still are a number of open questions. Thus, the articles in this section attempt to throw additional light on some of the questions that have been raised.

The first article, "Cohabitation in the United States," takes a thorough look at the body of research that has been accumulated on cohabitation and goes on to look at the nature of the relationships involved, the ways in which these relationships come about, and the ways in which they end. The author then summarizes the research related to the effects of cohabitation on the individuals, on marriage, and on the society. Although this article is now about ten years old, it was retained in this new edition because it is still the most comprehensive summary of research on the topic. Furthermore, at about the time this article was written, research interest on cohabitation waned so that few new findings on the topic have been published since this summary was written.

The second article, "It Pays to Get Your Affair in Order," takes a practical look at some of the possible consequences of couples' living together. It focuses mainly upon the potential legal and financial difficulties that can arise from couples living together without the normal legal protections that go with marriage. One means of protection is through contracts that spell out who owns what or how jointly owned real and personal property is to be divided in the event that the couple part company. However, even carefully drawn agreements do not completely solve all of the possible problems because, just as in the case of so-called prenuptial contracts, some of the agreements might not hold up under court scrutiny. Nevertheless, plenty of good advice is contained in the article.

The final brief article in this part is a more personal account, written from the points of view of both the man and the woman in a cohabitation relationship. A number of difficulties, as well as some of the positive features of such relationships, are illustrated.

NOTES

1 U.S. Bureau of the Census, *Current Population Reports*, "Households, Families, Marital Status, and Living Arrangements: March 1985 (Advance Report)," Series P-20, No. 402, October 1985, p. 9.

2 Ibid.

3 Ibid.

4 U. S. Bureau of the Census, *Current Population Reports*, "Marital Status and Living Arrangements: March 1984," Series P-20, No. 399, July 1985, pp. 47-8.

5 Ira L. Reiss, *Family Systems in America*, 2nd ed. (Hinsdale, Ill.: The Dryden Press, 1976), p. 88.

6 Michael P. Johnson, "Courtship and Commitment: A Study of Cohabitation on a University Campus," unpublished master's thesis, University of Iowa, 1969; cited in Reiss, op. cit., p. 87.

7 Judith L. Lyness, Milton E. Lipetz, and Keith E. Davis, "Living Together: An Alternative to Marriage," *Journal of Marriage and the Family*, 34 (May 1972), pp. 305-311.

8 Eleanor P. Macklin, "Heterosexual Cohabitation Among College Students," *The Family Coordinator*, 21 (October 1972), pp. 463-473; Charles Lee Cole, "Cohabitation in Social Context," in Roger W. Libby and Robert N. Whitehurst, *Marriage and Alternatives: Exploring Intimate Relationships* (Glenview, Ill.: Scott, Foresman and Company, 1977), pp. 62-79.

9 Reiss, op. cit., p. 88.

10 Lyness, et al., op. cit.

11 Macklin, op. cit.

5.

Cohabitation in the United States

Eleanor D. Macklin

During the past decade, observers of the social scene and researchers in the area of marriage and courtship have become ever more aware of the rising number of unmarried heterosexual persons living together. Although the phenomenon of men and women living together without "benefit of marriage" is not new, either in this country or in other cultures (Berger, 1971; Rodman, 1961, 1966), it certainly has not been common to Western middle-class society. In fact, nonmarital cohabitation still is held to be a crime, complete with fine and jail sentence, in many states in this country (see Massey and Warner, 1974; Weitzman, 1974; King, 1975; Hirsch, 1976; Lavori, 1976 for a review of the legal situation).

As the adult world argued pro and con, there was increasing evidence that young persons (and some not-so-young persons) were not sitting patiently waiting for the verdict. Quietly, and on their own, they were beginning to experiment with new ways of living together and relating to one another. The public media were the first to report ("Unstructured Relationships," 1966; Grant, 1968; "Linda, the Light Housekeeper," 1968; McWhirter, 1968; Schrag, 1968; Bloch, 1969; Karlen, 1969; Sheehy, 1969). And slowly, on many different campuses around the country, researchers also began to note the changing mores, and simultaneously and independently, to gather data suggesting that a new dimension was being added to the traditional courtship pattern. In 1968 the first graduate thesis on cohabitation was completed (Johnson, 1968), and in 1972 the first published research appeared (Lyness et al., 1972; Macklin, 1972).

Excerpted from "Review of Research on Nonmarital Cohabitation in the United States," in Bernard I. Murstein (ed.), *Exploring Intimate Lifestyles*, New York: Springer Publishing Company, 1978.

Attitudes Toward Cohabitation

There have been a number of studies designed primarily to measure attitudes of college students to the new life styles and to determine factors associated with these attitudes, and many of the more general surveys have included questions regarding attitudes. All available evidence suggests that, in general, students tend to approve of cohabitation outside marriage.

At City College in New York in the early 1970's, almost 80 per cent of a large convenience sample said they would live with someone of the opposite sex if given an opportunity to do so (Arafat and Yorburg, 1973). At Arizona State University at about the same time, almost 60 per cent of the men who had not cohabited and 35 per cent of such women answered "yes" when asked if they would want to (Henze and Hudson, 1974). Bower and Christopherson (1977), in their national survey of convenience samples in sixteen state universities, found that more than 50 per cent of those who had not cohabited indicated they would consider doing so. At the University of Delaware, only 28 per cent of the undergraduate random sample said they probably or definitely would not cohabit (McCauley, 1977). At Illinois State University in 1972, only 23 per cent of the females and 8 per cent of the males in a large convenience sample said they definitely would not cohabit, even if in love (Huang, 1974). At Cornell University in 1972, only 7 per cent of those who had not cohabited said it was because of moral reasons. The most common reasons indicated for not having cohabited were: "Have not yet found a partner with whom I would like to stay for four or more nights a week" and "Am geographically separated from partner" (Macklin, 1976b).

Drawing upon these varied data, one is tempted to project that, across the country as a whole, probably about 25 per cent of the undergraduate population has cohabited; 50 per cent would if they were to find themselves in an appropriate relationship and in a situation in which they could; and 25 per cent believe they probably would not do so even if it were possible (more of these being females and underclassmen).

A majority of the student population not only apparently approves of cohabitation outside marriage and would cohabit given an opportunity and the right circumstances, but in addition, most feel no long-term commitment to the person is necessary before doing so (see Table 1). The most commonly held attitude appears to be that cohabitation is acceptable as long as there is a strong, affectionate, preferably monogamous relationship between the two persons involved. There is some suggestion, again depending upon the institution, that males as a group might be somewhat more accepting of cohabitation than females and might not feel the need for as strong an emotional involvement before cohabiting.

TABLE 1. Relationship That Should Exist Before a Person Cohabits with Someone of the Opposite Sex*

	Macklin (1976b) N: 299	Cole ** N: 190	Kalmbach (1973) N: 40	McCauley (1977) N: 397
Married	5%	2%	5%	14%
Officially engaged	1	10	19	3
Tentatively engaged	6	16	0	14
Strong affectionate, monogamous relationship	45	42	38	34
Strong affectionate relationship, but might be dating others	13	13	18	10
Good friends	10	7	17	8
No relationship need exist	19	10	3	17

*Data are from surveys of random or systematic samples of various undergraduate populations using the same questionnaire items.
**Personal communication.

How do those who approve of cohabitation differ from those who do not? Religion and personality factors have been the two differentiating variables most frequently discussed in reports to date. As well as being one of the best predictors of who will cohabit, religion (in particular, present religious preference and strength of that preference) has been found to be one of the most powerful predictors of attitude (Arafat and Yorburg, 1973; Huang, 1974; Strong and Nass, 1975). Those who receive high religiosity scores are less likely to approve of cohabitation, whereas those who indicate they have no current religious affiliation are more likely to approve.

Personality, and in particular, self concept also might be important variables. For instance, Strong and Nass (1975) found that females who viewed their mothers as being more rejecting and less satisfied in the marital relationship, and who held less traditional sex-role orientations, tended to be more accepting of cohabitation. This would appear to fit well with the Arafat and Yorburg (1973) finding that those women who approved of cohabitation were more likely to characterize themselves as independent, outgoing, and aggressive. It also is consistent with the finding by Guittar and Lewis (1974) that cohabiting females tend to see themselves as more managerial, competitive, and aggressive than do engaged, noncohabiting women and are more likely to report less closeness to the same-sex parent. It frequently has been hypothesized that women who are more independent, have more need to achieve, and are less accepting of traditional femininity tend to see their mothers as colder and less supportive (Bardwick, 1971). It would make sense that these less traditional women more easily would accept nontraditional courtship patterns. Mosher's finding

(1975) that disbelief in romantic love and value placed on self-actualization were major personality variables related to the endorsement of trial and contract marriage would seem consistent with these general conclusions.

Although students have been found to have generally positive attitudes toward cohabitation, parents have not. Three studies are known to have compared the attitudes of parents and students (Macklin, 1974a; Smith and Kimmel, 1970; Steiner, 1975), and in all three cases, the gap between the generations has been dramatic. When the attitudes of seventy students (mostly female) at a northeastern university were compared with those of their parents, 6 per cent of the students and 63 per cent of the parents indicated that persons should marry before living together (Macklin, 1974a). When a more conservative group of women was surveyed at a north central university, the difference was equally significant, with 41 per cent of the daughters and 88 per cent of the mothers indicating that cohabitation without marriage was morally unacceptable under any circumstances (Steiner, 1975). In neither study did a single parent indicate she would approve of her daughter's cohabitation (although some would accept it). Interestingly enough, when students were asked to predict their parents' attitudes, they were able to do so with considerable accuracy (for example, in the Steiner research, 80 per cent of the daughters correctly predicted their mothers' response regarding cohabitation).

Nature of the Relationship

It has become clear that there is no single entity known as the cohabitation relationship. The concept as now used covers a wide variety of relationships, differing not only in amount of time spent together and nature of the living arrangement, but also in the partners' degree of commitment.

Several attempts have been made to develop a useful typology of cohabitation relationships. The cohabitation research group that met at the Groves Conference on Marriage and the Family in 1974 sought to classify cohabitation relationships along a continuum of dyadic commitment and identified the following six points: (1) temporary convenience or mutual benefit; (2) affectionate relationship but open to other simultaneous relationships; (3) affectionate, monogamous relationship (i.e., "going steady"); (4) trial marriage or the conscious testing of a relationship; (5) temporary alternative to marriage (e.g., while awaiting divorce settlement or graduation); and (6) permanent alternative to marriage (*Cohabitation Research Newsletter*, No. 4, June 1974, p. 2). Others, for ease of analysis, have reduced the types to three: casual or temporary involvement, preparation or testing for marriage, and substitute for or alternative to marriage (Lewis et al., 1975; Petty, 1975). It now is generally accepted by most researchers that it is unrealistic to treat all unmarried cohabitants as one homogeneous group, but there still is a strong tendency to do so.

The percentage of cohabitants who fall within each of these categories is not clear. When college cohabitants have been asked in surveys to identify the nature of their relationship at the time they began living together, a small number described themselves as simply friends or persons living together purely for convenience (probably under 10 per cent). A somewhat larger group (somewhere between 10 and 20 per cent generally) indicated that they were seriously contemplating marriage or living together until it was convenient to marry. The great majority fell between these two extremes, describing themselves as involved in a strong, affectionate, but as yet uncommitted relationship (with between 50 and 60 per cent indicating that they were monogamous or "going steady"). Rarely did undergraduate cohabitants see themselves as involved in a permanent alternative to marriage. Consistent with this perception was the fact that most college cohabiting couples maintained two separate residences, at least during the first year of their relationship, and did not spend every night together.

It is this information that has led researcher after researcher to declare that cohabitation on the college campus is merely an added step in the courtship process—a kind of "living-out of going steady" (e.g., Henze and Hudson, 1974; Johnson, 1968; Macklin, 1972;1974b, 1976b; Bower and Christopherson, 1977). The partners generally share a deep emotional relationship with each other but have not yet reached a point of long-term commitment. Most have not even considered marriage as a viable alternative to their present relationship, not because they disapprove of marriage (study after study has confirmed that the great majority of cohabiting students see themselves as being married at some point in their lives), but because they do not feel personally ready for marriage or are not ready to commit themselves to that particular person. As Bower and Christopherson indicate when reporting their national survey: "Cohabitation, as it seems to be practiced today by middle-class college students, is defined as a replacement for marriage by only a small minority of its participants. . . . Cohabitants seem not to be rejecting marriage itself but merely adding to some of the processes by which the marriage bond is formed" (1977, pp. 450-51).

Formation of the Cohabitation Dyad

Living together, at least on the college campus, is seldom the result of a considered decision, at least not initially. Most relationships involve a gradual (and sometimes not so gradual) drifting into sleeping together more and more frequently. Only 25 per cent in one study (Macklin, 1974b) indicated that they had discussed whether to live together before starting to do so. If and when a decision with conscious deliberation is made, it usually is precipitated by some external force (e.g., need to make plans for the summer or next fall, graduation, unexpected pregnancy, or a necessary housing or room change). Until that time, there is only a mutual, often unspoken, recognition of the desire to be together—a natural progression of the relationship.

Some attention has been given to identifying those factors that influence, encourage, or facilitate this drift into living together. At the first meeting of the cohabitation research group (at Groves Conference in 1973), it was suggested that the variables most predictive of cohabitation were: low perception of social disapproval, low internalized guilt regarding premarital sexuality and living together, and high availability of opportunity (*Cohabitation Research Newsletter*, No. 3, October 1973). Working from this idea, Clatworthy (1975) suggested that if one were to place amount of guilt and perceived degree of social disapproval on separate scales from one to ten points each, and if an individual received a total of more then ten points from the two scales together, he or she would find living together to be more anguish than benefit. This is an interesting idea that awaits testing.

Meeting again in 1974, the research group further delineated those factors that might be predictive of drift. The following were among those hypothesized (see *Cohabitation Research Newsletter*, No. 4, June 1974, pp. 2-3):

1. Factors that affect the degree to which an individual *experiences or perceives the opportunity to cohabit*:
   a. Environmental opportunity (e.g., availability of potential partners; geographic distance from partner; permissive housing regulations).
   b. Sociocultural norms within immediate environment (e.g., peer norms, salience of peer norms, perception of reference group support, awareness of others cohabiting).
   c. Isolation from conventional social control agents (e.g., geographic distance from parents; predictability of parental visits). Importance will be conditional upon degree of financial and emotional independence of these agents.
   d. Interpersonal attractiveness (e.g., interpersonal competence, physical attractiveness).
2. Factors that affect the likelihood that an individual *will avail him/herself of the opportunity to cohabit*:
   a. Religiosity (degree to which one identifies with religious groups or beliefs that are consistent with cohabitation).
   b. Personality variables (e.g., degree of need for autonomy, capacity for intimacy, disbelief in romantic love, acceptance of nontraditional sex roles, value placed on self-actualization, aggressiveness, comfort with ambiguity and change); will vary somewhat with gender.
   c. Degree of previous sexual or dating experience.
   d. Degree of affection for partner and perceived happiness when with individual.

The above are, in general, factors that research to date has found tend to differentiate between cohabitants and noncohabitants or that have been reported by individuals as reasons for or for not cohabiting. No attempt has been made yet to weigh the variables or to develop some path analysis indicating which variables might be more basic and determinant than others.

Montgomery (1973) also has given some thought to the path by which relationships move from their typically casual beginnings to deeper and more permanent involvements. He argues that cohabitation requires more commitment ("internally generated cohesion") than does marriage in order to continue, for there are fewer external unifiers and numerous external forces that work against the relationship. And because commitment is evident only through some behavioral manifestation, there must be behavioral manifestations of gradually increasing commitments if the cohabitation relationship is to grow and survive. Each step toward increased commitment requires that the individual experience some evidence that his increased commitment is going to be worth it to him. Evidence of the other's deepening commitment provides that reassurance. Montgomery suggests the following hierarchy of "commitment evidence":

1. Sharing fun and pleasant social activity.
2. Limiting of social activity to the one other person.
3. Establishment of joint residence.
4. Sharing of activities necessary for the continuation of the relationship (e.g., the sharing of household tasks).
5. Sharing expenses.
6. Working out personal problems in ways that strengthen the relationship.
7. The making of marriage plans.
8. Marriage.
9. Having children.

Dissolution of the Cohabitation Dyad

Ganson (1975) surveyed a sample of thirty male and forty-one female students who had experienced the termination of a cohabitation relationship, in an effort to identify the causes of termination and the differences between males and females in their reasons for breaking up. Respondents were given a list of forty-three possible reasons for the termination of a living-together relationship and were asked to indicate the extent to which they believed each factor had contributed to their own breakup. Factors related to infringement on freedom and personal incompatibility were seen most often as the cause of dissolution, with women more likely than men

to believe that the factor has played a role. The following items were those
on which men and women differed significantly in their responses:

	Per Cent Indicating Reason for Terminating	
	Males	Females
Infringement on personal freedom		
I felt trapped	32	63
There were times I couldn't be me	32	58
My partner wanted me to be different	36	48
I believed I was losing my identity	32	48
My partner dominated me	24	43
Personal characteristics of partner		
We just grew apart/our personalities no longer were compatible	39	73
I got bored with my partner	13	45
Our sexual needs weren't compatible	16	33
Inability to cope with situation		
Parents dead set against relationship	7	19
My values opposed to cohabitation	0	10
Living situation		
Didn't have privacy I needed	32	45
Insufficient income	13	35
Commitment discrepancy		
I was too dependent on partner	19	41

Why females consistently were more likely than males to believe that
a factor had contributed to dissolution is not clear. Ganson hypothesized
that women are more emotionally involved in relationships than men and
hence more sensitive to problems. Noting that many of the reasons given
by women for breakup revolve around infringement on personal freedom,
she hypothesizes that women traditionally have given up more autonomy
than men when they move into a relationship and that women are increasingly unwilling to do so. If indeed their relationships were as traditional
as has been suggested earlier in this chapter and women are indeed more
interested in androgynous relationships than men (as suggested by
McCauley, 1975), then perhaps these women did feel unduly trapped and
inhibited and were in fact more in need of freedom from the relationship
than their male partners.

One is reminded of the findings reported by Zick Rubin (1975), who followed a sample of 231 college-age couples for two years. Like Ganson, he also
noted that when the relationships dissolved, the women tended to see more
problems in the relationship than did the men (74 per cent of the women
and 61 per cent of the men mentioned "my need for independence" as a

contributing factor). Like Ganson, Rubin hypothesized that women might be more sensitive to the quality of their interpersonal relationships, but he suggested a somewhat different reason. Rubin argued that because a woman's future status in our society is so dependent upon the kind of husband she marries, she must evaluate her courtship relationship more frequently and more carefully than a man. Rather than finding women to be more emotionally involved than men, his data suggest that men fall in love more quickly and suffer more emotional pain at dissolution than do women. Although his research dealt only peripherally with cohabitation, he did report that those of his couples who lived together were not more or less likely to stay together than couples who had not lived together—suggesting once again that the mere fact of cohabitation might be somewhat irrelevant.

In a paper based on interviews with six cohabiting couples, Hennon (1975a) theorized about the role that conflict-management plays in the development and maintenance of cohabitation relationships. Building on concepts developed originally by Jetse Sprey, Hannon argued that any pair-bond relationship, including the cohabitation relationship, must be seen as "a system in conflict." How conflict is dealt with will vary with the degree of mutual desire to maintain the relationship and with the extent to which there are shared procedural rules for negotiating the conflict. This, in turn, will determine whether conflict leads to dissolution or to enhanced intimacy and pair-bond strength.

Hennon raised the following important, but as yet unanswered, questions: Are cohabiting couples, because they cannot take the relationship for granted and must "work" in order to maintain it, more likely than married couples to be aware of areas of disagreement and their techniques for dealing with these? Or do they tend to be in a romantic stage and hence less able to face their conflicts realistically? Or because they are less secure in their relationship (with less perceived mutuality of commitment and less conviction that the partner will cooperate to negotiate the conflict in a way that will preserve the relationship), will they be more hesitant to disclose and confront areas of conflict? These are interesting research questions, deserving attention, but one could predict that the answer will vary with the particular skills and personality attributes of the individual couple and that it will be difficult to generalize about cohabiting couples as a group.

How many cohabitation relationships break up and how many continue on as permanent relationships is not known yet, and the answer awaits more longitudinal research. One study of college cohabitation (Macklin, 1976b) reported that at time of data collection, 5 per cent of the relationships had resulted in marriage, 25 per cent were at the point of tentative or formal engagement, 50 per cent still were ongoing but not as yet committed, and 20 per cent had dissolved.

Effects of Cohabitation

ON THE INDIVIDUALS INVOLVED

Most of the research to date on effect of cohabitation on the individuals involved has been a matter of self-report, with the cohabitants indicating by either questionnaire or interview what they considered to be the pros and cons of the cohabitation experience. By and large, cohabitants have given overwhelmingly positive ratings to their experience. In one study (Macklin, 1976b), when college cohabitants were asked to indicate the degree to which their cohabitation was successful, pleasurable, and maturing, 78 per cent indicated that it was successful or very successful (10 per cent, unsuccessful); 93 per cent rated it pleasurable or very pleasurable (1 per cent, unpleasurable); and 91 per cent rated it as maturing or very maturing (no one rated it as "not at all maturing"). When asked to rate the effect of the experience on a number of specific growth areas (e.g., self-confidence, emotional maturity, ability to understand and relate to others, and insight into the opposite sex), 80 per cent or more indicated that the experience had had a positive effect in each area. More than three quarters indicated that they never would marry without living with the person first and no one said that they never again would cohabit outside of marriage.

These findings are corroborated by other research. When Bower (1975) asked a similar question of his 126 cohabitants, 66 per cent said that they never would marry without cohabiting first, and 68 per cent said they would cohabit again with the same person. Shuttlesworth and Thorman (1973) report that 64 per cent of their sample of college cohabitants rated the relationship as "very happy," 30 per cent as "pretty happy," and only 6 per cent as "not very happy." Eighty per cent checked that "the experience gave me a deeper understanding of myself" and "fostered my own emotional growth." Eighty-three per cent indicated that they held no regrets about having cohabited; only 3 per cent regretted having done so. Fifty-six per cent indicated that they would "not consider marriage without first having lived with the prospective marriage partner."

Peterman, Ridley, and Anderson (1974) conclude their report on college cohabitation by saying, "There are no immediately obvious negative effects of cohabitation, at least in terms of self-described personal adjustment or functioning as a student. If anything, cohabitation is associated with more positive self-attitudes and heterosexual relating." Lautenschlager (1972) concludes, on the basis of her survey of college students, that although "there are risks involved to the individual as there are in any human relationships. . .consensual union for the young college student appears to have definite functional value" (e.g., providing emotional support, financial practicality, sexual fulfillment, opportunity for personal growth, and the chance to assess compatibility).

In reviewing all available data, one is impressed repeatedly by the very strong positive attitudes toward cohabitation that are held by those who have experienced it. The main message that one gets consistently from cohabitants is the many ways in which the experience served to foster their own personal growth and maturity. Yet to date, no one has attempted to develop or apply over time any objective measures to test to what extent cohabitation does in fact lead to enhanced personal growth.

Ridley and Peterman (1975) have hypothesized that cohabitation is most likely to be a growth-producing experience and to lead to improved heterosexual competence when the following conditions are present: (a) the individuals do not have strong needs for emotional security, which might serve to prevent them from openly acknowledging and dealing with any disagreements for fear of endangering the relationship; (b) the couple enters the relationship with increased self-understanding as a goal; (c) one has a basis of prior heterosexual experience on which to build; and (d) one does not isolate oneself from a broader network of friends. They suggest that should a termination result, it will be less traumatic if (a) the individual already has affirmed his/her social desirability and developed good interpersonal skills in earlier relationships; (b) the step into cohabitation was a natural developmental extension from earlier relationships; and (c) the individuals maintain a "cushion" of friends to fall back upon. All of these are hypotheses that deserve to be tested.

ON MARRIAGE

The critical issue for many laymen has been: What effect does cohabitation have on later marriage? Does it, by serving as a screening device and laboratory for personal growth, enhance the chances of later marital success? Or does it instead encourage persons to place a priority on self-fulfillment and personal happiness and hence make them less likely to make the sacrifices necessary for a successful relationship? To answer this question will require agreed-upon criteria of marital success (longevity and lack of evident conflict are not necessarily adequate criteria) and longitudinal research on carefully matched samples of unmarried cohabiting and noncohabiting couples. At present, we must rely instead on comparisons of currently married couples who had and had not cohabitated before marriage. Four such studies come to mind.

Lyness (1976b) compared eleven married couples who had cohabited before marriage with thirteen married couples who had not, on sixteen variables representing concepts from "open marriage" and found few differences between the groups. Olday (*Cohabitation Research Newsletter*, No. 5, p. 38) surveyed 184 married students who had cohabited before marriage and 524 who had not, controlling for such variables as income, length of marriage, and relationship to parents, and also found practically no significant difference between the groups. Specifically, cohabitation before marriage did not seem to be related to degree of emotional closeness, satisfaction, conflict, or egalitarianism in marriage. The only significant difference was age of marriage, with the premarital cohabitants marrying about a year later than the others.

Budd (1976) studied 151 volunteer couples (fifty-four cohabiting couples, forty-eight marrieds who had cohabited, and forty-nine marrieds who had not). Like Olday, when she compared those marrieds who had cohabited with those who had not on problems experienced, amount of self-disclosure, and degree of commitment, she found few significant differences. Marrieds who had cohabited did indicate less social commitment to the relationship (i.e., opinions of others would have less influence on making them stay together); males showed less concern about their partners not loving them as much as they used to; females indicated more concern about feeling trapped; and males indicated their partners more often had seen them use "poor communication" methods (e.g., walking out or refusing to talk). But caution is urged in interpreting these results, for they were not strong differences and could well be due more to personality factors than to the experience of having cohabited.

Clatworthy and Scheid (1977), though noting many similarities between couples who had and had not lived together before marriage, also found important differences: Those who had cohabited premaritally were less likely to acquiesce in disagreement; disagreed more often on such things as finances, household duties, and recreation; were less dependent on their spouses; considered their marriage a less intrinsic part of their lives; had broken up more often; and a higher percentage had sought marriage counseling. Again, it seems likely that these differences might well have existed even if the couples had not cohabited and more likely are due to pre-existing personal predispositions than to the experience of cohabitation per se. In fact, the very factors that led them to be attracted to cohabitation in the first place (more liberal attitudes and greater tendency toward independence and assertiveness on the part of the females) might lead them to reveal less acquiescence in marriage and to see marriage as less essential to their well-being.

Clatworthy and Scheid go on to report that, although all the married couples studied who had cohabited before marriage considered the experience to have been beneficial, there was no evidence that their marriages were any better or any less conventional than the marriages of those who merely had dated. They conclude that, although there is no evidence that cohabitation causes any problems in later marriage, it certainly should not be seen as a cure-all for the problems facing marriage in today's society.

There has been as yet no research that will let us say with any certainty what effect the movement from cohabitation to marriage has on a relationship. Berger (1974) concludes, on the basis of retrospective data gained from interviews with twenty-one middle-aged couples who had cohabited premaritally, that marriage leads to no dramatic change in the relationship. The quality of the relationship after marriage duplicates to a large extent the apparent quality of the relationship before marriage. One finds no real consensus on this point, however (see, for example, Keaough, 1975). Some observe that marriage made things better by removing social and parental pressure; others complain that they found themselves falling into traditional roles and expectations with a resulting loss of identity. On the basis of what evidence we do have, it seems likely that in many cases movement into marriage brings escalation of commitment and increased ease with relatives and other members of the larger community. However, because of our socialization, marriage also brings an increased tendency toward role-playing, possessiveness, and reduction in personal identity and autonomy unless the couple make a strong effort to counteract this tendency. How the couple define the relationship for themselves might well be more important than the legal label attached to it.

ON SOCIETY

Many have feared that cohabitation will lead to erosion of the family, reduction in marriage rates, and an increase in children born without the security of committed parents. However, these fears have not been validated. Although there has been a decrease in the percentage of women currently married over the past fifteen years (62.1 in 1960; 58.4 in 1970; 57.5 in 1974), and an accompanying increase in single and divorced women (28.6 per cent of women aged twenty to twenty four were single in 1960, whereas 39.6 per cent were single in 1974), there is no reason to think that large numbers are permanently substituting nonmarital relationships (Bernard, 1975).

When students are asked about their attitude toward marriage, the vast majority continue to indicate that they hope to marry someday. In Bower and Christopherson's national survey (1977), only 4 per cent of the cohabitants and 1 per cent of the noncohabitants indicated they wished never to marry. This is consistent with findings of surveys at two large eastern universities (Macklin, 1976b; McCauley, 1977), where only about 1 per cent indicated no desire ever to marry. Although about 25 per cent said they might marry someday but did not think marriage was necessary for their happiness, the great majority plan to marry at some point in their life.

We cannot say yet whether cohabitation before marriage eventually will reduce the divorce rate in this country. It is true that it might provide for more effective screening and lead to persons marrying at a more mature age. But the mere fact that a couple have had an opportunity to test their initial compatibility through living together, even if they make maximum use of that opportunity, might have little effect on whether that couple manage to spend a lifetime together. There are so many factors that affect the course of relationships in our society that cohabitation before marriage logically would play a very minor role when compared to the multitude of other influences.

As yet, there are no data to tell us what effect growing up with cohabiting parents will have on children. Bernice Eiduson and her associates currently are involved in a longitudinal comparison of two hundred children reared in cohabiting, communal, single-parent, and two-parent nuclear families. Evidence to date suggests that the needs of the infant are such strong determiners of how children are reared during the first year of life that caretaking practices in nontraditional and traditional families do not differ significantly during this period. At the end of one year, the development of the total sample generally fell within the normal range, with life style not a differentiating factor (Eiduson, personal communication, 1977). It will be interesting to see the extent to which life style appears to affect the later development of these children.

REFERENCES

Arafat, I. and B. Yorburg. "On Living Together Without Marriage." *Journal of Sex Research* 9 (1973): 97-106.

Bardwick, J. *The Psychology of Women: A Study of Bio-Cultural Conflict.* New York: Harper & Row, 1971.

Berger, M. E. "Trial Marriage Harnessing the Trend Constructively." *The Family Coordinator* 20 (1971): 38-43.

Berger, M. E. *Trial Marriage Follow-Up Study.* Unpublished manuscript, 1974. Bernard, J. "Note on Changing Life Styles, 1970- 1974." *Journal of Marriage and the Family* 37 (1975): 582-93.

Bloch, D. "Unwed Couples: Do They Live Happily Ever After?" *Redbook* (April 1969): 90, 140-44.

Bower, D. W. *A Description and Analysis of a Cohabiting Sample in America.* Unpublished master's thesis. University of Arizona, 1975.

Bower, D. W. and V. A. Christopherson. "University Student Cohabitation: A Regional Comparison of Selected Attitudes and Behavior." *Journal of Marriage and the Family* 39 (1977): 447-53.

Budd, L. S. *Problems, Disclosure, and Commitment of Cohabiting and Married Couples.* Unpublished doctoral dissertation. University of Minnesota, 1976.

Clatworthy, N. M. "Couples in Quasi-Marriage." *Old Family/New Family: Interpersonal Relationships,* edited by N. Glazer-Malbin. Princeton: Van Nostrand, 1975.

Clatworthy, N. M. and L. Scheid. *A Comparison of Married Couples: Premarital Cohabitants with Nonpremarital Cohabitants.* Unpublished manuscript. Ohio State University, 1977.

Ganson, H. C. *Cohabitation: The Antecedents of Dissolution of Formerly Cohabiting Individuals.* Unpublished master's thesis. Ohio State University, 1975.

Grant, A. "No Rings Attached: A Look at Premarital Marriage on Campus." *Mademoiselle* (April 1978): 208.

Guittar, E. C. and R. A. Lewis. *Self Concepts Among Some Unmarried Cohabitants.* Unpublished manuscript. Pennsylvania State University, 1974.

Hennon, C. B. *Conflict Management Within Pairing Relationships: The Case of Nonmarital Cohabitation.* Unpublished manuscript. University of Utah, 1975.

Henze, L. F. and J. W. Hudson. "Personal and Family Characteristics of Non-cohabiting College Students." *Journal of Marriage and the Family* 36 (1974): 722-26.

Hirsch, B. *Living Together: A Guide to the Law for Unmarried Couples.* Boston: Houghton Mifflin, 1976.

Huang, L. J. *Research with Unmarried Cohabiting Couples: Including Nonexclusive Sexual Relations.* Unpublished manuscript. Illinois State University, 1974.

Johnson, M. P. *Courtship and Commitment: A Study of Cohabitation on a University Campus.* Unpublished master's thesis. University of Iowa, 1968.

Karlen, A. "The Unmarried Marrieds on Campus." *New York Times Magazine* (January 26, 1969): 31.

Keaough, D. "Without Knotting the Tie." *The Arizona Republic* (July 27, 1975): 8-15.

King, M. D. *Cohabitation Handbook: Living Together and the Law.* Berkeley, California: Ten Speed Press, 1975.

Lautenschlager, S. Y. *A Descriptive Study of Consensual Union Among College Students.* Unpublished master's thesis. California State University at Northridge, 1972.

Lavori, N. *Living Together, Married or Single: Your Legal Rights.* New York: Harper and Row, 1976.

Lewis, R. A., G. B. Soanier, V. L. Storm, and C. F. LeHecka, *Commitment in Married and Unmarried Cohabitation.* Unpublished manuscript. Pennsylvania State University, 1975.

"Linda, the Light Housekeeper." *Time* (April 26, 1968): 51.

Lyness, J. F. *Open Marriage Among Former Cohabitants: "We Have Met the Enemy: Is It Us?"* Unpublished manuscript. Pennsylvania State University. 1976.

Lyness, J. F., M. E. Lipetz, and K. E. Davis. "Living Together: An Alternative to Marriage." *Journal of Marriage and the Family* 34 (1972): 305-11.

Macklin, E. D. "Heterosexual Cohabitation Among Unmarried College Students." *The Family Coordinator* 21 (1972): 163-72.

Macklin, E. D. *Comparison of Parent and Student Attitudes Toward Nonmarital Cohabitation.* Unpublished manuscript. Cornell University, 1974.

Macklin, E. D. "Students Who Live Together: Trial Marriage or Going Very Steady?" *Psychology Today* (November, 1974): 53-59.

Macklin, E. D. "Unmarried Heterosexual Cohabitation on the University Campus." *The Social Psychology of Sex,* edited by J. P. Wiseman. New York: Harper and Row, 1976.

Massey, C. and R. Warner. *Sex, Living Together and the Law: A Legal Guide for Unmarried Couples (and Groups).* Berkeley, California: Nolo Press, 1974.

McCauley, B. *Sex Roles in Alternative Life Styles: Egalitarian Attitudes in the Cohabiting Relationship.* Unpublished manuscript. University of Delaware, 1975.

McCauley, B. *Self-Esteem in the Cohabiting Relationship.* Unpublished master's thesis. University of Delaware, 1977.

McWhirter, W. A. "The Arrangement at College." *Life* (May 31, 1968): 56.

Montgomery, J. P. *Commitment and Cohabitation Cohesion.* Unpublished manuscript. University of Edmonton, 1973.

Mosher, J. B. *Deviance, Growth Motivation and Attraction to Marital Alternatives.* Unpublished doctoral dissertation. University of Connecticut, 1975.

Peterman, D. J., C. A. Ridley, and S. M. Anderson. "A Comparison of Cohabiting and Noncohabiting College Students." *Journal of Marriage and the Family* 36 (1974): 344-354.

Petty, J. A. *An Investigation of Factors Which Differentiate Between Types of Cohabitation.* Unpublished master's thesis. Indiana University, 1975.

Ridley, C. A. and D. J. Peterman. *Beyond Cohabitation: A Case for Heterosexual Competence.* Unpublished manuscript. Pennsylvania State University, 1975.

Rodman, H. "Marital Relationships in a Trinidad Village." *Marriage and Family Living.* 23 (1961): 166-70.

Rodman, H. "Illegitimacy in the Caribbean Social Structure: A Reconsideration." *American Sociological Review.* 31 (1966): 673-83.

Rubin, Z. *Dating Project Research Report* (Vol. 2, No. 1). Cambridge, Massachusetts: Harvard University, 1975.

Schrag, P. "Posse at Generation Gap: Implications of the Linda LeClair Affair." *Saturday Review.* (May 18, 1968): 81.

Sheehy, G. "Living Together: The Stories of Four Young Couples Who Risk the Strains of Nonmarriage and Why." *Glamour* (February 1, 1969): 136-137, 198-202.

Shuttlesworth, G. and G. Thorman. *Living Together: Unmarried Relationships.* Unpublished manuscript. University of Texas at Austin, 1973.

Smith, P.B. and K. Kimmel. "Student-Parent Reactions to Off-Campus Cohabitation." *Journal of College Student Personnel* 11 (1970): 188-93.

Steiner, D. *Nonmarital Cohabitation and Marriage: Questionnaire Responses of College Women and Their Mothers.* Unpublished master's thesis. North Dakota State University, 1975.

Strong, L. and G. Nass. *Correlates of Willingness Among College Students to Participate in Prolonged Cohabitation.* Unpublished manuscript. University of Connecticut, 1975.

"Unstructured Relationships: Students Living Together." *Newsweek* (July 4, 1966): 78.

Weitzmann, L. J. "Legal Regulation of Marriage: Tradition and Change: A Proposal for Individual Contracts and Contracts in Lieu of Marriage." *California Law Review.* 62 (1974): 1169-1288.

6.

It Pays to Get Your Affair in Order

Patricia O'Toole

Mention that you know a couple living together without benefit of clergy and you're likely to raise more yawns than eyebrows. This year [1983] 1.9 million couples fit the Census Bureau description of POSSLQ (persons of the opposite sex sharing living quarters)—more than triple the 1970 figure. Add to that a sizable but unknown contingent of same-sex couples and the total could surpass 2.5 million.

Although sheer numbers have helped render unconventional relationships more socially acceptable, unmarried couples still live in a cloudy and unpredictable legal climate. State courts are recognizing their rights, but, says New York attorney Doris Jonas Freed, an authority on family law, "The country still is riddled with old-fashioned judges."

Until the law catches up with the facts of unmarried life, couples who by choice or necessity leave the knot untied will operate at a distinct disadvantage compared with married partners. Among the major problems:

Inheritance. When a husband or wife dies without a will, state laws typically assure that the bulk of the person's property will pass to the surviving spouse. But when an unmarried person leaves no will, all of his or her earthly goods can be claimed by the next of kin. Even a loathsome great-aunt thousands of miles away stands ahead of a POSSLQ in the inheritance line.
Health insurance. Plans that cover a spouse almost never extend to an unmarried mate.
Children's rights. To protect their child's future claim to financial support and inheritance, both unmarried parents have to take the extra step of acknowledging in writing the paternity of the child.
Separation. In a divorce, state laws offer guidance for dividing property, but unmarried couples who split up are left to slug it out on their own.

Spread over these difficulties is a crazy quilt of state laws ranging from outright bans on cohabitation to various shades of permissiveness. In Georgia, unwed cohabitants risk a $1,000 fine and a year in jail. Although such laws rarely are enforced, they can tilt the way judges settle other legal problems. In a court dispute with a landlord, for instance, an unmarried couple with an entirely justified gripe may find themselves out on the sidewalk because their living arrangement is against the law.

Archaic statutes can stymie other seemingly just claims. In Illinois a few years ago, the state supreme court denied a woman's pleas for an equal share of the assets accumulated by the man with whom she had lived for 15 years—even though she had borne him three children while he was establishing a dental practice. The court ruled that their relationship amounted to a common-law marriage, which the state outlawed back in 1905.

It's usually possible for couples to plug the holes in a legal system that predates POSSLQs and gay lib, but the remedies they have to take will mock their deliberately casual way of life. These involve drawing up contracts or agreements—precisely the kind of thing that the resounding majority of such couples find odious. "Contracts just don't go with moonlight and roses," sighs San Francisco lawyer Melvin Belli. Observes Elliot L. Evans, a lawyer in New York: "People who live together often do so because they don't want to define their relationship. They think that if they don't write things down, they won't lock themselves in."

Alas, by not writing things down, unmarried couples may inadvertently lock themselves out. Without written contracts, they often forfeit the legal protections of married couples. If disputes arise over an inheritance, ownership of property or financial obligations, POSSLQs may end up in court, where the outcome could have scant relation to what either wants done. And the absence of written agreements leaves the door wide open for the spurned lover to go to court to argue the existence of an unwritten contract. Michelle Triola Marvin established that precedent in California (but failed in her own claim) when she sued her ex-lover, actor Lee Marvin, for "palimony."

Mere utterance of the word *contract* calls up visions of inflexibility (ironclad, written in stone) and complexity (party of the first part and party of the second part). But contracts don't have to be complicated or, for that matter, permanent. In one common type of agreement, couples simply waive all financial claims on each other: what's his is his and what's hers is hers, period.

Contracts also can provide for regular revision. Dick Merritt and Mary Gannaway of Raleigh, North Carolina review their agreement every year. The latest changes deal with Gannaway's return to college, which Merritt is underwriting with a long-term 7 per cent loan. She has guaranteed to repay him whether or not the two continue living together.

Nor is there any need for contracts to cover every aspect of couples' lives. Advises Doris Freed: "Focus on money and property. Don't get into who empties the garbage and who walks the dog." Instead of drawing up a single, comprehensive contract, many couples write several agreements, each one focused on a specific bit of business. That is how Ralph Warner and Toni Ihara, two lawyers who live together in Berkeley, California handle ownership of their house and their interests in Nolo Press, which publishes *The Living Together Kit* ($12.95 at bookstores or from the publisher, 950 Parker St., Berkeley, California 94710) and other self-help legal material. Says Warner: "She and I have a written agreement covering the house. And every time we do a book together, we write that down. We don't have an agreement about things in the house because if we put them all out on the lawn, they probably wouldn't be worth more than $2,000."

As for how to draw up contracts, many lawyers say that couples with little money and no major assets usually can get by with the fill-in-blanks legal forms found in books on living together. If a couple's financial picture is more intricate, they should see an attorney—but first they should compose a rough draft as a way of clarifying their financial expectations of each other. When serious questions arise over individual interests, each partner should consult a different lawyer.

Whether prepackaged or tailor-made, contracts between unmarried couples generally are recognized by courts as long as they violate no laws and as long as both parties enter into them freely. Leave out of the contract the nature of your relationship, especially in states where cohabitation and homosexuality are illegal. Never put in writing any words that could be construed as an agreement to exchange money for sex, lest you run afoul of prostitution laws. Living-together documents should be signed, witnessed and notarized in triplicate: one copy for each of you and the third entrusted to a relative or lawyer.

With or without contracts, unmarried couples make dozens of decisions that can have legal reverberations. The major considerations:

DAY-TO-DAY FINANCES

Wedded or not, as soon as couples set up housekeeping, they begin accumulating possessions—from stereo rigs to Cuisinarts. If a married couple call it quits, their divorce decree will spell out who gets what. For unmarried couples who split, the best protection against a needlessly bitter end is separate ownership. He buys the car, she buys the computer. "They should acquire as little as possible together and keep receipts or other records of what each of them buys," says New York matrimonial lawyer Raoul Lionel Felder. Unmarried couples should not have joint bank accounts or credit cards. Each person is 100 per cent responsible for debts incurred by the other in joint charge accounts, and creditors can seize bank assets that are deposited in both names.

The tidiest way to split household expenses is down the middle, which many POSSLQs do quite simply by initialing receipts, tossing them into a drawer and squaring accounts once a month. But if one person quits work, the situation may call for a written agreement.

Cindy Ornstein, a public relations account executive in Manhattan, says she and her ex-POSSLQ divided expenses evenly until he left his job to attend law school. Then, she says, "we wrote a contract that was basically a loan agreement. I was to pay considerably more of our living expenses while he was in school, and the contract set the terms for paying me back." Their romance eventually came apart, but because of their clear-cut agreement, his debt of about $6,000 was one thing they didn't argue about. He has agreed to start paying her back in January.

"Couples also need to plan what financial support they will provide each other in case one of them loses a job or gets sick," says Merle Horwitz, a Los Angeles lawyer and author of *Love Is Love but Business Is Business: The Essential Guide to Living Together* (William Morrow, $4.95). "These plans should be part of their written contract. It's fine to make promises, but feelings change when there's stress on a relationship."

In prince-and-pauper partnerships, a proportional sharing of expenses may feel more comfortable than a fifty-fifty split, but the American Bar Association cautions that the law generally respects cash more than services. So if the prince contributed mostly money and the pauper mostly elbow grease, a judge might well view the toil as a gift—and deny the toiler's claim to any possessions paid for by the prince. In a written contract, however, the pair could spell out their intentions for sharing the fruits of their individual contributions.

HOUSING

The legal hazards facing POSSLQs here range from shared leases to disagreements over jointly acquired real estate. Roberta Springer and Michael Spitalnik leased an apartment together a few years ago, hoping to make a profitable investment if the building was converted to a co-op or condo. The building eventually was converted, but by then the couple had broken up and Springer had moved out. Since her name was still on the lease, though, the landlord insisted that the two of them would have to buy the apartment jointly to get the favorable price available to existing tenants. When he and she each pressed for the individual right to buy at the insider price, Spitalnik asked a New York State court to rule that he alone, as the occupant, should be allowed to buy the apartment. Their legal tiff, which is still going on, might have been avoided had they spelled out each person's share of any profit in case the place was bought and later sold.

"Business partners make these buy-sell agreements all the time," says Judith Zabalaoui, head of Resource Management, a financial-planning firm in Metairie, LA. "The idea is that you negotiate the exit as you're making the entrance. That's when everybody has a nice, rosy glow and a concern for each other's interests."

TAXES

Here's one positive inducement for living together unwed. Even with recently enacted deductions for two-career couples, the tax code still requires many married people to pay more than their unmarried counterparts. The more nearly equal the unmarried partners' earnings, the bigger the benefit. A couple with two $30,000-a-year incomes and average deductions can keep the IRS smiling with about 15 per cent less tax if they're single.

But the rules turn against unwed couples if only one partner works. You can claim your POSSLQ as a dependent only by passing a stiff IRS test. Among the conditions for the $1,000 exemption: the state doesn't ban cohabitation, the taxpaying partner furnishes more than half of the other's support, and the dependent earns under $1,000 a year. State income tax laws might not look on unmarried couples even that tolerantly.

CHILDREN

The rights of children, especially to inheritances and financial support, are the same whether their parents marry or not. And child custody disputes usually are not decided on the basis of marital status. But parents should write a statement acknowledging the father's parenthood to assure that neither a parent nor a child will have to go to extravagant lengths to prove paternity.

A divorced mother who moves in with another man should know that her cohabitant's contributions to the household may cost her the loss of child support from her ex-husband. "If the unmarried couple have a written contract stating that the man does not contribute to the children's support, that would be a helpful piece of evidence if the issue went to court," says lawyer Merle Horwitz.

INSURANCE AND WILLS

Unmarried couples' problems with most types of insurance are minimal as long as they tell the truth on application forms. Homeowners' and renters' policies should carry both names so the possessions of both are clearly covered. One temptation to resist: registering his car in her name to escape the high premiums paid by unmarried men under 25. Says Bill Malcolm, president of the Professional Insurance Agents Association of Connecticut: "If there's an accident, she'll be liable even if he's driving. Judgments these days can be enormous, and any such award would stay on her insurance record." Settlement of a negligence claim would sharply raise her premium or perhaps cause the insurance company to cancel her policy.

Because employer-provided family health insurance does not extend to POSSLQs, unmarried couples have to buy their own protection against catastrophic medical costs if either of them isn't covered by a group plan. One advantage of unmarried couples over marrieds: they are not liable for each other's medical bills. One disadvantage: if an unmarried person is hospitalized with a serious illness, the hospital may grant visiting privileges only to kin. To get around such rules, draft a medical power of attorney that permits an unrelated person not only to visit but also to make medical decisions for a totally incapacitated patient.

Don't neglect to name your POSSLQ the beneficiary of your life insurance policies. Also arrange for your partner to receive the death benefits if you die before you collect your pension or profit-sharing proceeds. You should hit no obstacles with pension and profit-sharing plans, but life insurers have balked at making one unmarried person the beneficiary of another. An easy, perfectly legal way out is suggested by Bill Malcolm, the insurance agent: "Name a family member when you take out the policy, and change the beneficiary later." The owner of the policy can make such a change anytime—and many an ex-lover has done so.

Pension plans frequently offer a joint-and-survivor annuity, which allows the widow or widower of a pensioner to continue collecting at least part of the retirement benefit. But POSSLQs don't qualify for the joint-and-survivor option. An unmarried pair's only safe passage through the pension maze is to explore with the company's employee-benefits counselor other annuity options that provide a survivor benefit.

While money from life insurance and pensions goes directly to the beneficiaries, most other assets acquired over a lifetime are destined for the owner's estate. That's the domain ruled over by his or her last will and testament. To make sure their wishes are carried out in probate—and that no kinfolk, especially that loathsome great-aunt, inherit undeserved assets—an unmarried couple had better write their wills. A few years ago, when a New York writer died intestate, the apartment that he owned went to his co-op association instead of to his male live-in lover of 10 years.

SOCIAL SECURITY

The federal old-age system no longer pays higher retirement income to unmarried couples than to husbands and wives. People wed or unwed can draw their benefits from the individual accounts they built up during their working years. Although individual benefits earned while you're working are the same for unmarrieds as for marrieds, the Social Security system generally favors those who wed.

When a husband or wife is the only one getting retirement benefits and then dies, the spouse gets survivor's income; a POSSLQ has no such right. If one spouse worked only a short time and accrued only a small individual benefit, the law allows that person the option of drawing half the other spouse's benefit instead. So a wife entitled to $200 a month married to a man receiving $700 could raise her benefit to $350.

Unmarried couples cannot take advantage of this option. Nor do they qualify for the $255 lump sum paid at a spouse's death, except in states permitting common-law marriage. But children under 18, whether their parents marry or not, are entitled to monthly income if a parent dies or is totally disabled.

Proper documents, from wills to statements of who owns what, can yield peace of mind as well as legal and financial benefits, says Baila Zeitz, a New York City psychologist with a special interest in money problems. "Contracts form a basis for constructive discussion when things go wrong—as they invariably do. Even more important, they give people a way of knowing what's going to happen, which feels much better than not knowing." Until the law gives the same shelter to unmarried partners that it does to spouses, putting your intentions in writing is the best way to protect a joint venture of the heart.

7.

Why Living Together Was Not Enough

Judith Barnard and Michael Fain

"Come live with me and be my love," begins a sixteenth-century sonnet, and although we don't know the result of the poet's entreaty, it's clear that today, some four hundred years later, an invitation to set up house together has undeniable appeal. According to a recent report by the U.S. Bureau of the Census, the number of unmarried couples living together more than doubled between 1970 and 1978 and increased more than eight times among people under thirty-five.

The trend clearly is upward, with no sign of leveling off. And what about marriage? The rate is going up too. Among those who are exchanging vows are many couples who previously have lived together. What, barring the desire for children, moves these young men and women to change their status? Isn't it true, as so many cohabiting couples affirm, that living together is "just the same as being married," that it's "only a question of a piece of paper"?

For us there *was* a difference. We lived together for a year and a half and then decided that for us, it wasn't enough; we wanted to be married. Here, from each of us, is how it happened—and why.

JUDITH'S POINT OF VIEW

Michael moved in and I felt like one of the three bears discovering traces of Goldilocks. I heard his footsteps. Drawers were left open. Books traveled mysteriously from room to room.

He'd invaded my private space. That took getting used to after three years alone, especially because it also involved cooking for two, scheduling for two, thinking in terms of two. It's amazing how much room one other person takes when you're well organized.

Reprinted by permission of the authors. First appeared in June 1980 *Redbook*.

That's what occupied my thoughts the first months we lived together. I'd been the one to invite him to move in—though at the time I didn't know his idea of domestic happiness was sitting at the oak table in the kitchen with his feet up on another chair (mine), munching oyster crackers, the crumbs floating about like dandelion seeds, while we read the newspaper together. But who can know such things until they share bed, board, and kitchen?

I wasn't sure I was in love with him. We did have wonderful times together, though, and going out on dates suddenly seemed silly—playing games when we were grown up. We all reach a time when we're ready for our next step, and I was ready for more than dating.

Was I thinking about marriage? Probably. Don't we all when we find someone who makes each day golden? But I didn't want it. I'd been married, and my image of myself as successful wife had been shaken. I wasn't in a hurry to try out a new husband. Besides, I enjoyed living alone. I had friends, places to go, and private space for sorting out thoughts. In short, I didn't invite Michael out of desperation to nestle his toothbrush next to mine.

I did want friendship, sharing, a good time, as much security as I could hope to get from one person—maybe even love. These seemed reasonable goals, and one advantage of being a single woman of sound mind and body in the 1970's was that I didn't need a marriage license to achieve them.

By the time Michael and his toothbrush moved in, we knew each other fairly well. We settled in like old-timers. We didn't swing, we didn't switch, we didn't even cast roving eyes. We probably disappointed "experts" who "explain" living together as the indulgence of infantile needs or as an acting-out of transitory sexual fantasies, because we acted—well, we acted as if we were married.

It's amazing how swiftly we adapt to new circumstances. Michael moved in on Sunday; Monday we awoke and went to work and that night he came home for dinner; Tuesday we accepted a dinner invitation for the weekend; by Wednesday, the only unusual item was the curious fact of footsteps in my private space.

No, there was one more. Suddenly I was a dedicated domestic. I baked, I brewed, I stirred. I cleaned, I mended, I shopped. The fragrance of baking bread and simmering creole dishes was wafted through our rooms. Furniture and hardwood floors gleamed; sunlight poured through dazzling windows onto plump cushions and rugs shaken to within a thread of their life. The house was a model of order. I was exhausted. Michael was amused. "It's called the nesting instinct," he said.

Had I, for three single years, been waiting to make a nest for a man? It's possible, but I wasn't aware of it until Michael arrived and settled into the niches of my single home.

But soon the domestic frenzy quieted, and I was congratulating myself on how easy new lives can be when Michael's six-year-old son, Eric, came for his first week-long visit. On the first day, Eric and I went to the local public library. "Your mother will have to help you carry all these books," the librarian said cheerfully. Eric responded promptly, "She's not my mother; she's my baby sitter."

A small explosion went off in my head. Michael and I had been living together three months; and not only had we fallen in love, we'd discovered a quality and depth to our sharing that we'd never known before. Also we made a good threesome with Eric—a real family unit. What I'm saying is, we were having a marvelous time and here was this child casually saying I was just the baby sitter.

I tried to straighten him out, but more was needed. That night I talked to Michael; the next day Michael talked to Eric and I heard no more of baby sitters. But I knew Eric was keeping his thoughts to himself, and I wasn't even sure he approved of me.

We knew there were many who did not approve of living together without marriage. When our neighbors Martha and Joe bought an apartment, their lawyer frowned. "You're taking awful chances," he said, "without a permanent relationship." They'd lived together for five years; how long does "permanence" take? The answer is *immediately* if there's a ceremony; a *lifetime* if there isn't. (Martha and Joe began making other investments and found the paperwork would be less complicated if they were married, so they did indeed become "permanent," and their lawyers nodded with approval.)

We'd bought property together too, but it hadn't seemed complicated. We thought we had no problems. Friends were casual; co-workers didn't comment; our parents awed us with their silence. We were what is called a "happy couple."

But still I wasn't as comfortable as I thought (if I were sensible) I should be. I had a man who loved me and respected my independence, a man I deeply loved; a career, good friends, good food, good sex, a happy, shared life. What more could even a greedy person possibly want?

A few things, I found. For one, I needed a feeling of completion. The situation was sloppy; it had no real beginning, no formalization. As silly as it sounds, I didn't know what our anniversary was. The day we met? The day Michael agreed to move in? The day he brought over his suitcases?

Well, obviously these weren't overwhelming issues, but they nagged at me. I felt we were "playing house," that we weren't responsible—which was ridiculous, but try to make all your feelings seem logical.

Our friends Jane and Paul came to dinner and announced they were marrying after living together for three years. "It's been okay," Jane said, "but we want children, and how can we have a family without being married?" We understood. We sympathized. If we'd wanted children, we said later, we too. . . . "But for us, it isn't necessary," Michael said, and I looked at him. Really?

Suddenly when I thought about marriage, wherever I looked I saw women with rings. Where were the living-together couples? Were we the only ones left? Friends with whom we bicycled on Sundays got married because their embarrassed families begged them to. That seemed to us a poor reason; marriage should be rooted within the couple. We would not marry to cure the disapproval of families or attorneys or even to convince Eric that I was more than a baby sitter. Reasons for marriage (other than having children) should be intimate, almost inexpressible.

But we did express them; we started to talk seriously about marriage. Michael had doubts; he wondered if I wanted marriage because our culture "programmed" me to want it. Could be, but it was too late to change the program. I loved him; I wanted to marry him. We'd been "playing marriage;" I wanted it to be formalized as a way of stating the depth of our feelings.

Michael, for his own reasons, soon came to the same conclusion. So in a small gathering in our home we said publicly what we'd said privately for so long—that we were merging our separate worlds to stand together, to look outward from one shared spot, to look inward with love and caring and joy.

Marriage was our acceptance of tradition: a reaffirmation of our continuity in a world where there's plenty of uncertainty. We didn't expect it to create or change anything—and it didn't. We cannot find a single alteration in any of our words or activities. Sometimes I find that the tiniest bit disappointing. *Something* should be different. But then, thinking about it, I'm satisfied. It's true that Michael as husband might have given up oyster crackers, but he might have given up helping with the housework too. On balance, it's fine if everything stays the same. At least I know what to expect.

MICHAEL'S POINT OF VIEW

Judy popped the question, asking me to move into her apartment after we'd known each other for a couple of months. I was pleased but felt a strong inner pull of caution. You don't really know her, I thought; I wasn't sure I'd ever know a woman again after the suddenness of my divorce and the empty days and nights that followed. That had been only a year ago; I still was trying to put my life together and I thought I needed to do that alone. So I said no. Thank you and I like you, but no.

She didn't push, but as the months went by and we spent good times together, I realized how important it was to me to share completely with a woman. But I also wanted to love, and I didn't know if I was ready for that. Judy, strong and independent though she was, needed love and caring as much as I did. Two people needing what only one might be able to give could lead to disaster, and I'd had enough of that. But we had so much in common that finally it seemed foolish not to have a home in common as well. Caution fled. I moved in.

I wasn't in love. I never thought of marriage. We were two mature people who enjoyed each other and so decided to live together. No one asked for how long.

Caution, it seemed, hadn't been necessary. Each step felt natural and right—carrying in suitcases and books; putting my feet up to read the paper in Judy's kitchen (later it would feel like our kitchen); more important, being myself. Judy was ahead of me in her readiness for sharing and being able to talk about fears and anxieties as well as successes; her honesty made it easier for me to admit my own needs. I opened up. All the feelings I'd been guarding as if they were the crown jewels tumbled out; it seemed I was conducting a monologue; about myself, my family, my hopes. But it wasn't a monologue; Judy was opening up too, and I found myself caring about what she said, worrying if she was unhappy, exulting if she had a triumph in her work. It was thinking about her as much as about myself. I was falling in love.

I raised my glass in a toast at our favorite restaurant about three months after I'd moved in: "To our permanence." She raised an eyebrow. Well, it was true our separate pasts hardly constituted a recommendation for permanence, but I wasn't looking for guarantees. I wanted us to be together forever—which meant as long as we could see into the future and as far beyond as our feelings could let us dream.

We already had merged most of our finances, with joint checking and savings accounts and the purchase of land for a someday house. My friend Bill, splitting from Norma after two years of living together, warned me that was a mistake. "Stay loose everywhere but at meals and in bed," he said. "Otherwise you'll feel trapped—no place to escape if things get bad. The more you're forced to turn to another person for security, the more you resent that person for having power over you."

I shrugged. I was deeply in love and I was happy. I grinned at Bill. "The family that saves together," I said, "stays together."

In fact, we did, with every day better than the last. Then my son, Eric, came for a visit, his first since I had moved in, and it was a tense one. Judy got upset at little things; Eric kept finding ways to annoy her. One night she asked me if I'd told Eric I loved her. I hadn't—how could anyone, even a child, miss how I felt about her?—but the next day I did.

Eric listened in silence. It occurred to me that he might be wondering when Judy would go home (like a baby sitter) and leave us together, as we'd been before I met her. "Listen, Eric," I said, "we're a family." And I told him carefully (because I figured he'd understand at least some of it) what it meant to me in love and strength and security to live with this woman.

"Well," Eric said when I finished, "but she isn't my stepmother because you aren't married."

I paused. That was true but unimportant. "We don't need to be married to love each other and be a family," I said. I was absolutely sure of it. I didn't want marriage; nothing I'd had before was as good as what Judy and I had now, which was reason enough to leave things as they were. We'd built a life from private feelings, without legalities or ceremonial mumblings.

I wanted to preserve that—just us, holding ourselves together because we wanted to be together.

Our friends Marie and Dan came over one evening. "We're getting married," they announced. We were surprised; they had seemed happy, living together. "Because of my job," Marie said. "I have to entertain and go to parties and I'm expected to bring my husband. Not my friend, not my roommate—my husband. We aren't going to lie; it's simpler to get married."

I didn't think marriage was simple; I had serious doubts about it. Too many people, especially men, still saw it as ownership, with rights and privileges automatically conferred by a ceremony. Judy and I were separate and independent; I didn't want a symbol of dependency to influence us. As for the protections marriage provides, Judy never said she wanted or expected any and I didn't need guarantees of my share of our property or my access to sex.

Society's images of "husband" and "wife"—how they behave to each other, how they act as a couple—were based on dominance and dependence, and that was damaging, witness our crazy divorce rate. I didn't want them to spill over into our home, bumping into the images, conscious and unconscious, we'd formed of each other. I didn't want Judy to become a "wife"; she didn't fit the images the word conjured up for me.

I don't know whether more men feel this way than women, and I don't know if this attitude is more usual after a divorce. But I felt this way, and when the subject of marriage crept now and then into our conversations, I forcefully gave my views, which prevented discussion.

"But what do I call you?" Judy's mother asked. "My sin-in-law? My common-law son? Judy's pal?" True—this was a problem. My father, we learned later, called Judy "that woman" to his close friends and "Michael's um..." to others. Judy's parents settled on calling me her "companion." We used "the man (or woman) I live with." ("Girl friend" and "boy friend" were out; okay for teen-agers but not for us.) None of this, however, was serious; hardly cause for changing a satisfactory way of life.

In short, I was happy, I was comfortable, I was secure. We'd built a home by acting on our own convictions rather than joining the crowd. That pleased me; it made us stronger, our commitment more binding.

But nothing is static. Like Judy, I was ready for the next step, and she helped me see it. I began thinking seriously about marriage— rethinking old ideas—not because I felt something was missing in our lives but because I felt we already had all the important things. Using marriage to fill a gap is not a statement of love but an admission of failure.

We'd been together a year and a half, and I'd come to a point where I could make a public pledge of love. Living together had given me time and space to come to terms with myself, to believe in myself, to learn to love and to give. Living together gave me the courage to marry. My doubts had come from my own insecurities, but I didn't have to accept the attitudes others had toward marriage; I could make it *my* symbol, with my own meanings, to be shared with Judy. And I could accept it as society's ultimate symbol of commitment—the only symbol we had not yet embraced. I could join Judy in the traditional public promise—something I wanted very much to give her and receive from her—because now I trusted myself and the promise we'd made *and lived* in private.

So we had our ceremony, standing before our living-room fireplace, saying the words we'd written to fit our circumstances: We've already begun a life together, we said, and join now not in hope but in confirmation of what we have created. We declare our community in the midst of the larger community; we pledge to each other love and cherishing and shared growth. And we become husband and wife—with our own definitions of those ancient terms.

The next morning we got up at the usual time and went to work.

Unexpected aftermath: Friends and acquaintances who'd been so casual about our living together beamed with delight at our marriage. Our parents practically cheered. (Eric didn't say much, at the wedding or later, but he's clearly more relaxed, satisfied that now we're a real family.) No one visibly had disapproved of our living together, but everyone's enthusiastic approval made it clear they had had doubts about our being truly "serious."

Well, we didn't get married to prove anything to anyone, but we're always glad to be seen as "serious." If I'd been asked earlier, however, I'd have given a straight answer: Marriage to Judy is as right and natural as living with her, but I felt serious and permanent almost from the beginning. How could I ever leave a woman who is tolerant of oyster-cracker crumbs?

Part

Three

Changing Marital and Family Roles

Family scholars usually describe the family as being strong and resilient, both as an institution and as a social group, and as being amazingly consistent over time in its functions and organizational structure. Nevertheless, family historians sometimes point to particular events or eras in history that have had some degree of impact upon the family, with attempts to describe and explain how the family may have changed as a result. These events may be of the long-term variety, such as the spread of Christianity or the discovery of the New World, or they may be of more recent occurrence, such as wars or economic recessions.

Many scholars are beginning to agree that nothing since the turn of the century has had as significant an impact upon the family as are the changes resulting from the Women's Movement of the last two decades. The major manifestation of this movement with regard to the family is the shift of women away from the home and into the workplace. Women are increasingly taking on the additional role of work outside the home, while retaining, for the most part, their role responsibilities related to the home. Although many attribute this shift to the Women's Movement, it is probably more likely that the Women's Movement, at least in its more recent manifestations, is itself partially a result of women's increasing presence in the work force. Furthermore, efforts by women to change various aspects of their lives have been going on for decades, perhaps centuries.

Also predating the contemporary Women's Movement is the scholarly study of men's and women's roles in society and in the family, and the ways in which their roles are related to each other. This topic generally is referred to as the study of gender or *sex roles*. The term sex role refers to those components of a role, apart from the more general expectations that make up the role, that are attached to a role solely on the basis of the sex of the person assumed to be playing or expected to play the role. The term most often is used in discussions of the *division of labor* within the family, division of labor referring to the manner in which the various domestic tasks are allocated according to sex. Of course, the concept of sex role has application outside the family as well, particularly in the occupational world.

Western culture traditionally has viewed the different roles required of men and women as being based upon ascriptive qualities, that is, those qualities related to inherent or natural differences between the sexes. However, we now are being made increasingly aware, through the findings of both biological and social research, that the two sexes might not be as different as formerly thought and that the nature of the differences that do exist might vary considerably from what was traditionally thought to be the case. Currently, in both the academic world and the popular media, the debate rages over just what differences actually do exist between the sexes and over the precise nature of the differences. One obvious difference is that women bear children and men do not. The extremists of the Women's Movement would have us believe that there are no important differences between men and women and that childbearing is a relatively minor one. A less radical and more rational position is that childbearing is important but women should not be the objects of discrimination because of it.

On the other hand, many of those who are opposed to changes in women's roles attribute to women a number of distinct psychological and emotional characteristics that are not seen as applying to men. Presumably, the truth lies somewhere between these various points of view. In any event, the informed person today sees far fewer differences between the sexes than was traditionally the case, and this can mean only that many of the differences of the past were based on social and cultural factors.

Most sociologists view roles, and especially sex roles, as being defined in terms of other reciprocal or *complementary roles*. For example, the husband role exists and is defined mainly in terms of its complement, which is the wife role. This complementarity applies to almost all situations in which men and women interact because of the condition that, as with almost all social roles, the sex of the role player is assumed to be a part of the definition of role. Thus, all social roles are colored by the sex of the person playing the role, although one's sex might be of no intrinsic importance to the actual role performance. This probably is the most crucial issue being raised by contemporary feminists, and it also is the issue that makes the current movement different from the earlier women's movements. The concern now is with informal social customs that, for the most part, are unrelated to sex in the biological or physiological sense, whereas in the past the concern was more with legal restrictions and inequalities related to the more basic freedoms and activities of citizenship.

Many people, both men and women, understand the goals of those who are seeking change in women's roles, and quite a few also are in sympathy with those goals. However, many of those who claim to understand and sympathize have not yet fully grasped all the implications and ramifications of the proposed changes in women's roles. Perhaps the most important ramification is related to the complementary nature of roles. If most roles are in fact complementary, it must follow that *any change that occurs in any one role must bring about a change also in all those roles that are reciprocal or complementary to it.* Therefore, if the role of the wife changes, it necessarily follows that the role of the husband must change also in order to maintain some sort of workable accommodation or agreement between the two roles and consequently between the persons playing the roles. The same would hold true for other basic female roles, such as mother and daughter, as well as for their various role reciprocals. And what is more important, this same principle of related change also would apply to those roles that might have been held traditionally by one sex or the other, such as occupational or professional roles.

This situation, in which changes in one role affect the other roles related to it, probably is the reason why many men, even those in sympathy with the ideals of sexual equality, find themselves a little bewildered by the changes. In the past, men and women were able to interact with each other in a fairly standardized and predictable manner. That is, most men reacted to most women in the same expected and predictable ways. However, as more and more women are changing their own style of behavior (changing their roles), a man might find himself in an increasingly ambivalent position, often not knowing precisely how to react to a specific woman because he is unable to determine whether she is "liberated" or "traditional." Unclear expectations often result in role confusion and sometimes in interpersonal conflict.

On the other hand, the "new" woman might have similar problems. If she treats all men as if they held what she considers to be the outdated traditional views of women's roles, she might create difficulties when she encounters a man who is in sympathy with her newer ideas. Eventually she also would reach a point at which she would have the same problem as the bewildered males, in that she would not know how best to react to or interact with a particular man until she first had ascertained his views with respect to women.

Thus, it becomes clear that solving the problems of discrimination and differential behavior toward women involves far more than simply having men change their basic attitudes about what behaviors are appropriate or inappropriate for women. The solution actually requires, at least theoretically, four shifts with respect to sex role expectations. Just as both men and women must make shifts in the ways in which they view each other's roles, they also must make shifts in the ways in which they view their own roles. Interaction problems and social maladjustments arise from the fact that we as a society are unable to make all these shifts simultaneously. In a game of musical chairs, if no chairs are removed when the music stops, there are no problems. But if one or two chairs are taken away, there ensues great confusion and maybe even some conflict. It is increasingly evident that our society is in for a period of confusion and conflict on the question of men's and women's roles as the uncoordinated shifting goes on.

One of the most often mentioned discussions of sex roles in the family, and especially concerning the roles of women, is one formulated by Clifford Kirkpatrick.[1] His view is that women actually have had a wider range in the choice of possible roles because our society had not allowed men to do anything other than hold jobs. Except for the very rich and the very poor, the only legitimate dominant role for a man is his occupational role. On the other hand, says Kirkpatrick, many women have had a choice about the roles that they may occupy as well as the option of changing their major roles at various times throughout their lives. Among these choices are the *housewife-mother* role, the *equal partner* role, and the *companion* role. The major distinction among these roles is the woman's degree of involvement with her own career on the one hand or with her husband's career on the other.

This analysis of women's roles is not meant to imply that women have total or even very much freedom in their choice of roles, but rather that there is probably more latitude in women's roles than in men's, and of course, some women have more freedom than other women have. Kirkpatrick certainly is not complaining about the fact that women have greater freedom in their choice of roles, for he believes that this role flexibility creates problems for both men and women, similar to the interaction problems mentioned in the previous few paragraphs. He says that a man tends to develop the expectation that his wife should be able to perform all the various women's roles well. Rather than allowing her to choose only one of the possible roles, he believes she should be able not only to hold a full-time job but also to keep the house spotless as well as to take excellent care of the children. Of course, the average woman cannot meet these expectations, so her husband might berate her or withhold rewards.

With respect to the wife's own expectations about her roles, says Kirkpatrick, she tends to believe that she is meeting adequately the expectations of her husband and performing all the roles well. Therefore, she is dissatisfied with her husband's response to her performance. The result of all this is a great deal of discord on the part of both men and women, all of it centered upon the woman's role.

The conclusion must be drawn that the problems of determining the appropriate roles for both men and women, as well as the problem of changes in these roles, are very complex issues that defy simple answers. The articles in this section which address these issues certainly do not contain all or even very many of the answers, but they express some interesting viewpoints and present some useful research findings.

The first article of Part Three illustrates the type of role conflict that has become all to common with many marriages today. In "Having It All," the author presents her own experiences, as well as those of several young women whom she interviewed, with regard to the problems of attempting to have not only a career, but a marriage and children as well. This is, without question, the major issue facing marriages today, and dealing with it is particularly difficult for the women involved. Conflict in these marriages is very common, and this problem must certainly be a contributor to the continuing high divorce rate. It is clear that the solution to this kind of conflict lies in both attitudinal and behavioral changes with regard to the roles of both partners, and consequently to the manner in which they relate to each other. The author of this article concludes on a positive, and apparently successful, note. However, the question as to whether most women can realistically "have it all" still remains, and more and more women are finding that the costs may not be worth it.

The opening commentary for this section stated that it would be impossible for women's roles to change without causing changes to come about also in the roles of men. The second article deals with this matter. "Their Turn: How Men are Changing," was written with unusual perception and sensitivity by Betty Friedan, who is credited with being one of the founders of the current Women's Movement through her well-known book *The Feminine Mystique*. In the article reprinted here she focuses particularly on the feelings and attitudes of men and the ways in which these are changing in response not only to the changes that are occurring with women, but also in response to the increasing opportunities men now have for taking a closer look at themselves, at who and what they are. Much of the discussion here centers around the question of how dependent or independent men and women, and particularly those who are husbands and wives, should be upon each other. Beyond the obvious changes in work and family roles, Friedan is concerned with what happens when women no longer have to depend on men for their status and security and the effects of this new situation on men and their self-images. She believes that men now might become freer to define themselves and their roles in terms other than those of work and occupations, and this is seen as a major positive outcome of the sexual equality movement.

The third article of this section, "Changing Sex Roles and Changing Families," is concerned with the relationship between changes in men's and women's roles and changes in the structure of the family. It is not altogether clear which area of change precedes the other, but the author believes that in order for major changes to occur in the dominant roles of men and women, there must be significant changes made in family structure. On the other hand, many of the changes the family is experiencing these days occurred as a result of changing sex role definitions. The author also sees some of the changes in the roles of women coming about as a result of demographic changes in their lives, such as a shorter childbearing period and a longer life span. Both these changes mean that women are not now as necessary for family-related operations as they were in the past, and they now are freer to engage in activities outside the home. One result of these changes is the decline in the traditional division of labor both inside and outside the home. The major structural characterization of families in the near future is what has been termed the "symmetrical family," one in which there is greater equality and more sharing of the various duties, whether they be keeping house or earning the living.

NOTE

1 Clifford Kirkpatrick, "The Measurement of Ethical Inconsistency in Marriage." *The International Journal of Ethics,* 46 (July 1936): 444-460.

8.

Having It All

Sara Davidson

Nothing is working out the way we expected, of course. It is four in the morning and I lie in bed, listening to my son's cries echo in the dark house.

"Sara," my husband says.

"I hear him."

I wait, hoping against hope that the cries will stop.

"Could you take this feeding?" I ask. "I'm so exhausted, and I was just falling asleep."

"I have to be at work at eight."

"I have to work, too."

"You agreed to get up nights."

This is true. I stumble into the nursery, pick up my son, so small, so perfect, and as he fastens himself to me like a tiny, sucking minnow I am flooded with tenderness. This baby was the great missing link for me, the one thing I have longed for in my life that, once realized, brought the satisfaction I'd hoped for. I change him, rock him, sing him to sleep, and am just dozing off myself when, at seven a.m., the phone rings. It is my help saying she is sick and can't come in. I burst into tears.

"You can do it," my husband says. "My mother raised three children without help." He begins getting dressed for work, and I reach for the phone to cancel my appointments.

"Your mother wasn't working then," I want to say, but it is irrelevant. I have chosen this road, and I must find a way to walk it.

The notion that a woman might have it all—an absorbing career, a loving marriage, children—continues to grip me with an almost mystical power. The woman who can balance family and career—love and work—is the woman most men say they desire and most women say they want to be. Yet I do not know such a woman. I do not yet understand how a woman can successfully split herself between home and the marketplace. Fifteen years of feminist theory and action have taught us that sacrificing one for the other does not satisfy, but having both together simultaneously is so difficult that no one I know has found anything but the most quirky and incomplete solution.

How to reconcile family and career is the crucial, unresolved issue in women's lives. It is an issue men are not required to struggle with, and it is the reason many women still believe that in this world, men have the better deal.

I am sitting with three women who recently graduated from Yale. All three are dark, attractive, lively. Becky wants to earn her doctorate in English, Jan will start medical school in the fall, and Kate has just finished her first year at Columbia Law School. They are spending the summer at a workshop on Judaism and values run by the Brandeis-Bardin Institute, and they have been giving serious thought to what they want from their lives.

"Before I went to Yale," Kate says, "my mother told me, 'When I was your age, I didn't have a choice, I became a housewife. But you! Nothing stands in your way. You can have a career, money of your own, marriage, travel, exciting people and places. Do it all!' "

The other girls nod their heads. Each received a similar speech from her mother, and then they arrived at Yale, where the evidence of women's emancipation was tangible. Kate says: "Yale had been exclusively for men—all the dorms had urinals in the bathrooms—and there we were, nearly fifty per cent women. It was utopia! We had a woman editor of the paper. Everyone was equal. Then I went into law and discovered Yale was unreal."

Kate says she worked as an intern one summer for a major New York law firm. "There were three women partners, which was good, but their personal lives were terrible. One woman was forty and had never been married. One had been divorced twice, and one was married and had just decided to have her tubes tied." Kate says there was a young woman associate who was pregnant, "and every time I peeked in her office, I wondered, What will she do when the baby comes? Will she be able to work sixteen-hour days and push herself to make partner? The men attorneys could have wives and children, but I didn't see how the women attorneys could *be* wives and have children."

Kate and her friends say they are reacting against the "excessive careerism" of the past decade. Becky says, "Careers are not holy. My parents were divorced, I didn't have a good family life, and I want one so badly, to make up for what I missed out on."

The problem, of course, is that family happiness is less clearly definable and often more elusive than career success. Jan says, "I know a good marriage will be harder for me to find than a good job. I want to marry a man who's at least as bright as me, who's outstanding at what he does, and who'll go fifty-fifty with me in the house."

The others laugh. "Forget it," Becky says. "Have you met guys who are willing to stay home with children? I have, and I wouldn't want to marry them. I don't think men can become successful men—strong in the world—and still do fifty per cent of the female roles."

Kate hits the table. "But women who do the male roles still have to do all the female things. It's unfair, and I *burn* that every man doesn't have to worry about splitting himself."

I ask if they think their lot is better than that of their mothers and grand-mothers. They are silent—a telling silence. "Feminism is great as an idea," Kate says, "but the reality isn't always so pretty."

What is the reality?

"It's holding your best friend's hand while she's having an abortion because she can't pursue her career and have the baby."

"It's crying in the women's bathroom because you're in a male environment and men don't cry."

"It's being successful and being alone because men don't respond that well to assertive women."

"It's running from Columbia Law School to Elizabeth Arden to make yourself beautiful for the handful of men available to women like you."

If you *had* to choose, I say, posing the impossible question, between having a family and having a career, which would you choose?

Instantly the future doctor, lawyer, and English professor say, "Family."

I am stunned. At their age, I would have given the opposite answer.

When I was in my twenties, I had no interest in children. I saw babies as blobs who made irritating noises, and staying at home with them all day was a frightening vision. I wanted to make my mark as a reporter, a writer, and was willing to work endless hours, to drop everything and go anywhere for little or no pay if it meant gaining ground in my profession.

I had nothing but disdain for bourgeois homes in the suburbs and the women who came and went in station wagons. I wanted to propel myself forcibly from everything I associated with those women: card games, golf dates, charity lunches.

Remember, if you can, the shocking and intoxicating rhetoric of the first women's liberation groups in 1968. "Leave your husbands." "Avoid having children." "The nuclear family is oppressive to women." "Don't wear lipstick or shave your legs to please a man." The ideal was to become "independent," "whole," a strong woman who was nobody's sex object and who found salvation through achievement in the world. In the years that followed there were scores of runaway wives and men who blamed the women's movement for the breakup of their homes. By the end of the Seventies there were more unattached women and men in this country than ever before in history.

At some point along the way a number of us woke up and found that we were wonderfully self-sufficient and successful and our lives were empty. There was no one to share it with, no living, growing ties to the future. Something vital had been discarded, and we scurried to recapture it.

About the time I turned thirty, I began to cast surreptitious glances at children playing in the park, at families eating potato salad at picnic tables. Before long I could not attend a baby shower—it was too painful.

The scurry, for me, turned into a panic. I was emotionally and financially ready to have a baby, but I did not have a partner. Other women I knew came to accept with varying degrees of sadness that "I won't be having children." It seemed some terrible justice of the gods; what we now wanted most was what we once had cast aside.

I remember a night when it was raining and I was alone in my house, talking on the phone with a man I had met recently—a virtual stranger. For some reason, I began to weep at my predicament, and he said, "I'll give you a baby, okay, if it comes down to the wire and you have no other options. You raise it, but I'll provide the sperm." Laughing with embarrassment, I added his name to a mental list I was keeping of potential donors. I knew, in my heart, I would never use the list, but it was a great comfort to have it.

Women's Medical Group in Santa Monica is a new-style obstetrics group. The doctors are all women, except for one. They call themselves Karen and Patty, not Doctor, wear casual clothes, deliver babies in alternative-birth centers in hospitals, and give their patients a great amount of information and time. Medically, though, they are conservative, and specialize in high-risk pregnancies.

Sitting in the waiting room on a sunny April morning, I marvel at my fortune. I feel I have sneaked in under the wire—getting married for the second time at thirty-eight and having a baby at thirty-nine. Across from me are two women with very young babies. They discover that they both had to stay in bed for most of their pregnancies. A chill runs through me. "You couldn't get up, not even to eat? That's horrible."

My husband reaches for my hand. "Don't worry," he says with his wonderful optimism, "it won't happen to you."

Ha.

One of the things people don't tell you about having a baby late in life is that the chances of having trouble carrying the baby are greatly increased. Women's Medical Group has a high proportion of patients over thirty, and at times 30 to 40 per cent of them are in bed.

I was in excellent health when I became pregnant, and I expected to jog and work up to the last day. In a routine visit during my fourth month the doctor said I appeared to be having problems. I would have to lie on my back with my hips elevated for the rest of my term, or the force of gravity might bring the baby out prematurely.

I was incredulous. I felt fine, and I could not believe anything was serious-ly wrong. So I cheated. I got out of bed, first for one thing, then for another, until I was walking about more than half the day. During my sixth month I went in for a checkup and was sent straight to the hospital in premature labor.

They strapped a fetal monitor around my stomach, put my head down and my feet up, and pumped me full of intravenous drugs to stop the con-tractions. The drugs made my heart race 120 beats per minute. My neck was pulsing, my gums, fingers, stomach—everything had the rapid ham-mer beat. I was short of breath, sweating; the sheets came off steaming, as if from an iron.

From the rooms on either side I could hear women screaming, "It hurts, oh God, my insides are coming out! Heeeellp!" They were delivering babies, but I thought I was in the gulag, hearing the other prisoners being tor-tured. What had happened? I had walked into the hospital, looking radiant in a Laura Ashley dress, and now I was weak, panting for breath, with sheet burns on my back and bruises on my arms from the IV. I wanted to pull out the tubes and rip off the belts and run out of the hospital, and just as I was cracking, one of the nurses brought in a tiny baby from the nursery.

"This is what you're working for," she said.

I was startled. I had forgotten I was pregnant.

After this my husband virtually moved into the hospital to keep my spirits up. He brought in our stereo and video recorder and meals from restaurants. When he did go home, he would call and play the piano and sing Cole Porter songs. "Birds do it, bees do it . . . ."

Together we managed to weather it out until my condition had stabiliz-ed and I could go home. Everyone told me, "As soon as the baby comes, you'll forget the pain." Not a chance, I thought, I won't forget this.

But I did. At this moment I am pregnant with our second child, lying on a rented hospital bed with my hips up and a word processor positioned over my stomach.

This time I am not cheating.

Nothing in my life prepared me for the happiness, the wholeness I felt when my son was born. I am embarrassed to tell you how many nights I would walk into his room and just stand at the crib, my heart brimming.

One day my husband and I took the baby to a restaurant. For the first time, the baby sat upright in his Sassy Seat and ate with us, like a com-panion. He looked about with his enormous eyes, and we tasted each other's food. It was so simple, and yet it was one of those moments when life is as good as it gets.

I wonder if I possibly could have felt this way if I had had the baby when I was younger. I doubt it. I am sure I would have been frustrated and resentful if I had not had the opportunity to satisfy certain professional yearnings first.

Behind every great woman, the proverb goes, there is another woman: a domestic.

I always said I would not have children until I could afford help. Many women I meet still say this, and I want to tell them the equation is not so simple. You do not snap your fingers, hire help, and go on with your life without a hitch. You can hire almost anyone to clean your house and cook, but caring for your child is one area that cannot be so successfully delegated. Anyone who has tried live-in help will tell you it is a more difficult adjustment than having a baby. They are not telling you the half of it.

The day before my son was born, I hired a British nanny. She turned out to be a magpie, who yammered and complained without mercy, and before long I was taking my meals in my bedroom huddled over my desk with the door closed. I next tried a Danish *au pair* girl, who was soft-spoken but left without notice to go to Hawaii with her boyfriend. The third young woman I hired was marvelous with the baby. His personality seemed to change when she moved in; he laughed and flourished, but after two months the young woman disappeared with thousands of dollars' worth of our property.

A few days later I went to see my dermatologist. The doctor is a woman, and on this morning her waiting room was overflowing. The receptionist explained, "Her housekeeper quit this morning, so she was late and had to bring her son along."

A chorus of empathy rang out from the women in the room.

"My help's quitting tomorrow—she's pregnant."

"I have to fire mine, she leaves the baby wet and crying."

"Please, could we change the subject? All we ever talk about is help."

I was shown into an examining room and when the doctor came in, I caught sight of a toddler in the hall with a pacifier in his mouth. The little boy howled as he watched his mother, in her white lab coat, disappear.

"It's hard to shut the door on him," she said.

We consoled each other with our stories. "You feel so vulnerable, so dependent on your help," the doctor said. "You have to be ready, at any moment to drop your work and take your child." I had come, reluctantly, to perceive this. Having help makes it *possible* for a woman to work, but you cannot be complacent. Even with the most responsible baby-sitter, you must be watchful and on call.

I have not seen my friend Jack in ten years. He is visiting town on business, and we are sitting in a bar late at night, catching up. Jack teaches at a midwestern college, has two children and has been married for what in our scattered circle is a record—sixteen years. But it has not been easy.

"There's a lot of bitterness in our marriage because of a covenant that wasn't fulfilled," he says. "We promised each other we would take responsibility for the children fifty-fifty, and it's never been like that."

Jack says he hasn't been able to find a part-time job teaching. "I'd like to quit and stay home with the kids, but Kathy couldn't make enough money in the work she's trained for to support us. We don't want to give up our house and our lifestyle, so we're stuck.

"I feel for Kathy," he says. "Sometimes on the weekend I'll have both kids by myself all day, and by dinnertime I'm ready to down four bourbons and watch soap operas."

I ask if he knows any men who are doing 50 per cent of the childcare. He doesn't. Neither do I, though I have read about such men in magazines. Most of the men I know love their babies and are far more involved with them emotionally than their fathers were with them. They go to Lamaze classes and want to be in the delivery room, but the following day they go back to work.

I am lucky, for my husband has played an increasingly larger role in raising our son, and there is an electricity, a special bond between them.

To be honest, I would not completely switch roles with the man, even if I could. When I started working again, I would often go to the window of my study and look down into the yard, where the sitter was playing with the baby. One day the baby was lying on his back, wiggling his arms and legs, and suddenly he grew still. I didn't think he could see me from that distance, but he did, and broke into piteous tears.

I ran downstairs in anguish. Why am I working, I thought? My son needs me, he won't be a baby very long and I don't want to miss these crucial years. I cuddled him and played with him, but after a while I began to feel a nagging pull to be working.

"I've decided I want a woman who'll be a housewife," says David, who is thirty-six and has never married. Instead he has had a succession of affairs with beautiful and ambitious women.

"I don't believe you," I say. "You don't even like paying for a woman's dinner, let alone supporting her."

"If she devotes herself to making me comfortable and raising our children, I'll support her."

"What will you talk about?"

"Maybe she'll have some good hobbies."

I laugh.

"I'm serious," he says. "I'm tired of leathery career women. Do you know how long it's been since anyone fixed me a meal?"

I imagine this is a reaction to David's last girlfriend, a circuit court judge who kept nothing in the refrigerator except vaginal suppositories. But I hear something else in David's lament, something I hear in women: the longing for a vanished simplicity.

And what of the young men—those in their early twenties—the counter-parts of the women I met from Yale? I have arranged to speak with a group from the University of California, all seniors and honor students. Mark is a sociology major, Kevin plans to be an investment counselor, and Dan is in a rigorous program leading to an M.D. and Ph.D. They say that they support women's rights, but when it comes to envisioning their own lives with women, they express an astonishingly romantic view of wives and mothers.

"I don't fear a woman who has a career," says Mark. "I support that as an alternative, but I would *prefer* the other kind of woman, the one who'll be home for me and my child, because I missed that. Both my parents work-ed, and when I was in second grade, I came home to an empty house. My mother would leave instructions for me to start dinner."

Kevin's experience was different—his mother stayed at home—and he, too, would like a wife who devotes herself to the family. "As much as people say roles are changing, I see my wife as *the mother*. I mean there's nothing like your mother. The bond between a mother and child is so special—it's in the soul. The mother *bore* the child."

"Your mom is your mom," agrees Mark. "No nanny or day care can substitute for your mom. When people talk about a woman sacrificing for her children, I don't see the sacrifice, I see it as a gain."

Dan, unlike the others, says he wants to marry a woman with a profes-sion. He also wants children, though. "My wife could stop working to have babies and go back when they're in school. That's what my mother did."

None of the men is interested in taking over part of the mothering role. "If I'm bringing in the money, bearing the pressures of a career," says Kevin, "I don't want to come home and deal with another incredible responsibility."

I wonder how these men will get on with the women of their generation.

Ten years ago I would have been appalled at the life I am leading. We have moved into a large tract house in the suburbs, a house I do not admire aesthetically but that is perfectly engineered for a family. We are consider-ing getting a van or station wagon.

I have created the form I wanted, but sometimes I feel I'm dying inside it. Gone are an active social life, travel, hobbies, recreational activities. All my time is spent on three things: baby, work, and keeping the marriage going.

I find I can handle two beautifully. When my husband is out of town, or when I'm between projects and not working, things go smoothly. But three pushes me to the edge. Someone is unhappy, something is always get-ting short shrift.

"Do you want to know the sex of your baby?" says the counselor at the laboratory, calling with the results of my amniocentesis. "It's a girl." I yelp with joy, but a few moments later I feel flickers of apprehension. What wisdom, what guidance will I be able to offer my daughter? Freud wrestled with the question, What do women want?, but I am pondering, What can women have, dear God, what can women have?

The only answer I come up with is that you can have it *sequentially*. At one stage you may emphasize career, and at another, marriage and nurturing young children, and at any point you will be aware of what is missing. If you are lucky, you will be able to fit everything in.

My cousin is about to be married, and relatives have descended from east and west. My sister and her daughter are here from Hawaii, and my father-in-law from Chicago, and there are seven people sleeping in our house.

The night after the wedding we have a potluck supper for thirteen. The children are overexcited, shrieking and running through the rooms. My husband is playing the piano and my parents are carrying in platters of food. My sister herds the children to their own little table and the adults to a larger one, and the decibel level is so high that I cannot hear anyone speak.

As I lie on my hospital bed, watching the chaos, I feel a sense of well-being. I, who for so many years was the guest in other people's homes, the extra woman, have a family of my own creating. I thank God for this—for what I very nearly missed. It's worth it.

9.

Their Turn: How Men Are Changing

Betty Friedan

I believe that American men are at the edge of a tidal wave of change—a change in their very identity as men. It is a change not yet clearly visible, not really identified or understood by the experts and not even, or seldom, spoken about by men themselves. Yet this change will be as basic as the change created for women by the Women's Movement, even though it is nothing like the Women's Movement. Nobody is marching or making statements. There is no explosion of anger, no enemy to rage against, no list of grievances or demands for benefits and opportunities clearly valuable and previously denied, as with women.

This is a quiet movement, a shifting in direction, the saying of no to old patterns, a searching for new values, a struggling with basic questions that each man seems to be going through alone. At the same time, he continues the outward motions that always have defined men's lives, making it (or struggling to make it) at the office, the plant, the ball park ... making it with women ... getting married ... having children ... yet he senses that something is happening with men, something large and historic, and he wants to be part of it. He carries the baby in his backpack, shops at the supermarket on Saturdays, with a certain showing-off quality.

It started for many men almost unwillingly, in response to the Women's Movement. The outward stance of hostility and bristling defensiveness that the rhetoric of the first stage of the Women's Movement almost demanded of men obscured the reality of the first changes among them, the real reasons those changes were threatening to some men, and the surprising relief, support—even envy—many men felt about the Women's Movement. At first glance, all it looked like was endless arguments about his doing a fair share of the housework, the cooking, and the cleaning; and his responsibility for helping with the children, getting them to bed, into snowsuits, to the park, to the pediatrician. Because now it wasn't *automatic* that her job was to take care of the house and all the other details of life while his job was to support everyone. Now she was working to support them too.

But then, even if she didn't have a job outside the home, she suddenly had to be treated as a person too, as he was. She had a right to her own life and interests; at night, on weekends, he could help with the children and the house.

He felt wronged, injured. He had been working his can off to support her and the children and now he was her "oppressor," a "male chauvinist pig," if he didn't scrub all the pots and pans to boot. "You make dinner," she said. "I'm going to my design class."

He felt scared when she walked out like that. If she didn't need him for her identity, her status, her sense of importance, if she was going to get all that for herself and have a life independent of him, wouldn't she stop loving him? Wouldn't she just leave? He was supposed to be the big male oppressor, yeah? How could he admit the big secret—that maybe he need- ed her more than she needed him? That he felt like a baby when he became afraid she would leave. That suddenly he didn't know what he felt, what he was *supposed* to feel—as a man.

I believe much of the hostility of men comes from their very dependence on our love, from those feelings of need that men aren't supposed to have— just as the excesses of our attacks on our male "oppressors" stemmed from our dependence on men. That old, excessive dependence (which was sup- posed to be natural in women) made us feel we had to be *more* indepen- dent than any man in order to be able to move at all. Our explosion of rage and our attacks on men masked our own timidity and fear at risking ourselves, in a complex and competitive world, in ways we never had had to before.

And the more a man was pretending to a dominant, cool, masculine superiority he didn't really feel—the more he was forced to carry the burden alone of supporting everyone against the rough odds of that grim, outside economic world—the more threatened and the more hostile he felt.

Sam, a foreman for an aerospace company in Seattle, Washington, believes that the period when his wife "tried to be just a housewife" was the worst time in his marriage. "If you decide you're going to stay home and be taken care of," he says, "and you have to depend for everything on this guy, you get afraid. *Can he do it?* It all depended on me, and I was in a constant panic, the way our business is now, but I'd say, 'Don't worry.'

"Susie was tired of her job anyhow," explains Sam. "It wasn't such a great job—neither is mine, if you want to know—but she had an excuse. She said she wanted to be home with the children. The pressure was on me. But it was crazy. Here I was, not knowing where the next paycheck was com- ing from after our government contract ran out, suddenly supporting a wife and children all by myself.

"It's better now that she's working and bringing some money in," Sam insists. "And I don't just help with the kids. She has to be at work before I do, so I give them breakfast and get them off to school. The nights she works late, I make dinner, help with homework, and get everyone to bed. But I don't feel so panicky now—and she isn't attacking me any more."

Phil Kessler, a young doctor who started out to be a surgeon but who now has a small-town family practice in New Jersey, talks to me as he makes pickles and his children run around underfoot in the country kitchen that is next to his office. "I was going to be a surgeon, super cool in my gleaming white uniform," he says, "the man I was supposed to be but knew I wasn't. So I married a nurse and she stayed home to raise our children, and she was supposed to fulfill herself through my career. It didn't work for either of us.

"I went through torture before every operation," Phil explains. "Then Ellen started turning against me. I always said the children needed her at home full time. Maybe because I was so scared inside. Maybe she didn't have the nerve to do her own thing professionally. All she seemed to want was revenge against me, as if she were locked into some kind of sexual battle against me, playing around, looking elsewhere for true love.

"When Ellen finally got up the nerve to do her own thing—she's a nurse-midwife now—it was a relief," says Phil. "The other stuff stopped. She could come back to being my wife. And I'm *redefining myself,* no longer in terms of success or failure as a doctor, although I still am a doctor, and not as superior or inferior to her. It was a blow to my ego, but what a relief to take off my surgical mask! I'm discovering my own value to the family.

"Now that I'm not so hurt and angry and afraid that she'll leave me, I can see that it's a hell of a fight for a woman to be seen as a person. I think she was afraid of trying to accomplish something on her own, so she made me the villain. But it's as hard for me to feel like a person as it is for her. We couldn't—either of us—get that from each other."

The new questions are harder for men because men have a harder time talking about their feelings than women do. That's part of the masculine mystique. And after all, because men have the power and the top-dog position in society that women are making all the fuss about, why should men want to change—unless women make them?

"Maybe men feel more need to pretend," says a sales engineer in Detroit, Michigan, who is struggling to take "equal responsibility" for the children and the house, now that his wife has gone to work in a department store. "I don't think men thought much about what it was to be a man," he explains, "until women suddenly were talking about what it was to be a woman—and men were left out of the equation.

"Now men are thinking about what it means to be a man. The Women's Movement forced us to start rethinking the way we relate to women and to our families. Now men are going to have to rethink the way they relate to their work. Our sense of who we are always was based profoundly on work, but men are going to begin to define themselves in ways other than work.

"In the '80s," this man says, "we're going to see more men dropping away from traditional male roles, partly because of the economy, partly because men are beginning to find other goodies at the table, like their children—areas from which men were excluded before. Being a daddy has become very important to me. When I used to see a man on the street with his children on a weekday, I assumed he was unemployed, a loser. Now it's so common—daddies with their children, at ease."

The truth is that many of the old bases for men's identity have become shaky. If being a man is defined, for example, as being *dominant, superior*—as *not-being-a-woman*—the definition gets shaky when most of the important work of society no longer requires brute muscular force. The Vietnam War probably was the beginning of the end of the old caveman-hunter, gun-toting, he-man mystique. The men I have been interviewing around the country these past months are the men who fought in Vietnam or who went to graduate school to stay out of the war.

Vietnam was somehow a watershed. If men stop defining themselves by going to war or getting power from jobs women can't have, what is left? What does it mean to be a man, except *not-being-a-woman*—that is, physically superior and able to beat up everyone else? The fact is, when a man admits to those "messy feelings" that men as well as women have, he can't *play* the same kind of man any more.

Tony Kowalski, of the Outer Banks of North Carolina, was a pilot in Vietnam when it started for him. "I was a captain, coming up for major," he says. "I had all the medals, and I would have gone on for twenty years in the Air Force. Sitting up there over Nam, the commander, under heavy fire, the guys screaming into the mikes, the bombers and fighters moving in, me giving the orders, I was caught up in it, crazy-wild, excited. And then I woke up one day, coming out of Special Forces camp, and found myself clicking my empty gun at civilians. I knew I had to get out."

Tony can fly any piece of machinery. He took a job with an airline. "All I wanted was security," he says. "After one year I was furloughed because the company was having financial difficulties. There was no security. So I came back to this town where I grew up and took a job as a schoolteacher, working with seventh and eighth graders who were reading at the second-grade level. It was the 'reading lab,' the pits, the bottom—and traditionally a 'woman's job.' It's the hardest job I've ever done and it gets the least respect. Flying a 323,000-pound Lockheed Starlifter can't compare." As a pilot Tony made $34,000 a year; as a teacher he makes $12,000.

"But maybe now," he says, "with the ladies moving in and picking up some of the financial slack—my wife works for a florist and as a waitress nights—a guy can say, 'I'm not going to get much of anywhere with the money anyhow. Why don't I do something really worthwhile from a human point of view?' "

Another man, a West Point graduate of the class of '68, whose father and grandfather were Army men, insists: "Men can't be the same again after Vietnam. It always defined men, as against women, that we went to war. We learned it in the locker room, young. The worst insult was to be called all the four- and five-letter words for women's sex. Now that women are in the locker rooms at West Point, how can that work?

"Women have a powerful advantage," this man adds, "because they aren't brought up to believe that if someone knocks you down, *he* has the courage, so you have to knock *him* down. Women aren't stuck with the notion that that kind of courage is necessary. It seems to me, ever since the Vietnam War more and more men are reaching a turning point, so that if they don't get beyond these games, they start to die. Women will make a mistake if they reach that turning point and start to imitate men. Men can't be role models for women, not even in the Army. We badly need some new role models ourselves."

At first it seems as if men and women are moving in exactly opposite directions. Women are moving out of the home and into the men's world of work and men are shifting toward a new definition of themselves *in* the home. As we move into the '80s, social psychologist and public-opinion analyst Daniel Yankelovich is finding that a majority of adult men in the United States no longer are seeking or are satisfied by conventional job success. Only one in every five men now says that work means more to him than leisure.

"Men have come to believe that success on the job is not enough to satisfy their yearnings for self-fulfillment," says Yankelovich. "They are reaching for something more and for something different."

Certain large signs of this movement are reported in the newspapers almost daily. Corporation heads complain that young executives refuse to accept transfers because of "the family." Economists and government officials bewail increased absenteeism and declining productivity among workers. In the past ten years, more than half of West Point's graduates have resigned as Army career officers. College and graduate-school enrollments are dropping among men (as they continue to increase among women), and not just because it isn't necessary for men to evade the draft any more.

In the book *Breaktime*, a controversial study of men "living without work in a nine-to-five world," Bernard Lefkowitz reports a 71 per cent increase in the number of working-aged men who have left the labor force since 1968 and who are not looking for work. According to Lefkowitz, the "stop-and-go pattern of work" is becoming the predominant pattern, rather than the lifetime jobs and careers men used to pursue both for economic security and for their masculine identity.

"In the depression of the '30s," says Lefkowitz, "men were anxious because they were not working. In the '70s men became anxious because their work was not paying off in the over-all economic security they had expected."

Bob O'Malley, 33, quit his rising career in a big New York City bank to sell real estate on the tip of Long Island.

"I asked myself one day, if my career continued going well and I really made it up the corporate ladder, did I want to be there fifteen years from now, with the headaches of the senior executives I saw being pushed off to smaller offices, their staffs, secretaries, status taken away, or having heart attacks, strokes? Men who had been loyal to the company twenty-five years–it governed their whole lives–and to what end? I didn't want to live my life like that. I wanted to be more independent–maybe not making so much money but living more for myself."

The trouble is that once men disengage themselves from the old patterns of masculinity and success, they are just as lost for role models as women are. Moreover, if a man tries to get out of his own bind by *reversing roles* with his wife–if he yearns for a superwoman to support him as she used to yearn for a strong man who would take care of her–it makes his wife uneasy.

"My husband wants me to have another child, and he says he'll quit his job and stay home to take care of the children," a woman in Vermont tells me. "But why should that work for him when it didn't work for me? And maybe I don't want him to take over the family that much. Maybe I'd resent it–just working to support him."

It's a situation that didn't work when Dr. Phil Kessler, in the first flush of relief after dropping his surgical mask, tried reversing roles with his wife. In the first place, his wife couldn't make as much money as a nurse-midwife as he could make as a doctor. And somehow when she came home from work, the house was never "clean enough," the meat loaf wasn't seasoned "right" and he'd also forgotten to put the potatoes on. So she would rush around, tired as she was, doing everything over, making him feel just as guilty as she had in the old days.

"Then I began to feel like a martyr," he says. "Nobody appreciated how hard I worked, taking care of the house and the children. Now that I'm doing my own work again–and bringing money in–I don't have to feel guilty if the house isn't all that clean. And now that they're treating her like a professional at the hospital, she doesn't notice the dust on the windowsills so much, either."

It takes trial and error, of course, to work out the practicalities, the real trade-offs, of the new equality between the sexes when both try to share home and work responsibilities. And it might be harder for men because the benefits of the trade-offs for them aren't that obvious at first. Women, after all, are fighting for an equal share in the activities and the power games that are rewarded in this society. What are men's rewards for giving up some of that power?

Jimmy Fox, a blue-collar worker in Brooklyn, New York, won't admit that there are any rewards for him in the trade-offs he's been "forced" to work out with his wife. "In our community," says Jimmy, "men don't freely accept women's equality. It's got to be slowly pushed down their throats. Men are the ones who go to the bar on the corner, drink, come home when the heck they want, and expect supper to be on the table, waiting for them. When that starts changing, it scares them to death. It scared me.

"I didn't know what was going on," he says. "First thing I knew, my wife is going out to a women's organization, the National Congress of Neighborhood Women, and she wants to go do this, do that. She's learning, letting me know that things are wrong with our marriage. What am I supposed to do? It took five years before we got to the point where she went out to work and found her own role."

Today Jimmy makes $9,000 a year and his wife makes $9,000. "And when she's out working," says Jimmy, "I'm taking care of the baby. It's no picnic. Any man who wants to change places with his wife when his wife stays home and takes care of the house and children has got to be a maniac. Her job in the house was twice as hard as mine at the plant. I work ten, twelve hours. She works from when she gets up in the morning until she goes to bed."

When Linda Fox first started working, she says, "there were many, many battles between Jimmy and me. I wanted equality, which I thought meant that if he put three hours and twenty-two minutes into housework, then I would put in three hours and twenty-two minutes. I wanted a blow-by-blow division and I was fanatical about it. Jimmy was so happy to be relieved of some of the burden of being the only one with the paycheck that he was willing to do that, although I know he was teased by the guys at the bar."

The first payoff for men then, obviously, is economic survival. Unfortunately, few of the other big trade-offs of equality can be measured as mechanically as men's and women's making exactly the same amount of money (women on the average still earn only 59 cents to a man's $1.00) or their spending exactly the same amount of time on housework.

"What I've gained," says Avery Corman, who wrote the novel *Kramer versus Kramer*, on which the movie was based, from his own experience of taking over the children when his wife started a business, "is the joy—and it is a joy—of having my children really rely on me. I've gained this real participation in their upbringing because I've been active in it on a daily basis."

Unlike the Kramers, the Cormans remain happily married, and he says, "What I've given up is being waited on myself. There are times when I'd really like to be the prince of patriarchs and sit around with my pipe and slippers with my wife and children tiptoeing around, but it sure isn't like that now and it never will be again. A secret part of me would sometimes like a less-equal marriage, would like to be catered to the way guys used to be.

"But the real payoff," he says, "is that men can begin to think about who they are as *men*. I can ask myself what I really want in life. With my wife out there earning, I don't have to be just a breadwinner." Another big trade-

off for men while women become more independent is more independence—
more "space"—for them. An Atlanta cotton broker, now married at thirty
to a woman with her own career, recalls his first marriage, to a woman
who depended on him for everything.

"She made me feel suffocated," he says. "Living with a completely dependent woman is debilitating. You don't know why, but you just feel awful.
She's breathing your air. She's passing her anxiety on to you. She's got no
confidence in herself and she's looking to you for everything; but what she
does is always put you down, make you feel you won't make it.

"She may be very sweet," he explains further. "She may be lovely, but
all you know is that you don't have room to breathe. I never heard of any
ruling class resigning, but as men realize that it's better to live with a
nondependent woman, the change will come about because the payoff is
real—economic and emotional."

Paradoxically, part of the trade-off is that when women share the economic
burden—and declare themselves equal persons in other ways—men are able
to put a new value on personal qualities once considered the exclusive domain of women. It's the new American frontier for men, this exploration
of their inner space, of the "messy feelings" we all have but that for too
long were considered awesome and mysterious and forbidden territory for
men.

When women share the work burden and relieve men of the need to pretend to false strengths, men can open up to feelings that give them a real
sense of strength, especially when they share the daily chores of life that
wives used to shield them from. "It grounds me—I have to admit it," says
a man named Bernie, who for the first time, after thirty years of his mother's
and wife's doing it for him, is cooking, shopping, and washing clothes. "I
like the relief from always thinking about my job, feeling like a disembodied
head chained to a typewriter."

Or as a man named Lars Hendrix, of Oakland, California, expresses it:
"It makes me feel alive. I don't have to pretend to be so strong because I
feel good. I feel grounded. The silence that most men live with isolates them
not only from women but also from other men. My wife's assault on my
silence was at first extremely painful. She made me share my feelings with
her. It brought an incredible sense of liberation, and maybe for the first
time in my adult life a sense of reality, that I can *feel* my feelings and share
them with her.

"But there'll still be a loneliness, for me and for other men," says Lars,
"until we can share our feelings with each other. That's what I envy most
about the Women's Movement—the way women share their feelings and
the support they get from each other. Do you know how isolated and lonely and weak a man feels in that silence, never really making contact with
another man?"

There is another, major problem. As men seek for themselves the liberation that began with the Women's Movement, both men and women have

to confront the conflict between their human needs—for love, for family, for purpose in life—and the demands of the workplace.

A family therapist in Philadelphia, Pennsylvania, the father of a three-year-old son, talks about the conflict in terms of his own profession and personal needs. "I was working at one of the top family-training centers in the country," he says. "There was constant theoretical discussion about getting the father back into the family, but the way the jobs were set up there, you had to work fifty, sixty hours a week. To really get anywhere you had to put in seventy hours and work nights, weekends. You didn't have time for your own family. I won't do that. My family is number one—my job is only to be a good therapist."

Recent managerial studies have shown that the long working hours and the corporate transfers that keep many men from strong daily involvements with their families or with other interests are not always necessary for the work of the company. But the long hours and the transfers do serve to keep a man *dependent* for his very identity, as well as his livelihood, on the corporation—dependent as a "company man."

Recently, at the National Assembly on the Future of the Family sponsored by the NOW Legal Defense and Education Fund, corporation heads and union leaders joined feminists and family experts in confronting the need for "practical and innovative" solutions to balancing the demands of the workplace and the family. The agenda for the '80s must include restructuring the institutions of work and home to make both equality livable and workable—for women and men.

Women can't solve the problem alone by taking everything on themselves, by trying to be "superwomen." And women don't have the power to change the structure of the workplace by themselves. But while more and more men decide that they want some self-fulfillment beyond their jobs and some of the life-grounding that women always have had in the family—as much as women now need and want some voice and active power in the world—there will be a new combined force for carrying out the second stage of liberation for us all.

It seems strange to suggest that there is a new American frontier, a new adventure for men, in the struggle for *wholeness*, for openness to feeling, for living and sharing life on equal terms with women. But it is a new frontier where both men's and women's needs converge. Men need new role models now as much as women do.

Men also need to share their new questions and feelings about work and family and self-fulfillment with other men. To help each other. To begin to break out of their isolation and become role models for each other, as women are doing in the second stage of the struggle for liberation.

The dialogue has gone on too long in terms of women alone. Let men join women in the center of the second stage.

10.

Changing Sex Roles and Changing Families

Janet Zollinger Giele

There is a close tie between the change in men's and women's roles and the change in family structure. But the relative status of women in family life is more difficult to measure than their status in public affairs. Political, economic, or educational activities operate in "markets" that assign the individual a formal status and pay a stated income. The family by contrast is "associational" (Weinstein and Platt, 1969:1-19). The status of each member is enmeshed with facts of birth and death, marriage or divorce. Participation in the family hinges on the emotional life of others as well as on individual accomplishment. Laws and public policies directed at child care, the elderly, tax rates, or public welfare affect not only one member or one sex but also the whole family unit. Consequently, examination of the relative status of women and men in the family very quickly leads to considering the structure of the family unit and the situational realities that determine its form.

Women's and men's roles will not really change unless family institutions also change, but it is not at all clear in what order and in what direction family life will be transformed. Maybe, as some economists suggest, the next steps to be taken are public measures that will support a new occupation of consumer maintenance or allow tax deductions for household costs, such as heat, light, or childcare, much as corporations are allowed tax deductions for their expenses (Bell, 1975; Lekachman, 1975). Or perhaps the next steps must be personal and ideological, through commitment to the idea that the family is the responsibility of both men and women.

No matter what change comes first, it is clear now that the traditional sex-typed division of labor between women's work at home and men's work at a job is under strain in every major industrial nation. Although 40 to 60 per cent of women are employed in such countries as the United States, Russia, Poland, and Japan, they pay a penalty of being overburdened by both domestic *and* paid work (Blake, 1974). Employed American women who have families average a total of seventy hours of work a week (Gauger, 1973: 23). Each week they have a few hours less leisure time than men for sleep or relaxation (Szalai, 1973). Thus more women have entered employment without having secured the needed adjustments in family life.

The balance of work and leisure is only one issue raised by changes in sex roles. Other issues are related to problems that emerge when individuals deviate from the preferred life cycle. The poverty of female-headed households is one example. If through divorce, widowhood, or desertion a woman is left alone to head a household with children, her children are about six times more likely to grow up in poverty than children living in male-headed families (Bane, 1976:118).

Family issues become especially significant for changing sex roles as the boundary between public and private life becomes more permeable. Demographic shifts (lengthening of life, the changing life cycle of women and families) are behind such current public-policy issues as childcare or homemaker allowances. However, current extension of government supports into various functions of private life such as health care and care of the elderly gives public policy potential power to influence the shape of family life and sex roles in the future.

Two major demographic changes have taken place that affect the life cycle and women's role within it. The childbearing period has been compressed, and adult women's average length of life has increased. As a result, the typical American woman in this century bears fewer children and has her last child at the age of thirty; that child leaves home when a woman is in her late forties, and she still can expect to live thirty more years. As recently as the turn of the century women were bearing their last child when they were thirty-three, seeing their last child married when they were fifty-six, and themselves living only ten or fifteen years more.

Each major demographic trend affecting women points to the uncertainty of following any single prescribed route over the life course. Marriage may end in divorce; a woman may have to support herself and children; a man may have to work out complicated schedules and relationships with children by a former marriage. Rather than be confined to sex-stereotyped activities or try to meet rigid timetables of accomplishment, men and women may do best to adopt a flexible time perspective that permits them to negotiate twists and turns as they appear. By this perspective the family is not so much a distraction from work as the primary social system for synchronizing the achievement and affiliative needs of both sexes.

Given the changing demographic realities for women's lives—they are through raising children sooner, live longer, and are more likely to combine paid work with family life—what will be the shape of family life that will allow them a more equitable share in leisure as well as in work and family? How are family forms changing even now to show us the outlines of a more egalitarian arrangement to come? The answers are important, for they suggest not only how younger generations should be prepared to select from the available alternatives, but also how practical legislation or voluntary efforts may be undertaken that will support the forms that seem most desirable to us now.

If recent books and articles on family life can be taken as any trustworthy guide, there is remarkable convergence on a new, more egalitarian family form, which Young and Willmott (1973) term the *symmetrical family*. Changes in the industrial and ecological order as well as limited fertility and feminism have brought about this change. The phenomenon is observable not only in the managerial and professional class but also among shift workers in the manufacturing and service trades. Yet at the same time as marriages are becoming less hierarchical—husbands being asked to share more housework, and wives working more outside the home— another development is taking place alongside. Alternative family forms are springing up here and there: female-headed families that result from separation, divorce, or unwed pregnancy; or households made up of unrelated individuals living together. These new forms challenge the assumption on which the traditional nuclear family is based. Alternative styles show, for example, how childcare or cooking arrangements can be modified. But they also illustrate that any social system lives with constraints of one kind or another.

Evolution of Family Forms

Changing patterns of participation in family life precipitate strains in the established patterns. As we have seen in the case of higher divorce rates, remarriage, and the increase in dual-worker families, new "scripts" for action are being tried out as each family experiments with its internal division of labor and timing of decisions.

One sign of ferment in the family division of labor comes from American opinion surveys conducted between 1964 and 1974. Over that decade women's attitudes toward the traditional division of labor between husbands and wives showed a consistent trend. In every major segment of the population, the proportion of women supporting the traditional pattern declined. At the same time, the proportion supporting women's rights in the labor market and their options for a life without marriage or motherhood increased (Mason et al., 1976: 585).

Newspapers report instances of commuting professional couples, one of whom may work in Cleveland, the other in New York City, yet who manage to share a marriage and perhaps even children. Less attention has been given the life patterns of husband and wife in the blue-collar classes. Historical studies, however, suggest that the sharing of work and family responsibilities between husbands and wives employed in the mills may have had some of the characteristics of the modern symmetrical family. Children were expected to help with household tasks and care for younger siblings. Schedules were stretched and complicated. People found various adaptive routines for making do (Hareven, 1975).

Symmetrical families are a phenomenon of modern society, not just in the United States but in Europe as well. Househusbands are not common in Sweden, but they do exist there and their roles are accepted. Dual-career families in Great Britain are the subject of a major study by Rhona and Robert Rapoport (1976). Other countries of Eastern and Western Europe with high numbers of women in the labor force have put women, for the time being, under a heavy overload if they have both families and careers. The way out of this stressful situation has not resulted yet in full institutionalization of the symmetrical family. But a rising divorce rate and growing insistence by women on revising the roles within marriage point in that direction (Fogarty et al., 1971: 96; Sokolowska, 1977; Silver, 1977).

Why is the symmetrical family the likely wave of the future? The answer comes from an analysis of modern society and the kind of capacity for role flexibility that a highly differentiated structure requires. Moreover, when society is changing rapidly and circumstances are uncertain, a high degree of flexibility is more adaptive than rigid adherence to one pattern of activity or another. This is true not only of individuals but of the family itself as well. The family performs its function best when it handles nonuniform tasks that are not easily farmed out to bureaucratic institutions, which can perform them more expertly or more efficiently. But as Litwak (1970: 354-359) has pointed out, what are defined as nonuniform functions change as fast as technology and the social environment change. For the family to perform at its best, it therefore must be able to take on functions that at the moment are defined as nonuniform and to drop them when they become routine.

For example, early in the century, laundry was a routine menial task, and there were outside laundry establishments prepared to provide the service; even working-class women sent out their wash. When, however, the home washing machine appeared and new fabrics and automatic washers were introduced, laundry returned to the home. The household then could meet the special requirements of each individual's laundry needs and care for each fabric type better than could the commercial establishment. Litwak (1970: 358-359) concludes analysis of the laundry example with a general rule that gives a clue to the type of family that can be best adapted to our rapidly changing society:

> [The] one key structural need of the family–given a rapidly changing technology–is the capacity to deal with changing functions, the capacity to rapidly change what are legitimate and what are nonlegitimate activities, or most generally the capacity to be flexible.

One of the main sociological consequences of flexibility in the family is role substitutability between husband and wife rather than fixed sex-typed roles. The wife cannot be just an expressive leader in the family and let the husband be the instrumental leader in the world of work outside. She may be the instrumental leader in bringing up the children or managing household affairs. She needs the husband's expressive help to handle the tensions that may result, just as he needs her expressive help with anxieties about work. Furthermore, by Litwak's reasoning, the family has major commitments in all areas of life, not just to the care of young children. It is the most effective agent for handling other types of nonuniform problems, such as peculiar circumstances of health or emotional depression, sudden loss of income by some member, some failure in school or work, or some threat to the local neighborhood. To meet such unexpected needs, the "family clockwork" must be able to respond appropriately.

As each family experiments to produce a workable formula of interaction, certain common themes emerge. One is that couples still are more likely to put primary emphasis on the husband's job as a basis for choosing a residential location or for timing major family events. The wife's role more often contains the compromises that keep the family flexible. Yet even this pattern may characterize only one point in time, when the children and couple are relatively young. Later on, the wife's career might, in fact, take precedence. Families move in and out of different forms, and it is difficult to keep remembering that their very flexibility makes it difficult to capture a snapshot of them that is true for more than a moment. It therefore is important to examine some of the forms that families may take over a period of time.

DUAL-CAREER FAMILIES

Numerous studies of professional couples of whom the wife also has a career have shown consistently that even in this type of marriage the husband's career is accorded somewhat greater priority than that of the wife. Yet Holmstrom (1972: 40), who interviewed twenty two-career couples, notes:

> The wives accommodated to their husbands' careers, more than vice versa, when deciding where to live. But the more surprising finding is how much the husbands' decisions were affected by the career interests of their wives. In quite a departure from middle-class norms, many husbands went out of their way to live in places where their wives also could obtain desirable employment.

In addition, the internal division of labor evolves so that some husbands and children are drawn into household tasks. As a wife goes to work, the husband takes on more chores around the house, and the wife's power in the household domain diminishes somewhat (Bahr, 1974: 185). One of the couples described by the Rapoports was very effective in getting each of their two boys to pitch in as needed. According to the wife,

> the main rule we've tried to work to ever since we were married is that if there is a job to be done, we do it together so that there isn't one person working and feeling "There's me slaving over a hot stove and there's him sitting with his feet up." Unless the person who is specifically doing the job says "Right, you go and sit down," we do it together and nobody sits down and does nothing until everybody sits down and does nothing. The children join in this plan and they are expected to work when we are working and we don't expect them to work and us sit down but we do it together. [Rapoport and Rapoport, 1976: 65]

In some families a wife's work may become more important later in the life of the couple than it was at the beginning. Established male professors, for example, have been known to relocate in another, sometimes less famous, university center because it offered more opportunity for the wife's career. Data on women's labor-force participation by age certainly suggest that the life pattern whereby older married women are employed is rapidly becoming the norm.

However, it would be a mistake to suppose that the ideal patterns of role symmetry and sharing that occasionally are realized in a few dual-career families are yet in fact a reality for the great majority of two-worker families. With respect to sharing of household work, data reported in 1969 and 1970 by Kathryn Walker are sobering: women at that time still performed considerably more home work than men—4.8 hours a day for the married women employed 30 hours a week or more as compared with 1.6 hours for the employed men who were married to working wives. Childcare routines still assume that the mother is the parent primarily responsible for coming to school conferences, delivering the child to weekday extracurricular activities, and being at home when the child is sick. Joseph Pleck (1977) perceives the differential permeability of men's and women's careers to the demands of family as patterned in such a way as to reinforce the priority of husband's commitment to work and wife's commitment to family.

WORKING-CLASS FAMILIES

New efforts to understand working-class families in the United States closely parallel the findings of Young and Willmott in London. Working-class people in some ways give more devotion to family than middle-class people, presumably because their work lives are less stimulating and all-consuming. The 1974 Virginia Slims Poll found, for example, that when women were asked what they wanted most for a son, a happy marriage or an interesting career, far more of the less-educated women gave priority to family over work.

Of course, it also is true that the older respondents gave more priority to family than to work, and to the extent that age and lower education are associated, differential responses by education may be related not just to social class but to age as well. Yet such results seem to make sense out of what some have found to be the puzzling rejection by working-class women of women's liberation. College women and their husbands have the education that would open interesting careers to them. Educated women thus feel frustrated when doing housework, because they compare it with the work that they might do for pay. But working-class women, whose alternatives are repetitive factory work or menial service occupations, find their liberation through independence in home life, cooking, and household work. To them, being a good wife and mother is one of the few routes to significant satisfaction, and the middle-class women's liberation rhetoric seems to them to be devaluing a world they consider to be of primary importance (Seifer, 1975; Levison, 1974; Meade, 1975; Coles 1973: 106).

Nevertheless, there may soon be a convergence between the working class and the middle class in their attitudes toward family life and the roles of husbands and wives. In reviewing what is known about blue-collar women, Victoria Samuels (1975) finds signs that there has been some change since Rainwater and Komarovsky surveyed working men's wives in 1959. At that time working-class women lived a routine life segregated from much companionship with men. One day was pretty much the same as another. Husbands resisted wives' working, and wives seemed to lack self-confidence (Rainwater et al., 1959; Komarovsky, 1964). In the 1970s more working-class women view themselves as being competent in the role of housewife than the number reporting such competency in 1959. They show more interest in work and freedom to work. And they seem to feel that they can be more assertive in the home (Samuels, 1975). Even in the drabness and frustration that Rubin finds in the lives of working-class women, there is an underlying theme that more egalitarian relationships within the family are desired. The implicit ideal is more talking, more understanding, and more sharing of emotional life between wives and husbands. Ann Oakley (1975) contends that housework also is boring to working-class women. And among the working class, Lein et al. (1974) find that a significant number of husbands share in housework and childcare when their wives are working.

In her studies of working-class women, Nancy Seifer (1975) got to know a few women in various parts of the United States—for example, the wife of a coal miner in Alabama and a secretary in a steel mill in Gary, Indiana. Each of these women became an activist for women's rights through some catalyzing experience that touched her own job or her family's interests. They all had been turned off by middle-class feminist rhetoric that devalued the wife and mother role, but when they perceived their common interests with other women over such issues as equal pay, opportunities for promotion, or the family health-insurance plans of their unions, they became involved.

Just why such changes have occurred still is hidden. Many have speculated that a wife's working actually changes the power relationship in any couple. The husband has less opportunity to dominate when the wife also brings in a paycheck (Bahr, 1974: 184-185). In the past a wife's employment might have threatened a husband's self-esteem. But rising participation of women in the work force now apparently is changing that norm. Short-term unemployment or a cutback in working hours or overtime is such a common threat to the working class that a wife's work is unquestionably an asset for tiding the family over lean times. Seifer (1975: 14) recently has estimated that the *majority* of women in working-class families now are employed during at least some part of the year. Dougherty et al. (1977) found in a study of fourteen Boston area dual-worker blue-collar families that *every family had experienced at least one layoff* of either husband or wife in the recession period since 1972-1973. Husbands tremendously valued a wife's contribution when her wages helped keep the family income up to the standard they desired.

Other Emerging Family Forms

High rates of marital breakdown have put large numbers of women "at risk" of forming single-parent households. Divorce also has given rise to remarriage and reconstituted nuclear families. In addition, communal experiments and individuals in transition between single and married states have created intimate networks and other variant forms. Of these we shall give most attention to the single-parent households, reconstituted marriages, and experiments with communal and modified extended families because they have the most far-reaching implications for women's status. Each of these variant forms can provide information on the structural conditions that are conducive to equality in household and work roles, legal provisions, child-care arrangements, and leisure.

SINGLE-PARENT HOUSEHOLDS

From the point of view of women, the significant feature of single-parent families, particularly when a woman is head of the household, is that resources can be less than in the nuclear or extended form, and as a result, the woman head may be unusually burdened with responsibility. Much effort has been devoted to lowering the number of such women on the welfare rolls by means tests or by getting them into the labor force. But not even the majority of single heads of family are on welfare. Those not on welfare also have needs that should be met for the sake of the family and the children.

The proportion of white families headed by women has not changed in forty years, although it has doubled for blacks. What has changed markedly is the proportion of these families in younger age groups *with children*. It is the presence of children that makes the difference between poverty and an adequate standard of living for the families with a single head. In 1972 the Michigan Panel Study of Income Dynamics studied five thousand families over a period of several years and found that 65 per cent of all families with mother heads had *no* income from welfare, and no more than a fifth of all mother heads received as much as half of their income from welfare. Only 47 per cent received any alimony or child support from fathers, and the median amount of such support was only $1,350 (Heclo et al., 1973: 12-13). But a relatively high percentage of even college-educated female heads of family are poor—18 per cent as compared with 3 per cent of college-educated male heads. Lack of male support coupled with women's frequent lack of marketable skills and much lower earning power, even if they are fully employed, makes it more likely that a female-headed family will be poorer than either the male-supported nuclear family or the reconstituted family.

How do these women and their families survive then? More than half (56 per cent) derive at least $500 or more from their own earnings and receive no welfare income. Furthermore, many of these female-headed families (10.2 per cent of all families with children) reconstitute themselves into nuclear families with a husband and wife within five years. The single-parent state thus seems definitely transitional.

But the possibility that single headship is a transitional state should not make us forget that, in the difficult years, parents without partners need emotional support, help with household chores, flexible working hours so that they can meet their dual-family and work responsibilities, and publicly available provision for childcare so that they can meet emergencies, get away on occasion, and see that their children get proper attention while the parent attends to other responsibilities. Cogswell and Sussman (1972) note the prevailing assumption that a mother will be available to come to school during the day for a parent-child conference, take time off to get children to the doctor or dentist, chauffeur children to recreational areas, or be available to fix lunch and supper. For some working women, heading a household and meeting these expectations can prove a loss to working hours and needed income. Rather than impose on such persons the system designed for the nonemployed wife in the husband-wife family, Cogswell and Sussman suggest that mobile health-care units come to school yards, recreational facilities be in walking distance for young children, round-the-clock child care be available for emergencies, and eating facilities be present in the neighborhood, where children can take morning and evening meals either accompanied or unaccompanied by parents. Although there might not be sufficient demand for such services in suburban middle-

class areas to be feasible, one easily can imagine what a boon such facilities
would offer to poor working-class or middle-class single-parent families in
regional subgroupings of large urban areas.

RECONSTITUTED FAMILIES

Although the income outlook for reconstituted families definitely is better than for single-parent families, other problems remain in legal im-
pediments and psychological drain. Established legal routines generally
have given custody to the mother, thereby causing fathers a sense of loss
of their children. If custody is not awarded to the mother, there is a common tendency to assume that something must be wrong with her. Visitation rights for either parent can provoke inconvenience and further conflict.

Division of property between the former spouses is likely to be a further
bone of contention, particularly when a couple entered the marriage arrangement unprepared for any possible termination and so merged their
assets that an equitable reckoning at the end is made difficult.

Finally, continuing provision for support of children or a dependent wife
of a former marriage can constitute an almost intolerable burden for the
husband who also has to contribute support to a second marriage. Undoubtedly in a few cases fathers do not support their legitimate offspring
by a former marriage because of such a dual burden. However, this reason
should not be exaggerated. One study done in 1970 in five California counties found that nonsupporting fathers were similar in their occupational
distribution to the entire male population, neither predominant in low-
income occupations nor more heavily represented among the unemployed:
10 per cent were professional or managerial and 8 per cent were craftsmen
or foremen. Usually these fathers were living in the same county as their
children. And they were not supporting any other children; 92 per cent of
the nonsupporting fathers had a total of three or fewer children, and only
13 per cent were married to other women. Furthermore, the amount of child
support awarded was not unreasonable, typically on the order of $50 a
month (Winston and Forsher, 1971: 15-16). Heclo et al. (1973: 33-36),
however, explain nonsupport largely as the inability of fathers to pay. They
note that four fifths of the fathers involved receive less than $10,000 a year.
Many administrative and legal factors also contribute to nonsupport—the
attitudes of the judges who make the awards, the lack of incentive for officials to enforce the order, and the lack of legal interest in the problem.

Aside from these economic complexities, which might underlie
reconstituted marriages, there also are knotty interpersonal issues that
can arise. The kinship terms are lacking for referring to one's spouse's
children by another marriage or to the second wife whom one's father married. Household avoidance patterns and the incest taboos have to be redefined (Bohannan, 1970). As with the communes and extended family

experiments that we consider next, the structural problems have just begun to be identified. Satisfactory solutions have to be found.

EXTENDED-FAMILY EXPERIMENTS

In the last decade a number of variant family forms have arisen. Their sheer variety and the amount of popular attention they have aroused suggest that their significance is larger than the mere curiosity factor. Some students of the phenomenon in fact contend that these experiments are a sign of strains in the traditional nuclear family and a clue to the mutations that it must undergo if it is to be adapted to contemporary society (Cogswell, 1975: 391).

A great deal of interest has centered upon the unconventional sexual arrangements that are found in the new family forms. Some people have tried "swinging," intimate networks, and multilateral marriage as alternatives to the sexual exclusivity of the nuclear family. However, it turns out that sexual activities have lower priority than obligations of work, childcare, and home duties even in the new intimate networks (Ramey, 1975). It is with respect to these daily household obligations that the new family experiments offer the most innovative alternatives for the changing domestic roles of women and men.

Betty Cogswell (1975: 401) makes the insightful observation that traditional family forms emphasize constraints, while the participants in the experimental forms speak primarily of freedom and opportunity. Yet any viable social system sets constraints as well as offers opportunities. Both age-old limits and new possibilities have been discovered by experimentation. The main innovations revolve around (1) flexible work opportunities for female and male alike, (2) ways of sharing cooking, cleaning, shopping, and other household duties, and (3) new approaches to maternity, pregnancy, and childcare.

Shared living arrangements among a group of adults or couples can result, for example, in rotation of responsibility for meal preparation and home maintenance, thus particularly freeing women for job responsibilities. Such experiments have been tried most notably in the kibbutzim, the Chinese collective enterprises, and the contemporary urban communes in the United States.

There is a tendency, however, toward a more traditional assignment of women to the home and kitchen tasks when children arrive. This happened when the Israeli kibbutzim were transformed from revolutionary frontier communities to more settled establishments that began to have families with young children. Women were more and more assigned to the kitchens and nurseries as part of their communal work (Talmon, 1972). Contemporary rural communes in the United States generally have had a more traditional division of labor from the beginning (Schlesinger, 1972; Berger et al., 1972). When the contemporary urban communal households begin to have children, there is some tendency for men to desert, leaving women to handle the responsibility (Bernard, 1974: 309-310). Or people do not choose to have children and are ambivalent about their care. Kanter found that there were remarkably few (only ten) "full-time children" in fifty-eight Boston area communes that she studied (Kanter, 1972: 27). It may also be that, viewed in terms of the life cycle, the experimental marriage or commune is primarily a transitional state and that people will leave when they decide to set up their own households or marry and have children (Giele, 1976). Nevertheless, recent feminist interest in public childcare facilities has drawn considerable impetus from foreign communal experiments in childcare, particularly in China, Israel, and the U.S.S.R. (Sidel, 1972; Bettelheim, 1969; Bronfenbrenner, 1970).

Curiously, the idea of communal eating facilities never has caught on to the same degree among the noncommunal family population. One of the leading theorists of feminism, Charlotte Perkins Gilman (1898; 1966), in the last century visualized a day when there would be neighborhood kitchens that would save each family's making its meal separately. Perhaps the hamburger chains, the frozen dinner, prepared mixes, and other convenience foods, together with advanced household appliances, such as the gas or electric stove and the refrigerator, have obviated this alternative. By contrast, no such comparable shortcut for childcare has appeared yet, or for that matter, is likely to.

Although communes have received considerable attention, there is one family form to which perhaps more examination is due than it has yet received, what Litwak (1970) has called the "modified extended family." If we picture that many of the needs families are called to fill are personal, emotional, and physical and that the individuals who fulfill them are at best in a trusting and intimate relationship to those receiving help, it is usually a relative or group of relatives who turn out to have the deepest and longest-lasting loyalties that will sustain these demands. One possibility for modifying the nuclear family, therefore, is to extend it in ways that activate and maintain these ties with a larger group of relatives. This would not be the traditional extended family of patriarchal legend, but a more flexible and egalitarian group, able to help its kin with crises of childcare, illness, or financial distress. It probably would be maintained by geographical proximity, impromptu visiting, and perhaps even common economic or ethnic ties that prevail in certain farming, mining, manufacturing, or professional milieux. The nineteenth-century pattern of taking in roomers and boarders may have helped to sustain such an extended network in a tight economy. Communes in the Canadian West (which are similar to those in the United States) apparently even now take in former members on a temporary basis, much as a kinship group would have operated in the past (Gagné, 1975). There may be other networks sustained through church, lodge, or colleague relationships that operate in similar fashion and of which social scientists as yet have little formal knowledge.

Affluence might allow people to buy services and support separate living arrangements in a way that diminishes the human ties based on noneconomic exchange. Or geographical mobility might be so great that even relatives who wish to maintain helping ties are prevented from doing so by their distance from each other. If this is so, we will have to decide whether such a trend is to be allowed or encouraged or whether it in the end promotes an antifamilial policy.

REFERENCES

Bahr, Stephen J. "Effects on Power and Division of Labor in Family." *Working Mothers*, edited by L.W. Hoffman and F.I. Nye. San Francisco: Jossey-Bass, 1974.

Bane, Mary Jo. *Here to Stay: American Families in the Twentieth Century*. New York: Basic Books, 1976.

Bell, Carolyn Shaw. "The Next Revolution." *Social Policy* 6 (September-October 1975): 5-11.

Berger, Bennett M., Bruce M. Hackett, and R. Mervyn Miller. "Childrearing Practices in the Communal Family." *Family, Marriage, and the Struggle of the Sexes*, edited by H.P. Dreitzel. New York: Macmillan, 1972.

Bernard, Jessie. *The Future of Motherhood*. New York: Dial Press, 1974.

Bettelheim, Bruno. *The Children of the Dream*. New York: Macmillan, 1969.

Blake, Judith. "The Changing Status of Women in Developed Countries." *Scientific American* (September 1974: 137-147.

Bohannan, Paul, ed. *Divorce and After*. Garden City, N.Y.: Doubleday- Anchor, 1970.

Bronfenbrenner, Urie. *Two Worlds of Childhood: U.S. and U.S.S.R.* New York: Russell Sage Foundation, 1970.

Cogswell, Betty E. "Variant Family Forms and Life Styles: Rejection of the Traditional Nuclear Family." *Family Coordinator* 24 (October 1975): 391-406.

Cogswell, Betty E., and Marvin B. Sussman. "Changing Family and Marriage Forms: Complications for Human Service Systems." *Family Coordinator* 21 (October 1972): 505-516.

Coles, Robert C. "Statement." *American Families: Trends and Pressures, 1973: Hearings before the Subcommittee on Children and Youth*, U.S. Senate. Washington, D.C.: U.S.G.P.O., 1973.

Dougherty, Kevin, Gail Howrigan, Laura Lein, and Heather Weiss (Working Family Project). *Work and the American Family*. Chicago: National Parent Teachers Association, 1977.

Fogarty, Michael P., Rhona Rapoport, and Robert N. Rapoport. *Sex, Career, and Family*. London: Allen and Unwin, 1971.

Gagné, Jacques. Interview with Janet Zollinger Giele at the Vanier Institute of the Family, Ottawa, Canada, February, 1975.

Gauger, William. "Household Work: Can We Add It to the GNP?" *Journal of Home Economics* (October 1973): 12-23.

Giele, Janet Zollinger. "Changing Sex Roles and the Future of Marriage." in *Con-*

temporary Marriage: Bond or Bondage, edited by H. Grunebaum and J. Christ. Boston: Little, Brown, 1976.

Gilman, Charlotte Perkins. *Women and Economics*, edited by C.N. Degler. New York: Harper and Row, 1898; 1966.

Hareven, Tamara K. "Family Time and Industrial Time: Family and Work in a Planned Corporation Town, 1900-1924." *Journal of Urban History* 1 (May 1975): 365-389.

Heclo, Hugh, Lee Rainwater, Martin Rein, and Robert Weiss. "Single-parent Families: Issues and Policies." Prepared for the Office of Child Development, Department of Health, Education, and Welfare, 1973.

Holmstrom, Lynda Lytle. The Two-Career Family. Cambridge, Massachusetts: Schenkman, 1972.

Kanter, Rosabeth Moss. "Communes, the Family, and Sex Roles." Paper presented at the annual meeting of the American Sociological Association, New Orleans, August 1972.

Komarovsky, Mirra. *Blue-collar Marriage*. New York: Random House, 1964.

Lein, Laura, M. Durham, M. Pratt, M. Schudson, R. Thomas, and H. Weiss. *Final Report: Work and Family Life*. Cambridge, Massachusetts: Center for Study of Public Policy, National Institute of Education Project no. 3-33074, 1974.

Lekachman, Robert. "On Economic Equality." *Signs* 1 (Autumn 1975): 93-102.

Levison, Andrew. "The Working-class Majority." *New Yorker* (September 1974): 36-61.

Litwak, Eugene. "Technological Innovation and Ideal Forms of Family Structure in an Industrial Democratic Society." in *Families in East and West*, edited by R. Hill and R. Konig. Paris: Mouton, 1970.

Mason, Karen Oppenheim, John Czajka, and Sara Arber. "Change in U.S. Women's Sex-role Attitudes, 1964-1974." *American Sociological Review* 41 (August 1970): 573-596.

Meade, Ellen. "Role Satisfaction of Housewives." Paper presented at Annual Meeting of Eastern Sociological Association, New York City, August 1975.

Oakley, Ann. *The Sociology of Housework*. New York: Pantheon, 1975.

Pleck, Joseph H. "The Work-Family Role System." *Social Problems* 24 (1977): 417-427.

Rainwater, Lee, Richard P. Coleman, and Gerald Handel. *Workingman's Wife*. New York: Oceana, 1959.

Ramey, James W. "Intimate Groups and Networks: Frequent Consequences of Sexually Open Marriage." *Family Coordinator* 24 (October 1975): 515-530.

Rapoport, Rhona and Robert N. Rapoport. *Dual-Career Families Re-examined*. New York: Harper and Row, 1976.

Roper Organization. *The Virginia Slims American Women's Opinion Poll. Vol. 3: A Survey of the Attitudes of Women on Marriage, Divorce, the Family, and America's Changing Sexual Morality*. New York: Roper Organization, 1974.

Samuels, Victoria. "Nowhere to Be Found: A Literature Review and Annotated Bibliography on White Working-class Women." New York: Institute on Pluralism in Group Identity, 1975.

Schlesinger, Benjamin. "Family Life in the Kibbutz of Israel: Utopia Gained or Paradise Lost?" in *Family, Marriage, and the Struggle of the Sexes*, edited by H.P. Dreitzel, New York: Macmillan, 1972.

Seifer, Nancy. "The Working Family in Crisis: Who Is Listening?" Project on Group Life and Ethnic Americans, American Jewish Commission. New York: Institute on Pluralism in Group Identity, 1975.

Sidel, Ruth. *Women and Child Care in China.* New York: Hill and Wang, 1972.

Silver, Catherine Bodard. "France: Contrasts in Familial and Societal Roles." *Women: Roles and Status in Eight Countries*, edited by J.Z. Giele and A.C. Smock. New York: Wiley, 1977.

Sokolowska, Magdalena. "Poland: Women's Experience Under Socialism." *Women: Roles and Status in Eight Countries*, edited by J.Z. Giele and A.C. Smock. New York: Wiley 1977.

Szalai, Alexander. "The Quality of Family Life–Traditional and Modern: A Review of Sociological Findings on Contemporary Family Organization and Role Differentiation in the Family." Paper presented at the United Nations Interregional Seminar on the Family in a Changing Society: Problems and Responsibilities of its Members, London (July 18-31, 1973): ESA/SDHA/AC. 3/6.

Talmon, Yonina. *Family and Community in the Kibbutz.* Cambridge, Massachusetts: Harvard University Press, 1972.

Walker, Kathryn E. "Time Spent in Household Work by Homeworkers." *Family Economics Review* (September 1969): 5-6.

Walker, Kathryn E. "Time Spent by Husbands in Household Work." *Family Economics Review* (June 1970): 8-11.

Weinstein, Fred, and Gerald M. Platt. *The Wish to Be Free.* Berkeley, California: University of California Press, 1969.

Winston, Marian P., and Trude Forsher. "Nonsupport of Legitimate Children by Affluent Fathers as a Cause of Poverty and Welfare Dependence." Santa Monica, California: Rand Corporation, 1971.

Young, Michael, and Peter Willmott. *The Symmetrical Family.* New York: Pantheon, 1973.

Part

Four

Having

Children

Ours is a society that has encouraged, worshiped, and sometimes even demanded large families. Until recently, the idea that wives invariably should bear children was taken as the normal course of events for a family. The only families who did not have children were those with medical problems and those with grave sexual incompatibilities. Even in the face of increasing levels of industrialization, only within the last two or three decades has the trend to smaller families taken hold in America. Nations that experience high levels of industrial development usually experience an immediate decline in the size of families. Some, like Japan, even have experienced slight declines in total population. But the United States was unusually slow in responding to industrialization, at least in this particular aspect. Perhaps part of the reason was that while industry was expanding at a rapid pace, agriculture also was continuing to expand, rather than to decline, until the 1920s. The beginning of the trend toward smaller families seems to be concomitant with the decline in agriculture, both changes having begun in the 1920s.

Actually, the tradition of large families is not an exclusively American tradition. Many of the immigrants to this country brought with them their Old World traditions that encouraged large families. Also, much of the expansion of business was dependent upon an expanding population, so that the business world encouraged large families in any number of ways. Our society has placed a great value upon population growth for the purpose of occupying the seemingly endless frontier. This emphasis upon growth apparently had gained so much momentum that it was not until several decades after the closing of the frontier that we began to have second thoughts about the value of growth.

Most of the major social institutions have done their part to encourage large families, either directly, as has been the case with a number of religious groups, or indirectly, as was the case with education. Religions have encouraged having children both for ideological reasons, such as the admonition to "be fruitful and multiply," and for the practical reason of increasing the size of the religious body. Education has encouraged the bearing of children in a more indirect fashion by providing free public education for all children and requiring them to attend. This relieved the parents of constant childcare responsibility and assured to some degree that their children would be prepared to earn a living.

Until recent years, few families ever explored their reasons for having children. Having children was as much a part of marriage as it was for the man and woman to live together. The question of whether or not to have children rarely was asked because few people ever thought to ask it, and those who did violated the prevalent norms. With the increased knowledge and effectiveness of contraceptives and the spread of their use during the 1920s and 1930s, especially among the middle class, the idea of limiting family size began to be acceptable and later on reached the point of being almost mandatory. However, it was not until the last decade that the idea of having no children at all began to gain some acceptance. Concomitant with and perhaps related to the Women's Movement is the present trend among more and more young married couples to at least ask questions of themselves about whether or not they want children and to explore in depth just why they reach the conclusions they come to. Because it is the wife who has to bear and usually rear the child, women are demanding a larger role in the decisions about having children, with the result that in many cases they are having fewer children and occasionally they are deciding to have none.

Also having a tremendous impact upon families' decisions in this area have been the increased awareness of and sensitivity to the issues of overpopulation and environmental pollution, which have emerged as major social, political, and economic issues in the last few years. Concern over these issues certainly has made the choice not to have children a more socially acceptable one for many families. However, few couples make such a personal decision based solely upon these kinds of considerations.

Whatever the causes, there is no doubt that the average family size is decreasing, as evidenced by the decline in the fertility rate, that is, the number of babies born to women of childbearing age. The decline in the fertility rate averaged about 7 per cent per year between 1970 and 1973, with the decline slowing to about 2 per cent per year from 1973 to 1976. During 1976, the fertility rate was the lowest in our history at 65.0 per 1000 women of childbearing age. Since then, fertility has fluctuated up and down for several years, with no strong trends being established. However, since about 1980 there has been a slight increase in fertility among women 30-39 years of age with a concurrent decrease among women 20-29 years old.[1] Thus, we still are in a period of low fertility, producing fewer than two children per family. It is unclear what trends will develop in the short or long term, and much depends upon the course of the domestic economy and other world events.

Although there likely will be continued fluctuations in birth and fertility rates, it also is likely that the small family will be the dominant mode, at least for the foreseeable future, and that an increasing minority of married couples will choose to remain childless. Because it is necessary for families to have an average of 2.1 children in order to maintain the population at an even size from one generation to the next (not counting the effects of immigration), the population actually could begin to decline in about twenty-five years if current trends held. Most experts, however, are unclear as to what changes might occur in the immediate future, and there is no way to foretell what impact national and world events might have. There are some indications that women who deferred having babies during the mid-seventies have begun having them now, which might account for the slight increase in the birthrate.

But the longterm trend is still likely to be toward smaller families because some of the factors that have contributed to the decline of births will remain. These are: improved birth control techniques, liberalized abortion laws and procedures, increased numbers of women in the work force, a sluggish economy, and as stated earlier, the increased social acceptance of childless marriages. In the last ten years, the proportion of women 18 to 44 years of age who have remained childless increased from about 35 per cent to just over 38 per cent. However, among women 25 to 39 years of age, childlessness has increased considerably.[2]

Another indication of the current trends is found in Census Bureau data concerning the number of children young women expect to have during their lifetimes. In 1967, wives eighteen to twenty-four years of age expected to have an average of 2.85 children. In 1976, wives in this same age category expected to have only 2.03 children. And by 1985, there had been virtually no change since 1976 in this expectation.[3] An interesting sidelight is that in most of the similar studies done in the past, a majority of the women questioned ultimately had fewer children than they had expressed an expectation of having earlier in their marriages. It probably is safe to say, therefore, that at least for the immediate future the one- or two-child family will become the more prevalent family unit, with larger families becoming a rarity.

The question of family size, and especially the trend toward the smaller family, is not really very much of an issue. What is much more at issue is the question of whether to have children at all. This question is dealt with in the first article of this section, "Coping with the Decision Not to Have Children." It looks at several cases of women who have chosen not to bear children, detailing some of the motivations behind and consequences of their decisions.

The second article in this section takes an unusual approach to the question of whether or not to have children: it looks at the presence of children in purely economic terms, carefully analyzing the various monetary costs involved in bearing and rearing children. Although this article was revised to reflect the value of 1980 dollars, the numbers are still fairly close because there has been less inflation in recent years than was previously the case. This approach might seem rather cold and calculating, but there is no question but that a family's economic situation has an important influence on its decisions concerning children. Readers will likely find the article interesting and informative, if not startling.

The final article of this section is rather unusual in that it attempts to delineate and classify all of the various reasons why people might want to have children. And it succeeds admirably. The author, Bernard Berelson, constructs a taxonomy of reasons for wanting children that covers the biological, cultural, political, economic, familial, and in greater detail, the personal reasons that might be seen as rationales behind procreation. The article concludes with a brief history of the differing evaluations that have been made of children.

NOTES

1   National Center for Health Statistics, *Monthly Vital Statistics Report*, "Advance Report on Final Natality Statistics, 1984," U. S. Department of Health and Human Services, September 1986; and National Center for Health Statistics, *Annual Summary of Births, Marriages, Divorces, and Deaths: United States, 1985*, U. S. Department of Health and Human Services, September 1986.

2   U. S. Bureau of the Census, *Current Population Reports*, Series P-20, No. 406, "Fertility of American Women: June 1985," U. S. Government Printing Office, June 1986.

3   Ibid.; and U. S. Bureau of the Census, *Current Population Reports*, Series P-20, No. 300, "Prospects for American Fertility: June 1976," U. S. Government Printing Office, June, 1977.

11.

Coping With the Decision Not to Have Children

Joan Iaconetti

"Every woman wants a child, once she admits it to herself. What else would be as meaningful and fulfilling?"

"Women are programmed to have babies—it's in the genes; it's innate."

"These girls who reject motherhood—they're just being selfish, materialistic, and immature."

"I feel sorry for them...no sweet baby to play with, no one to take care of them when they're old!"

If all this sounds like your Great-Aunt Mildred (mother of eight) talking, be aware that hers is only one voice in a very large crowd. The group includes not only "traditional" generations past but also legions of new and expectant mothers your own age (and younger) who can't wait for you to join their exclusive club. Being *unable* to have children is cause for sympathy and pity, but to *deliberately* reject becoming a mother? Sacrilege! Unnatural!

Yet, despite the cultural push toward motherhood, the number of women who are opting not to have children is startlingly high. Charles Westoff, director of Princeton University's Office of Population Research, projects that as many as 25 per cent of women now in their twenties will remain childless by choice. Possibly, they are ignoring what "everybody else" does and making a truly informed, personal decision. Or they may simply be seduced by the lifestyle of leisure activities, travel, and a new wardrobe every season. But no matter how frivolous or well-considered their choice

Reprinted from *Cosmopolitan*, January 1985, by permissison of the author.

may be, will these women discover, when it's too late, that they've denied themselves a very basic, needed female experience? Just how high a price will they pay?

"It's important that people who decide to remain childless know what they are *not* doing," says Erik Erikson, renowned psychoanalyst, author, and former professor at Harvard and Yale. "The danger is that they will repress the sense of frustration and loss that comes with the rejection of procreativity, so that a new kind of unconscious repression develops in place of the sexual repression of the Victorian age."

Erikson believes there is an instinctual human wish to have children and that women (and men, for that matter) who fail to do so may be cutting themselves off from a major experience in adult development. Rejecting parenthood may suit them now, but it *will* have a lasting effect on their lives. Erikson's theory echoes that of Sigmund Freud, who flatly asserted that "anatomy is destiny"; to wit, *real* women had babies, and those who didn't were doomed to a life of anxiety, sexual neurosis, and general unhappiness, as a consequence of denying their "true" feminine role.

Freud's pronouncements seem laughably outdated today, but Erikson's views are harder to dismiss and uncomfortably thought-provoking. Most girls, no matter *how* insistent they are about not wanting children, still hear a tiny lingering doubt whispering in the back of their minds: Are you *positive* about this? Are you *sure* you won't be missing out on something wonderful? And how can you ever know for certain if you haven't tried?

Quite a dilemma! And as those who've made the wrong choice – either way – know only too well, babies aren't exactly returnable, and adoption in later life is a long, trying process. Is the only alternative, then, that childless women must resign themselves to living a pale imitation of the earth-mother's social and sexual fulfillment? Just what has happened to the women who decided twenty or so years ago that the experience of children really wasn't for them?

"I've never had any regrets about not having had a family," says Belinda, an attractive, elegantly dressed blond of forty-eight. "I always wanted a career and never felt particularly drawn to motherhood." Belinda is the director of marketing for a Fortune 500 firm in San Francisco. Like many successful women, she identified more strongly with her father than with her mother as a girl and was always work-oriented. "Besides," she continues, "I felt it would be unfair to me *and* the child if I were split between working and parenting. But believe me, twenty-five years ago, deciding not to have children was a very unpopular stance to take."

Still, Belinda feels that were she to begin again in 1985, she might consider having a baby along with a career: "I do enjoy kids – my husband and I are very close to our godchildren in many ways. At Christmastime, I'll see them gathered with their parents around the tree and wonder what it would have been like to have had a family of our own. But then I think, if we had, I wouldn't be where I am today. It's a trade-off I'm satisfied with.

And I'm lucky—our godchildren provide us with a chance to know and care for young people that I might not otherwise have sought out."

Belinda's story sounds almost too good to be true. She has an interesting job, leads an affluent life, and is happily married (for the second time) to a man who agrees they are happier childless. Why *should* she regret having no children of her own? She has just about everything else!

Yet Belinda is, in fact, a typical childless (or childfree, as many prefer to call it) woman: She has given the issue a great deal of intelligent thought, is involved in rewarding work, and is blessed with accepting, supportive parents who encouraged her in a career. Obviously, however, not all of the childless have had these advantages. When they look back on their decision, do they feel differently?

Therese, forty-nine, was divorced over twenty years ago and has been pursuing an acting career in New York City ever since. Her financial situation, like that of most performers, has always been precarious. Though she has close friends, there have often been times when she has had no special, ongoing relationship with a man, someone to support her through exhausting rehearsals or the struggle to find work.

One can't help wondering if Therese regrets having bought youthful independence at the cost of a close family attachment in her life. Had she given birth as a young woman, her child would be an adult by now.

"I never feel alone when I'm acting; when I work, whether it's in a role or in acting class, I'm doing exactly what I want to do," she says. "A theater career is terribly difficult in New York, but I'd never give it up—I've loved acting since I was five years old. My role, my successes, are *like* my babies," she adds, echoing a feeling voiced by many childfree women.

"I never made a conscious decision not to have kids," Therese continues. "It's just that the responsibilities of childcare always seemed an impossible burden to me. I know I would have taken the whole thing much too seriously for anyone's good. Actually the world is probably better off that I'm *not* a mother!"

Therese, like Belinda, reports feeling "like a real outcast" at times, because she has no children. "Occasionally, when work isn't going well, I'm keenly aware that I'm alone, out of step with the rest of the world, but it's the sort of need for attachment I can usually satisfy through a friend or a lover." And what of her own need to nurture others? "For me, acting *is* nurturing and creation. And besides, I have the freedom to enjoy any child I come in contact with—on my own terms."

Therese's life is a good example of what Erik Erikson calls *sublimation*: the channeling of the procreative drive into either creative expression or socially fruitful channels. Working for the good or enjoyment of others, whether through the arts, volunteer work, political action, is more than fulfilling; according to Erikson, it's *necessary* for a balanced life.

As you can see, the instinct to nurture does not have to be directed toward one's own children, or even toward children at all; there are many ways a person can satisfy the need to care for and about other human beings. And, surprisingly, many experts feel the satisfaction derived from raising a child is the same as that experienced in any caring relationship. The need to *nurture*, they say, is indeed universal; the need to *mother*, however, is not.

Manhattan psychotherapist Elaine Ruskin also points out that many mothers, especially those who are single and working, simply lack adequate time to nurture their children in a truly positive, creative way. Those who extol motherhood as the ideal for every woman rarely mention that the majority of early childcare tasks—unless you're able to afford help—are routine, often boring. "Child rearing is an extremely stressful occupation, and some women lead much happier lives without taking on motherhood," Ruskin comments.

Adds Marian Faux, author of *Childless by Choice: Choosing Childlessness in the '80s*: "It became clear to me as I did my research that the drive to nurture and the drive to create are separate. Any woman can fulfill her creative needs on the job or through outside activities, as men traditionally have. And plenty of opportunities exist to nurture others, children or adults, briefly or in ongoing relationships. There's no reason for childless women to think they can't do both of these things."

Some women, in fact, manage to combine both in almost every aspect of their lives. Annemarie, thirty-nine, is a printmaker and kindergarten teacher who also does occasional commercial artwork. She is president of her block association, has numerous friends, and is rarely without a loving relationship with a man. Annemarie is also "just crazy about kids! Knowing that the four hours a day I spend with my students has a truly significant effect on their lives is enormously satisfying, and by allowing myself to become close to them and love them, I *get* as much out of nurturing the children as I give."

You'd think that someone with Annemarie's attitude and enthusiasm would rush to have a baby of her own, but "I don't feel any compelling reason to do that. Though I wanted a child badly when I was twenty-four, I knew my art was taking too much of my time and energy. Also, none of the men in my life at the time were stable or committed enough to be good parents. And to be honest, at that stage, I'd have to say the same thing about myself.

"I might still reconsider and have a child *if* all the issues—health, money, relationship, career—were resolved. But so far I've been very happy just giving myself carte blanche to be as close to *every* child as I choose to be. If I were a mother, nurturing would be a demanding full-time job as well as a joy; this way, it's all joy."

Not all childfree women adore children, obviously; many decide not to become mothers simply because they're not particularly interested in children or childcare. Others had unhappy childhoods themselves, and their memories of poverty, mistreatment, and neglect are powerful deterrents to having children of their own; rationally or not, they are afraid of exposing their own children to such pain. The cliche' about "not wanting to bring a child into this terrible world" can certainly be a tired excuse, but it can also be a very valid reason for remaining childless.

Sandra, a manager in a public-relations firm, cites such a reason for not having had a child. "I've been a mother since I was five years old," she says. "As a girl I had major responsibility for both my little brothers. My own mother was a child herself and didn't care adequately for any of us. I'm glad I was there to raise them, but by the time I grew up, I'd had my fill of mothering.

"I've noticed over the years that women who share the same sort of past have either no children or a flock of them. In my own case, even now my brothers treat me more like a parent than like a sister, so in a very real way they're still 'my kids.' "

Another reason women decide to remain childfree has to do with the men in their lives. Interestingly, all the married women I spoke with mentioned that they felt their mates, although often not opposed to having children, weren't sufficiently stable, mature, well-to-do, or otherwise suitable as "parent material." "Even if I'd decided I wanted a child, I knew he would never have lifted a finger to help. He would have been pleased, but that's about it," said Jane, a forty-seven-year-old magazine editor.

Still, Sandra *did* have the luxury of making a conscious choice: She was married during her childbearing years and was free, as far as she knew, from fertility problems. Though a few women today opt for single parenthood (sometimes through artificial insemination), they are a tiny minority. The fact is that most women who never marry, for whatever reason, also forego the chance to have a child. What are the repercussions for them?

"I always liked kids and expected to have several of my own, but somehow I never found anyone I wanted to marry," says Rosa, a forty-eight-year-old legal secretary. "Single parenthood was out of the question when I was twenty-five, so without really planning what I was doing, I became close to my best friend's children. I liked being around them so much that as they grew up, a real relationship formed, and it's continued now that they're young adults.

"Sometimes I think maybe I was lucky not to have had the work and worry of having children—just the fun. Maybe that's a rationalization; I don't know. But I have the satisfaction of having been a positive influence on these kid's lives, and that's a great feeling."

Maybe Rosa *is* rationalizing, but there's no way to determine that for sure—any more than the millions of mothers in the world could ever determine how happy they would have been if they *hadn't* had children. Surprisingly few women are absolutely, unerringly sure of their choice to mother or not to mother: "Ambivalence about whether or not you want a child doesn't necessarily stop once you've given birth," says author Marian Faux. The best you can do is weigh the pros and cons, pay attention to your own feelings, and reasure yourself that whatever the decision, the opportunity is *always* there to fill your life with people and activities that have real meaning for you.

12.

Raising a Child Can Now Cost $85,000

Thomas J. Espenshade

How much does it cost to raise a child in the United States? In 1977 the Population Reference Bureau published "The Value and Cost of Children," a *Population Bulletin* by the author, containing estimates of the cost of rearing American children in 1977 dollars and prices.

Since that time, inflation has pushed up the U. S. Consumer Price Index nearly 40 per cent, and these earlier estimates now are out of date. To satisfy a continuing demand for these figures, therefore, I have updated my estimates to reflect the cost of having and rearing a child in 1980.

Seeing a child through birth, eighteen years under the parental roof, and four years at a public university now costs the average middle-income U.S. family some $85,000 in 1980 in direct, out-of-pocket expenditures. (This is up about 33 per cent from 1977's figure of some $64,000.) For low-income families the cost of having and raising a child through college now is estimated at some $58,000. (This is about 32 per cent higher than 1977's figures of $44,000.)

These figures represent only the *direct maintenance costs*, consisting of out-of-pocket expenditures on a child's birth, items such as food, housing, clothing, medical care, and education to age eighteen, and four years of college. The economic cost of children also is considered to include a second part: the *opportunity costs*. These costs are perhaps less tangible, but no less important, and refer to the income the mother (typically) forgoes by reducing her labor force participation below what it otherwise would be without the advent of a child. Assuming that the better educated a wife is, the higher the family income will be, and adding direct and opportunity costs together we obtain a total economic cost confronting American families in 1980 that varies on a per-child basis from slightly

Reprinted by permission from *Intercom*, Vol. 8, No. 9, September 1980.

more than $100,000 at the low-income level to nearly $140,000 for middle-income families. These figures for 1980 are up about 30 per cent over their corresponding 1977 levels.

As I discuss below, there are several reasons for treating these figures with caution. Improvement in the ways we estimate child costs are being made. Consequently, the numbers I present should be interpreted only as *interim* estimates of the cost of children.

BACKGROUND

One of the first efforts at estimating what it costs to raise a child was a paper by Ritchie Reed and Susan McIntosh on "Costs of Children" prepared for the 1970-1972 U. S. Commission on Population Growth and the American Future.[1] They used data from a U. S. Department of Agriculture report for their estimates of direct costs and information on wife's labor force participation to construct the opportunity costs. The USDA estimates were of direct expenditures on children in 1961, and Reed and McIntosh updated these to 1969, using price inflators from the U. S. Bureau of Labor Statistics.

The Reed-McIntosh methodology was reapplied in the 1977 PRB *Population Bulletin* to bring the data to 1977 prices. For opportunity costs, Reed and McIntosh computed the difference in hours worked by childless women and by mothers with children of different ages and then multiplied by the difference – representing hours of mothers' time lost from work – by wives' wages in 1969 to measure opportunity cost. An essentially similar procedure was used in the 1977 PRB study. Female wages were estimated for 1977 by years of women's schooling and applied against the number of hours presumed to be lost from work because of children.

In the current report the only adjustments to the 1977 figures are those for price and wage inflation. The overall increase in the Consumer Price Index during the past three years is not applied; rather, each component of cost (food, clothing, housing, etc.) is inflated separately, using disaggregated CPI data, then recombined for 1980. Female wage rates are estimated for 1980 on the basis of earnings-by-education data during the 1970s.

DIRECT MAINTENANCE COSTS

Like the 1977 *Bulletin*, this report distinguishes three components of direct maintenance costs: expenses associated with childbirth, other maintenance costs to age eighteen, and the cost of a four-year college education. The largest of these are the maintenance costs to the end of high school, excluding those surrounding birth. Our updated estimates are shown in Table 1. Children evidently are most expensive to rear in Western states, although the type of residence, whether farm, rural, nonfarm, urban, is not consistently correlated with expenditures. The family's standard of living is one of the most important determinants of child-related purchases. To rear children at a level corresponding to the USDA's moderate-cost food plan costs approximately 50 per cent more than rearing them on the low-cost plan. The USDA uses food costs to determine family living standards. The "low-cost food plan" corresponds roughly to family incomes after taxes of $14,000 to $18,000 in 1980 dollars; the "moderate cost food plan," to family incomes after taxes in the $22,500 to $27,500 range. (Comparable figures in the 1977 study were $10,500 to $13,500 for the low-cost food plan and $16,500 to $20,000 for the moderate-cost food plan.)

With these sources of variation considered, Table 1 shows that the expense involved in rearing a child to age eighteen in different U.S. regions currently varies from $43,032 for a low-cost-plan farm family in the North Central region to $79,215 for a moderate-cost-plan rural nonfarm family in the West. In 1977 the comparable range was from $31,675 to $58,255, or approximately 26 per cent below today's figures.

As in 1977, housing is the leading item in child-rearing expenses, followed by food and then transportation. For example, of the $68,898 it would cost a typical North Central city family to raise a child at a moderate standard of living, in 1980 prices, 33.9 per cent would go to housing, 24.6 per cent to food, 16.5 per cent to transportation, 7.8 per cent to clothing, 5.1 per cent to medical care, 1.4 per cent to education, and 10.6 per cent to "all other" expenses.

TABLE 1. Direct Cost of Raising a Child to Age 18 in the U. S. at 1980 Prices (Excluding Childbirth)

| | Farm Costs | | Rural Nonfarm Costs | | Urban Costs | |
	Low	Moderate	Low	Moderate	Low	Moderate
Total U. S.	$44,910	$66,490	$47,591	$73,222	$47,940	$72,894
North Central	43,032	63,800	43,056	64,246	50,109	68,898
South	47,973	71,478	46,768	75,027	47,068	74,568
Northeast	44,024	62,328	51,202	77,952	43,312	72,878
West	na	na	55,019	79,215	52,057	76,288

Sources: United States Department of Agriculture, "Cost of Raising a Child," CFE (Adm.)—318, September 1971; Consumer Price Index data from the U.S. Department of Labor, Bureau of Labor Statistics.

Data on the cost of childbirth come from the Health Insurance Institute. The estimated total of $2,485 for 1978 is broken down into $888 for hospital costs, $543 for medical expenses, $762 for a layette, and an estimated $292 for maternity clothing.

The final component of direct costs is an allowance for the cost of a college education. We have used a conservative assumption that a child will attend a public school and not a private one. Specifically, it is assumed that a child from the moderate-cost standard of living will attend a four-year public university. This expense totaled $9,784 in 1980, according to the most recent data available from the U. S. National Center for Education Statistics.[2] Educating a child from a low-cost background is presumed to cost somewhat less ($8,664) because it is assumed that a person of this type would attend a state-supported undergraduate institution.

The three items of direct cost are added together in Table 2, showing that the estimates of total direct maintenance cost range in 1980 from $58,238 at the low-cost level to $85,163 at the moderate-cost standard. (When Reed and McIntosh made similar estimates for 1969, the range was from $27,109 to $39,924. The 1977 range was between $44,156 and $64,215.) As pointed out in the 1977 report, actual expenditures by any particular family probably will deviate from these estimates. The figures clearly would be less if children did not go to college, and they would be much greater if they elected to attend a private college or university without the aid of a scholarship. Beyond that, expenses will depend upon the region of the country in which the family lives, the race of the head of the household, educational levels of the parents, and tastes and preferences for alternative lifestyles. In sum, the estimates in Table 2 need to be interpreted as rough orders of magnitude and should not be taken to represent an immutable "sticker price" for children.

TABLE 2. Total Direct Costs of a Child in the U.S., About 1980 (by Cost Level)

Cost Level	Childbirth	Cost to Age 18[a]	4 Years College	Total
Low-cost	$1,634[b]	$47,940	$8,664	$58,238
Moderate-cost	2,485	72,894	9,784	85,163

[a]Based on U.S. average for urban areas.

[b]Assumed to be in the same proportion to the moderate-cost childbirth figure as the respective costs to age 18.

OPPORTUNITY COST

Opportunity cost of children refers to the value of the lost work time that mothers experience if they reduce their labor force participation to bear and rear a child. The size of the opportunity cost thus depends upon how much time is lost from work and on the value of each hour lost. For our updates we make adjustments for the fact that female wage rates have increased since 1977, but we continue to rely on the earlier figures on hours lost from work.

The revised estimates are shown in Table 3. Column 2 reflects the annual number of hours lost from work owing to the presence of a child at various ages, on the assumption that a typical wife of childbearing age who

TABLE 3. Average Opportunity Cost of a First Child for U. S. Wives, 1980, by Wives' Education

Age of Child (yrs.)	Hours Worked (1)	Lost Work Time (2) = 1000^a - (1)	All Women (3) = (2) × \$5.60^b	Elementary (4) = (2) × \$4.01^b	High School (5) = (2) × 5.29^b	College 4 yrs. (6) = (2) × \$6.55^b	College 5 yrs. and Over (7) = (2) × \$8.19^b
<1	106	894	$ 5,006	$ 3,585	$ 4,729	$ 5,856	$ 7,322
1	191	809	4,530	3,244	4,280	5,299	6,626
2	219	781	4,374	3,132	4,131	5,116	6,396
3	237	763	4,273	3,060	4,036	4,998	6,249
4	279	721	4,038	2,891	3,814	4,723	5,905
5	289	711	3,982	2,851	3,761	4,657	5,823
6	620	380	2,128	1,524	2,010	2,489	3,112
7	620	380	2,128	1,524	2,010	2,489	3,112
8	620	380	2,128	1,524	2,010	2,489	3,112
9	620	380	2,128	1,524	2,010	2,489	3,112
10	620	380	2,128	1,524	2,010	2,489	3,112
11	620	380	2,128	1,524	2,010	2,489	3,112
12	620	380	2,128	1,524	2,010	2,489	3,112
13	620	380	2,128	1,524	2,010	2,489	3,112
14	620	380	2,128	1,524	2,010	2,489	3,112
Total			$45,355	$32,479	$42,841	$53,050	$66,329

[a] Assumed average hours worked per year by married women with no children under age 14.
[b] Estimated hourly earnings for 1980.

had no children would work an average of one thousand hours per year (i.e., twenty hours a week for fifty weeks). Lost work time is greatest in the year following birth and declines as the child ages, with a large reduction occurring when the child enters first grade. Hourly market wage rates for women having attained various levels of education are computed by dividing estimated yearly earnings of full-time female workers by two thousand hours of work (i.e., forty hours a week for fifty weeks). The resulting dollar figures are assumed to represent the 1980 value of each hour withdrawn from paid work. These are tabulated across the top of columns 3 through 7 in Table 3, and when multiplied by the hours of lost work time, they yield the dollar opportunity cost corresponding to various ages of children. Opportunity cost increases as education does, and when totaled for fifteen years, rises from $32,479 for wives with an elementary school education to $66,329 for those who have gone beyond their bachelor's degree.

For mothers who would choose to work full time if they had no children under age fifteen, assuming one thousand hours of work per year will not be relevant, and for these women we should be calculating opportunity cost by subtracting the number of hours worked by women with children from two thousand not from one thousand. Recomputing the data in Table 3 on this basis boosts the opportunity cost of a first child to about $93,000 for the least well-educated mothers and to $189,000 for those with a postgraduate education, with an average value for all women of approximately $130,000.

Both the direct maintenance costs and the opportunity cost attributable to American children are substantial. Assuming that the better educated a wife is the higher the family income will be and adding direct and opportunity costs together, we obtain a total economic cost confronting American families in 1980 that varies on a per child basis from slightly more than $100,000 at the low-cost level to nearly $140,000 at the moderate-cost standard. (These figures are based on data in Tables 2 and 3 and assume that wives in "low-cost plan" families will be high school graduates, whereas those in moderate-cost plan" families have a college education.) These combined direct and opportunity cost figures for 1980 are up by about 30 per cent over their corresponding 1977 levels.

CONCLUSIONS

Several qualifications must be mentioned in connection with the interpretation of these estimates. With regard to the derivation of opportunity cost, using the going wage rate to put a dollar value on the wife's time computes gross opportunity cost, or income forgone before taxes. Net opportunity cost, or income forgone after taxes, is more relevant. The net figure could be substantially less than the gross because the extra family income contributed by the wife will be taxed at higher rates than the husband's income. The economic loss from reduced work is lessened further if the mother, by returning to work, would have to pay child-care expenses.

Moreover, the calculations of direct cost and opportunity cost are flawed in important ways. The direct cost estimates are based on spending patterns measured in the Bureau of Labor Statistics 1960-1962 Survey of Consumer Expenditures. The most recent BLS survey, conducted in 1972-1973, reveals significant shifts in spending patterns. Food expenditures, for example, fell from 24.4 per cent of total consumption in 1960-1961 to 20.1 per cent in 1972-1973. Housing rose from 28.4 to 31.4 per cent and transportation increased from 15.2 to 21.4 per cent.[3] These shifts will be taken into account in later estimates of child expenditures.

Second, the rapid rise in female labor force participation in the United States has been accompanied by striking changes in participation rate differentials, and these have implications for the number of hours lost from work owing to the presence of children. In particular, it no longer is as true as it once was that the presence of children, especially younger children, detracts from the mother's labor force participation. Table 4 presents data from 1950 to 1978 on the labor force participation rates of married women (husband present) according to whether there were no children under age eighteen in the home or whether there were children under six years. By 1978, women with young children still have lower participation rates, but the twenty-eight-year perspective reveals that the differential has converged in a dramatic fashion. Thus it is likely that measurements of opportunity cost on the basis of current female labor force participation rates would yield smaller figures than those reported in Table 3.

TABLE 4. Labor Force Participation Rates (%) for Married Women (Husband Present), by Presence and Age of Children: 1950 to 1978

Presence and Age of Children	Year				
	1950	1960	1970	1975	1978
No children under 18 yrs.	30.3	34.7	42.2	43.9	44.7
Children under 6	11.9	18.6	30.3	36.6	41.6

Source: U.S. Bureau of the Census, Statistical Abstract of the United States: 1979. (100th edition). Washington, D.C. 1979.

Finally, our estimates, because they are in terms of 1980 prices, make no allowance for subsequent inflation. They could not be used to gauge what parents could expect to spend on a child born in 1980. To be more realistic, these estimates should be adjusted for expected future inflation.

Work on remedying some of these deficiencies is underway and the results will be reported in the not-too-distant future.

NOTES

1   Ritchie H. Reed and Susan McIntosh, "Costs of Children," in *Research Reports*, Vol. 2, Commission on Population Growth and the American Future. Washington, D.C.: USGPO, 1972

2   W. Vance Grant and Leo Eiden, *Digest of Education Statistics, 1980*, U.S. Department of Health, Education, and Welfare, National Center for Education Statistics, 1980, Table 133.

3   U.S. Department of Labor, "Changes in Consumer Spending Patterns," *News*, USDL: 77-428, May 10, 1977.

13.

The Value of Children: A Taxonomical Essay

Bernard Berelson

Why do people want children? It is a simple question to ask, perhaps an impossible one to answer.

Throughout most of human history, the question never seemed to need a reply. These years, however, the question has a new tone. It is being asked in a nonrhetorical way because of three revolutions in thought and behavior that characterize the latter decades of the twentieth century: the vital revolution in which lower death rates have given rise to the population problem and raise new issues about human fertility; the sexual revolution; and the women's revolution, in which childbearing and -rearing no longer are being accepted as the only or even the primary roles of half the human race. Accordingly, for about the first time, the question of why people want children now can be asked, so to speak, with a straight face.

"Why" questions of this kind, with simple surfaces but profound depths, are not answered or settled; they are ventilated, explicated, clarified. Anything as complex as the motives for having children can be classified in various ways, and any such taxonomy has an arbitrary character to it. This one starts with chemistry and proceeds to spirit.

Taxonomy

THE BIOLOGICAL

Do people innately want children for some built-in reason of physiology? Is there anything to maternal instinct, or parental instinct? Or is biology satisfied with the sex instinct as the way to assure continuity?

Reprinted from *The Population Council Annual Report—1972*, used by permission of the author.

In psychoanalytic thought there is talk of the "child-wish," the "instinctual drive of physiological cause," "the innate femaleness of the girl direct(ing) her development toward motherhood," and the wanting of children as "the essence of her self-realization," indicating normality. From the experimental literature, there is some evidence that man, like other animals, is innately attracted to the quality of "babyishness."

> If the young adults of several species are compared for differences in bodily and facial features, it will be seen readily that the nature of the difference is apparently the same almost throughout the phylogenetic scale. Limbs are shorter and much heavier in proportion to the torso in babies than in adults. Also, the head is proportionately much larger in relation to the body than is the case with adults. On the face itself, the forehead is more prominent and bulbous; the eyes large and perhaps located as far down as below the middle of the face, because of the large forehead. In addition, the cheeks may be round and protruding. In many species there is also a greater degree of overall fatness in contrast to normal adult bodies. . . . In man, as in other animals, social prescriptions and customs are not the sole or even primary factors that guarantee the rearing and protection of babies. This seems to indicate that the biologically rooted releaser of babyishness may have promoted infant care in primitive man before societies ever were formed, just as it appears to do in many animal species. Thus this releaser may have a high survival value for the species of man.[1]

In the human species the question of social and personal motivation distinctively arises, but that does not necessarily mean that the biology is completely obliterated. In animals the instinct to reproduce appears to be all; in humans is it something?

THE CULTURAL

Whatever the biological answer, people do not want all the children they physically can have—no society, hardly any woman. Everywhere social traditions and social pressures enforce a certain conformity to the approved childbearing pattern, whether large numbers of children in Africa or small numbers in Eastern Europe. People want children because that is "the thing to do"–culturally sanctioned and institutionally supported, hence about as natural as any social behavior can be.

Such social expectations, expressed by everyone toward everyone, are extremely strong in influencing behavior even on such an important element in life as childbearing and on whether the outcome is two children or six. In most human societies, the thing to do gets done, for social rewards and punishments are among the most powerful. Whether they produce lots of children or few and whether the matter is fully conscious or not, the cultural norms are all the more effective if, as often, they are rationalized as the will of God or the hand of fate.

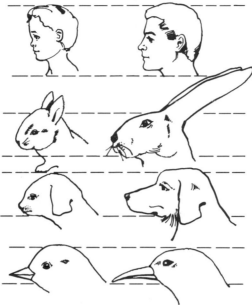

FIGURE 1. Comparison of visual features provided by morphological characteristics of infantile and adult forms of four different species: human, rabbit, dog, and bird. Although the infantile characteristics release parental responses, the adult ones do not. (Drawing after Lorenz in Musser, op. cit.)

THE POLITICAL

The cultural shades off into political considerations: reproduction for the purposes of a higher authority. In a way, the human responsibility to perpetuate the species is the grandest such expression – the human family pitted politically against fauna and flora – and there always might be people who partly rationalize their own childbearing as a contribution to that lofty end. Beneath that, however, there are political units for whom collective childbearing is or has been explicitly encouraged as a demographic duty – countries concerned with national glory or competitive political position; governments concerned with the supply of workers and soldiers; churches concerned with propagation of their faith or their relative strength; ethnic minorities concerned with their political power; linguistic communities competing for position; clans and tribes concerned over their relative status within a larger setting. In ancient Rome, according to the *Oxford English Dictionary*, the proletariat – from the root *proles*, for progeny – were "the lowest class of the community, regarded as contributing nothing to the state but offspring": and a proletaire was "one who served the state not with his property but only with his offspring." The world has changed since then, but not all the way.

THE ECONOMIC

As the "new home economics" is reminding us in its current attention to the microeconomics of fertility, children are economically valuable. Not that that would come as a surprise to the poor peasant who consciously acts on the premise, but it is clear that some people want children or not for economic reasons.

Start with the obvious case of economic returns from children that appears to be characteristic of the rural poor. To some extent, that accounts for their generally higher fertility than that of their urban and wealthier counterparts: labor in the fields; hunting, fishing, animal care; help in the home and with the younger children; dowry and "bride-wealth"; support in later life (the individualized system of social security).

The economics of the case carries through on the negative side as well. It is not publicly comfortable to think of children as another consumer durable, but sometimes that is precisely the way parents do think of them, before conception: another child or a trip to Europe; a birth deferred in favor of a new car, the *nth* child requiring more expenditure on education or housing. But observe the special characteristics of children viewed as consumer durables: they come only in whole units; they cannot be evaluated quickly; they do not come in several competing brands or products; their quality cannot be pretested before delivery; they usually are not available for appraisal in large numbers in one's personal experience; they themselves participate actively in the household decisions. And in the broad view, both societies and families tend to choose standard of living over number of children when the opportunity presents itself.

THE FAMILIAL

In some societies people want children for what might be called familial reasons: to extend the family line or the family name; to propitiate the ancestors; to enable the proper functioning of religious rituals involving the family (e.g., the Hindu son needed to light the father's funeral pyre, the Jewish son needed to say Kaddish for the dead father). Such reasons may seem thin in the modern, secularized society but they have been and are powerful indeed in other places.

In addition, one class of family reasons shares a border with the following category, namely, having children in order to maintain or improve a marriage: to hold the husband or occupy the wife; to repair or rejuvenate the marriage; to increase the number of children on the assumption that family happiness lies that way. The point is underlined by its converse: in some societies failure to bear children (or males) is a threat to the marriage and a ready cause for divorce.

Beyond all that is the profound significance of children to the very institution of the family itself. To many people, husband and wife alone do not seem a proper family—they need children to enrich the circle, to validate its family character, to gather the redemptive influence of offspring. Children need the family, but the family seems also to need children, as the social institution uniquely available, at least in principle, for security, comfort, assurance, and direction in a changing, often hostile, world. To most people, such a home base, in the literal sense, needs more than one person for sustenance and in generational extension.

THE PERSONAL

Up to here the reasons for wanting children primarily refer to instrumental benefits. Now we come to a variety of reasons for wanting children that are supposed to bring direct personal benefits.

Personal Power. As noted, having children sometimes gives one parent power over the other. More than that, it gives parents power over the child(ren)—in many cases, perhaps most, about as much effective power as they ever will have the opportunity of exercising on an individual basis. They are looked up to by the child(ren), literally and figuratively, and rarely does that happen otherwise. Beyond that, having children is involved in a wider circle of power:

> In most simple societies the lines of kinship are the lines of political power, social prestige and economic aggrandizement. The more children a man has, the more successful marriage alliances he can arrange, increasing his own power and influence by linking himself to men of greater power or to men who will be his supporters. . . . In primitive and peasant societies, the man with few children is the man of minor influence and the childless man is virtually a social nonentity.[2]

Personal Competence. Becoming a parent demonstrates competence in an essential human role. Men and women who are closed off from other demonstrations of competence, through lack of talent or educational opportunity or social status, still have this central one. For males, parenthood is thought to show virility, potency, *machismo*. For females it demonstrates fecundity, itself so critical to an acceptable life in many societies.

Personal Status. Everywhere parenthood confers status. It is an accomplishment open to all, or virtually all, and realized by the overwhelming majority of adult humankind. Indeed, achieving parenthood surely must be one of the two most significant events in one's life—that and being born in the first place. In many societies, then and only then is one considered a real man or a real woman.

Childbearing is one of the few ways in which the poor can compete with the rich. Life cannot make the poor man prosperous in material goods and services but it easily can make him rich with children. He cannot have as much of anything else worth having, except sex, which itself typically means children in such societies. Even so, the poor still are deprived by the arithmetic: they have only two or three times as many children as the rich whereas the rich have at least forty times the income of the poor.

Personal Extension. Beyond the family line, wanting children is a way to reach for personal immortality—for most people, the only way available. It is a way to extend oneself indefinitely into the future. And short of that, there is simply the physical and psychological extension of oneself in the children, here and now—a kind of narcissism: there they are and they are mine (or like me).

> Look in thy glass and tell the face thou viewest,
> Now is the time that face should form another; . . .
> But if thou live, remember'd not to be,
> Die single, and thine image dies with thee.
>   Shakespeare's Sonnets,III

Personal Experience. Among all the activities of life, parenthood is a u-nique experience. It is a part of life, or personal growth, that simply cannot be experienced in any other way and hence is literally an indispensable element of the full life. The experience has many profound facets: the deep curiosity as to how the child will turn out; the renewal of self in the second chance; the reliving of one's own childhood; the redemptive opportunity; the challenge to shape another human being; the sheer creativity and self-realization involved. For a large proportion of the world's women, there was and probably still is nothing else for the grown female to do with her time and energy, as society defines her role. And for many women, it might be the most emotional and spiritual experience they ever have and perhaps the most gratifying as well.

Personal Pleasure. Last, but one hopes not least, in the list of reasons for wanting children is the altruistic pleasure of having them, caring for them, watching them grow, shaping them, being with them, enjoying them. This reason comes last on the list but it is typically the first one mentioned on the casual inquiry: "because I like children." Even this reason has its dark side, as with parents who live through their children, often to the latter's distaste and disadvantage. But that should not obscure a fundamental reason for wanting children: love.

There are, in short, many reasons for wanting children. Taken together, they must be among the most compelling motivations in human behavior: culturally imposed, institutionally reinforced, psychologically welcome.

History

What of the broad, historical trends in the evaluation of children? The central trend can be embodied in a conundrum: over the long run, as children have become less valuable they have become more valued. That is, as children have lost their economic value to the parents, under the impact of modernization, they have gained value in a qualitative sense – in the provision of health and particularly education and training. In this sense, the world seems to move from quantity to quality in the evaluation of children.

Surely the modern response – modern not simply in the chronological but in the social sense – is in this direction: the child as a consumption not a production good; the child as deserving consideration in his own right; what the parent owes the child rather than what the child owes the parent. That adjustment currently is being worked through, and on the whole it probably means less wanting of children and fewer children (particularly as the available technology for fertility control gets more evenly distributed). So under man's newly emerging conditions, already realized in some parts of the world, wanting few children is as natural as wanting several: after all, people can satisfy the reasons for wanting children without having many.

In the classical literature of Greece and Rome there appears to be little serious reference to children and childbearing except for the continuation of royal lines. According to George Boas, in the *The Cult of Childhood*, the "ancients had a low opinion of children if they appraised them at all." According to Philippe Aries in *Centuries of Childhood*, "in medieval society the idea of childhood did not exist"; only in the eighteenth century are "not only the child's future but his presence and his very existence . . .of concern: the child has taken a central place in the family." And according to Peter Coveney in *Poor Monkey: The Child in Literature*, the emergence of the child is sharply visible in English literature:

> Until the last decades of the eighteenth century the child did not exist as an important and continuous theme in English literature. Childhood as a major theme came with the generation of Blake and Wordsworth. There were of course children in English literature before the Romantics. . .But in the Elizabethan drama, in the main body of Augustan verse, the major eighteenth-century novel, the child is absent, or the occasion of a passing reference; at the most a subsidiary element in an adult world. . .Within the course of a few decades the child emerges from comparative unimportance to become the focus of an unprecedented literary interest, and in time, the central figure of an increasingly significant proportion of our literature.

Why does the child in literature emerge only then, with the romantic period? There were some great events at work – the industrial revolution was changing the economy, the French Revolution was changing the politics. But there was another revolution of lower death rates (especially of infants and children) and increasing population. There were thus more children around, simply on a statistical basis, and hence more visible and accountable for. Children were living who previously would have died. Is it only historic accident that the literary interest and the demographic trends came together in this way?

Over the succeeding century one can identify a rough progression from the innocent child of Wordsworth through the child employed for the social criticism of industrialized institutions in Dickens, through the sentimentalized and redemptive child of *Silas Marner* and worse, to the realistic child (and family) of Butler and Lawrence. So in about a century, the whole literary position of the child changed from romantic to glorification to realistic appreciation. What Rousseau and Wordsworth started, Freud and the post-Freudian writers finished.

Man has come a long way in a short time in his evaluation of children: from nonappreciation of childhood, through innocent primitive and social cause, to obsession and problem. Many have remarked on our own "child-centered society," our "cult of children," yet even that may be changing now in response to the three revolutions.

In the end, we may need to rely on those old standbys, rationality and responsibility: not everyone is equally talented to be a parent any more than a pianist or a mathematician or a tennis player, although the parental talent may not be as rare as those; and concern is owed the developmental possibilities for the individual child beyond the parental or social gratifications. If a society has full information on personal and collective consequences of childbearing, full opportunity to control fertility and thus divorce reproduction from sexuality, productive alternatives for women, no undue social pressures with regard to marriage or parenthood, and genuine concern for the produced child, that is about the best we can do.

The currency is not debased, although modern conditions affect both numbers and values. For whatever else it is, wanting children remains a restart for man, and for individual men, another chance to try for "the good life," a revitalization in both the literal and the symbolic sense. On the title page of *Silas Marner*, George Eliot quoted these lines from Wordsworth:

> A child, more than all other gifts
> That earth can offer to declining man,
> Brings hope with it, and forward-looking thoughts.

NOTES

1   Eckhard H. Hess, "Ethology and Developmental Psychology," in Paul H. Musser, ed., *Carmichaels's Manual of Child Psychology*, vol. 1 (New York: Wiley, 1970), pp. 20-21.

2   Burton Benedict, "Population Regulation in Primitive Societies," in Anthony Allison, ed., *Population Control* (London: Penguin, 1970), pp. 176-177.

As solutions to the problems of unwanted pregnancies and births have been found and made available with increasing effectiveness and decreasing cost, more and more attention has been given to the problems of those married couples whose desire is not to avoid pregnancy and birth, but rather to overcome problems of infertility so as to have children of their own. Success with the control of unwanted children, however, has gone a long way toward eliminating what was in the past the major solution for infertile couples wanting children — adoption. More particularly, the availability of adoptive children has declined drastically owing for the most part to three developments: first is the widespread use and effectiveness of contraception among unmarried young women who traditionally have been the major source of adoptive children; second is the dramatic increase in abortions among those young women who do become pregnant; and third is the desire among an increasingly significant number of unmarried young women who get pregnant to keep and rear their children.

Thus, with the decreasing likelihood of adoption as a solution for infertile couples desiring children, there have arisen several new and controversial alternatives that have the potential for providing relief to at least a few such couples. Actually, several of these alternatives are not really so new. For example, artificial insemination has been practiced for several decades, but because of the ease and secrecy with which it can be undertaken, it has not received a great deal of public attention until recent years.

On the other hand, such alternatives as surrogate motherhood and *in vitro* fertilization (which produces so-called test-tube babies) are relatively recent developments. Another fairly recent development is the technology that allows couples to know the sex of their child early in the pregnancy. This, of course, allows for the possibility of indirect sex selection through selective abortion. Of these childbearing alternatives, perhaps the least controversial is artificial insemination, particularly with the husband as the semen donor. The most controversial, from a social and legal standpoint, is surrogate motherhood. (Of course, anything involving abortion is controversial, but that topic is the focus of the next section.) *In vitro* fertilization was at first somewhat controversial because it was based on new and limited medical technology. However, as it has become more common, it has also become less controversial.

It is certainly no coincidence that the least controversial of these alternatives are those that involve only the married partners, e.g., artificial insemination with the husband as donor, whereas the most controversial are those involving third parties, e.g., surrogate motherhood. There are some who argue that both surrogate motherhood and *in vitro* fertilization could be defined as acts of adultery, depending upon whose sperm is combined with whose ovum. These difficulties grow out of our traditional manner of connecting parenthood with sex and the view that parenthood is essentially a biological fact rather than a social relationship. This view places supreme importance upon real (read *biological*) parenthood and lessens the value of any other type of parenthood, whether it be through illegitimacy or, for that matter, through adoption. It is unfortunate that we have failed to give sufficient importance to the social nature of parenthood. It is sadly ironic that so many people can and do produce children in the biological sense, while relatively few biological parents are capable of truly excelling in the social aspects of parenthood. The real significance of parenthood should be placed upon how children are reared rather than upon the circumstances of their birth. These are problems of social definition and probably serve as the root causes of the controversies surrounding these childbearing alternatives.

This section of the book will not view each alternative in terms of its pros and cons—these issues are much too new for that. Rather, a general review will be presented on each of several alternatives, seeking to illustrate some of the major questions and concerns that are being raised at the present time. The opening article of the section, "Making Babies: The State of the Art," does, in fact, present a description of most of the possibilities available to persons who wish to avail themselves of ways other than the ordinary one for having children. It also covers some new procedures and practices that might be brought into play as a part of the normal childbearing process.

Of the various childbearing alternatives, this commentary will look briefly at the three most controversial: artificial insemination, surrogate motherhood, and sex selection. With the exception of the potential problems mentioned above, *in vitro* fertilization has not proved to be particularly controversial, although there might be some premature concerns about what might happen to sex itself, and what will happen if men no longer are necessary for childbearing. If this practice becomes more widespread, these concerns could develop into significant issues, but as yet, this has not occurred.

ARTIFICIAL INSEMINATION

There are two types of artificial insemination, one in which the husband provides the sperm (AIH) and the other in which one or more donors (usually anonymous) provide the sperm (AID). Use of the husband's sperm is relatively rare simply because the most common reason why couples resort to artificial insemination is the lack of enough viable sperm in the husband's ejaculate. Thus, most babies born in this manner are conceived through AID. Sometimes, however, when the husband's sperm count is low, attempts are made to use it by concentrating it so as to improve the chances of impregnation.

Artificial insemination is the least controversial of the various childbearing alternatives because it allows for the most privacy, and few people even know of its occurrence. If the couple choose not to tell anyone, as is often the case, only the doctor knows and he might keep no records of the transaction. Thus, even the closest friends and relatives easily are led to believe that the resulting child is the biological child of both parents. Furthermore, it is likely that very few children conceived in this manner ever are told the details of their origin.

SURROGATE MOTHERHOOD

As used here, the word surrogate means substitute; thus surrogate motherhood is the situation in which a woman becomes the substitute mother, in the biological sense, for another woman who is unable to conceive a child but whose husband is fertile and serves as the biological father of the child. Conception ordinarily would take place through artificial insemination performed in a medical setting. The child produced therefore would be the biological offspring of a least one of the new parents, a point of significance for many would-be parents. One case was reported in which the surrogate was the sister of the adopting mother, thus making the child even more genetically akin to the couple.[1]

The usual procedure upon the birth of the child is for the biological mother to terminate legally her parental rights, just as in a normal adoption, and for the married couple to adopt the child. One of the major problems lies in the fact that about half the states allow adoptions only through public agencies, disallowing any money changing hands between the biological mother and the adopting parents. However, some states do allow private adoptions and the payment of fees, and in some cases these fees are hidden in other legal fees that are charged for private adoptions.

There are myriad moral, legal, and theological questions raised by the phenomenon of surrogate motherhood. Most of the concerns are of the "what would happen if. . .?" variety. For example, what if the surrogate decided to keep the baby? Or what if the couple decided they did not want the child because it was deformed? Could the father be held responsible for supporting the child? Or what if the same woman served as a surrogate for two different couples? Would the children be siblings? Or isn't this the same as selling and buying babies? Or isn't this another form of adultery? And there are certainly many more.

Most of these questions are waiting to be answered and some quite simply are unanswerable. The article "Surrogate Parenting: Legal Labor Pains," looks at a number of the legal problems, both real and potential, that can develop, focusing upon the first of the questions asked above—what happens when a surrogate mother decides to renege on the contract and keep her baby. The article covers a specific case now in the courts, and also describes what is fast becoming an "industry," the producing of babies for infertile couples who desperately desire children.

SEX SELECTION

One of the effects of the increasing preference for smaller families, i.e., fewer children, has been a concurrent rise of interest in the preselection of the sex of the children. When families desire only two children, they generally want one child of each sex, and when financial, career, and other pressures exist to keep childbearing limited, people desire a method of ensuring their getting one of each sex. Thus, it is easy to understand why couples would like to be able to select the sex of their children prior to conception. At the same time, there are others who strongly oppose sex selection for a number of reasons.

In recent years, the popular media have publicized several "scientific" methods that have been advocated as increasing the chances of having a child of one sex or the other.[2] Kits are now being marketed which are advertised as increasing a couple's chances of having one sex or the other as much as 80 per cent. Nevertheless, the only certain method available at this time is through the use of selective abortion based on the information provided by a procedure called amniocentesis. The use of amniocentesis for purposes of sex selection is highly controversial, as is the whole question of sex selection.

Amniocentesis is a relatively simple medical procedure in which a needle is inserted through the abdomen of a pregnant woman, relatively early in the pregnancy, for the purpose of drawing off a small sample of fluid from the amniotic sac in which the fetus is developing. Prior to inserting the needle the fetus is located in the uterus through sonography, which uses sound waves to construct an x-raylike picture of the interior of the uterus. Thus, the danger of injuring the fetus with the needle is lessened considerably. When the amniotic fluid is obtained, it is submitted to a laboratory process called karyotyping, in which some cells are removed and allowed to grow so that the chromosomes of those cells then can be inspected. Scrutiny of these cells can indicate the presence or absence of several genetic disorders that might exist in the fetus and might cause the child to be deformed in some manner. The wife then is in a position to make an informed choice about whether or not to end the pregnancy. One of the "by-products" of karyotyping is that it indicates the sex of the fetus.

The major medical indication for amniocentesis is when there is a risk of producing a deformed or damaged child, while its use solely for purposes of sex selection is highly controversial. The article included in this section, "Is Amniocentesis Justifiable in Selecting Baby's Sex?" directly addresses this particular controversy. This whole topic is doubly an issue because it dovetails with the abortion issue. The use of abortion as a means of negative choice regarding the sex of a potential child is, to many people, an abhorrent idea, whereas to others it might seem a better reason than many upon which abortions are based.

NOTES

1   *Intercom*, Population Reference Bureau, Inc., Vol.9, No.10, p.2.

2   For example, D. Rorvick and L. B. Shettles, "You Can Choose Your Baby's Sex," *Look Magazine*, April 1970; E. M. Whelan, *Boy or Girl? The Sex Selection Technique That Makes All Others Obsolete* (Indianapolis: Bobbs-Merrill, 1977); L. B. Shettles and D. Rorvick, "How to Choose the Sex of Your Baby," *Family Circle*, March 6, 1984.

14.

Making Babies: The State of the Art

Robert H. Blank

Before the advent of the new reproductive technologies, we largely accepted human reproduction as an inevitable natural process, for better or worse. Now, however, reproduction-aiding technologies offer childless couples the chance to have children, while reproduction-control technologies provide the means to terminate or temporarily limit fertility. Genetic-screening techniques, along with prenatal diagnosis and treatment, promise to give us "quality control" over our offspring, reducing genetic disorders and even offering future generations the capability of direct genetic control over progeny.

Let's look first at the reproduction-aiding technologies. The human reproductive system has a high rate of failure. In about 16 per cent of cases where human ova are exposed to sperm, fertilization does not occur. When fertilization does take place, the embryo is lost during the first week in about 18 per cent of the cases and during the second week in 32 per cent. Only 37 per cent of human zygotes survive to be delivered as live infants.

In addition to these relatively high rates of embryonic loss, it is estimated that 15 per cent of all married couples in the United States are infertile; it is not surprising, then, that the demand for reproduction-aiding technologies is escalating.

ARTIFICIAL INSEMINATION

The most widely used form of reproduction-aiding technology today is *artificial insemination* (AI). Semen is deposited by a syringe in or near the cervix of a woman's uterus in an effort to achieve conception. AI is a relatively simple medical procedure; in fact, one researcher suggests that a "home insemination kit" might not be far off.

Reprinted, with permission, from *The Futurist*, published by the World Future Society, 4916 St. Elmo Ave., Bethesda, Maryland 20814.

Biologically it is irrelevant whether the sperm used is the husband's or a donor's, but the ethical, psychological, and social problems surrounding the latter are more severe. Artificial insemination by donor (AID) is usually used when the husband is wholly infertile, when there is severe RH incompatibility, or when the husband is known to suffer from a serious hereditary disorder such as Huntington's disease. AID is also used for single women wishing to bear a child.

Cryopreservation—freezing and preserving sperm by immersion in liquid nitrogen—enlarges the potential for artificial insemination. "Cryobanks" make it possible for a man to store his semen prior to undergoing a vasectomy and for a woman to have a child by a man who is dead. Recently, a French woman went to court to obtain her late husband's semen.

IN-VITRO FERTILIZATION

In-vitro fertilization (IVF) is the procedure by which eggs are removed from a woman's ovaries, fertilized outside her body, and reimplanted in her uterus. This procedure is called for when the oviducts are blocked, preventing the egg from passing through the fallopian tubes to be fertilized. The National Academy of Sciences estimates that between 0.5 per cent and 1 per cent of all American women who are otherwise unable to bear children might be able to do so through IVF.

In order to be successful, IVF entails a series of well timed and executed procedures. The first stage is to obtain an egg from the woman's ovary. A small incision is made in the woman's abdomen and a fine hollow needle is inserted, aspirating the mature egg contained in follicular fluid. The fluid is then deposited in a medium that allows the ovum to mature completely prior to fertilization.

Similarly, sperm is placed in a carrier solution that capacitates it so that it is able to fertilize the egg. The two mediums containing the egg and the sperm are then diluted to simulate the conditions found in the fallopian tubes. A few hours after the fertilization occurs, the zygote is transferred to a solution that supports cell division and embryo maturation. When the embryo reaches the 8- to 16-cell stage, it is transferred to the uterus of the egg donor—or to another woman.

CLONING AND EGG FUSION

In looking toward the future, we see that current technologies pale in comparison with what may be possible. Here are a few innovations in researching with animals.

In *cloning*, the nucleus of an egg is removed and replaced with a nucleus from a somatic (body) cell, which contains the entire genetic code of the organism from which it is taken. In the case of humans, cloning would require the acquisition of eggs from the woman, the destruction of the nucleus (chemically or by laser), and the "fertilization" with the nucleus of a somatic cell. The "fertilized" egg would then be implanted in the womb and brought to term. The result of successful cloning is an exact duplicate of the organism from which the somatic cell was taken.

A technique related to cloning but one that appears to have more potential human application is fertilization of one mature ovum with another. *Egg fusion* would eliminate the need for male genetic material and would always produce a female. In an extension of this technique, both eggs could be obtained from the same woman, thus producing a daughter who is totally hers genetically.

Another possibility is the production of *chimeras*. A chimera is an animal created with cells from several species. This is done by fusing two or more early embryos or by adding extra cells to the embryo. To date, chimeras of two species of mouse have been created, resulting in a mouse with four or six parents instead of two.

NEW FORMS OF PARENTHOOD

A clinic in Chicago is reported to be offering *artificial embryonation*, where a childless husband and wife pay a fee to a fertile woman who agrees to be inseminated with the husband's sperm. Then, four to five days after fertilization, the embryo is flushed out and implanted in the wife. A variation of this procedure, *embryo adoption*, uses sperm from a donor rather than the husband.

One social innovation culminating from technological breakthroughs is the phenomenon of *surrogate motherhood*. An infertile woman and her husband enter into an agreement with another woman (the surrogate) by which she will be artificially inseminated with the sperm of the husband. After fertilization, she carries the fetus to term, and after the baby is born she relinquishes her rights to it and gives it to the couple.

Surrogate motherhood raises new legal and moral problems because the surrogate must be willing to be inseminated by the sperm of a stranger, carry his baby for nine months, and then give the baby to the couple. The commitment of a surrogate mother is substantial, both physically and emotionally. The couple must rely totally on the good faith of the surrogate to keep her promise since they cannot be assured of any legal rights to the child.

Another possibility for a childless couple is a *fetal transfer* from a woman considering abortion. Theoretically, abortion does not preclude substitution of another life-support system for the developing fetus. Intensive-care innovations for the newborn are constantly improving the odds that artificial wombs might become available in the not-so-remote future.

With the availability of such technologies, abortion would not result in the death of the fetus but merely its transfer to another womb—mechanical or human. The technique of fetal transfer, if successful, would allow a woman who no longer wishes to carry her child to have it transferred to the womb of a woman who wants it. Under these circumstances, fetal adoption might replace abortion.

REVERSING STERILIZATION

Sterilization is viewed by growing numbers of Americans as a safe and sure form of contraception. But many individuals choosing sterilization would like to be able to reverse the operation if they change their minds later.

Important advances have been made in the last decade in reversing "permanent" sterilization, but current research focuses on techniques designed to be reversible from the start.

Although most attention on the reversible methods is being directed toward women, some efforts are being made to make male sterilization simple and reversible as well. Procedural prospects for male sterilization include nonsurgical methods of chemical sterilization, pharmacological sterilizing agents, vas deferens-blocking plugs and prosthetics, and reversible valves or other devices that can be switched on or off to regulate passage of the sperm through the vas.

The reversible sterilization techniques increase the reproductive options that couples (and individuals) will have in the future. They also raise the possibility that the forced sterilization of certain groups–inmates of mental institutions, for example–might become more "acceptable."

PRENATAL INTERVENTION

Each year, in the United States alone, between 100,000 and 200,000 infants are born with congenital disorders, which play a key role in fetal and infant mortality, mental retardation, and chronic disability. The substantial human suffering and social costs have motivated significant efforts to identify and eventually treat a wide array of chromosomal abnormalities, metabolic disorders, and other hereditary diseases. Among the major prenatal diagnostic technologies that are now available to meet this growing need and demand to reduce genetic disease are amniocentesis, ultrasound and fetoscopy.

Amniocentesis. In this procedure, a long thin needle attached to a syringe is inserted through the lower wall of the woman's abdomen and amniotic fluid, which contains some live body cells shed by the fetus, is withdrawn. The chromosomes are karyotyped to identify any abnormalities and to determine the sex of the fetus. If a fetus is diagnosed as having severe chromosomal or metabolic disorder, therapeutic abortion is offered to the mother.

Ultrasound. A technology that has become indispensable in prenatal diagnosis is ultrasound or "pulse-echo" sonography. This procedure uses sound waves directed into the abdomen of the pregnant woman to gain an echo-visual image of the fetus, uterus, placenta, and other inner structures.

It is a non-invasive technology that is painless for the woman and reduces the need for X-ray scanning procedures.

Fetoscopy. Detection of a wide variety of hereditary disorders (including hemophilia, sickle-cell anemia, and possibly Duchenne muscular dystrophy) might be possible through fetoscopy. Fetoscopy is an application of fiber-optics technology that allows doctors to look at the fetus inside the uterus. The fetoscope is inserted through an incision in the woman's abdomen, usually under the direction of ultrasound. Fetoscopy, now used to give blood transfusions to diseased fetuses, has considerable potential for introducing medicines, cell transplants, or genetic materials into fetal tissues in order to treat genetic diseases.

RIDDLES FOR LAW AND ETHICS

The rapid advances in reproductive technology may force us to modify our beliefs about human life and our definition of what it is to be a person. The legal and ethical questions are numerous and difficult.

Who ultimately has legal and moral responsibility to care for the products of "artificial" procreation? Who are the rightful parents, and who decides what is best for a child when the traditional mother-father combination is no longer clear? What psychological effect might the knowledge that one is the product of the fertilization of an anonymous donor sperm and donor egg in a petri dish have on a person?

What are society's responsibilities to future generations when the technology is available to "perfect" the human species? In an overpopulated world, can the right to reproduce remain inviolate? Should the right of parents to procreate become a secondary consideration to the right of children to be born with a sound physical and mental genotype?

From now on, prospective parents will have the opportunity to draw upon knowledge and techniques of reproductive research. How far ought they to go in that regard: selective abortion, sex preselection, trait selection, cloning? More importantly, how far are we as a society going to go in encouraging, facilitating, or mandating such decisions?

Today's actions have impressive potential to constrain or broaden the alternatives open in the future. Decisions made in the near future will unalterably either limit or expand the health of future generations.

TWO SCENARIOS

Two scenarios can be developed for the future: (1) a "brave new world" scenario based on increased societal control over reproduction and (2) a scenario featuring expanded choices for individuals.

In Aldous Huxley's novel *Brave New World*, human breeding technologies are used by the state for social control. This results in a genetic caste system

and the creation of standardized humans "the principle of mass production at last applied to biology."

It is easy to see why critics of genetic engineering and reproductive intervention often cite *Brave New World*. Eugenic programs of an extreme
variety contradict even the most narrow conventional definitions of individual autonomy. Social control of reproduction could–if pushed to
extremes–lead to:

- Constraints on reproduction for particular groups of people such as the poor, minorities, and welfare mothers.

- Further separation of sex and reproduction.

- Creation of a new social class–surrogate mothers and
  fathers.

- Policies aimed at licensing parents on genetic and social
  grounds.

- Forced sterilization, abortion, genetic screening, infanticide, and so forth.

The second scenario–that of expanded individual choice–features the
same advances in technology but in a context of personal choice and volun-
tarism. Some potential uses of the technologies include:

- Artificial placentas and surrogate mothers for women
  who cannot–or choose not to–carry their own fetuses.

- Semen and embryo banks for parents who desire these
  services.

- Gene marking and splicing technologies allowing
  parents to choose the genetic traits of their children.

- A wide variety of safe and effective contraceptive
  methods, including a one- or two-year pill that
  simultaneously immunizes against venereal disease.

The major differences in these two scenarios are political and social–
not technological. In the "brave new world" scenario, reproductive innovations have been developed in order to maximize social stability and effi-
ciency by controlling and institutionalizing human procreation. But in the
expanded choice scenarios, priorities are established on the basis of the
extent to which they enhance reproductive options available to individuals.
Ironically, both scenarios severely challenge contemporary notions of
human reproduction and represent social settings at variance with currently accepted notions of what the future ought to be.

HOPE FOR THE FUTURE

The scope of the problems raised by the advent of reproductive technologies is awesome, but there is hope for the future. Diligent and cautious policymaking is required to ensure that potential benefits are realized to the maximum extent possible while the less desirable applications and unintended consequences are channeled into manageable problems. The alternative could be the gradual slippage into a scenario similar to a "brave new world."

No longer is human life the product solely of natural happenings, fate, or even manipulation of the environment. We now hold the keys to direct intervention in the most fundamental aspects of human life. However, as we acquire the capacity to control and direct the human condition, we also assume an awesome responsibility, whether willingly or not, for the choices we make.

15.

Surrogate Parenting: Legal Labor Pains

Malcolm Gladwell

Almost one and one-half years ago, New Jersey housewife Mary Beth Whitehead agreed to bear a child for Elizabeth Stern, an infertile New Jersey pediatrician, and her husband, William. Mary Beth was artificially inseminated with William's sperm and in return for carrying the child to term she was given $10,000.

But there was a hitch. When Mary Beth Whitehead first saw the baby she calls Sara, she says her "emotions just overwhelmed me." She decided she wanted to keep the girl. Elizabeth Stern, who calls the baby Melissa, says, "She's mine." And now the Sterns and the Whiteheads are in a Hackensack, N.J., courthouse battling over the child the courts call "Baby M."

Mary Beth Whitehead is not the first surrogate mother to decide to keep her child. Noel Keane, the Detroit attorney who is responsible for more surrogate contracts than anyone else in the country, says that in the 118 births he has arranged, two mothers have decided to withhold their children and break the surrogate contract. But this is the first case that has ever gone to court, the first time a judge has had to play Solomon over a baby born to one couple by another woman.

What makes it a landmark case is that at present, there is no legislation on the books anywhere in the United States—nor any significant legal precedent—dealing specifically with the question of surrogate motherhood. Most states have laws against baby selling, but there is some dispute about whether they apply in the case of surrogate motherhood. After all, what is being sold for $10,000? The child? Or the services of the surrogate? No one knows, and since the practice of surrogate motherhood became more common about five years ago, the business has been conducted in a legal gray area. "You screen potential mothers, and you cross your fingers," says

Reprinted by permission from *Insight*, September 22, 1986.

one law professor of the manner in which the "infertility industry" has conducted itself so far. "You hope no one makes trouble."

Mary Beth Whitehead made trouble.

The showdown over custody of Baby M in New Jersey is not at all what the supporters of surrogate motherhood wanted. For years they have tried to pass legislation on the state level that would avoid the possibility of such messy judicial resolution. They have always wanted the issues of parenthood clarified. "Do we have to wait for the first baby to be born deformed, and the first father to say, 'I don't want it,' so some judge who knows nothing about surrogate parenting has to decide what happens to that baby?" asks Harriett Blankfeld, who runs Infertility Associates International Inc. in Chevy Chase, Md.

She points out that with proper state regulation of the surrogate process, the Baby M case might never have arisen. "Right now we have to be self-regulating, and hopefully we're as good as government regulation might be," the surrogate parenting broker says. In this case, however, Harriett Blankfeld says there is a "tremendous difference" between the screening process at the Infertility Center in New York that handled the Whitehead-Stern contract and that used by her own agency. She would have immediately rejected Whitehead as a high-risk applicant, she says. The surrogate mothers "must have a high school diploma, not to demonstrate their intelligence, but to prove they have made a commitment." Whitehead would not qualify there. "Money can't be the number one factor," as it may have been in this case, says the head of Infertility Associates. The bonding that Whitehead claims with her child Blankfeld says "could have been resolved during pregnancy" if infertility agencies were required by law to provide counseling to birth mothers.

Surrogate motherhood, explains Vicki Michel, a law professor at Loyola Marymount University, "is an industry, and with any industry you've got problems that require regulation. You've got lawyers writing contracts, psychologists counseling people. People getting a vested interest in the business. I know of a case where people have been pushed toward surrogate motherhood when other means were not exhausted." Sheila Kuehl, head of the Women Lawyers Association of Los Angeles, says that she once came out of a baseball game and found a flier advertising for surrogate mother applicants on her windshield.

But every time surrogate motherhood legislation has been proposed around the country, it has failed. In Michigan, state Rep. Richard Fitzpatrick has introduced a bill dealing with reproductive alternatives in every session since 1981. His bill sets out clear guidelines for a legitimate surrogate contract, requires full psychological and medical screening for all parties to the contract and recognizes the societal parents of the child as its legal parents while opening a legal avenue for surrogates who want to keep their baby.

Fitzpatrick has advanced his Alternative Reproduction Act because he thinks that surrogate motherhood is here to stay.

"There is no way to let the genie back into the bottle," he told the Wayne State School of Medicine last fall. "Even assuming there was some way we could marshal enough law enforcement officers and public opinion to drive all of those who wish to involve themselves in these practices from the state of Michigan, it is reasonable to assume that these procedures will take place in other states and countries." Says a Fitzpatrick aide, "It's the proper role of government to set down basic guidelines for things like this." But HR 4554-4557 has gone nowhere in the Michigan Legislature, and similar bills in California and Maryland have met the same fate.

"It's hard to be rational about surrogate motherhood," says Detroit psychiatrist Philip Parker, who is not surprised by the reluctance of lawmakers to touch the subject. "We're talking about a combination of reproduction, sexuality and marriage, things that trigger feelings from childhood, feelings and fantasies about sexuality and where babies come from."

In California, the charge against recognizing and regulating the practice has been led by the former Southern Baptist preacher W. B. Timberlake and his lobby group, the Committee on Moral Concerns.

"The whole idea of legalizing surrogate parenting puts man's law above the law of nature," says committee lobbyist Art Croney. He says that giving up a baby goes against natural motherly love, which "is one of the strongest emotions in the world, not only in humans but in animals as well."

"When you mess with a bear's cubs," Croney says, "that's when you get into real trouble." He, like many others in the religious community, is not surprised by the Baby M case. Mary Beth Whitehead "didn't change her mind," Croney says. "A natural process took over." He thinks she was exploited by the infertility industry, and if surrogate parenting becomes more widespread, "thousands and thousands" of women will share her predicament.

Parker, who has conducted extensive psychological tests on more than 500 surrogate applicants, disagrees. Many of the women who become surrogate mothers are motivated by strong altruistic feelings about giving someone else the gift of a child. "A third of the women I've studied have had a prior voluntary loss of a child," Parker says. "They feel the need to repeat the trauma in order to master it." Yes, he adds, giving up the child is nearly always associated with some kind of "grief experience," but that is to be expected. In its most severe forms it can be dealt with through therapy. So far experience bears out his analysis. Out of nearly 300 surrogate births in America, birth mothers have tried to hold on to the children in only a handful of cases. "The overwhelming majority of our surrogate arrangements go off without a hitch," says Keane.

But if the Whitehead case is the exception rather than the rule, that does not faze the religious opponents of alternative reproduction. Their opposition, ultimately, is philosophical. When Biorna and James Noyes, an infertile couple from Rochester, N.Y., went on television's "Donahue" show a few years ago to explain their search for a surrogate mother, one comment from a self-described born-again Christian in the audience was representative: "I feel that God gave you your difference when you were born, so that you could adopt a child that had a difference or maybe just an older child."

To the two million parents in the United States who want to have children but cannot, Croney says the same thing: Adopt. And he does not see the notorious seven-year waiting lists for adoptable children as a problem at all. "There's an abundance of minority children, older children or children with physical or mental handicaps out there in need of homes," he says. "Most people just want to buy a healthy white baby. It's unfair, when there are all those kids out there who are desperate."

Occasionally the surrogate parenting debate degenerates to mudslinging. Fitzpatrick used to begin his frequent speeches on the subject by recalling the biblical story of Abraham, Sarah, and Hagar. This, he claims, is the first recorded surrogate birth: Sarah was infertile and agreed to use her handmaiden Hagar to bear her husband's child. In testimony before the California Legislature, the Committee on Moral Concerns attacked Fitzpatrick and his proposal, claiming it was the cause of the entire Arab-Israeli conflict. The line of reasoning was that the sons of Ishmael (the surrogate child) are the Arabs and the sons of Isaac (the "traditionally conceived" child) are the Jews—the groups' animosity was caused by surrogate parenting. "I have been accused of many things," Fitzpatrick responds, laughing, but he says he did not know he was "responsible for war in the Middle East."

Religious groups want a flat ban on surrogate parenting, but legal experts question whether that would be constitutional. "There's a real good argument that the procreative liberty of a married couple includes the constitutional right to engage a reproductive collaborator to provide an egg, sperm or gestation," says John Robertson, A University of Texas law professor. He does not think that religious arguments about the "sacredness of the marital bond" have a chance against constitutional considerations of reproductive freedom. "Why," asks Fitzpatrick, "should the right of a couple to raise a child of their own depend on their luck in a biological lottery, if they can obtain the missing factor of reproduction from other consenting adults?"

The bottom line is that the real barrier to explicit legislative recognition of surrogate parenting may have less to do with fundamental moral objections than the relative novelty of the practice. After all, there have still been only a few hundred surrogate births in America. "It's a new issue," explains Robertson. "We haven't had enough experience with it, not enough disputes or problems," he says, adding that the Whitehead-Stern case may provide just the impetus for serious public consideration of surrogate motherhood that the infertility industry has been looking for.

Another practical stumbling block to legislation dealing with alternative reproduction, say some observers, is that until now surrogate parenting advocates have been asking for too much, too soon. That certainly was true in California. "We were concerned because the impetus for this legislation came entirely from the attorneys for adoptive parents," explains Sheila Kuehl, who was heavily involved in fighting sections of the bill. The original proposals would have stacked the deck against birth mothers in any custody dispute by, among other rules, denying state child support to the surrogate mother if she decided to keep her baby. Says the women lawyers association president, "They wanted to give the adoptive parents all the rights of biological parents but none of the responsibilities."

Some of the same criticisms have also been leveled at Fitzpatrick's proposed Michigan law. The legislation was drafted with the help of surrogate motherhood mogul Keane. And he is not known for his tact in dealing with opponents. "We haven't had a public policy debate in Michigan," Keane says of the legislation's fate. "Our definition of public policy in this state comes from a time when they wouldn't let blacks buy houses in white neighborhoods."

The biggest concession the infertility industry will probably have to make is over its insistence on the inviolability of the contract between the birth mother and the adoptive parents. Harriet Blankfeld says that "there is no gray area. Either you're a surrogate mother or you're not. Either you have a contract that is legally binding or you don't." That position, however, is clearly unacceptable to many other interested parties, particularly women's groups. Sheila Kuehl says that a contract involving a human being cannot be considered in the same light as a contract involving something inanimate. Besides, she points out, "there is always the expectation that any contract will be broken if there is an economic gain to be made. If I'm selling you a thousand balloons and I find I can get a better price elsewhere, I try and break our contract. In some cases of surrogate motherhood, there's an emotional advantage to be gained from keeping the baby."

Vicki Michel just hopes that when the Hackensack court makes its decision, it will remember one thing: "This is a child, not a commodity. Whenever there's a conflict, the interest of the child should be paramount."

* * *

EDITOR'S UPDATE: *

Since this article was written, the case of Baby M has been to trial and a decision has been handed down. Although there will likely be appeals of the current ruling, it also seems likely at this point that the essential elements of the decision will stand.

The trial was divided into two segments, reflecting the two major issues which emerged from the dispute: the question as to the validity of the surrogate contract, and the question of who should gain custody of the child. These issues were seen as being separate, and the decision in either was not seen by the court as having a major influence upon the other. That is, the judge could uphold the contract and still give custody to the birth mother, or he could declare the contract invalid, yet give custody to the father. On March 31, 1987, after a lengthy trial, the decision was handed down. Although the ruling is binding only in New Jersey, it will likely set important legal precedents that will carry over to other states, affecting both court decisions and potential legislation.

As to the validity of the contract, the ruling stated that the contract was essentially valid, in that, if men have the right to sell their sperm, then women also have the right to decide what they will do with their wombs. In regard to the question as to whether or not surrogate motherhood amounts to the selling of babies, the ruling stated that since the child is already the father's, he is then incapable of purchasing that which is already his.

The custody issue was decided solely on the basis of the "best interests of the child," a long-standing doctrine that is usually applied in child custody disputes. Independently of the contract decision, the judge found that the Sterns (the biological father and adoptive mother) were the more capable and stable of the couples wanting custody, and that Mrs. Whitehead (the surrogate mother) had been inconsistent and unstable, as well as impulsive and exploitive.

This decision by no means settles all of the issues involved. However, it should spur state legislatures to begin looking at the potential problems that can occur, and to begin to draft legislation that will protect rights that need legal protection, particularly the rights of potential children produced in these situations.

*These comments are based upon numerous press reports concerning the "Baby M" case.

16.

Is Amniocentesis Justifiable in Selecting Baby's Sex?

John C. Fletcher

Two types of parents request fetal sex identification by amniocentesis: The first group risk transmitting a sex-linked hereditary disorder, and the second want to select the gender of their next child. Physicians generally encourage the first type of parent but discourage the second.

Prenatal diagnosis for sex choice is controversial because of ethical objections to the use of abortion for such a reason and because of the question of whether amniocentesis, a scarce medical resource, can be used prudently for this purpose. The issue is complex and involves many competing ethical claims.

I have re-evaluated my position on this issue as a result of participation in a Hastings Center study group and consultation with staff of the Prenatal Diagnostic Center of the Johns Hopkins Hospital on their policy on amniocentesis for sex choice.

My earlier position was based on four main points. In the first place, I argued that parents with this request ought to be discouraged because sex is not a disease. I saw prenatal diagnosis as a tool that ethically could be used to diagnose hereditary diseases or congenital defects in the fetus. Second, I stressed that abortion for sex choice could contribute to social inequality between the sexes because of a preference for male offspring.

Third, I criticized sex choice as a "frivolous" reason for abortion that could not be defended successfully in the company of serious moral persons. My fourth point was that amniocentesis was a scarce resource in the light of the total number of pregnancies at risk. Requests for fetal sex identifica-

Reprinted by permission from the *New England Journal of Medicine*, vol. 301 (1979), pp. 550-553.

tion could swamp an already overloaded system or delay laboratory work in cases of serious genetic diseases.

A legal and a public-relations consideration buttressed these reasons and secured my position. Physicians cannot be forced legally to provide procedures that are not "lifesaving." Furthermore, if parents were accommodated in this request, anti-abortion forces might raise a public outcry that would discourage parents genuinely at risk from seeking prenatal testing. I supported the prevailing policy of discouragement and defended the practice in some laboratories of refusing to do karyotyping when fetal sex alone was the presenting indication.

ON RE-EVALUATION...

My re-evaluation assumes that the basis for the policy of discouragement is the belief of most physicians who perform prenatal diagnosis that abortion for sex choice is morally unjustifiable. Those who reason as I did also use the scarce-resource argument and are wary of the use of prenatal diagnosis for "social engineering" to plan the sex of children.

In practice, however, discouragement based on opposition to abortion for sex choice is weightier than the other two reasons. Most of us have an uneasy conscience about the number of abortions performed in the United States and about the lack of moral seriousness with which abortion sometimes is requested and carried out. We have preferred to use prenatal diagnosis in the context of saving fetal lives. I personally believe that sex choice is not a compelling reason for abortion. The first moral response of most who think about the issue is close to queasiness.

Yet, the issue does not turn on the validity of opposition to abortion for sex choice. The issue turns on the validity of the legal rules on abortion defined by the Supreme Court, which do not require that a woman state reasons in a public or medical forum for early to midtrimester abortion. No one is presumed to be a public judge of her reason except herself. Family, friends, counselors, or physicians may challenge her reasons if she chooses to confide in them. But the rule is that no public test of reasons is required.

Is this the best rule to apply in abortion? Yes, if one holds, as I do, that the woman's right to decide is the overriding consideration in the abortion issue. The rationale for the legal rule omitting a test of reasons is that a woman has the right to control her reproduction and the risks involved in a pregnancy. To employ public or medical tests of reasons provides opportunities to obstruct and defeat society's obligation to grant women the freedom to determine their own reproductive futures. To prevent obstruction of self-determination, it is better to have no public tests of reasons.

The Supreme Court took the position that the state has no interest in refusing an adult woman the right of self-determination in reproduction through the second trimester of pregnancy. Although a Supreme Court decision is not itself an ethical consideration, the legal guideline on abortion points beyond itself to the principles of justice and respect for persons.

Justice in the modern state requires that women be freed from restrictions on their freedom and opportunity to compete for the social and economic rewards of citizenship. Respect for persons requires that a woman's autonomy and personal responsibility be the standards that govern the final resolution of conflicts about reproduction and abortion.

The Supreme Court justices probably did not imagine in 1973 that their decision on abortion was related to the right of parents to choose the sex of children through amniocentesis. However, even if the justices were aware then of the potential use of amniocentesis for this purpose, it did not figure in their reasoning. The position that they took made abortion on request a legal practice and the conscience of the individual woman the sole arbiter of the reasons. Abortion for sex choice is legal, and if we are to act in accordance with the principles that now should inform decision making on abortion, all forms of tests should be removed.

Given the ethical and legal posture discussed above, one must be willing to accept the fact that some abortions will be performed for trivial reasons. The existence of some trivial reasons should not deter us from the larger goal of protecting the right of women to make such decisions in the first place. That is what is at stake in the issue under discussion. My major argument is that it is inconsistent to support an abortion law that protects the absolute right of women to decide, and at the same time, to block access to information about the fetus because one thinks that an abortion may be sought foolishly on the basis of the information.

AN EXAMPLE

Another way to measure the degree of ethical inconsistency in the policy of discouragement is to reflect on an example. An obstetrician-gynecologist is asked by a thirty-year-old woman in the second month of gestation to perform an abortion. The physician does not inquire about her reasons. As it turns out, she desired the abortion so that she could make a trip to Europe.

The same physician is a cooperating member of a prenatal diagnostic center in a university hospital with a policy of discouraging access for prenatal sex identification and a prohibition against laboratory cultures for this purpose. The mother of three children of one gender requests fetal sex identification in the fourth pregnancy. The physician must either refer her to another center at some distance or do the amniotic tap in the office and send the sample to a commercial laboratory where no questions are asked.

If the sometimes trivial reason for abortion must be accepted to protect the rights of many women, how could it be acceptable for the same physician to participate in a system that discriminates because of reasons for abortion? To hold to this inconsistency is morally self-defeating and leads to hypocrisy. Furthermore, amniocentesis and laboratory work should be done under the very best of conditions, if done at all. The physician should not be forced to defend an inconsistent policy and practice less than optimum medicine and science.

INFORMED CONSENT

When the physicians counsel parents who want to know the sex of the fetus, they should inform them carefully about several areas of risk.

Amniocentesis carries a small but nonetheless real risk of death to the fetus and injury to the mother. The risk of fetal death from amniocentesis has been shown to be less than 1 per cent in controlled studies in the United States and Canada. A British study that suggested a 1.5 per cent fetal loss has been challenged on the ground that selection of controls was biased. Until this controversy is resolved, the previous risk figures and the fact that risk factors still are being studied should be communicated to the parents.

A very small number of technical errors still are made in laboratories. A recent review of three thousand consecutive amniocenteses showed the karyotyping error rate to be 0.07 per cent, or seven in ten thousand.

Midtrimester abortion is a major procedure, and depression has been reported in both parents after genetically indicated abortions.

Finally, an unknown risk of insult to other members of the family and to the wider society is involved in a decision to abort for sex choice. The physician can, if he or she chooses, state an opposing view in moral terms. What the physician should not do is withhold amniocentesis if informed parents desire to proceed. To do so would be to test the parents' reasons for abortion. The parents may or may not decide on abortion on the basis of the information gained. In any event, that decision remains theirs to make, legally and morally.

PUBLIC AND PRIVATE OPPOSITION

Individuals and groups who want to test the reasoning of those who might seek abortions are free to do so within the limits of the law. Religious groups opposed to abortion can attempt to convince anyone in society that abortion is morally wrong. Any group is free to work toward amending the Constitution so that public tests of reasons on abortion are required.

Parents are free to instruct children about human sexuality in a manner that reduces the likelihood that abortion ever will be needed in their families. Spouses and companions are free to challenge the reasoning used in any instance of contemplation of abortion. Social critics and moralists are free to write and speak against the current rules on abortion and the ethical perspective behind the rules. What none of these persons is free to do is to construct a public or medical test of a woman's reasons.

COMPETING ETHICAL CLAIMS

Wherever possible, competing ethical claims should be acknowledged in practice. There are three major ethical claims on the other side of the issue: scarcity of amniocentesis, risks and costs of the procedure, and social engineering without full appreciation of the consequences.

When there is a genuine scarcity of amniocentesis in any center, its use for sex choice should be given the lowest priority. Parents who request amniocentesis for sex choice should bear all expenses, since society is not confronted with a disease in the fetus that should be prevented in the interest of the family in society. Because of risks to the mother and fetus, the procedure should be performed only when there is adequate counseling and access to high-quality laboratory work.

Forecasting the long-range consequences of sex preselection is a complex task that deserves more encouragement and support. An earlier study based on data from the 1970 National Fertility Survey showed that the major consequence of sex determination would be planning the order of children (male first, female second) rather than increasing the number of boys. An excellent study of the preferences for sex of children among American couples showed that wives are much more likely to prefer a son than a daughter and more likely to prefer either one than to have a positive underlying desire for an equal number of boys and girls. The exceptions to this finding were wives of Hispanic heritage, who preferred girls.

These findings suggest that if a safe, inexpensive preconception method of sex selection were available, first-borns increasingly would be male. Would these first-born boys receive such a disproportionate share of the emotional and economic resources of their parents that second-born girls would be seriously disadvantaged? More work needs to be done connecting forecasts of technological advances in sex control with psychological research in gender roles and birth order. The immediate ethical question is whether a more permissive policy on amniocentesis for sex choice will precipitate a social experiment in sex selection before there is sufficient study of the consequences.

The parents who now need amniocentesis for sex choice presumably are motivated to have one child of the opposite gender from their living children. If this is true, these parents and their needs are not accurate predictors of the long-range consequences of sex determination in a planned birth order. Those consequences should be researched in the framework of sex-control methods that are more easily diffused and involve fewer risks than abortion.

CONCLUSIONS

In my revised view, it is not ethically required that physicians withhold amniocentesis from fully informed parents who might use the results in deciding to abort for sex choice. Even though the physician might dis-

approve personally of the request, it is fairer to the parents to grant it within
the limits of availability of amniocentesis. Physicians who agree with the
social-ethical perspective that informs the legal rules on abortion will want
finally to keep faith with the moral intent of the law.

Part

Six

The

Abortion

Controversy

The status of legalized abortion in the United States has changed considerably since the January 1973 landmark decision of the U.S. Supreme Court, which essentially prohibited state governments from outlawing abortions for women who wanted them, no matter what the grounds. This decision was a capstone in the trend toward increased liberalization of abortion laws, which had been occurring already in several states. Coming as it did and saying what it said, the Supreme Court decision produced surprise among the pro-abortion forces and dumbfounded the anti-abortion groups, who were attempting to stem the tide of liberalization. The pro-abortion groups had not expected quite so sweeping a decision, and the anti-abortion groups, feeling that they had begun to slow the trend toward liberalization, were thoroughly shocked and dismayed by the extent of the decision.

Since this major Court decision, there have been a series of supplementary decisions that have served to clarify further the exact meaning and extent of the original decision. A number of state laws passed both before and after the decision sought to place further restrictions on abortion and raised a number of side issues. For example, there was the question as to whether or not a minor female needed her parents' permission to obtain an abortion. Another issue was whether or not a woman's husband had to comply with her decision to have an abortion. There are questions also as to the circumstances under which an abortion may be refused and the hotly debated issue of whether or not federal funds should be used to pay for the abortions of poor women.

However, the major question, at least from a legal standpoint, has been settled by the Supreme Court. But the issue is by no means dead since the anti-abortion forces now have adopted the approach of supporting a constitutional amendment that would negate the Court's decision. Also, some feel that the more conservative Court that is emerging at this time might turn around some of the decisions of the past.

What makes the abortion issue such a heated one is the fact that it is actually a dual issue, or at least one with two or more facets that overlap in such a manner as to create a great deal of confusion and controversy. On the one hand is the legal question and on the other is the moral-religious one. The former has to do with privacy, civil liberties, and personal freedoms; the latter has to do with the question of when life begins and what constitutes a human being. Of course, the question of when life begins might be considered from a medical stand-point as well, an aspect that could be seen as a third side of the controversy. However, apart from this possibly unanswerable question, there is actually very little at issue with regard to the medical aspects of abortion except for the variations in degrees of danger related to the stages of pregnancy at which an abortion might be induced.

Those on either side of this controversy, at least in extreme instances, rarely recognize or admit to the dual nature of the issue. Those in favor of liberalized abortion see it as being solely a matter of civil liberties and a private patient-physician decision. They believe that the whole question of whether or not a fetus is a human being with all the rights of other citizens is an unanswerable one and probably an irrelevant one as well. In addition, they often take a point of view similar to the one held by those who favor liberalizing other types of laws—those laws concerned only with private behavior that poses no threat to others. For example, the argument is made that the use of marijuana in the home or varieties of sexual behavior between consenting adults harm no one, do not threaten society, and that laws attempting to regulate such behavior are unenforceable anyway. Abortion is seen as a similar type of situation, and an often-heard statement from this side of the issue is that it is impossible to legislate private morality.

From the anti-abortion side, the most extreme view would reject totally the civil liberties argument, with the idea that abortion is the same as murder and that there is certainly no question about the illegality of murder. This view states that at the point of conception there exists a human being who has an equal status with all other humans. Those with less extreme views simply state that the unborn child, no matter at which stage of development, is a potential person and that it therefore has a right to life. Those of this persuasion also would reject the private morality argument, again based on the fact that the potential human life means that there is no longer just one individual, the mother, involved, but also the helpless fetus who has no one but the society to turn to for protection.

Underlying the morality argument against abortion is the rarely spoken but widely believed view that pregnancy is a just punishment for illicit sexual behavior and that allowing easy abortion lets the "sinner" escape deserved punishment. Persons with this belief, however, fail to recognize that many illegal abortions of the past were sought by married women rather than single women.

This presentation of two sides of the issue is admittedly sketchy and necessarily oversimplified, but many of these arguments are developed further in the articles that follow, and no position is taken here with respect to the issue. However, one further bit of explanation should be offered at this point. It concerns the meaning and the usage of the term *legislation of morality.* From a sociological standpoint, all legislation is in fact the legislation of morality in that laws always reflect the basic norms of a society, and the norms in turn are the embodiment of the society's morality. Thus, when a state legislature tries to regulate drugs, abortion, prostitution, pornography, or other sexual behaviors, it is in fact attempting to inject into the law its own, or perhaps its conception of the society's, moral viewpoints. This is the case no matter what the laws are attempting to ban or regulate. Therefore, it is important that those who question the legislation of morality specify that they are referring to attempts to regulate private, consensual behavior involving adults that does no harm to anyone else. Many lawmakers fail to make even these distinctions, however, believing that any behavior that violates society's basic norms should be banned, no matter what the circumstances. Furthermore, this explanation does nothing to solve the question of whether or not abortion is a purely private matter.

One thing is certain: Laws that attempt to regulate or ban certain kinds of private moral behavior actually do a great deal of harm to individuals and to society and rarely accomplish the goals for which they are enacted. They more often drive the behavior in question underground, create a black market, and often make criminals of otherwise ordinary citizens. This certainly was the case with laws against easy abortion. And specifically with abortion, an indirect result of restrictive laws was the high mortality rate of those who were forced to seek out amateur practitioners for release from an untenable situation. One of the most significant changes that occurred in those states which liberalized their abortion laws prior to the Supreme Court decision was the sharp decline in fatalities related to abortion. In New York City alone, during the first year of the new liberal abortion law, there were only three deaths as a result of illegal abortions and the overall maternal death rate declined 50 per cent to the lowest maternal death rate ever recorded in that city. Other locations with new abortion laws reported similar occurrences.[1]

Medical authorities indicate that an abortion up to the twelfth week of pregnancy is a relatively minor procedure that takes only a few minutes and usually does not require a hospital stay. The method most commonly used for this type of abortion is called *vacuum aspiration* because it employs the use of a small suction pump to remove the placental material that contains the fertilized egg. This recently developed method is far superior to the older *dilation and curettage* method in that it is safer and much easier on the patient, usually requiring no general anesthetic.

For the period of thirteen to sixteen weeks of pregnancy, abortion is slightly more dangerous, and many doctors are reluctant to perform the operation during that period, preferring to wait until after the sixteenth week. Beyond the twelfth week the operation is also more difficult and more expensive. The method used for later abortions is generally the *saline* method, in which a salt solution is injected into the uterus, which causes it to reject the fetus within several hours in much the same manner as childbirth. For this procedure the patient usually has to remain in the hospital for two or three days. Because of its similarity to actual childbirth, many women find this method more traumatic, but it is still the safest method for later abortions.

As far as the safety factor is concerned, having an abortion actually is safer than going on to have the baby at full term. For example, during one year New York recorded a death rate of 4.2 per 100,000 legal abortions;[2] during the same period, the general maternal mortality rate (deaths resulting from childbirth) was around four or five times greater.

How extensive have legal abortions become in the years since the Supreme Court's decision? The data available on abortions are, on the one hand, rather complex, and, on the other, not always totally accurate or reliable. The complexity lies in the fact that there are a number of methods of counting, measuring and reporting abortions. For example, one might find in various government reports such data as absolute numbers of abortions, abortion rates, and several types of abortion ratios, and all of these might be broken down according to the age, sex, race, or marital status of the women involved. Inaccuracy and unreliability grow out of the fact that very few states report data on abortions, and some abortions go unreported because they are masked behind or included in other medical procedures. Inaccuracy also grows out of both pro- and anti-abortion groups developing their own statistics which are designed mainly for ideological or propagandistic purposes.

The best available data probably come from federal government compilations of state reports, although these are somewhat limited. Best estimates are that possibly as many as one million abortions were performed during the peak year, which was probably in the early 1980s. After the Supreme Court decision in 1973, there was a steady and rapid increase in abortions, that increase being mostly among unmarried white women. For example, in 1979, for this particular category, there were slightly more than two abortions for every live birth. For unmarried black women, the ratio was less than one abortion for every two live births.[3] Prior to the Court decision, abortion statistics were dominated by older married women rather than younger single women. Data for 1983 (the most recent available), however, show a marked turnaround. Ratios for white single women had declined to three abortions for every two live births, whereas ratios for black single women had increased to one for every two live births. Even with these changes the data indicate an overall decline of about 16 per cent in the total number of abortions since 1979.[4]

One would think that changes in abortion rates would be related to changes in the number of illegitimate births. However, this relationship has been neither clear nor consistent. Although the abortion rates declined since 1979, the illegitimacy rates have continued to increase. Currently, almost 20 per cent of all births in the United States occur out of wedlock, a 17 per cent increase over 1979. Although 60 per cent of all babies born to black women are born out of wedlock, the greatest increase in illegitimacy has been among white women, from 4.7 per cent of all births in 1970 to 12.8 per cent in 1983.[5] Furthermore, increasing numbers of unmarried mothers are keeping their babies, a phenomenon that severely has affected the adoption market, as was indicated in a previous section of this book.

And what about public opinion regarding abortion? Opinion polls going back more than a decade indicated that the general public favored freedom of choice in this matter, believing that it should be settled between each individual woman and her doctor. However, most people also were opposed to abortions for themselves. Over the years, these opinions favoring freedom of choice have grown to the extent that an Associated Press-NBC News poll indicated that 78 per cent of those questioned in a carefully drawn representative sample of the country believed that the decision to have an abortion should be left to the woman and her doctor. Also two-thirds of the respondents in this poll opposed a constitutional amendment to ban abortions.[6]

The abortion issue has become increasingly politicized. During the 1980 national elections, there was a strong attempt to create a conservative coalition bringing together those who were opposed to a number of things, such as the Equal Rights Amendment, legal abortions, gun control, and the teaching of evolution in the schools. Although at the time of the election it seemed that this coalition was having some impact, after the election it was unable to translate these political views into action in the U.S. Congress. Concerning abortion, two methods of legally limiting abortion were proposed to the Congress: one was a constitutional amendment to ban abortions except in extreme situations, such as a threat to the life of the woman, and the other was a bill that would define human life as beginning with conception, which would make abortion tantamount to murder. As of this writing, neither of these moves has made any significant headway.

In recent years, the legal and political maneuverings over this issue have become increasingly dominated by moral and religious arguments coming from a wide spectrum (politically speaking) of denominational groups. Most of the current arguments center around the nature and meaning of human life and also the question of when a fetus becomes a "human." In the first article, "Taking Life Seriously: The Case Against *Roe v. Wade*," Richard Stith takes an anti-abortion position from a "left" political position. Much of his position revolves around a civil liberties point-of-view, stating among other things that civil liberties should apply to the unborn just as they do to others. Professor Stith, who has authored articles in prior editions of this book, can be counted on for interesting and thought-provoking arguments that are usually quite different from those that are ordinarily heard.

The second article, "Concerning Abortion: An Attempt at a Rational View," takes a careful look at the question of when human life begins, based on a pro-choice point of view. The writer effectively calls into question many of the statements made by those who claim that a potential human is the same as a viable, fully developed human.

The third article is a first-person account of a young, unmarried woman's experience in obtaining a legal abortion in a well-run clinic. The article is amazingly neutral on abortion in general. The writer is obviously in favor of having one herself, although her own feelings seem to be ambivalent.

NOTES

1   "Legal Abortion: How Safe? How Available? How Costly?" *Consumer Reports,* 37 (July 1972), p. 467.

2   *Consumer Reports,* op. cit., p.469.

3   National Center for Health Statistics, *Monthly Vital Statistics Report,* "Induced Terminations of Pregnancy: Reporting States, 1977 and 1978," Vol. 30, No. 6, (Supplement), U.S. Department of Health and Human Services, 1981.

4   National Center for Health Statistics, *Monthly Vital Statistics Report,* "Induced Terminations of Pregnancy: Reporting States, 1982 and 1983," Vol. 35, No. 3 (Supplement), U. S. Department of Health and Human Services, July 1986.

5   *Intercom,* Population Reference Bureau, Inc., Vol.9, No. 11, November/December 1981, p. 11; and National Center for Health Statistics, *Monthly Vital Statistics Report,* "Advance Report on Final Natality Statistics, 1983," U. S. Department of Health and Human Services, September 1985.

6   *The Clarion Ledger/Jackson Daily News,* Sunday, October 18, 1981, p. 16E.

17.

Taking Life Seriously:
The Case Against Roe v. Wade

Richard Stith

(Editor's Note: What follows is the testimony of Professor Stith before the U. S. Senate Subcommittee on Constitutional Amendments on the subject of proposed amendments relating to abortion.)

Let me first remark in passing that I am not entirely satisfied with any of the proposed amendments. As someone sympathetic both to the pro-life position and to democratic socialism, I would like to see both the unborn and the born guaranteed a right to life in the full sense: that is, a right not only against public or private violence, but also against the evils of poverty, disease, ignorance, class prejudice, and the like. The right to life ought to include a right to that level of welfare minimally necessary for a decent existence. However, I realize such a right is not under consideration today, so I will go on to the matters here at issue.

As you know, the *Roe v. Wade* decision grants a constitutional right to abortion throughout pregnancy. More specifically, there is a right to end what the court calls the "potential life" of the fetus for any reason whatsoever prior to viability, and for any reason of maternal health (including "familial" or "psychological" "well-being") thereafter.[1] This decision and its progeny (ironic term) turn the early stages of our common human species into absolutely private property—virtually unlimited by public, fetal, or even paternal interests.[2]

As a teacher of comparative law, I find this decision unique in the world. No other modern domestic state or foreign nation has ever, to my knowledge, privatized the value of new human life to this degree. No one, except our

Reprinted from *The Cresset* by permission of the author.

Court, has ever left the unborn entirely without public protection for the first six months of gestation and with only nominal protection even just before birth. Moreover, this extremist position has been imposed on our country not as a matter of temporary legislative experimentation, but by practically unchangeable judicial fiat—and this with scarcely any principled basis in the Constitution.[3]

All this, however, is beside my main point today: Whatever criticisms may be levelled at the outcome of *Roe v. Wade*, far worse in my opinion is its reasoning. In order to sustain its new right to abortion, the Court pretends not to know whether actual human life ever exists prior to birth. Indeed, it treats, and requires the states to treat, unborn members of our species as merely the "potentiality of human life," even in the last trimester of pregnancy, with the lethal consequences detailed above.

To me, the greatest wrong done the unborn is just this failure to take them into consideration as actual living human beings. The Court has closed its eyes to the reality of abortion and has blindfolded our legislatures. I am not arguing for absolutism: I can understand (though I disagree with) someone who favors capital punishment as a necessary evil, arguing that the interests of felons are outweighed by the interests of society. But I would be dismayed and dumbfounded by someone who claimed that felons had lost the right to be considered actual human beings whose interests should at all be taken into account. Similarly, I can respect and live in disagreement with those who admit and regret that abortion destroys a little human being, but who honestly believe private freedom to be more important than a young life.[4] But if we have any compassion for what we ourselves once were or any sense of the intrinsic dignity of life, we ought at least to acknowledge the unborn we cannot or will not save.

Nor is this callousness toward the unborn without its effect on the moral and legal rights of the rest of us. For consider: the court is saying that after eight months of gestation a child in the womb is still only a potential life which can be intentionally destroyed for the sake of familial or psychological well-being, while another eight-month-old fetus born prematurely is an actual human life with full human rights. But the two beings are developmentally identical, differing only in location and mode of nutrition and oxygenation. Would an I.V. and an oxygen tent make someone not alive or not human? Clearly not. Would someone who really cared about the rights of new-born infants completely ignore identical infants endangered in the womb? I think not. He or she would take them into account to the same degree in or out of the womb,[5] even if other interests (say, privacy) provided a greater counterbalance of value prior to birth.

Therefore, and this is my fundamental point, if we do not take the interests of the unborn as actual living human beings into consideration, we cannot logically claim to really care about the right to life even *after* birth. If we are willing lethally to ignore someone when he or she is hidden from sight, we cannot care sincerely and in principle about his or her life when it is in full view. In graphic terms, the nurse who both cares for premature babies and does quasi-elective late-term abortions is involved in a contradiction which cannot be resolved except by either ceasing to do abortions or by becoming equally callous to life after birth.

Put more generally, *Roe v. Wade*, by arbitrarily ignoring the actual existence of life prior to birth, commits us to a nominalist or conventionalist view of human rights.[6] If the definition of when a human being exists can be arbitrary, then the human rights which supposedly accompany that existence likewise are recognized arbitrarily. Such rights are subject to rescission at any time.

Of course, as long as we are strong enough or valuable enough, we are no doubt not in personal danger of losing our rights. But the safest as well as the highest path in the defense of civil rights is to patrol the perimeters of principle, to close up every single opening. For to affirm a single arbitrary exception to a principle, such as the right to life, means that the whole remaining structure can no longer *logically* be defended. Indeed, already anyone who arbitrarily disregards human life can rightly claim that he is only doing what the Court has done. If he is punished, this can seem to him only an act of power rather than one of equal justice.

REASON AS A WEAPON AGAINST POWER

There is one further harm done by *Roe v. Wade* to civil rights in general: it eliminates reason as a weapon against power. If the fundamental facts on which the law is based are to be finally and arbitrarily defined by the court to suit its wishes, then no one can even sensibly object to the laws which govern us. Pro-lifers, for example, argue that certain facts (such as the heartbeat, brainwaves, or physical appearance of the unborn) indicate that abortion kills a human being, and they are frequently met with the response that there is no point in claiming abortion kills since the Court has decided the issue once and for all. Such a world is an Orwellian nightmare, just as in *1984* one could not sensibly be a pacifist because war was officially defined as peace. If the factual concepts on which legal decisions are based are stipulatively defined in ways which can support only the results reached, the possibility of reasoned public criticism is eliminated.

What can be done to reverse these effects of *Roe v. Wade*? To my mind, the simplest and best would be simply to recognize the developing human embryo and fetus to be a constitutional person under the Fifth and Fourteenth Amendments. As a person, he or she would have to be taken into consideration in all legislation related to pregnancy, and could no longer be declared officially to have only a potential or doubtful existence. Of course, even persons do not have absolute rights, and equal protection does not mean identical treatment but only non-arbitrary treatment. Calling the unborn legal persons for purposes of the right to life means only that their lives cannot be surrendered without a compelling state interest. And, to my mind, the unique conditions of pregnancy—such as privacy, emotional distress, and sexual inequality—together with public concerns such as the difficulty of enforcing child protective laws make it reasonable, for example, not to punish the woman criminally at all—and instead to focus on other ways to limit abortion (such as by requiring prior counselling, as was done in West Germany, or by penalizing the abortionist).

Personhood for the unborn, in other words, would not lock us into some kind of rigid policy of treating abortion legally as murder. It would ensure only that the unborn's interests are taken into account like anyone else's, that we make a good faith effort to protect them as part of our community, not that their interests become the whole of our concerns. Even calling the right to life "paramount" or adding the phrase "no unborn person shall be deprived of life by any other person," in my opinion, can express no more than an ideal. It does not mandate the enforcement of this ideal by absolute means which do not take into account the other interests at stake.

Unfortunately, however, a personhood-conferring amendment may be politically difficult to pass. This is so not because such an amendment would be in fact overly rigid, but because it can easily be distorted in the minds of non-lawyers to appear to be absolutist. By acting as though the word "equal" meant "identical," opponents of fetal personhood are already claiming that passage of a Human Life Amendment would cause every woman having an abortion to be prosecuted for murder, and everyone miscarrying to be liable for manslaughter. We may well regret such scare tactics, which are reminiscent of the equally misleading claims so far used to defeat the ERA (such as the argument that it would require coeducational bathrooms). But they are nevertheless real and, in my opinion, make the success of a personhood Human Life Amendment highly doubtful at this time.

It is the great merit of SJR 110, the "Human Life Federalism Amendment," that it cannot be accused of locking the nation into any kind of absolutism in either direction. By leaving abortion up to Congress and the state legislatures to regulate, it permits divergent and evolving legislation, the correction of mistakes, and open-minded debate by all concerned. And, alone among all the proposals before you, it clearly rebukes the Supreme Court for intruding into the realm reserved for legislation.

REMOVING THE BLINDFOLD OF *ROE V. WADE*

Does it also overcome the greatest flaw in *Roe v. Wade* to which I have pointed: pretending, and requiring the states to pretend, not to know whether actual human life exists prior to birth? Now, the amendment proposed does not point to the unborn child and say "Look, there is a person." But it does remove the blindfold fastened onto all of us by *Roe v. Wade*. It does permit us to look and see and conceptualize the facts for ourselves. And I am confident that for the most part the unborn will be acknowledged and protected—primarily because (in the absence of religious myth) there is no non-arbitrary way to exclude unborn children from the concept of "human being" without also excluding newborn infants, an exclusion which is still intuitively unacceptable to most people.

An arbitrary or nominalist definition of who is a human being will thus no longer be required by our Constitution. The precedent for further mandatory dehumanization is excised.

At the same time, reason can again appeal to facts against power. The *1984* axiom that "war is peace" is no longer official policy. Of course, neither is it stated in the amendment that "war is war," but frankly I am satisfied to be able to argue the issue by appealing directly to the facts and concepts at issue.

Under this amendment, we may find ourselves in the minority, but we will not find ourselves excluded from debate by prior stipulated definitions of the beings whose interests are at issue. We may disagree with our fellow citizens, but we will not find ourselves alienated from the fundamental law of our land. And even in disagreement there is a bond to our neighbors in the hope of persuasion: political dialogue and accommodation become once again worthwhile because local political decisions can and must be made. Free speech itself can again matter because it can be effective speech.

NOTES

1   *Roe v. Wade*, 93 S. Ct. 705, 732-33 (1973) and *Doe v. Bolton*, 93 S. Ct. 739, 746 (1973). In the recent funding decision, *Harris v. McRae*, 100 S. Ct. 2671, 2687-2688 (1980), it was taken for granted by all parties and by the Court that even in the third trimester maternal health broadly defined outweighs the "potential life" of the fetus.

2   See *Planned Parenthood of Central Missouri v. Danforth*, 96 S. Ct. 2831 (1976).

3   See the consensus of most academics on this matter well summarized by Senator Orrin Hatch in the *Congressional Record* for September 21, 1981, at S10195.

4   Most of the rest of the world appears to admit that abortion takes a human life, even when the practice is defended. For example, a West German Constitutional Court dissenting opinion supported the decriminalization of abortion in the first trimester, but nonetheless stated: "[T]he value of each individual human being is self-evidently a central value of the legal order. It is *uncontested* [emphasis added] that the constitutional duty to protect this life also includes its preliminary stages prior to birth." "West German Abortion Decision," translated by J. D. Gorby and R. E. Jonas, 9 *John Marshall Journal of Practice and Procedure* 605, 663 (1976).

5   I am assuming here that neither ignorance nor religious revelation can be invoked here constitutionally to allege that the minor physical differences in and out of the womb are metaphysically major. Other ages may well have been able honestly to draw lines which modern medical knowledge and the secular state prevent us from doing.

6   The conventionalism of *Roe v. Wade* is also known by the fact that Justice Blackmun appeals to the conclusions of past ages and religions to support

his position, without inquiring into the validity of the fact and value premises supporting such conclusions. If he wanted to find out a true or right answer regarding abortion, he would obviously have to make such an inquiry. (We would not think it a sufficient argument for the permissibility of slavery that most ages have thought it justified.) Instead, he seems to treat the definition of life as a matter of mere social convention. See *Roe* at 715 ff., 730. *Cf.* footnote 5 *supra*.

18.

Concerning Abortion: An Attempt at a Rational View

Charles Hartshorne

My onetime colleague T. V. Smith once wrote a book called *Beyond Conscience*, in which he waxed eloquent in showing "the harm that good men do." To live according to one's conscience may be a fine thing, but what if A's conscience leads A to try to compel B and C to live, not according to B's or C's conscience, but according to A's? That is what many opponents of abortion are trying to do. To propose a constitutional amendment to this effect is one of the most outrageous attempts to tyrannize over others that I can recall in my long lifetime as an American citizen. Proponents of the anti-abortion amendment make their case, if possible, even worse when they defend themselves with the contention, "It isn't my conscience only— it is a commandment of religion." For now one particular form of religion (certainly not the only form) is being used in an attempt to tyrannize over other forms of religious or philosophical belief. The separation of church and state evidently means little to such people.

IN WHAT SENSE "HUMAN"?

Ours is a country that has many diverse religious groups and many people who cannot find truth in any organized religious body. It is a country that has great difficulty in effectively opposing forms of killing that *everyone* admits to be wrong. Those who would saddle the legal system with matters about which consciences sincerely and strongly differ show a disregard of the country's primary needs. (The same is to be said about crusades to make things difficult for homosexuals.) There can be little freedom if we lose sight of the vital distinction between moral questions and legal ones. The law compels and coerces, with the implicit threat of violence; morals seek to persuade. It is a poor society that forgets the difference.

What is the *moral* question regarding abortion? We are told that the fetus is alive and that therefore killing it is wrong. Since mosquitoes, bacteria, apes, and whales are alive also, the argument is less than clear. Even plants are alive. I am not impressed by the rebuttal, "But plants, mosquitoes, bacteria, and whales are not human, and the fetus is." For the issue now becomes, *in what sense* is the fetus human? No one denies that its origin is human, as is its *possible* destiny. But the same is true of every unfertilized egg in the body of a nun. Is it wrong that some such eggs are not made or allowed to become human individuals?

Granted that a fetus is human in origin and possible destiny, in what further sense is it human? The entire problem lies here. If there are pro-life activists who have thrown much light on this question, I do not know their names.

One theologian who writes on the subject—Paul Ramsey—thinks that a human egg cell becomes a human individual with a moral claim to survive if it has been fertilized. Yet this egg cell has none of the qualities that we have in mind when we proclaim our superior worth over the chimpanzees or dolphins. It cannot speak, reason, or judge between right and wrong. It cannot have personal relations, without which a person is not functionally a person at all, until months—and not, except minimally, until years—have passed. And even then, it will not be a person in the normal sense unless some who are already fully persons have taken pains to help it become a human being in the full value sense, functioning as such. The anti-abortionist is commanding some person or persons to undertake this effort. For without it, the fetus *never* will be human in the relevant sense. It will be human only in origin but otherwise a subhuman animal.

The fertilized egg is an individual egg but not an individual human being. For such a being is, in its body, a multicellular organism, a *metazoan*—to use the scientific Greek—and the egg is a single cell. The first thing the egg cell does is to begin dividing into many cells. For some weeks the fetus is not a single individual at all, but a colony of cells. During its first weeks there seems to be no ground for regarding the fetus as comparable to an individual animal. Only in possible or probable destiny is it an individual. Otherwise it is an organized society of single-celled individuals.

A possible individual person is one thing; an actual person is another. If this difference is not important, what is? There is in the long run no room in the solar system, or even in the known universe, for all human eggs—even all fertilized eggs, as things now stand—to become human persons. Indeed, it is mathematically demonstrable that the present rate of population growth must be lowered somehow. It is not a moral imperative that all possibilities of human persons become actual persons.

Of course, some might say that the fertilized egg already has a human soul, but on what evidence? The evidence of soul in the relevant sense is the capacity to reason, judge right and wrong, and the like.

GENETIC AND OTHER INFLUENCES

One also might say that since the fertilized egg has a combination of genes (the units of physical inheritance) from both parents, in this sense it is already a human individual. There are two objections, either one in my opinion conclusive but only one of which is taken into account by Ramsey. The one he does mention is that identical twins have the same gene combination. The theologian does not see this as decisive, but I do.

The other objection is that it amounts to a very crude form of materialism to identify individuality with the gene combinations. Genes are the chemical bearers of inherited traits. This chemical basis of inheritance presumably influences everything about the development of the individual – *influences* but does not fully determine. To say that the entire life of the person is determined by heredity is a theory of unfreedom that my religious conviction can regard only as monstrous. And there are biophysicists and neurophysiologists who agree with me.

From the gene-determined chemistry to a human person is a long, long step. As soon as the nervous system forming in the embryo begins to function as a whole – and not before – the cell colony begins to turn into a genuinely individual animal. One might suppose reasonably that this change is accompanied by some extremely primitive individual animal feelings. They cannot be recognizably human feelings, much less human thoughts, and cannot compare with the feelings of a porpoise or chimpanzee in level of consciousness. That much seems as certain as anything about the fetus except its origin and possible destiny. The nervous system of a very premature baby has been compared by an expert to that of a pig. And we know, if we know anything about this matter, that it is the nervous system that counts where individuality is concerned.

Identical twins are different individuals, each unique in consciousness. Though having the same genetic make-up, they will have been differently situated in the womb and hence will have received different stimuli. For that reason, if for no other, they will have developed differently, especially in their brains and nervous systems.

But there are additional reasons for the difference in development. One is the role of chance, which takes many forms. We are passing through a great cultural change in which the idea, long dominant in science, that chance is "only a word for our ignorance of causes" is being replaced by the view that the real laws of nature are probabilistic and allow for aspects of genuine chance.

Another reason is that it is reasonable to admit a reverse influence of the developing life of feelings in the fetus on the nervous system, as well as of the system upon the feelings. And since I, along with some famous philosophers and scientists, believe in freedom (not solely of mature human beings but—in some slight degree—of all individuals in nature, down to the atoms and further), I hold that even in the fetus the incipient individual unconsciously is making what on higher levels we call "decisions." These decisions influence the developing nervous system. Thus to a certain extent we *make our own bodies* by our feelings and thoughts. An English poet with Platonic ideas expressed this concept as follows:

> The body from the soul its form doth take,
> For soul is form and doth the body make.

The word soul is, for me, incidental. The point is that feelings, thoughts, experiences react on the body and partly mold its development.

THE RIGHTS OF PERSONS

Paul Ramsey argues (as does William Buckley in a letter to me) that if a fetus is not fully human then neither is an infant. Of course an infant is not fully human. No one thinks it can, while an infant, be taught to speak, reason, or judge right and wrong. But it is much closer to that stage than is a three-month fetus. It is beginning to have primitive social relations not open to a fetus; and since there is no sharp line anywhere between an infant and a child able to speak a few words, or between the latter and a child able to speak very many words, we have to regard the infant as significantly different from a three-month or four-month fetus. Nevertheless, I have little sympathy with the idea that infanticide is just another form of murder. Persons who already are functionally persons in the full sense have more important rights even than infants. Infanticide can be wrong without being fully comparable to the killing of persons in the full sense.

Does this distinction apply to the killing of a hopelessly senile person (or one in a permanent coma)? For me it does. I hope no one will think that if, God forbid, I ever reach that stage, it must be for my sake that I should be treated with the respect due to normal human beings. Rather, it is for the sake of others that such respect may be imperative. Symbolically, one who has been a person may have to be treated as a person. There are difficulties and hazards in not so treating such individuals.

Religious people (I would so describe myself) might argue that once a fetus starts to develop, it is for God, not human beings, to decide whether the fetus survives and how long it lives. This argument assumes, against all evidence, that human life spans are independent of human decision. Our medical hygiene has altered radically the original "balance of nature." Hence the population explosion. Our technology makes pregnancy more and more a matter of human decision; more and more our choices are influencing the weal and woe of the animals on this earth. It is an awesome responsibility, but one that we cannot avoid. And after all, the book of Genesis essentially predicted our dominion over terrestrial life. In addition, no one is proposing to make abortion compulsory for those morally opposed to it. I add that everyone who smokes is taking a hand in deciding how long he or she will live. Also everyone who, by failing to exercise reasonably, allows his or her heart to lose its vigor. Our destinies are not simply "acts of God."

I might be told that if I value my life I must be glad that I was not aborted in the fetus stage. Yes, I am glad, but this expression does not constitute a claim to having already had a "right," against which no other right could prevail, to the life I have enjoyed. I feel no indignation or horror at contemplating the idea that the world might have had to do without me. The world could have managed, and as for what I would have missed, there would have been no such "I" to miss it.

POTENTIAL, NOT ACTUAL

With almost everything they say, the fanatics against abortion show that they will not, or cannot, face the known facts of this matter. The inability of a fetus to say "I" is not merely a lack of skill; there is nothing there to which the pronoun properly could refer. A fetus is not a person but a *potential* person. The "life" to which "pro-life" refers is nonpersonal, by any criterion that makes sense to some of us. It is subpersonal animal life only. The mother, however, *is* a person.

I resent strongly the way many males tend to dictate to females their behavior, even though many females encourage them in this. Of course, the male parent of a fetus also has certain rights, but it remains true that the female parent is the one most directly and vitally concerned.

I shall not forget talking about this whole matter to a wonderful woman, the widow of a philosopher known for his idealism. She was doing social work with young women and had come to the conclusion that abortion is, in some cases, the lesser evil. She told me that her late husband had said, when she broached the subject to him, "But you can't do that." "My darling," she replied, "we *are* doing it." I see no reason to rate the consciences of the pro-lifers higher than this woman's conscience. She knew what the problem was for certain mothers. In a society that flaunts sex (its pleasures more than its serious hazards, problems, and spiritual values) in all the media, makes it difficult for the young to avoid unwanted pregnancy, and does little to help them with the most difficult of all problems of self-discipline, we tell young persons that they are murderers if they resort to abortion. And so we should not be surprised that Margaret Mead, that clear-sighted observer of our society (and of other societies), should say, "Abortion is a nasty thing, but our society deserves it." Alas, it is too true.

I share something of the disgust of hard-core opponents of abortion that contraceptives, combined with the availability of abortion, might deprive sexual intercourse of spiritual meaning. For me the sacramental view of marriage always has had appeal, and my life has been lived accordingly. Abortion is indeed a nasty thing, but unfortunately there are in our society many even nastier things, like the fact that some children are growing up unwanted. This for my conscience is a great deal nastier and truly horrible. An overcrowded world is also nasty and could in a few decades become truly catastrophic.

The argument against abortion (used, I am sorry to say, by Pearl Buck) that the fetus might be a potential genius has to be balanced against the much more probable chance of its being a mediocrity or a destructive enemy of society. Every egg cell is a possible genius and also a possible monster in human form. Where do we stop in calculating such possibilities?

If some who object to abortion work to diminish the number of unwanted, inappropriate pregnancies, or to make bearing a child for adoption by persons able to be its loving foster parents more attractive than it now is, and do this with a minimum of coercion, all honor to them. In view of the population problem, the first of these remedies should have high priority.

Above all, the coercive power of our legal system, already stretched thin, must be used with caution and chiefly against evils about which there is something like universal consensus. That persons have rights is a universal belief in our society, but that a fetus is already an actual person—about that there is and there can be no consensus. Coercion in such matters is tyranny. Alas for our dangerously fragmented and alienated society if we persist in such tyranny.

19.

Inside an Abortion Clinic

Pamela Dillett

Once inside the waiting room, with Saturday Pittsburgh traffic rumbling several stories below and my legs tucked cozily under my long corduroy skirt, I felt nothing but detachment. Until I glanced up from the magazine I wasn't reading and found four pairs of terrified eyes staring at me: 14-year-old Negro eyes; the weary eyes of a wizened welfare recipient; the analytical eyes of a well-dressed young socialite with two children; the hostile eyes of an attractive college coed.

The room was more accommodating than the usual doctor's waiting room. Yosemite Sam was six-shooting out of a color-TV set. There were davenports and carpeting of a soporific blue. But this wasn't a typical waiting room, for the patients were waiting to have an abortion.

I was in my junior year and majoring in English at a large university when I suspected I was pregnant. I wasn't on the Pill, even though I had been having sexual relations. Yet I wouldn't call myself a "pregnancy-prone" woman, that is, an emotionally distraught female who subconsciously wants to get pregnant to punish her parents or for various other neurotic reasons.

I think my negligence was attributable to the fact that by getting a prescription for the Pill, I would have been consciously admitting to myself that I was freely offering a sacred part of myself to someone whom I didn't even particularly like. At that time it was easier to quash all reasoning, thereby salvaging my self-respect.

I went to the infirmary, where I was given a urinalysis and a thorough inspection of my uterus. My uterus was bluish—a sign of pregnancy—and my urinalysis read positive. "Oh Pamela," moaned the doctor, shaking his head, "you're about seven weeks pregnant."

Stupefied, I managed only to peep a fragile, "Oh."

He referred me to CHOICE, a pregnancy-information organization that helps direct a woman when she has decided what route to follow. I knew abortion was my sole alternative, and the CHOICE representative gave me all the vital information. I would need a letter from the doctor certifying pregnancy. When we decided on Pittsburgh's Women's Health Services, an abortion clinic, I was told I also would need a sanitary belt, $140 by check or money order and transportation. The representative weighted me with pamphlets and sent me on my way.

All this time I was an automaton. some subliminal defense mechanism shielded me from the pain of feeling, allowing me only one evening's copious patronage of Kleenex. In a bed I would press my disappointingly flat stomach, trying to feel, or at least fathom, what dwelled there. During class I would draw Punnett squares, trying to determine the chances of the child's eyes being blue or brown. Most of the time, though, I wasn't overly concerned.

I called Women's Health Services to set up an appointment. The arrangement-making went smoothly–I had to wait only two weeks for my appointment, and no questions were asked. This surprised me, as I still was thinking in terms of illegal abortions and expected all sorts of complications and shady inquiries. I was relieved that they asked only how many weeks pregnant I was.

I confided my pregnancy to two or three girl friends, all of whom were horrified that I wasn't having an emotional earthquake or attaching a noose to my overhead light. But what could I do? My decision was firm, there were term papers to be written, and anyway, I didn't want to torture myself with notions of murder and the implications of premarital sex.

The night before my abortion I stayed with a friend in Pittsburgh. We ate pizza, discussed men, and watched the late movie as though we were going to a Pirates' game the next day instead of to an abortion clinic.

Saturday, May 4, 1974, was sunny and cold in Pittsburgh. We took a bus from Oakland to the inner city, where, in the mammoth office building, someone probably was having the contents of her womb uprooted at that very moment. Feeling we were still adolescent rebels, we rode up the elevator muttering outrageous allegations about our mothers and the milkman–just loud enough to arouse snorts and averted eyes from the other riders.

We found our floor and an unassuming door with "Women's Health Services, Inc." on frosted glass. I guess I expected a fist-sized black widow to sail down a pole of silk, cackling, "Come in, little girl–we've been expecting you."

The spacious room was pulsing with activity and people of both sexes and assorted ages, races, and income groups. The amicable receptionist asked to see the doctor's written verdict, then gave me a formidable list to fill out of vital information, including address, age, and comprehensive medical history. After relinquishing this portrait, I was told to wait until my name was called for a blood-pressure reading, a blood test for VD, and a urinalysis.

While waiting, I noted sundry boy friends, husbands, and whole families clustered around the feminine jewel who had suffered so much. Some women, like myself, were with girl friends; a couple were alone. One little black doll who looked frighteningly young sat silently with her mother— both staring straight ahead.

A professional voice called my name and I was whisked to a treatment room for those boring sorts of tests that the doctor gives once a year. There were several nurses bustling about with crimson-filled test tubes and little containers of urine. They didn't speak much or joke around, so I ventured some lamentably inane statement like, "Boy, I hope this is one scraping I get through all right."

One nurse looked interestedly at me, one frowned, and the others ignored me. "Roll up your sleeve, please," ordered one. I wished I'd kept my incorrigible mouth shut.

Then back to the reception room, where the receptionist told me the next time I'd be called back to pay my bill. I didn't think it was quite civil of them to continue taunting me with suspense, but at the same time I was relieved that I was spared the unknown for a while.

NERVOUSNESS SETS IN

Ten minutes later I handed over my $140 money order to a matron and returned to my restless friend to await my final calling, which would involve counselling from one of the youthful staff members. This was the part I dreaded, for I expected a maternal lecture on what I had gotten myself into and an intrusive probing into my mental condition. I asked the receptionist if my friend might accompany me in the recovery room. She replied that friends weren't permitted because there would be others recuperating there and the presence of a stranger who did not share their plight might be discomfiting. I was very disappointed because I had thought I at least would get to nurse my humiliation in private.

I unshackled my friend and instructed her to return in an hour and a half, for I'd certainly be finished by then. She left with well-wishings. Now alone, I started feeling a bit nervous.

Sometime later an attractive girl in her twenty's named Sally, with smiling face and sparkling eye, wandered among playing children and cigarette-puffing fathers and asked for me. She led me out the door I had entered first, down a narrow hall, in another door, and down another hall, so that when she finally showed me into a windowless, bathroom-sized room, I could have been in Outer Mongolia for all I knew.

THE PROCEDURE EXPLAINED

She sat down opposite me and began talking while my eyes kept slipping down to the prophylactics, IUDs, and birth-control pills on the table beside me. On the wall was a diagram of a woman's reproductive system—just like the one we used to chortle over in ninth-grade health class.

Sally gave a sketch of what happens to a woman when pregnancy occurs. Then she explained what was going to happen to me and about 900,000 others that year during the latest and safest method of abortion—vacuum aspiration.

The doctor makes four injections of a Novocain derivative, usually Xylocaine, on either side of the cervix. Called a paracervical block, this process anesthetizes the cervical area against the pain of what follows. These injections include medication that helps prevent hemorrhaging.

Next a plastic tube is inserted into the uterus, and a suction pump vacuums out the fetus and any other related tissue in the uterus. When the doctor sees that no more material is traveling through the tube, he turns off the pump. He then takes a curette and scrapes once around the uterus to make certain that the contents are removed. This is not the oft-used method of the past—D and C. D and C (dilation and curettage) involves scraping during the entire lengthy procedure. The vacuum-aspiration procedure takes no more than five to seven minutes.

Sally told me there was some danger of infection or hemorrhaging and (she hated to tell me, but) women have died from the effects of induced abortion. (At that date no woman ever had died from an abortion at Pittsburgh's clinic.)

My stomach danced a quick Charleston, but she reassured me that the chances of complications arising were fairly low and that infection could be detected readily if I took my temperature late every morning and early every evening for five days following the operation. If my temperature rose to 100.4 degrees or above twice in a row, a doctor should be called, as fever indicates infection may have occurred.

Profuse bleeding would be checked periodically during the recovery period, so any hemorrhaging that occurred would be treated right there in the clinic.

A month's supply of the Pill would be handed out. The first pill was to be taken the following day because a menstrual period would begin as a result of the abortion.

ANXIETY INTRUDES

I asked a bit incredulously if she wasn't going to test my emotional stamina. She laughed and showed me the place on my record where she was to check off whether I seemed anywhere from cheerful and self-aware to depressed and unconversant. She added that unless the patient showed all signs of unwillingness to abort, the abortion would be performed.

She took my doctor's verification, made sure I had a sanitary belt (because I'd have to wear a napkin afterward), and took me to the waiting room. I sat down among four other patients, who didn't even smile in greeting.

I felt my first sense of anxiety when I noticed all those terrified eyes penetrating me as though I were either their savior or their executioner.

The least Sally could have done was to wait here with me. There's that black nymphet; why does she flog me with those monstrously huge eyes? That blonde must be six feet tall; I wonder how her boy friend . . . oh, stop it, Pam! What's on TV? Why do they have a TV? To placate us, I guess. Sally sure was nice. Here's an article on Easter dinners. A little late, isn't it? "Instead of the traditional ham and cabbage this Easter, why not dazzle them with an exotic. . ."

THE FACELESS DOCTOR

"Mary Ann, come with me, please."

Oh-oh, there goes the blonde; I wonder how she feels; ". . .dazzle them with an exotic. . . ." I bet Orb Eyes still is watching me. I'll glance up now. Yes, she is! Why doesn't she stop haunting me? I should write an article about this. How big is this room? I have to give a speech for Speech 200: The digger wasp v. the tarantula. I better turn the page. I'm dying to laugh. There are several species of digger wasp. Why are the blinds closed? Oh, Orb Eyes.

"Pam, do you want to come with me?"

Oh, Orb Eyes!

Another girl, smiling and chipper like Sally, brought me to a tiny green operating room and instructed me to go behind a partition, shuck my skirt and panties, and put on my sanitary belt. This being done, I put the tablecloth-sized covering around me—an effort at discretion that I felt was terribly ironic. I hopped onto the rectangular table and inserted my feet in stirrups: I must have looked like the hapless Thanksgiving bird about to have her cornbread stuffing ripped out of her. These preliminaries were nothing unusual; any woman who's had a pelvic examination has endured this somewhat mortifying position.

In stormed the doctor—faceless, voiceless, devoid of emotion. He didn't say hello or even glance at my face. While the assistant, Jean, made small talk with me, the doctor expertly injected the four anesthetizing shots where I never dreamed a shot could be given. I'm no stoic, and that certainly hurt, but I continued to talk with my new-found confidante while never taking my eyes off the wordless robot trespassing down there on private property.

Next he inserted the plastic tube, which Jean warned would hurt a bit. He turned on the suction pump and the room was filled with what sounded like a jackhammer and then like a dentist's drill once I got used to the sound. The accompanying pain was exactly like a severe menstrual cramp— a shrill, persistent clamoring in the abdomen that bites the lower back and thighs as well.

AT THE END, TEARS

Jean took my hand, and I knew she was scanning her mind for something diversionary to talk about. To help her out, I told her about school through gritted teeth.

The infernal machine finally stopped. It probably took all of an eternal 120 seconds.

Next he scraped the uterine walls, and that hurt like blue blazes. While I frantically wriggled my feet, I asked Jean if she had to go to college in order to do this (yes) and where did she go (Pitt) and what was her major (psychology).

Then I erupted into tears. Here I thought I had been utterly composed. I suppose the days of suppressed anxiety, the guilt, the remote possibility of death, combined with the sound of my innards changing from solid to liquid, and that villain languidly watching my blood and tissue scurry through a tube must have come to my conscious realization. And during all this, here I was discussing Jean's educational history as though we were sitting over coffee and pound cake in Stouffer's. And still that brute never looked at me.

THE RECOVERY ROOM

After a few minutes the operation was over. The doctor left. I put on my skirt and napkin and hobbled with Jean to the recovery room.

The recovery room had an airy, sunny atmosphere of near gaiety, like the initial reception room. After I was checked for bleeding and temperature, I was placed on a couch next to a pleasant-looking girl my age. We took our choice of soda, juice, coffee, tea, and cookies that a jovial nurse offered us.

I spoke with the girl (a college junior from Delaware) about our pregnancies and abortions. She eyed me warily when I seemed jubilant at the fact that she cried during the vacuum pumping.

We were to stay in the recovery room for an hour, checking temperatures and the amount of bleeding every fifteen minutes. If a woman felt well enough, she was permitted to leave in forty-five minutes.

Assorted women around the room reclined or sat up, alone with their thoughts. Almost everybody had hot water bottles on their stomachs because they had menstrual cramps. I saw a couple of women from the waiting room, including the older welfare case, who rocked alone in a corner. One girl writhed about, moaning pitifully. I didn't see Orb Eyes.

I was anxious to get back to my friend, so after forty-five minutes I checked myself out and received a thermometer, birth-control pills, and a postabortion instruction sheet.

The reception room was twice as crowded as it was when I entered it the first time. I saw by my watch that I'd been gone for three hours. When I approached my friend I winked and said, "Sorry I took so long," to the horror of a middle-aged woman sitting nearby. As we pulled on our coats, we watched two girls emerge from the recovery room, solemnly embrace solicitous boy friends, and leave, arms intertwined.

Homeward bound on the bus, I mused about abortion—about how in the reception room and the waiting room I felt hostile toward the other waiting women around me, but how in the recovery room and back in the reception room I felt kinship and understanding that arise only from mutual suffering and persecution.

I thought of the hoary legislators who flung women's lives around cigar-fumed board rooms, mindlessly condemning them to perdition for the unfortunate results of mankind's fondest pastime.

I was grateful that I had to endure only minimal psychological and physical pain rather than the torture of bearing a child that I would have resented. I was grateful, too, that I could have my abortion in a sanitary hospital environment rather than in the dusty back rooms that housed deathbeds for many victims. As if to purge myself at last of subjugation and three hours of a knowledge that shouldn't have had to be known, I leaned out the bus window and vomited.

Part

Seven

Divorce and Remarriage

The topic of divorce generates a whole range of additional topics: child custody, single parenthood, remarriage, and reconstituted families, to mention the major ones. The earliest editions of this book focused upon the issue of reform of the divorce laws. A later edition added the issue of custody of children after divorce. The current edition now includes the additional topics of single parenthood and stepfamilies. Whereas, divorce reform and custody were clearly issues with several positions in contention with one another, single parenthood and, particularly, stepfamilies are less clear as issues, in that specific and opposing positions have yet to emerge on these topics. Nevertheless, they are topics of increasing concern to both the society and to family professionals.

Regarding divorce, the decade of the 1970s was one of significant reform, insofar as changes in the divorce laws and procedures were concerned. During this period most of the states made important changes in their laws, and these changes have gone far in making divorce a less traumatic and emotionally devastating experience than often was the case in the past. Nevertheless, divorce itself continues to be an important issue for American families in that it affects about 1.2 million families each year.[1] Of course, one reason why divorce has always created such concern is the fact that children are often involved, and children are profoundly affected by their parents' divorces. About half of all divorces involve no children, but those that do average almost 2 children per divorce.[2]

As divorce reform itself became less an issue, attention began to shift to one of the more difficult aspects of ending a marriage, the question of how to resolve disputes that arise over the custody of children, a question that has not been dealt with sufficiently in the course of the recent reforms. Furthermore, this is a growing issue because of the increasing number of fathers who are seeking custody of their children, in the face of judicial customs and habits that have tended to favor women in custody disputes. Although divorce reform as an issue still contains several unresolved questions, increased attention is being given to other major consequences of divorce, namely single parenthood and the formation of reconstituted families through remarriage. Therefore, reflecting the articles in this section, this opening commentary will center around the topics of divorce reform, child custody, single parenthood, and reconstituted families.

DIVORCE REFORM

The legal control of marriage, divorce, and child custody are areas left to the various states by the U.S. Constitution. Thus, each state has its own laws concerning divorce and the manner in which one might be obtained. Although there were a few significant differences from one state to the next, most state laws were basically similar until the early 1970s. At that time the divorce reform movement took off at full speed, starting with California's total overhaul of its statutes and procedures. In the ensuing decade, almost all of the states followed suit, and presently only two or three states have not yet made significant changes in their divorce laws.

Reform was brought about through variations on two basic approaches: one approach was to totally overhaul the old laws so as to institute what is termed a "pure no-fault" system; the other method was to simply "patch-up" the old statutes so as to institute some of the features of the no-fault approach, while retaining the basic structure of the old laws. Although most reformers preferred the former approach, most states chose the easier route of the latter method which, unfortunately, retained one of the major shortcomings of the old divorce laws, namely the *adversary system*. The old type of legal structure requires an "adversary" proceeding in which one party to the divorce must sue the other party, based on the misdeeds or "faults" of the party being sued. Thus, as in most court proceedings, there had to be an innocent party and a guilty party, these two being the adversaries. This term is simply a legal nicety for "enemies." Divorce, therefore, would proceed under the assumption that one spouse was at fault while the other was blameless. It does not require very much study of marital failure to recognize that divorce is almost never caused by one partner alone. Thus, this adversarial method of ending marriages had little to do with the realities of why marriages failed.

In going to the pure no-fault laws, some states chose to totally abandon the adversary system. Here, the "dissolution" of a marriage is based not upon any wrong-doing by one spouse against the other, but upon a determination that the marriage is "irretrievably broken." Furthermore, such matters as child custody, spousal maintenance, and property division are not supposed to be based upon any considerations of spousal misbehavior. Rather than suing one another, the couple petition the court for the dissolution of the marriage. Whereas the adversary system tended to generate conflict and animosity, the no-fault system allows a couple to end their marriage on a calmer note and without a lot of irrelevant accusations.

Reforms in those states that chose the "patch-up" method were brought about in one of two ways: either by adding the ground of "incompatibility," which would not require either spouse to be at fault, or by adding the ground of "irreconcilable differences." Either method, however, holds onto the basic adversary concept, and represents only limited reform. Thus, if a couple were unable to agree on one or more of the peripheral matters such as custody or maintenance, simply having the availability of the fault-finding adversary method creates a climate of coercion, conflict and tension. In many of these states, then, there has been only partial reform and there is still room for further improvement in the divorce laws.

The first article in this section presents an excellent contrast of the old divorce laws with the new ones. The author, Lenore Weitzman, a leading authority on this topic, argues that changing these laws not only changes the way in which marriages are ended, but also some of the basic elements of marriage itself. By changing the values and norms that undergird divorce, the values and norms of marriage are also subject to change. She further concludes that divorce reforms have not fully dealt with the problems presented by expecting women to immediately be able to assume roles of equality and independence.

CHILD CUSTODY

One of the desired consequences of divorce reform was a change in the manner in which child custody decisions would be made. However, although there have been some procedural changes, up to now there has not been a great deal of change in the *outcomes* of custody disputes. Most of the states that have revised their laws require that child custody be awarded without any regard to marital fault, and usually without any regard to the sex of the spouses. Reformers thought that the changes would result in more fathers getting custody. Nevertheless, these reforms have produced almost no change in the proportion of husbands and wives who obtain child custody, with the proportion of husbands gaining custody remaining at about 10-12 per cent.[3]

Even with new laws, custody decisions are still very much a judicial prerogative, and judges have shown a reluctance to change the way in which they have made those decisions in the past. Getting judges to operate without their traditional biases with respect to men as custodial parents probably will be far more difficult than it was to get legislatures to revise the laws. Thus, as an issue, the concern with divorce reform has shifted to the remaining problem of how to institute more equity into decisions regarding the custody and financial support of the children of divorce. Some improvements can be gained through the fine-tuning of some of the new no-fault laws.

However, more significant changes will require alterations of some of the traditional doctrines under which most courts reach their decisions, as well as continued pressure on the courts by men who desire to remain a viable part of their children's lives after divorce.

Custody decisions in the past were dominated by two major legal doctrines that created the current situation so far as child custody is concerned. These were the "tender years" doctrine and the "best interests of the child" doctrine. The first of these was the idea that a child was a delicate, sensitive, and impressionable creature in need of a great deal of direct care and attention during the early years of its life, a doctrine that favored mothers. The second was that any decision made concerning a child should reflect what the courts believed to be the best interests of the child, without regard to the personal wishes of either the father or the mother. Given the fault system of divorce, in which the husband usually was the one found to be "at fault," both legally and in the popular view of divorce, these two doctrines were bound to result in the automatic and habitual awarding of the custody of children to mothers, regardless of their fitness to rear children. Society and the courts simply could not conceive of a man *wanting* to rear his children after divorce, and furthermore, they did not think that he was capable of doing it anyway. In such a social and legal climate, few fathers ever went to the trouble to gain custody, and when they tried, most inevitably lost out in their efforts.

Today there is a changing view of fatherhood in which fathers increasingly are seen as playing a vital role in the lives of their children, as more than just the economic provider. As the new laws put more pressure on ex-wives to be self-supporting, some are beginning to decide that they and their children might be better off with the fathers having custody. In other cases, the courts are beginning to give a little more consideration to the interests of fathers in these cases. The "tender years" doctrine has begun to lose some of its influence, although the "best interest" doctrine is still quite strong. Nevertheless, these changes have not fully taken hold and as yet have had only a minimal impact upon the outcomes of custody disputes. Even in those states in which the laws specify that custody should be decided without reference to the sex of the parent, the vast majority of judges are still automatically awarding custody to the mother if she desires it.

A new alternative in the matter of child custody has emerged in recent years: the practice of *joint* or *shared* custody. These forms are more a product of parental initiative than of legislative or judicial reform. In fact, courts and lawyers have been somewhat reluctant in their acceptance of these kinds of custody arrangements. On the other hand, ex-spouses see these approaches as an improvement over a system that tends to cut one parent out of the life of their child, and these new alternatives are also seen as being more equalitarian. There are, however, enough unanswered questions and differences of opinion over joint and shared custody to create an issue that may take several years to resolve. The second article in this section, "The Debate Over Joint Custody," deals with some of the questions and issues related to the practice of joint or shared custody of children by both the ex-spouses.

SINGLE PARENTHOOD

One major consequence of divorce is the situation of single parenthood. This term usually brings up a picture of the divorced woman attempting to cope with the problems of raising children while at the same time trying to hold down a job and establish a new life without a husband. However, single parenthood includes many more lifestyles and situations than this common stereotype. In fact, divorced mothers represent 46 per cent of mother-child single parent families, and this is the largest single type, but there are also never-married mothers (20 per cent of mother-child families) and widowed mothers (9 percent).[4] Presumably, the remaining mother-child families include those without husbands/fathers due to separation, desertion, imprisonment, or other unknown reasons. Of course, there are also father-child families that constitute about 11 per cent of single parent families.

Contrary to the stereotype, many single parent families do not live alone. Rather, they live with one or more relatives or are a part of other households belonging to persons to whom they are not kin. Single parent families may also contain grown children. Membership in this single parent category is highly transitory. Many divorced mothers (and fathers) with children remarry, and many never-married mothers also eventually marry, although with limited levels of stability. Some evidence suggests that single mothers with several children actually marry quicker after divorce than do mothers with one or two children.[5] The presence of several children may put greater pressure upon the mother to reestablish a more financially stable family situation than is the case with the mother with fewer children.

Greatest growth among single parents is in the category of never-married mothers. Considerable media attention has been given recently to this situation among black women. Currently, one-half of all black families with young children are single parent families. Many of these are never-married mothers due largely to the fact that (in 1985) almost 75 per cent of all children born to black women were born to single mothers.[6] However, single parenthood among never-married white women has also increased significantly in recent years.

The third article in this section delineates a typology of single parent families. It is based more upon the lifestyles they attempt to create for themselves, rather than upon the household categories mentioned above. However, the circumstances that yield these categories, that is, household characteristics, do play an important role in determining the kinds of lifestyles available for single parent families.

RECONSTITUTED FAMILIES

Most people who divorce eventually remarry, many within a short period of time. Remarriages that involve children result in the creation of *reconstituted* families, also called stepfamilies or blended families. The type of family unit that evolves from a remarriage is dependent upon the structure of the household that is set up. For example, when two divorced people remarry, either or both might have children from the former marriage, and either or both might have custody of their children. Depending upon who brings how many children into the new household, there can be numerous possibilities as to what structure the reconstituted family might take. The term *stepfamily* usually refers to the remarriage in which only one spouse has children in the new household. The *blended family* usually refers to the situation in which both new spouses bring children into the household. In most cases, the more children involved, the more complicated will be the structure and the greater the possibilities for difficulties in adjusting to the new arrangements.

Almost a third of couples now marrying are entering remarriages, and a large portion of these involve children. More often than not, the children in the new family are those of the wife since wives usually get custody of children after divorce. Thus, the most common type of reconstituted family is the stepfamily in which a new husband sets up a household with a new wife and her children. This is probably also the least complicated structure compared to the other possibilities, but none of the types of reconstituted families is without its special problems and difficulties. The potential for problems is compounded by the residual effects of the former marital and parental relationships.

The last article of this section demonstrates the major aspects of the adjustment process faced by new members of these types of families. Recognition that there are new and different role needs and possibilities is crucial, and the article presents a sort of process through which new stepfamilies might move as they attempt to develop a cohesive household structure. In presenting the model, the authors reveal quite a bit about the workings of reconstituted families.

NOTES

1 National Center for Health Statistics, *Monthly Vital Statistics Report*, "Advance Report of Final Divorce Statistics, 1984," Vol. 35, No. 6 (Supplement), U.S. Department of Health and Human Services, September 1986.

2 Ibid.

3 U. S. Bureau of Census. *Current Population Reports*, "Household and Family Characteristics: March 1985," Series P-20, No. 411, November 1986.

4 Arthur J. Norton and Paul C. Glick, "One parent Families: A Social and Economic Profile," *Family Relations* 35 (January 1986):9-17.

5 Ibid.

6 U. S. Bureau of Census, Op. cit.

20.

The Transformation of Legal Marriage Through No-Fault Divorce

Lenore J. Weitzman and Ruth B. Dixon

Divorce and family breakdown constitute one of the major social problems in the United States today. In 1975 alone more than three million men, women, and minor children were involved in a divorce. In the future it is likely that one third to one half of all the adults in the United States, and close to one third of the minor children under eighteen, will be affected by a divorce or dissolution. These data reflect not only the numerical importance of divorce but its increased social significance as well. Whereas divorce might have been considered a "deviant family pattern" in the past, it rapidly is becoming accepted as a possible (though not yet a probable) outcome of marriage.

Since 1970 there has been a major reform in divorce law that attempts to institutionalize fundamental social changes in family patterns. Commonly referred to as no-fault divorce, this new legislation seeks to alter the definition of marriage, the relationship between husbands and wives, and the economic and social obligations of former spouses to each other and to their children after divorce.

In 1970, California instituted the first no-fault divorce law in the United States. Since then, fourteen other states have adopted "pure" no-fault divorce laws and an additional thirteen states have added no-fault grounds to their existing grounds for divorce. No-fault divorce has been praised as the embodiment of "modern" and "enlightened" law and heralded as the forerunner of future family law in the United States.

It also has been strongly attacked for "destroying the family" and for causing irreparable harm to women. This paper aims at analyzing the effects of this new legislation on both marriage and divorce.

The laws governing divorce tell us how a society defines marriage and where it sets the boundaries for appropriate marital behavior. One generally can examine the way a society defines marriage by examining its provisions for divorce, for it is at the point of divorce that a society has the opportunity to reward the marital behavior it approves of and to punish spouses who have violated its norms. In addition, in virtually all societies that allow divorce, it is assumed that people who once were married continue to have obligations to each other; and these obligations reflect the rights and duties of marriage itself.

This paper is divided into three sections. It begins with a discussion of traditional legal marriage, followed by a review of traditional divorce law. The last section examines the aims of the no-fault legislation and its implications for traditional family roles.

TRADITIONAL LEGAL MARRIAGE

The origins of Anglo-American family law can be traced to the tenth or eleventh century, when Christianity became sufficiently influential in Britain to enable the Church to assert its rules effectively (Clark, 1968: 281). Traditionally legal marriage was grounded firmly in the Christian conception of marriage as a holy union between a man and woman. Marriage was a sacrament, a commitment to join together for life: "to take each other to love and to cherish, in sickness and in health, for better, for worse, until death do us part."

The nature of the marital relationship and the legal responsibilities of the spouses were specified by law—by statute, case law, and common law. Although a thorough analysis of legal marriage obviously is beyond the scope of this paper (but see Clark, 1968; Kay, 1974; Weitzman, 1979), five important features can be summarized briefly as follows: First, legal marriage was limited to a single man and a single woman; bigamy, polygamy, and homosexual unions were prohibited. Second, legal marriage was monogamous. The spouses were to remain sexually faithful to each other and adultery explicitly was prohibited. Third, marriage was for procreation. One of the major objects of matrimony was the bearing and rearing of (legitimate) children (*Reynolds v. Reynolds*, 1862).

Fourth, legal marriage established a hierarchical relationship between the spouses: the husband was the head of the family, with his wife and children subordinate to him. The husband's authority was based on the common-law doctrine of coverture, which established the legal fiction that a husband and wife took a single legal identity upon marriage—the identity of the husband. At common law a married woman became a *feme covert*, a legal nonperson, under her husband's arm, protection, and cover (Blackstone, 1765).

Although most of the disabilities of coverture were removed by the Married Women's Property Acts in the nineteenth century, the common-law assumption that the husband was the head of the family remained firmly embodied in statutory and case law in the United States. The married woman's subordination was reflected most clearly in rules governing her domicile and name. In both cases the married woman assumed her husband's identity—taking his name and his domicile as her own. This basic assumption of traditional legal marriage has, of course, been challenged in recent years.

The fifth, and most important feature of traditional legal marriage, was its sex-based division of family roles and responsibilities. The woman was to devote herself to being a wife, homemaker, and mother in return for her husband's promise of lifelong support. The husband was given the sole responsibility for the family's financial welfare, while he was assured that his home, his children, and his social-emotional well-being would be cared for by his wife. Professor Homer Clark, a noted authority on family law, summarizes the legal obligations of the two spouses as follows:

> Specifically, the courts say that the husband has a duty to support his wife, that she has a duty to render services in the home, and that these duties are reciprocal. . . . The husband is to provide the family with food, clothing, shelter, and as many of the amenities of life as he can manage, either (in earlier days) by the management of his estates, or (more recently) by working for wages or a salary. The wife is to be mistress of the household, maintaining the home with resources furnished by the husband, and caring for children. A reading of contemporary judicial opinions leaves the impression that these roles have not changed over the last two hundred years (Clark, 1968; 181).

All states, even those with community property systems, placed the burden of the family support on the husband; he was legally responsible for providing necessities for his wife and his children. Similarly, all states made the wife responsible for domestic and childcare services: her legal obligation was to be a companion, housewife, and mother. As one court enumerated the services a man legally could expect from his wife:

> [she had a duty] to be his helpmate, to love and care for him in such a role, to afford him her society and her person, to protect and care for him in sickness, and to labor faithfully to advance his interest. . . [she also must perform] her household and domestic duties. . . . A husband is entitled to the benefit of his wife's industry and economy (*Rucci v. Rucci*, 1962: 127).

The wife also was assigned responsibility for childcare, both during marriage and after divorce, as the law viewed her as the "natural and proper" caretaker of the young.

While no one would claim that the law was responsible for the traditional division of labor in the family, it did serve to legitimate, sanction, and reinforce these traditional family roles. For example, the law reinforced the wife's subordinate status—and her economic dependency—by defining the husband as the only person who was responsible for (and capable of) supporting the family (Kay, 1974).

By promising the housewife lifelong support, the law provided a disincentive for women to develop their economic capacity and to work in the paid labor force. In addition, by making them legally responsible for domestic and childcare services, it reinforced the primacy of these activities in their lives, leaving them with neither time nor incentive to develop careers outside the home.

The law similarly reinforced the traditional male role by directing the husband away from domestic and childcare activities. Although the law did legitimate the husband's power and authority in the family it also encouraged a single-minded dedication to work, and to earning a living, for it made it clear that his sole responsibility was his family's economic welfare.

TRADITIONAL DIVORCE LAW

Since marriage was regarded as an indissoluble union, it could be ended only by the death of one of the parties (Rhinestein, 1972). "Divorce, in the modern sense of a judicial decree dissolving a valid marriage, and allowing one or both partners to remarry during the life of the other, did not exist in England until 1857" (Kay, 1970: 221).

A rare exception, originating in the late seventeenth century, allowed divorce (on the sole ground of adultery) by special act of Parliament. As a practical matter, however, few of these divorces were granted—and they were available only to the very rich, and to men (Clark, 1968: 281). The Church also permitted divorce *a mensa et thoro*, literally a divorce from bed and board, which allowed the parties to live apart. But this legal separation did not sever the marital bond.

The Ecclesiastical Courts retained their exclusive jurisdiction over marriage and divorce in England until 1857, when divorce jurisdiction was transferred to the Civil Court System, and divorces were authorized for adultery. But the underlying premise of divorce law remained the same: Marriage still was regarded as a permanent and cherished union that the Church—and then the state—had to protect and preserve. And it still was assumed that the holy bond of matrimony would be protected best by restricting access to divorce. As Clark observed:

> [They believed] that marital happiness is best secured by making marriage indissoluble except for very few causes. When the parties know that they are bound together for life, the argument runs, they will resolve their differences and disagreements and make an effort to get

> along with each other. If they are able to separate legally upon less
> serious grounds, they will make no such effort, and immorality will
> result (Clark, 1968: 242-43).

It should be noted also that these early divorce laws established a different standard for men and women: "wives. . .could obtain a divorce only if the husband's adultery was aggravated by bigamy, cruelty, or incest, while the husband could get his divorce for adultery alone" (Clark, 1969: 282).

Divorce laws in the United States were influenced heavily by the English tradition. In the middle and southern Colonies, divorces were granted by the legislature and were rare. However, New England allowed divorce more freely. The Protestant doctrines (and the absence of any system of Ecclesiastical Courts) resulted in statutes that authorized divorce for adultery, desertion, and in some cases, cruelty—sometimes by the courts and sometimes by acts of the legislature.

Although some diversity in the divorce laws of the states continued, in the nineteenth century most states gave the courts the jurisdiction to dissolve marriages on specified grounds (Kay, 1968: 221), and by 1900, most states had adopted what we shall refer to as the four major elements of traditional divorce laws.

First, *traditional divorce law perpetuated the sex-based division of roles and responsibilities in traditional legal marriage.* As we noted earlier, in legal marriage the woman presumably agreed to devote herself to being a wife, homemaker, and mother in return for her husband's promise of lifelong support. Although traditional family law assumed that the husband's support would be provided in a lifelong marriage, if the marriage did not endure, and if the wife was virtuous, she nevertheless was guaranteed alimony—a means of continued support. Alimony perpetuated the husband's responsibility for economic support and the wife's right to be supported in return for her domestic services. It thus maintained the reciprocity in the legal marriage contract.

Traditional divorce laws also perpetuated the sex-based division of roles with respect to children: the husband remained responsible for their economic support, the wife for their care. All states, by statute or by case law tradition, gave preference to the wife as the appropriate custodial parent after the divorce; and all states gave the husband the primary responsibility for their economic support.

Second, *traditional divorce law required grounds for divorce.* Divorce could be obtained only if one party committed a marital offense, giving the other a legal basis or ground for the divorce. Since marriage was supposed to be a permanent lifelong union, only serious marital offenses, such as adultery, cruelty, or desertion, could justify a divorce. As Professor Herma Hill Kay explains:

> The state's interest in marital stability, thus delegated to the courts, was to be guarded by the judge's diligence in requiring that evidence clearly established the ground relied on for a divorce, that the defendant had no valid defense to the plaintiff's suit, and that the parties had not conspired to put on a false case (Kay, 1970: 221).

The standards for judging appropriate grounds also reflected the sex-typed expectations of traditional legal marriage. Although the almost ritualistic "evidence" of misbehavior varied from state to state, husbands charged with cruelty often were alleged to have caused their wives bodily harm, whereas wives charged with cruelty more typically were charged with neglecting their husbands (showing lack of affection, belittling them) or their homes (leaving the home in disarray, neglecting dinner); impugning their husbands' self-respect or reputation (denigrating or insulting them in front of business associates or friends); or ignoring their wifely duties (what Clark calls the country club syndrome in which the wife "is entirely preoccupied with club and social life, is extravagant, drinks heavily, and wholly disregards the husband's desires for affection and comfort") (Clark, 1968: 349).

Cruelty was the most commonly used grounds for divorce, followed by desertion, which accounted for less than 18 per cent of all divorces (Jacobson, 1959: 124). Adultery rarely was used outside of New York, where it was the only permissible ground for divorce until 1967. Whereas the standards for desertion also varied from state to state, two sex-based standards were common to most: (1) If a wife refused to live in the domicile chosen by her husband, she was held responsible for desertion in the divorce action. In addition, if the husband moved and she refused to accompany him, *she* was considered to have deserted *him*, because he had the legal right to choose the family home. She then would be the guilty party in the divorce, and that had important economic consequences, which are discussed below. (2) A spouse's withdrawal from his or her marital roles might be considered desertion, and the standards for these withdrawals clearly were sex-typed. For example, a wife who showed "lack of affection" for the husband, had a relationship with another man (but did not commit adultery), refused to do housework, and nagged the husband would be guilty of desertion (see, for example, *Anton v. Anton*, 1955), but a husband who acted in a similar fashion would not—unless he also stopped supporting his wife financially.

Over time, in actual practice many divorcing couples privately agreed to an uncontested divorce in which one party, usually the wife, would take the *pro forma* role of plaintiff. Supported by witnesses, she would attest to her husband's cruel conduct and he would not challenge her testimony. But even if these allegations involved collusion and perjury, as many of them did, the type of behavior reported as grounds for divorce nevertheless reflected what the courts considered "appropriate violations" of the marriage contract. The husband, supposed to support and protect his wife, was sanctioned for nonsupport and physical abuse. The wife, obligated to care for her home and husband, was sanctioned for neglecting her domestic responsibilities.

Third, *traditional legal divorce was based on adversary proceedings.* The adversary process required that one party be guilty, or responsible for the divorce, and that the other be innocent. The plaintiff's success in obtaining a divorce depended on his or her ability to prove the defendant's fault for having committed some marital offense. Divorces had to be "won" by the innocent party against the guilty party. As the Tennessee Supreme Court (*Brown v. Brown*, 1955: 498) stated, "divorce is conceived as a remedy for the innocent against the guilty." If a spouse who was found guilty could prove the other was also at fault, or that the other had colluded in or condoned his or her behavior, the divorce thus might not be granted in order to punish both parties.

Finally, *traditional divorce law linked the financial terms of the divorce to the determination of fault.* Being found "guilty" or "innocent" in the divorce action had important financial consequences.

For example, alimony, or a "suitable allowance for support and maintenance," could be awarded only to the innocent spouse for his or her life, or for such shorter periods as the courts may deem "just" as a judgment *against* the guilty spouse (California Civil Code 139). Thus a wife found guilty of adultery typically was barred from receiving alimony, whereas a husband found guilty of adultery or cruelty could be ordered to pay for his transgressions with alimony and property. And many attorneys believed that justice was served by using alimony as a lever against a promiscuous husband or as a reward for a virtuous wife. As Eli Bronstein, a New York matrimonial lawyer, put it: "If a woman has been a tramp, why reward her? By the same token, if the man is alley-catting around town, shouldn't his wife get all the benefits she had as a married woman?" (Wheeler, 1974: 57).

Property awards similarly were linked to fault. In most states, the court had to award more than half of the property to the "innocent" or "injured" party. This standard easily led to heated accusations and counteraccusations of wrongs in order to obtain a better property settlement (Hogoboom, 1971: 687). It also allowed a spouse who did not want a divorce to use the property award as a lever in the negotiations. In practice, because the husband was more likely to be the party who wanted the divorce, the wife was more likely to assume the role of the innocent plaintiff (Friedman and Percival, 1976: 77); and she therefore was more likely to be awarded a greater share of the property. Of course, the proportion of her share (and the extent of the inequality) was related to both the amount and the type of property involved: significantly unequal awards were most likely to occur in cases in which the only family asset was the house, as the (innocent) wife typically was awarded the family home (Weitzman, Kay & Dixon, 1979).

Custody awards also could be influenced by findings of fault. A woman found guilty of adultery or cruelty might be deprived of her preference as the custodial parent—especially if her behavior indicated that she was an "unfit" mother.

By linking both the granting of the divorce and the financial settlements to findings of fault, the law gave the "aggrieved" spouse, particularly an "innocent" wife who wanted to stay married, a considerable advantage in the financial negotiations. In return for her agreement to the divorce, her husband typically was willing to be the guilty defendant (in a noncontested divorce) and to give her, as the innocent plaintiff, alimony and more than half of the property.

In summary, traditional divorce law helped sanction the spouses' roles and responsibilities in marriage—by both punishment and reward. On the negative side, if a wife was found guilty of adultery, cruelty, or desertion, she would have to pay for her wrongdoings by being denied alimony (and sometimes custody and property as well). And if the husband was at fault, he would be "punished" through awards of property, alimony, and child support to his ex-wife.

On the positive side, traditional divorce law promised "justice" for those who fulfilled their marital obligations. It guaranteed support for the wife who devoted herself to her family, thus reinforcing the desirability and legitimacy of the wife's role as homemaker and the husband's role as supporter. And it assured the husband that he would not have to support a wife who betrayed or failed him. Justice in this system was the assurance that the marriage contract would be honored. If not, the "bad" spouse would be punished, the "good" spouse rewarded, and the husband's obligation to support his wife (if she was good) enforced.

NO-FAULT DIVORCE

In 1970, California instituted the first law in the Western world to abolish completely any requirement of fault as the basis for marital dissolution (Hogoboom, 1971). The no-fault law provided for a divorce upon one party's assertion that "irreconcilable differences have caused the irremediable breakdown of the marriage." In establishing the new standards for marital dissolution, the California State Legislature sought to eliminate the adversarial nature of divorce and thereby to reduce the hostility, acrimony, and trauma characteristic of fault-oriented divorce.

The California no-fault divorce law marked the beginning of a nationwide trend toward legal recognition of "marital breakdown" as a sufficient justification for divorce. The new law not only eliminated the need for evidence of misconduct, it also eliminated the concept of fault itself. And thereby abolished the notion of interpersonal justice in divorce. With this seemingly simple move the California legislature dramatically altered the legal definition of the reciprocal rights of husbands and wives during marriage and after its dissolution.

Proponents of the divorce law reform had several aims. They sought to eliminate the hypocrisy, perjury, and collusion "required by courtroom practice under the fault system" (Kay, 1968: 1223); to reduce the adversity, acrimony, and bitterness surrounding divorce proceedings; to lessen the personal stigma attached to the divorce; and to create conditions for more rational and equitable settlements of property and spousal support (Hogoboom, 1970; Kay, 1970; Krom, 1970). In brief, the new law attempted to bring divorce legislation into line with the social realities of marital breakdown in contemporary society. It recognized that marital conduct and misconduct no longer fit rigid categories of fault. And it eliminated the punitive element of moral condemnation that had pervaded Western thought for centuries.

The no-fault legislation changed each of the four basic elements in traditional divorce law. First, *it eliminated the fault-based grounds for divorce.* No longer did one spouse have to testify to the other's adultery, cruelty, or desertion. And no longer were witnesses necessary to corroborate their testimony.

By replacing the old fault-based grounds for divorce with a single new standard of "irreconcilable differences," the legislature sought to eliminate both the artificial grounds for the breakdown of a marriage and the artificial conception that one party was "responsible" for the breakdown. Further, the criterion of "irreconcilable differences" recognized that whatever the reasons for marital failure they were best left out of the proceedings because they were irrelevant to an equitable settlement. Now the divorce procedure could begin with a neutral "petition for dissolution," with no specific acts or grounds needed as a justification.

Second, *the new laws eliminated the adversary process.* Divorce reformers believed that at least some of the trauma of a fault-based divorce resulted from the legal process itself, rather than from the inherent difficulties of dissolving a marriage. (See, for example, Rheinstein, 1972.) They assumed that husbands and wives who were dissolving their marriage were potentially "amicable" but that the *legal process generated hostility and trauma* by forcing them to be antagonists. The reformers assumed that if fault and the adversary process were eliminated from the legal proceedings, "human beings who are entitled to divorces could get them with the least possible amount of damage to themselves and to their families" (Proceedings from the California Assembly Committee on the Judiciary, 1964).

Each aspect of the legal process therefore was changed to reflect the new nonadversary approach to divorce: "Divorce" became "dissolution"; "plaintiffs" and "defendants" became "petitioners" and "respondents"; "alimony" became "spousal support"; and the court records read "*in re* the Marriage of Doe" instead of "Doe v. Doe." Standard printed forms written in plain English replaced the archaic legalistic pleadings. Residence requirements were reduced from one year to six months in the state before filing, and the minimum period between filing and the final decree was shortened from one year to six months. These revisions were designed in part to smooth the progress of a marital dissolution through the courts and to avoid some of the unnecessary legal wrangling and personal hostilities engendered by the adversarial model.

Third, *the financial aspects of the divorce were to be based on equity, equality, and economic need* rather than on either fault or sex-based role assignments. Proponents of no-fault divorce contended that it was outmoded to grant alimony and property as a reward for virtue, and to withhold them as punishment for wrongdoing. Instead, they advocated more realistic standards for alimony and property awards – standards based on the spouses' economic circumstances and a new principle of equality between the sexes. They argued that justice for both the wife and the husband would be served better by considering their economic situations, rather than by weighing their guilt or innocence. And they believed that men and women no longer should be shackled by the weight of traditional sex roles; new norms were necessary to bring the law into line with modern social reality.

With regard to the new economic criteria for awards, the no-fault law aimed at making the financial aspects of the divorce more equitable to facilitate the post-divorce adjustment of both men and women. Substantively, guidelines for financial settlements were changed to remove evidence of misconduct from consideration. For example, whereas alimony under the old law could be awarded only to the "injured party," regardless of that person's financial need, under the new law it was to be based on the financial needs and financial resources of both spouses.

With regard to the new norm of equality between the sexes, the advocates of the divorce law reform pointed to the changing position of women in general, and to their increased participation in the labor force in particular, and urged a reformulation of alimony and property awards that recognized the growing ability of women to be self-supporting. With a reformist zeal, they assumed that the employment gains of women already had eliminated the need for alimony as a means of continued support after divorce. Ignoring the fact that even full-time year-round female workers earn less than 60 per cent of what men earn, some advocates went so far as to declare that "it does seem somewhat anachronistic, in an era of increasing feminine [sic] equality, that the statutes providing for alimony have remained on the books for as long as they have" (Brody, 1070: 228).

The legislators also challenged the anachronistic assumption that the husband had to continue to support his wife – for life. They pointed to the difficulty that men face in supporting two households if they remarry and argued that the old law had converted "a host of physically and mentally competent young women into an army of alimony drones who neither toil nor spin and become a drain on society and a menace to themselves" (Hofstadter and Levittan, 1967: 55). Thus while the reformers were willing to consider support for the older housewife, they did not believe that the younger housewife deserved continued support; instead they saw her as a potential "alimony drone" who ought to be self-supporting.

Under the new law, California judges setting alimony are directed to consider "the circumstances of the respective parties, including the duration of the marriage, and the ability of the supported spouse to engage in gainful employment without interfering with the interests of the children of the parties in the custody of each spouse" (Civil Code 4801). California's no-fault divorce law thus is typical of new alimony legislation: It is concerned primarily with financial criteria, and although it specifically mentions the custodial spouse and the wife in a marriage of long duration, the thrust of the law is to encourage the divorced woman to become self-supporting (by engaging in gainful employment).

The implicit aim of the new alimony standard was to encourage (some would say force) formerly dependent wives to assume the responsibility for their own support. With the elimination of fault as the basis for alimony, the new standard explicitly excluded the granting of support awards to women just because they had been wives, or just because their husbands had left them, or just because they had spent years as homemakers. The new law recognized, in theory, the need for transitional support, support for the custodial parent, and support for the older housewife who could not become self-supporting.

Property awards under no-fault also are to be based on equity and equality and no longer are limited to findings of fault. For example, in California the community property *must be divided equally.* Underlying the new law is a conception of marriage as a partnership, with each person having made an equal contribution to the community property and therefore deserving an equal share.

The standards for child custody also reflect the new equality between the spouses. The preference for the mother (for children of tender years) has been replaced by a sex-neutral standard that instructs judges to award custody in the "best interests of the child." Finally, the new law makes both husbands and wives responsible for child support.

Fourth, *no-fault divorce redefined the traditional responsibilities of husbands and wives by instituting a new norm of equality between the sexes.*

Instead of the old sex-typed division of family responsibilities, the new law has attempted to institutionalize sex-neutral obligations that fall equally upon the husband and the wife. No longer is the husband the head of the family—both spouses now are presumed to be equal partners in the marriage. Nor is the husband alone responsible for support nor the wife alone obligated to care for the home and children.

Each of the provisions of the new law discussed above reflects these new assumptions about appropriate spousal roles. The new standards for alimony indicate that a woman no longer is supposed to devote herself to her home and family—rather, she now bears an equal responsibility for her own economic support. For the law has established clearly a new norm of economic self-sufficiency for the divorced woman. Similarly, the new standards indicate that men no longer will be held responsible for their wives' (and ex-wives') lifelong support.

The criterion for dividing property also reflects the new norm of equality between the sexes. There is no preference or protection for the older housewife—or even for the custodial mother (although some states do have a preference for the custodial parent to retain the family home while the children are living there). Instead, the two spouses are treated equally— each one receives an equal share of the property.

Finally, the expectations for child support are sex-neutral. Both parents are equally responsible for the financial welfare of their children after divorce. What previously was considered the husband's responsibility now is shared equally by the wife.

In summary, traditional divorce law and no-fault divorce reflect two contrasting visions of "justice." The traditional law sought to deliver a moral justice that rewarded the good spouse and punished the bad spouse. It was a justice based on compensation for *past* behavior, both sin and virtue. The no-fault law ignores both moral character and moral history as a basis for awards. Instead it seeks to deliver a fairness and equity based on the financial *needs* and upon equality of the two parties.

The law is based on the assumption that divorced women can be immediately self-supporting. This assumption stands in contrast to the Uniform Marriage and Divorce Act, which specifies that the court should consider the time necessary to acquire sufficient education or training to enable the party seeking temporary maintenance to find appropriate employment. Under this provision, a husband whose wife has supported him during his graduate education or professional training may be required to finance her education or training in order to place her in a position more nearly akin to the one she could have achieved (Kay, 1972). The lack of such provisions in the no-fault divorce laws adopted by most states, such as California, can incur a heavier burden on the wife and make post-divorce adjustment especially difficult for women.

Thus, while the aims of the no-fault laws, i.e., equality and sex-neutrality, are laudable, the laws may be instituting equality in a society in which women are not fully prepared (and/or permitted) to assume equal responsibility for their own and their children's support after divorce.

Public policy then becomes a choice between temporary protection and safeguards for the transitional woman (and for the older housewife in the transitional generation) to minimize the hardships incurred by the new expectations, versus current enforcement of the new equality, with the hope of speeding the transition, despite the hardships this might cause for current divorcees.

REFERENCES

Anton v. Anton
    1955   49 Del. 431, 118A.2d 605 (Supp. 1955).

Blackstone, William
    1765   *Commentaries on the Laws of England.*

Brody, Stuart
    1970   "California's Divorce Reform: Its Sociological Implication." *Pacific Law Journal*, 1.

Brown v. Brown
    1955   198 Tenn. 600, 381 S.W. 2d 492.

Carter, Hugh, and Paul C. Glick
    1970   *Marriage and Divorce: A Social and Economic Study.* Cambridge, Mass.: Harvard University.

    1976   *Marriage and Divorce: A Social and Economic Study.* Cambridge, Mass.: Harvard University. (Revised ed.)

Clark, Homer
    1968   *Domestic Relations.* St. Paul, Minn.: West.

Citizens' Advisory Council on the Status of Women
    1974   *Recognition of Economic Contribution of Homemakers and Protection of Children in Divorce and Practice.* Washington, D.C.: U.S. Government Printing Office.

Friedman, Lawrence M. and Robert V. Percival
    1976a   "Who Sues for Divorce? From Fault Through Fiction to Freedom." *Journal of Legal Studies* 5 (1): 61-82.

    1976b   "A Tale of Two Courts: Litigation in Alameda and San Benito Counties." *Law and Society Review* 10 (2); 267-303.

Foster, Henry H. and Doris Jonas Freed
    1974   "Marital Property Reform in New York; Partnership of Co-Equals?" *Family Law Quarterly*, Vol. 8; pp. 169-205.

    1977   *Family Law: Cases and Materials.* Boston: Little, Brown (3rd ed.).

Hofstadter, Samuel H., and Shirley R. Levittan
    1967   "Alimony—A Reformulation." *Journal of Family Law* 7:51-60.

Hogoboom, William P.
    1971   "The California Family Law Act of 1970: 18 Months' Experience," *Journal of Missouri Bar*: 584-589.

Krause, Harry D.
    1976   *Family Law: Cases and Materials.* St. Paul, Minn.: West.

Kay, Herma Hill
    1970   "A Family Court: The California Proposal." *Divorce and After*, edited by Paul Bohannan, Garden City, New York: Doubleday.

    1974   "Sex-Based Discrimination in Family Law," *Sex-Based Discrimination Text, Cases and Materials*, edited by Kenneth M. Davidson, Ruth G. Ginsburg and Herma Hill Kay, St. Paul, Minn.: West.

Reynolds v. Reynolds
    1862   85 Mass. (3 Allen) 605 (1862).

Rheinstein, Max
    1972   *Marriage Stability, Divorce and the Law.* Chicago: University of Chicago.

Rucci v. Rucci
    1962   23 Conn. Supp. 221, 181 a.2d 125.
Weitzman, Lenore
    1979   *The Marriage Contract.* Englewood Cliffs, N. J.: Prentice-Hall.
Weitzman, Lenore and Ruth B. Dixon
    1976   "The Alimony Myth." Paper read at the meeting of the American
                Sociological Association.

    1979   "Child Custody Standards and Awards." *Journal of Social Issues,*
                forthcoming.
Weitzman, Lenore J., Herma Hill Kay, and Ruth B. Dixon
    1979   *No-fault Divorce: The Impact of Changes in the Law and the Legal
                Process.* California Divorce Law Research Project, Center for the
                Study of Law and Society. University of California, Berkeley.
Wheeler, Michael
    1974   *No-fault Divorce.* Boston: Beacon Press.

21.

The Debate Over Joint Custody

Marilyn Webb

In 1977 when Jane Umanoff started Umanoff and Parsons, a chic wholesale bakery in New York, her daughters Becky (now 14) and Lila (now 11) were recent diaper graduates. The new business meant that Jane spent long weekends and late nights up to her elbows in flour while her husband, Fred Margulies, shared the childcare chores. "Fred was what you'd call 'an involved father,' " Jane says. "So when we separated several years later, he was so much a part of life with the kids that there was no question but that we'd continue sharing." Co-parenting was their solution.

Umanoff and Margulies are part of a new generation—the increasing number of former spouses who are making joint custody work. The labels vary—joint parenting, co-parenting, joint custody—but it all means that both parents share the rearing of their children. A joint-custody court order can refer only to sharing major decisions or it can also include joint physical custody—a version of the plan that Umanoff and Margulies have worked out.

Every two weeks Becky and Lila pack up their Walkmans and bookbags and move between Umanoff's Manhattan co-op and Margulies's, a few blocks away. "Get your schedule down so it's not a big thing," Becky tells other kids. "Just memorize it. If your parents were still married, you'd know where to go and when. Well, it's the same when you have two houses." Becky should know, since she's had two houses for the past seven years.

As more mothers become breadwinners and fathers take active roles in rearing their children, joint custody is quickly becoming a logical post-divorce solution. There are some drawbacks when it is compared with sole custody—it is more expensive, it imposes geographical restrictions, it can be a legal and financial risk for women and a problem when a parent remarries. But research is beginning to show that if former spouses can get along, it may well be one of the best ways to combine single-parent child rearing and a full-time career.

Legal statistics underscore this fact. In the past five years, joint-custody legislation has literally swept the nation. According to Doris Jonas Freed, a New York attorney and an American Bar Association expert on custody and family law, at least 30 states have replaced traditional sole-custody laws with statutes that also allow joint custody; legislation is pending in many others.

TWO LOFT BEDS, TWO PIANOS

Complicated as it sounds, double homes are already the norm for growing numbers of families. Going to the Umanoff and Margulies apartments is like having double vision. Becky has a loft bed in both of her homes. Each apartment has three bedrooms, a piano and a complete set of books and clothes.

"It's better than living with one parent, since you would feel the one you were visiting wasn't really your family," Becky says, sitting cross-legged atop the loft bed in her father's apartment. "It's not right. You don't visit your father and your mother; you live with them."

To live with both parents, she and Lila keep to a schedule. When the day to change comes, they just go to the other apartment after school. "Moving back and forth is sometimes fun," Lila says, "because you can get a chance to do things at different houses, but it's also hard because you forget things at the other house."

"We talk on the telephone a lot," Margulies says, "but each of us is The Parent when the kids are with us, which means we do the everyday things, like the cooking and the laundry [Margulies has cleaning help once every 2 weeks and Umanoff once a week] or writing a note when one of the kids is sick."

Obviously the arrangement also gives both parents time to date on off days and freedom to work late at the office.

Things are smooth now, but arriving at the plan wasn't so simple. When they first separated in 1980, Umanoff and Margulies had thought they'd let their children stay full-time in the co-op the couple had bought together and get a small second apartment for one parent to live in on the days away from child care. But they couldn't agree on which apartment to rent.

Margulies ended up moving into a place on his own, one everyone agreed was a "hole in the wall," so Becky and Lila just stayed there on Wednesdays and every other weekend. "In the beginning I felt jealous that Jane was giving them a home," he says. "I wanted to have something meaningful, so I did some research and came up with a few solutions." First he got a larger apartment within walking distance of Umanoff's, one where Becky and Lila could each have a room. Slowly they developed a schedule that worked, trying different combinations as the children grew older.

Rick and Phyllis Diamond came to joint custody in a more unusual way—through their son, Evan. Three years after their separation, Evan suggested that his parents give co-parenting a try. "When I got to be around 10," he says, "I wanted to see my dad more. I talked to my mom, and she said it was OK, so then I asked my dad. He liked it too, so we made up a kind of calendar." Evan, who is now 14, spends half the week living with each of his parents.

"At first I felt guilty about not being a full-time mother," Diamond says, "until I realized that as kids near adolescence, they can benefit from intimate contact with both a mother and a father." Diamond, a psychotherapist and president of a New York-based single-parent support service called Kindred Spirits, still works long hours on her business. Having joint custody has made her feel less guilty about taking time away from Evan. "I know he's being well cared for by his other parent," she says. "It's overwhelming being a single parent, so this has been a relief."

Not all joint-custody plans work out this well, though. A New Jersey father is considering putting an end to co-parenting his 8-year-old son because he feels it is too much for the boy to change lifestyles every two weeks from his home (where suits are the norm) to his wife's (where jeans are the more common way to dress). "He told his therapist," the man says sadly, that "he felt like a wishbone ready to break."

THE BATTLE OF THE EXPERTS

Despite plenty of opinions—pro and con—the jury of experts is still out on the ultimate effects of joint custody. Although many studies are under way, there is as yet no long-term research on how joint-custody kids turn out, and the issue is hotly contested. Robert Abramovitz, MD, chief psychiatrist at the Jewish Board of Family and Children's Services in New York, says that joint custody is a preferred solution after divorce because a child can continue to interact with both parents on an everyday basis. However, it definitely is not the solution for every youngster. "It does not alleviate problems that exist already, and it's very difficult logistically and emotionally. Divorced parents have to continue to deal with each other."

But powerful voices have spoken out against the practice. Perhaps the most influential is a 1973 book by Yale University law professor Joseph Goldstein, child psychoanalyst Anna Freud and Albert Solnit, MD, a child psychiatrist and the director of the Yale University Child Study Center. Called *Beyond the Best Interests of the Child*, it has had a great impact on family law, popping up in quotes and references in prestigious law journals, in testimony by experts at custody disputes and in judge's opinions. The book flatly states that a child needs one place to call home and only one parent to set all the boundaries (including the if and when of the other parent's visit).

Preliminary joint-custody studies now contest this thesis. If parents can cooperate, most kids do well–often better–than kids who grow up in sole-custody homes.

Perhaps the most powerful rebuttal comes from Mel Roman, PhD, a professor in the Department of Psychiatry at the Albert Einstein College of Medicine. "Although we cannot be certain that a joint-custody arrangement is the answer for all those who raise children after a divorce, it appears to be the most logical and emotionally sound choice," Roman says in his book *The Disposable Parent*. "Unlike sole (generally maternal) custody, it does not banish the father or overburden the mother, and, just as important, it does not sever ties between one parent and the children."

The importance of these ties was amply demonstrated by University of California at Berkeley researchers Judith Wallerstein, PhD, and Joan Kelly, PhD, in their now-famous long-term studies of children after divorce. Except when a child's relationship with an absent parent was destructive, children not visited by the parent often had lower self-esteem.

Early news from at least one researcher is good. In a much publicized study of 24 joint-custody families, Susan Steinman, DSW, director of the Joint Custody Study Project of the Jewish Board of Child and Family Services in California, found that this choice worked well for most children.

"Although they didn't like the inconvenience of going back and forth between two homes," Steinman reports, "most were able to master the practical problems of joint custody, and this, combined with a sense that both parents loved and wanted them, enhanced their self-esteem." For some children, though, loyalty to both parents became a burden, and they suffered considerable guilt. Adjustment depended on how comfortable the parents were with their joint-custody plan.

GOOD FOR CHILDREN, BAD FOR WOMEN?

While joint custody may work out well for the child and may even be the most practical solution following divorce, there may be real legal and financial risks for the working mother. Powerful women's groups–the National Organization of Women (NOW), for one–oppose legislation that would impose a joint-custody option, because most women can't afford to co-parent unless they have husbands willing to pay more than half of the bill.

Jane Umanoff and Fred Margulies each earn enough to contribute half the expenses, but their situation is rare. Phyllis Diamond's is more typical, and she readily admits that her plan works partly because her ex-husband, an executive with the Syms Clothing chain, pays two-thirds of their son's child-rearing costs.

When a father argues for joint custody yet is not willing to make the financial arrangement necessary to carry it off, both women and children can be hurt.

"Joint custody is a big lie," Carol Lefcourt, an attorney with the National Center on Women and Family Law, goes so far as to say. "What's really going on is that the man will ask for joint or sole custody so he can pay less child support, and there's no redress," she contends. "Let's say he doesn't show up. What are you supposed to do? You have less child support than you should—you can't force visitation."

The scenario of Susan and Frank Carter is one NOW and other women's organizations fear. When the couple decided on joint custody, their salaries were relatively the same. They both made about $15,000 when their daughter was a toddler in the mid-1970s. They had a co-parenting plan in which each would have their daughter half of the time and pay half her expenses, although Frank agreed to a token amount of support.

Over time Frank began spending more time and energy on his career and postponing his child-care time. Susan ended up with most of the parenting but was still expected to pay half the expenses. After negotiations she began receiving a slightly larger amount of token child support—about the cost of a pair of Reeboks and two sweaters from Benetton's each month. Since the added responsibility forced her to juggle her own career to take care of their child, she ended up with an adolescent fulltime and an income that was $40,000 as opposed to the estimated $100,000 Frank now makes as a real-estate executive.

The obvious solution would have been to return to court to seek more child support. But when faced with legal costs, Susan had a choice between defending herself (she figured she'd lose to the high-priced lawyers Frank could afford), putting herself in debt to borrow money to hire a lawyer or just concentrating on her career. She decided on the latter. "The heck with it," she says, "I decided I'd just make the money myself and see that he maintains a good relationship with our daughter."

Women's groups also worry that should joint custody replace sole custody as the legal preference, it would be imposed by courts on couples who have no hope of working it out. So far, however, that has not generally been the case. In California, the first state to pass joint-custody legislation (in 1979), judges report that couples who are at odds about other things can agree about raising their children, especially with help from professional mediators.

In one recent three-month period in Los Angeles, 42 per cent of 916 divorcing couples were given joint custody—and then, according to Hugh McIsaacs, director of the Los Angeles Conciliation Court, only when it made sense in terms of the families' dynamics. Forty-nine per cent of the mothers still received sole custody. Of the joint-custody couples, 62 per cent reached this decision on their own, and another 6 per cent decided on joint custody after mediation. California mediators report that once anger is resolved, finances are usually set up in an equitable way.

What's more, families who choose joint custody come back to court half as often as do sole-custody couples. According to a study conducted in Los Angeles, by District Commissioner John Alexander, of 138 joint-custody cases negotiated between 1978 and 1980, only 16 per cent came back to court because of further disputes. Nearly twice as many (32 per cent) of the sole-custody cases negotiated in that same period had to be dealt with again.

There's even good news about child support. A Canadian study by Howard Irving, PhD, at the University of Toronto, shows that joint-custody fathers have a much better record of making their support payments than fathers without custody, and they are generally paying about the same amount they would pay if their former wives had sole custody.

Meantime, the issue has forced a division among feminists. The majority of the New York and California chapters of NOW oppose joint-custody legislation; other state chapters favor it. "The position of opposing joint custody seems not only inconsistent," argues NOW's former president, Karen DeCrow, "but what would be better for a woman after a divorce than not to have sole and full responsibility for the children? Men's groups favor it, and it seems advantageous to children."

McIsaacs, of Los Angeles's Conciliation Court, goes one step further. "I see joint custody as the emergence of a new family system," he says. "It's like the old extended families, where kids are relating to a number of different adults in two homes. It may even be better than the nuclear family."

Better may be pushing it, but for families geographically, financially and psychologically equipped to handle it, joint custody could be the best choice. It may be especially good for a single mother who needs and wants the time to build her career without feeling she is cheating her children. If we believe that parenting is something mothers and fathers *share*, joint custody may be the fairest way to go. But to make it as safe a choice as possible, it's best to insert a clause into any joint-custody agreement that provides for more child support for the custodial parent should the plan fail.

22.

Single-Parent Families: A Typology of Lifestyles

Helen A. Mendes

With few exceptions, society expects parents to perform certain functions in behalf of their minor children. Parents are expected to feed, clothe, shelter, nurture, and socialize their young. The ideal, in this society, is for these parental functions to be carried out by two adults of the opposite sex who are married to each other. This ideal does not reflect the reality of over one-fourth of all families in the United States. Indeed, an estimated 4.9 million families do not conform to this ideal standard because the 11 million children in these families are cared for by only one of their parents.[1]

It is frequently assumed that because such families lack a second parent they are inevitably dysfunctional. In part, the assumption rests on the belief that single-parent families have available to them essentially only one lifestyle, or distinctive manner of functioning as a group over time, characterized by the single parents' inept attempts to be "both father and mother" to their children. Social scientists such as Glasser and Navarre take a dim view of this lifestyle that they assume that single-parent families adopt.[2] They view the functioning of such a family from the perspective of the two-parent model and assert that many of the family's needs go unmet or are poorly met when the family has only one parent.

Although their picture of life in the single-parent family undoubtedly captures the realities of some such families, it does not portray the realities of all. Single parents are not a homogeneous group. They exist in all social classes, among all racial and ethnic groups, and in age groups ranging from under 15 to over 50.[3] They become single parents through out-of-wedlock

births, divorces, separations, desertions, deaths, incarcerations, hospitaliza-
tions, military duties, out-of-state employment, or single-parent adoptions,
and their families differ in their resources, motivations, and opportunities
to function as viable family units. The diversity of single-parent families
is often blurred in the social science literature, where it is common for such
families to be referred to in the singular as "*the* one-parent family." Professionals who fail to see the diversity among single-parent families, while
attempting to help them, risk making use of stereotypes and deficit models,
that is, viewing the family in terms of who and what are missing rather
than who and what are present.

In spite of this diversity of life circumstances, the various lifestyles that
single-parent families adopt have some commonality fostered by the common tasks society assigns to parents. There is also mounting evidence that
single-parent families can be viable families.[4] This article offers a beginning conceptualization of some of the diverse and common components of
five lifestyles adopted by single-parent families. Because professionals need
to understand some of the psychosocial consequences of the various
lifestyles, this article will discuss some of the risks and opportunities
associated with each.

TYPE 1: SOLE EXECUTIVE

In the Type 1 lifestyle, the single parent is the only parental figure actively involved in the lives of the children. This "sole executive" is the only
adult who attempts to feed, clothe, shelter, nurture, and socialize the minor
children in the home. This often occurs in families in which the father has
died. However, in many families the other parent is alive but voluntarily
or involuntarily has no contact with the family and performs no parental
functions. With all of the parental responsibilities resting on him or her,
the sole executive risks psychobiosocial overload, a term that refers to the
stress resulting from trying to meet excessive psychological, physical, and
social demands.

Except for widows or widowers who receive insurance, social security, or
other benefits, and divorcees who receive adequate alimony and child-
support payments, sole executives must usually earn a living for their
families. Some are unable or unwilling to do so and receive public
assistance. Generally, public assistance affords an inadequate standard of
living, however, and this inevitably brings considerable stress to families.
Even when the sole executive is employed, the adequacy of her or his income is related to job skills and employment history as well as the degree
of race, sex, or age discrimination she or he encounters. The availability
and cost of child care also affect the net income of the family. Indeed, these
factors may determine whether the parent can take a job at all. The
employed sole executive must deal with the challenge posed by what Aldous
refers to as the synchronization of job and family responsibilities.[5] In part,

the problem is one of logistics. Failure to design an effective way of meeting what may sometimes be conflicting responsibilities can generate a great deal of stress within the family and between the family and the community. Families who fail to develop such an ability are at greater risk than those who do.

Tyrannized Single Parents. For many sole executives and their families, the problem of synchronization is compounded by their feelings about their status as single parents. In addition to any sorrow about the circumstances leading to this status, a frequent source of stress is what the author terms "the tyranny of the two-parent model." A tyrannized single-parent family is one that has never recovered from the absence of the other parent and feels broken or incomplete because of it. Although such feelings are common during the initial period of adjustment to being a single-parent family, some families eventually move beyond them. Those who do not are those who have never abandoned the cultural ideal of the two-parent family.[6] Anger, guilt, and anxiety are shared by the family members, each of whom, in varying degrees, may hold her- or himself responsible for the loss of the other parent.

The tyrannized sole executive tries to be "both father and mother" to the children in an effort to compensate for the loss. The children are permitted or encouraged to turn to the sole executive for needs previously met by the now-missing parent. The impossibility of one parent successfully performing the roles of two inevitably leads to stress, fatigue, anger, guilt, and failure. In her study of single fathers, the author reported that one man who tried to be both father and mother to his children—"superdad"—was eventually hospitalized for exhaustion.[7] Even when not driven to that extreme, some sole executives respond to the demands inherent in applying the two-parent model to a one-parent life situation by becoming overly involved with their children. Such sole executives feel guilty when they are away from their children and attempt to "mother" them all the time they are together. This encourages overdependence in both parent and child and exacerbates their feelings of low self-esteem and anger.

Fortunately, some sole executives have minimized the risks associated with this lifestyle and have taken advantage of some of the opportunities associated with it. Such parents and their children have evolved a sole executive lifestyle that is more realistic for one-parent families. Some have developed it intuitively, and others have attended workshops such as those sponsored by the One Parent Family Education organization in Santa Monica, California. These families have learned to develop alternatives to the inappropriate application of the two-parent model to the single-parent situation.

The role expectations of parents that emerge from analyzing the two-parent model are, in essence, to be suppliers, that is, to supply specified goods, services, and emotions for their children.[8] The roles that the children are expected to perform in the family are rarely described, but the common assumption is that they are to receive what the parents supply or provide and to react by becoming healthy and productive people.

Single-Parent Family Model. The alternative for a single-parent family is what the author calls simply the "single-parent family model." In this model, the single parent is essentially perceived as a "contributing coordinator." In this role, the parent contributes by doing for the children what she or he can manage without undue stress and to coordinate the allocation of some of the other functions usually assigned to parents to competent persons within and outside the family. For example, one single mother, whose capacity for loving was impaired by her own lack of sufficient mothering, sees to it that her 6-year-old daughter has frequent contact with an older woman in the neighborhood. This woman is warm and loving, and she and the child have a mutually gratifying, loving relationship. The neighbor's love for the child is a resource that the mother coordinates for the family's well-being. Utilizing this resource, the single mother loves her child as best she can, and her capability for loving has been growing since it has not been overtaxed. The child benefits from the love of both women.

In the single-parent family model, children are also regarded as contributing coordinators, not as recipients and reactors. Like the single parent, the children contribute to the family according to their abilities.

For instance, the 2-year-old who is taught to pick up his toys makes an age-appropriate contribution to the housekeeping tasks of his family. The 4-year-old who makes her own peanut butter and jelly sandwich lightens the single parent's task of preparing lunch. Children may also help to coordinate outside resources for their own and their family's benefit. For example, children who are sociable are more likely to be invited by other children and their parents to visit, go on trips, and the like. They are thus exposed to a wider variety of people and places than they might otherwise be. Children who function as contributing coordinators have opportunities to experience their own competence in making valuable contributions to their families.

Support System. An important dimension of those single-parent families that function in ways appropriate to their structure is the family's integration into an extrafamilial psychosocial support system. The components of such a system vary from family to family. The system may, for example, consist of relatives, friends, employment and child care resources, and community resources such as schools, clinics, social work agencies, and the like. Religious and philosophical beliefs held by the family and its significant others may also be important components of the psychological resources utilized by the family. The components of the system may vary over time as the family moves through its life cycle. For example, at one point in the family's life, child care resources may be more crucial than at a later period. During the initial adjustment to life as a single-parent family, relationships with social work and other agencies may be more important to the family than when it has stabilized and receives adequate psychosocial support from friends.

Establishing and maintaining good outside relationships may be difficult for some families, and they may require professional help. Without the assured support of extended kin groups and community, which single parents of earlier times presumably had, many of today's single-parent families are at risk of becoming socially isolated.[9] Sometimes the isolation is caused, in part, by neglect or outright rejection from others who disapprove of divorce or out-of-wedlock parenthood.[10] Even widows may find that they are socially in a "no-man's land," because, although no longer married, they are not quite single. Consequently, some widows have found it difficult to share common interests with other adults who are either married or single.[11]

Sometimes single-parent families become socially isolated because they have had to move to new communities. Economic necessity has forced many such families to seek cheaper places to live, and the loss of income from the husband and father sometimes causes the mother and children to move into a lower socioeconomic group. This can pose another barrier to satisfactory interaction with an extrafamilial psychosocial support system.

Single-parent families use a variety of means to meet the challenges posed by the risk of social isolation. Some join single-parent groups or live with other single-parent families; others strengthen preexisting family relationships.[12] Still others have become active in churches or communities. Some empirical evidence exists that a family's sense of remaining intact is related to the integration of its members into a viable extrafamilial psychosocial support system.[13]

TYPE 2: AUXILIARY PARENT

Not all single parents adopt a sole executive type of lifestyle. In the Type 2 lifestyle, the single parent shares one or more parental responsibilities with an auxiliary parent who does not live with the family. The auxiliary parent is usually the father of one or more of the children. This lifestyle is commonly adopted following a divorce that grants the mother custody of the children and the father visiting rights and orders the father to make child support payments. Another example of this type of single-parent lifestyle is when the parents have arranged legally or informally to share the custody of the children. The children live with one parent at a time for specified periods. In the shared custody arrangement, the parents take turns being auxiliary.

A Type 2 family can have several auxiliary fathers or mothers, for example, when the mother has been married several times or has had out-of-wedlock children by several men. Each father may assume some kind of parental responsibility for his children and play a significant role in the life of the family.

The auxiliary parent's degree of involvement may range from considerable to minimal. For example, Mr. S, an unwed father, does not live with the family but visits daily. He disciplines the children, makes major decisions affecting them, and supports them financially and emotionally. On the other hand, Mr. R, a divorced father, has very limited contacts with his daughter and former wife. He makes child support payments by mail and visits two or three times a year.

A common type of auxiliary parent is what Atkins and Rubin call the part-time father.[14] Usually he is a man who, after being divorced, discovers that he has lost many of his parental functions. Lacking clear guidelines about how to relate to his children in the postdivorce situation, he assumes the role of visiting uncle or part-time father. He makes child support payments and provides recreation for his children. The decision-making, disciplining, socialization, and other child-rearing functions are fulfilled by the mother.[15] Although the auxiliary parent is usually the father, it should be noted that in a growing number of families the mother is the auxiliary parent and that auxiliary mothers also vary in their degree of involvement with the family.[16] In short, the auxiliary parent's role in the family's life may complement or merely supplement the role of the single parent. The latter may hold more, equal, or less parental power and responsibility.

There are risks associated with the Type 2 family lifestyle. When the parents are separated or divorced, the active involvement of the auxiliary parent in the family's life may perpetuate the problems that led to the demise of the marriage. Frequently, the auxiliary and single parents compete for the children's love and loyalties. In their study of divorced families, Heatherington, Cox, and Cox found that the postmarital relationship between the parents affects the relationship between the single parent and the children. The more conflict that exists in the relationship between the single and auxiliary parents, the more stressful the relationship between the single parent and the children becomes.[17]

Risks are sometimes also inherent in relationships between single and auxiliary parents that are not characterized by conflict. The major risk is that amicable relationships may give unrealistic support to fantasies of reconciliation held by one of the parents or by the children. If the single and auxiliary parents find that their relationship has greatly improved in the postdivorce situation, it may keep one of the parents emotionally tied to the relationship. This may be a satisfactory state of affairs for some parents. For the majority, such attachments probably retard the necessary emotional divorce and the establishment of other meaningful and potentially satisfying relationships.[18]

The Type 2 lifestyle of single-parent families offers the opportunity for the children to continue to receive psychosocial support from both their parents. In some families, this support may have developed to a satisfactory level only after the auxiliary parent moved out of the home, thereby reducing the tensions and stresses engendered by a bad marital relationship. With the adoption of a Type 2 lifestyle, the single parent has an opportunity to receive psychosocial support in the rearing of children from someone who has as much or more commitment to them as he or she does. When the auxiliary parent is actively involved in the life of the family and discharges a considerable amount of parental responsibility, the single parent is spared the risks encountered by many sole executives who overtax themselves by trying to assume all such responsibilities themselves.

When the single and auxiliary parents can cooperate with each other as parents in the postdivorce situation, they may develop a new appreciation for each other. Such attitudes benefit the children. Some single and auxiliary parents find that their renewed friendship with each other does not rival the extrafamilial relationships each has as part of their psychosocial support systems. Some people work out their relationships over time so that no ambivalent messages are given about unrealistic reconciliation fantasies.

A special kind of auxiliary parent exists in some families. This is the fantasized auxiliary parent who is not actually present, but whose image is a potent force in the family's dynamics. Glick, Weiss, and Parkes discovered that some of the widows in their study actively kept alive the memories of their children's father and evoked the father's authority to help discipline the children.[19] In her study of single fathers, the author found that a mother who had abandoned her husband and two children was idealized by them for a number of years.[20] In spite of the fact that they had no contact with her whatsoever during that time, much of their thoughts and conversations were focused on the mother's imagined virtues. This prolonged their grief over her sudden desertion. Only after the mother came for an unexpected two-week visit did the family begin to reassess her realistically. Although confrontation with the reality of her immaturity was painful for the family members, it freed them to finish their grieving and to move beyond the point at which they had been fixated.

Fantasized auxiliary parents may also exist in single-parent families in which the children are adopted. For these children, fantasies or actual memories of natural or even foster parents may compete with the adoptive parent. If the fantasies or idealizations of the auxiliary parent remain uncorrected by a confrontation with reality or by therapeutic intervention, the family may become fixated and may not grow beyond the trauma of the loss of the actual parent.

Even when the auxiliary parent is not fantasized but is living and available, the single-parent family may not wish to involve him or her in their life. Sometimes the relationship with the children's other parent is so painful or dangerous that an auxiliary type of arrangement is counterindicated. Some single parents have, for a variety of reasons, adopted a third type of lifestyle.

TYPE 3: UNRELATED SUBSTITUTE

In the Type 3 lifestyle the single parent shares one or more parental functions with a person who is not related to the family. The unrelated parental substitute may or may not actually live with the family. An example of the Type 3 lifestyle is the family that has a live-in housekeeper who is "like a mother" to the children. Other examples are families in which the friends or lovers of the single parent assume some parental responsibilities for the children. In some black families, children receive considerable parental help from "play fathers" or "play mothers" who are friends of the family. Still other parental substitutes are found among the adult members of some communal families containing single parents and their children.[21]

One of the distinguishing features of the Type 3 lifestyle is that the parental substitute acts, on a temporary or long-term basis, "as if" he or she were the children's parent. The family has no legal or kinship claim on the person who performs this role. In his study of lower-class men, Liebow found that the relationship between a parental substitute and the children can be very close "where they [the men] have accepted day-to-day responsibility for the children, but where they have done so on a voluntary basis, that is, where the children are not their own."[22] He gives the following example:

> Robert, who had been living with Sistrene and her four children for a year and a half, had become, in that time, a primary source of aid and comfort to the children. When they fell or were hit or had an object of value taken from them, they ran to Robert if he was there. He comforted them, laughed with them, and arbitrated their disputes. He painted pictures for them, made plywood cutouts of the Seven Dwarfs for them, and brought home storybooks.[23]

As contributing coordinators, the children may bring parental resources into the family. For example, Charlene's boyfriend, Leroy

> looked after Charlene's little sister and brothers to such an extent that both their mother and the children themselves came to rely on him. . . . Leroy bathed the children, braided the girls' hair, washed their clothes, . . . played with them, and on their birthdays [gave] them gifts.[24]

Although the presence of an unrelated parental substitute may be a boon to the family, there are also risks involved in the Type 3 lifestyle. As Liebow found in his study, not all the men who took on the role of parental substitute "were able or even attempted to establish a warm personal relationship with the children they were living with."[25] The major risk of the Type 3 lifestyle is that the unrelated parental substitute may have no emotional attachment or commitment to the children or to their welfare. He or she may merely tolerate the children for the sake of a relationship with the single parent. Child abuse is one symptom of such extreme lack of commitment, and it is not unusual to find that a child has been abused by the mother's live-in boyfriend.

Another risk associated with the Type 3 lifestyle is that the children may be exposed to a series of unrelated parental substitutes. Over the years children may be cared for by a number of different housekeepers or baby sitters. How traumatic the serial experiences are, if at all, depends on the kind and degree of emotional attachments that exist between the family members and the parental substitutes. Since one assumes the existence of some emotional involvement with a live-in lover—at least on the part of the single parent—serious repercussions for the family are likely when a series of lovers function as parental substitutes. Hunt reported that a repeated loss of lovers who are parental substitutes can cause problems in the relationship between the single parent and her or his child.[26]

The Type 3 lifestyle offers an opportunity for the single parent who does not wish to marry or remarry to enjoy an intimate relationship with someone who will share some parental responsibilities. It must be recognized that there are people who do not wish to or are not able to successfully fill a marital role but who can, nevertheless, successfully fill a parental role. Some single parents who are ambitious in their careers but are also devoted to the welfare of their children have found that careful selection of a live-in housekeeper frees them to concentrate on their profession and their children without having to meet what for them are the unwelcome demands of a marital relationship.[27]

TYPE 4: RELATED SUBSTITUTE

The related parental substitute is a blood or legal relative who assumes a parental role, although he or she is not the actual parent of the children. This function can be assumed by grandparents, aunts, uncles, cousins, or siblings of the children.

A distinguishing feature of the Type 4 lifestyle is that the related parental substitute has two roles in the family. One is based on his or her actual relationship to the family, and the other is the "as-if" parental role assumed by that person. For example, the man who assumes a father's role with his sister's children has a longstanding sibling relationship with her, in addition to the co-parental one he has assumed more recently. The interplay between the two relationships creates a dynamic in this family that differs from the Type 3 lifestyle. The dynamics may be complicated by any rivalry that develops between the brother's wife and his sister, both of whom expect him to be a good father to their respective children.

The preexisting relationship between the single parent and the related parental substitute embodies one of the major risks associated with this lifestyle, particularly if the parental substitute is the mother or father of the single parent. Economic and other necessities prompt some single parents to return to their own parents' homes or to invite their parents or other relatives to live with them and the children. In this situation, the single parent may revert to functioning as a child in regard to her or his own parents. As a result, some single parents then act like older siblings in relationship to their own children.

Even when single parents relate to their own parents as adults, there is a risk that they may disagree about how the children should be raised. The generational differences predictably lead to some differences in perspectives on child-rearing. Resentment the single parents may have about their own upbringing can exacerbate any such disagreements they have with their parents, who are now functioning as parental substitutes to the grandchildren.

Another risk associated with the Type 4 lifestyle is that the related parental substitute may be a parental child, that is, one of the children who functions as a parent to his or her siblings. As Minuchin points out:

> A family with a parental child . . . may run into difficulty, if the delegation of authority is not explicit or if the parents abdicate, leaving the child to become the main source of guidance, control and decisions. In such a case, the demands on the parental child can clash with his own childhood needs, and exceed his ability to cope with them.[28]

The presence of a parental child can, however, provide important opportunities and benefits to the family.

> The allocation of parental powers to a child is a natural arrangement in large families, in single parent families or in families where both parents work. The system can function well. The younger children are cared for, and the parental child can develop responsibility, competence, and autonomy beyond his years.[29]

Another opportunity associated with the Type 4 lifestyle arises when the family is aided by parental substitutes who are members of a cohesive, extended kin system. The family's integration into such a system provides it with a stable psychosocial support system in which there is a lifetime commitment to the welfare of the family members. This may be especially beneficial to teenage single parents who need protection, nurturance, and security as they try to raise their children. Widows and others who were traumatized at the time they became single parents may also benefit from integration into an extended kinship system. The benefits afforded by such a lifestyle may exist simultaneously with the risks that have been discussed. However, the advantages may far outweigh the disadvantages for some families.

TYPE 5: TITULAR PARENT

In the Type 5 lifestyle, the single parent lives with the children but has, in effect, abdicated the parental role. Examples are single parents who are alcoholics, drug addicts, severely infantile, or actively psychotic and, as a consequence, are parents in name only. In the Type 5 lifestyle, the single parent acts like one of the children. Frequently, there is anarchy in the family as each member scrambles to have his or her needs met.

In some such families a parental child acts as parent, but he or she is in a very different situation from a parental child in the Type 4 lifestyle. The latter receives some support from his or her parent, whereas the parental child in the Type 5 lifestyle is chronically deprived of this support. As Brown vividly reports, the parental child almost inevitably fails as he or she tries to function as a kind of sole executive, but without the economic, social or emotional resources available to an adult sole executive.[30] Frequently, some agent outside the family intervenes temporarily or permanently. For example, concerned neighbors may offer food or shelter to the neglected children, or a public agency may remove them from the home. There are no genuine opportunities associated with this type of lifestyle for single-parent families.

IMPLICATIONS FOR PRACTICE

One of the most important tasks for social work practice with single-parent families, regardless of their lifestyle, is to help to liberate families that are tyrannized by the two-parent family model. This is especially important for those families with a sole executive lifestyle. They need to be helped to see that it is impossible for one parent to be both father and mother. This can sometimes be accomplished by having the family or the parent weigh the personal and interpersonal costs of a parent becoming overburdened trying to carry out this impossible task. Family members are more willing to become contributing coordinators when they are helped to see the value of their individual and collective contributions and when they perceive that by sharing family tasks they help to reduce the inevitable anger felt by an overburdened parent.

Crucial to the successful functioning of the family is its integration into a viable psychosocial support system. Again, this is especially important for families having a Type 1 lifestyle. This network provides resources in the form of people as well as material resources. People who function as resources may include the psychosocial family (both real and adopted relatives), friends, and acquaintances. These people can provide a single-parent family with a range of emotional, psychological, and material supports. They may also help the family obtain shelter, income, and educational, health, and recreational resources.

Social workers may have to help parents whose marriages have failed or who have not married to deal with the social rejections—real or imaginary—they sometimes experience as a result of a divorce or out-of-wedlock birth. They also need help to bolster their courage to reach out and form new relationships with supportive people. Friends, extended kin, and acquaintances can easily be neglected when the single parent tries to meet the demands of job and family. Social workers can help clients to evaluate the benefits of allowing other people into their lives. This may necessitate the family reordering its priorities or finding more efficient ways to manage time and responsibilities.

NOTES AND REFERENCES

1   Sandra Stencel, "Single-Parent Families," Editorial Research Report No. 10, *Congressional Quarterly*, 11 (September 1976).

2   Paul Glasser and Elizabeth Navarre, "Structural Problems of the One-parent Family," *Journal of Social Issues*, 21 (January 1965), pp 98-109.

3   Otto Pollak, "The Broken Family," in Nathan Cohen, ed., *Social Work and Social Problems* (New York: National Association of Social Workers, 1964), pp. 321-339; and U.S. Bureau of the Census, *Statistical Abstract of the United States: 1970* (Washington, D.C.: U.S. Government Printing Office, 1970).

4   Dennis Orthner, Terry Brown, and Dennis Ferguson, "Single Parent Fatherhood: An Emerging Life Style," *Family Coordinator* (October 1976), pp. 429-439; Helen A. Mendes, "Parental Experiences of Single Fathers," unpublished doctoral dissertation, University of California, Los Angeles, June 1975; Mendes, "Single Fatherhood," *Social Work*, 21 (July 1976), pp. 308-312; Mendes, "Single Fathers," *Family Coordinator*, 25 (October 1976), pp. 439-444; Mendes, "The Psychosocial Support System Utilized by Divorced Single Fathers and Mothers," unpublished research paper, University of Southern California, Los Angeles, 1977; Joan Shireman and Penny Johnson, "Single Persons as Adoptive Parents," *Social Service Review*, 50 (March 1976, pp. 103-116; Velma Jordan and William Little, "Early Comments on Single Parent Adoptive Homes," *Child Welfare*, 45 (October 1966), pp. 536- 538; Alfred Kadushin, "Single Parent Adoptions: An Overview and Some Relevant Research," *Social Service Review*, 44 (September 1970), pp. 263-274; and Linnda Caporeal, "Psychology and the Single Mother," in Karol Hope and Nancy Young, eds., *Momma Handbook: The Sourcebook for Single Mothers* (New York: New American Library, 1976), pp. 43-55.

5   Joan Aldous, "Occupational Characteristics and Males' Role Performance in the Family," *Journal of Marriage and the Family*, 31 (November 1969), pp. 707-712.

6   Mendes, "Parental Experiences of Single Fathers."

7   Ibid.

8   Leonard Benson, *Fatherhood: A Sociological Perspective* (New York: Random House, 1968); William Goode, *The Family* (Englewood Cliffs, N.J.: Prentice-Hall, 1964); Arlene Skolnick and Jerome Skolnick, *Family in Transition* (Boston: Little, Brown & Co. 1971); and Glasser and Navarre, op. cit.

9   Maurine Kornfeld, "A Support System for the Single Parent Family." Paper presented at the Annual Meeting of the American Orthopsychiatric Association, New York, New York, April 1977.

10 Robert Weiss, *Marital Separation* (New York: Basic Books, 1975); Orthner, Brown, and Ferguson, op. cit.; Helen Mendes, "Single Fatherhood"; Mendes, "Single Fathers"; and Rose Bernstein, *Helping Unmarried Mothers* (New York: Associated Press, 1971).

11 Ira Glick, Robert Weiss, and Murray Parkes, *The First Year of Bereavement* (New York: John Wiley & Sons, 1974).

12 Ibid.; Weiss, op. cit.; Patricia N. Clayton, "Meeting the Needs of the Single Parent Family." *Family Coordinator,* 20 (October 1971), pp. 327-336; and Harriet Stix, "One House, Eight Mothers, Twelve Children," *Los Angeles Times,* October 2, 1975, pp. 12-15.

13 Mendes, "Parental Experiences of Single Fathers"; Mendes, "The Psychosocial Support System Utilized by Divorced Single Fathers and Mothers"; and Caporeal, op. cit.

14 Edith Atkins and Estelle Rubin, *Part-Time Father* (New York: Vanguard Press, 1976).

15 E. Mavis Hetherington, Martha Cox, and Roger Cox, "Divorced Fathers," *Psychology Today,* 10 (April 1977), pp.42-46; and Hetherington, Cox, and Cox, "Divorced Fathers," *Family Coordinator,* 25 (October 1976), pp. 417-428.

16 Mendes, "Single Fatherhood"; Mendes, "Single Fathers"; Orthner, Brown and Ferguson, op. cit.; and Mendes, "Parental Experiences of Single Fathers."

17 Hetherington, Cox, and Cox, "Divorced Fathers," 1976; and Hetherington Cox, and Cox, "Divorced Fathers," 1977. See also Atkins and Rubin, op. cit.

18 Weiss, op. cit.

19 Glick, Weiss, and Parkes, op. cit.

20 Mendes, "Parental Experiences of Single Fathers."

21 Carol Klein, *The Single Parent Experience* (New York: Walker & Co., 1973).

22 Elliott Liebow, *Tally's Corner* (Boston: Little, Brown & Co., 1967), p. 84.

23 Ibid., p. 84

24 Ibid.

25 Ibid., pp. 84-85.

26 Morton Hunt, *The World of the Formerly Married* (New York: McGraw Hill Book Co., 1966).

27 Mendes, "Parental Experiences of Single Fathers."

28 Salvador Minuchin, *Families and Family Therapy* (Cambridge, Mass.: Harvard University Press, 1974), pp. 97-98.

29 Ibid., p. 97.

30 Claude Brown, *The Children of Ham* (New York: Stein & Day, 1976).

23.

A Model for Stepfamily Development

David M. Mills

There is currently no widely accepted, concrete model of how a stepfamily should function optimally. Consequently, most stepfamilies (and many professionals) base their notions of expected roles on models of the biological nuclear family. Failing to notice the profound difference between stepparent and parent, they move to recreate the original biological family. This attempt to create an instant family—with instant intimacy—leads to problematic family dynamics which tend to persist, and which can forever block the development of real intimacy. In most cases, these recursive cycles of interaction may be seen as the result of an inappropriate attempt to shift some parental functions from biological parent to stepparent. In order to avoid or break these (and other) problematic cycles of interaction, stepfamilies (and professionals helping stepfamilies) need to have a clear, concrete model of how an optimal stepfamily might function. This model must particularly stress how a stepfamily functions differently from a biological nuclear family.

A stepfamily model must focus on the appropriate development of the stepparent-child relationship. There is substantial research evidence in support of the view that the most prevalent problem experienced by remarried families is difficulty over the relationship between stepparent and child. Duberman (1975) found that in 35 per cent of eighty-eight nonclinical stepfamilies surveyed, conflict over childrearing was the most frequent major problem for the couple. Conflicts over money and "outsiders' influences" were cited only half as often. Walk (1970, 1981) found that stress between steprelations was the "most burdensome" problem reported in a clinical

From *Family Relations*, 33 (July 1986), pp. 365-372. Copyrighted 1984 by the National Council on Family Relations, 1910 West County Road B, Suite 147, St. Paul, Minnesota 55113. Reprinted by permission.

population. Even where marital difficulties were listed as a problem, these were most frequently seen as caused by tension between stepparent and child.

We will argue further that the appropriate goal for the stepparent-child relationship need *not* be based on the biological parent model. The model must allow that the stepparent role might never approximate that of a biological parent, and might be different with different children. For example, it seems improbable that a stepparent could achieve a full parental role with a teenager, given the lack of a common history over most of the teenager's life and the developmental push for the teenager to move away from the family. Based on their work with twenty-two stepparents, Walker and Messinger argue that nonparental roles are appropriate goals for stepparents, and that "roles most appropriate to interaction among remarriage household members clearly cannot be prescribed" (1979, p. 189). They reported that the stepparents in their groups typically "tried on" various roles until a comfortable fit was found. Unfortunately, this view is in contrast to nearly all of the published literature. There is general agreement that problems in stepfamilies most frequently arise when the stepparent begins to precipitously "act like a parent," and as a consequence stepparents should "go slow." However, the implicit or explicit eventual goal for "healthy" stepfamily functioning is still generally based on a model of the nuclear biological family. The stepparent is expected to eventually take on a parental role to the spouse's children, with components of nurturing and discipline. For example, Fast and Cain dismiss being a "friend" or "pal" to the child as a "nonparent" role and suggest that if "the stepparent does not appropriately carry out the role functions of a parent, the complementary roles and relationships of the natural parent will *also* suffer" (1966, p. 488, emphasis added). Ransom, Schlesinger, and Derdyn (1979) have suggested that the developmental task of the "reconstituted" family involves establishing the stepparent's *right* to function in the areas of discipline. Similar goals are stated by Visher and Visher (1979, 1982) and Wald (1981). Developmental models for stepfamilies are also presented by Goetting (1982), Kleinman, Rosenberg and Whiteside (1979), and Whiteside (1982), but there is not a specification of goals for the stepparent-child relationship in contrast to the model presented here. This issue, which is a key aspect of this model, will be further discussed throughout the paper.

Finally, a useful model for stepfamily development must take into account the nature of the problematic cycles of interaction typically caused by ignoring the differences between step and biological families, and show ways to interrupt these cycles. In our clinical experience, the majority of families caught in these cycles appear to fall into one of two groups (presumably because of perceived sex role differences in the biological family in our culture). In the first group are situations involving the mother's biological children, where there is an attempt to shift some of the parental limit-setting functions to the stepfather. In the second group are situations involving the father's biological children, where there is an attempt to shift many of the parental functions (including homemaking) to the stepmother. Within each group, the resulting dynamics are relatively independent of the particular starting point and tend to persist once started.

In the first group, a problematic cycle may begin when a stepfather moves to "correct" his stepchild's behavior, probably deriving his ideas of how to function in this stepfamily from his own biological father's example. The biological mother, who may or may not have been consulted, may not agree that the behavior needs changing, or that the husband's approach is the way to go about doing so. If she keeps her disagreement to herself so as not to threaten the new marital unit, the stepfather and child will generally fight over the behavior without resolution, as the child "knows" the biological parent doesn't agree. Or, the mother herself may push the child to change without real conviction, as it may be safer for her to struggle ineffectively with the child than to allow her husband to do so. Usually, the husband will eventually step in to "help" her with the disobedient child, and she will then be led to criticize him for his overbearing handling of the child. A similar sequence will occur even if the stepfather is invited to control the children by the mother, if she does so because she feels herself unable to control them. In his loyalty to his mother, the child can hardly allow the stepfather to succeed at being a better parent, and will continue to be disobedient. This leads the stepparent to escalate his demands to obey, and again the parent eventually comes in to criticize his methods. Regardless of how the cycle is begun, it continues unchecked, resulting in a stepfather who feels unappreciated and isolated and a mother who feels caught in the middle between her husband and her kids. The development of real intimacy between stepparent and child is the preferred resolution to this cycle, but its achievement is blocked by the very continuing cycles of conflict caused by its lack.

In the second group, the cycle may begin when a biological father acts on the assumption that his new wife will perform the same functions with his children as their mother once did. With his assistance she moves in to take over many of the nurturing and limit-setting functions in the family—organizing the household, cooking meals, arranging chores, reading bedtime stories, enforcing rules, and so on. The children miss the old relationship with their father and typically react to their stepmother's new role with indifference or hostility. She usually responds by trying harder to be more central, to which the children react by withdrawing more. The father's attempt to facilitate the relationship (for example, by demanding that the children show more gratefulness or obedience to the stepmother) usually makes matters worse. Again, a continuing cycle is begun which blocks the resolution of the problem. These problematic cycles occur in both noncustodial stepfamilies, where the father's children visit, but more importantly in father-custody families, where these interactions are particularly frequent and difficult to change (see Duberman, 1975; McGoldrick & Carter, 1980).

The model to be described here was initially developed through personal experience by the author and his spouse in forming a stepfamily. It has been further developed by them in conducting marital and family therapy with stepfamilies, short-term couples' groups for parents and stepparents over the past five years, and training for professionals working with stepfamilies. In the couples' groups (and usually in marital and family therapy as well) participants are introduced experientially to the stages of the model through the use of exercises practiced in sessions and at home. The specific exercises found helpful to couples in implementing the desired family processes or structures will be presented during the discussion of each stage.

A Stepfamily Model

GENERAL CHARACTERISTICS

The model presented here is a conservative one—a safe path to stepfamily development. It is certainly not the only path, and many stepfamilies develop adequately in very different ways, shortening steps or adopting entirely different family structures. Yet, stepfamilies and therapists assisting stepfamilies, need a concrete, step-by-step model that will work for the majority of families.

The general characteristics for such a model are asserted to be as follows. First, the marital pair needs to be the architect of the stepfamily system, to assume conscious executive control of the family. Drawing this boundary around the parental unit helps to cut across the pre-existing biological parent-child bonds. Second, the fact that the stepparent has few legal or customary obligations to the stepchildren can act to broaden the possibilities as well as to limit them. With cooperation of the biological parent, the stepparent can choose from a wide variety of possible roles, which may be different with different children. The potential variation in the stepparent-child relationships implies a wide range of potential structures for this family type (which is already characterized by an enormous amount of complexity and variability). Finally, this optimal stepfamily will need to select, out of the range of possible relationships and corresponding structures, that structure which best satisfies the individual needs of all its members. The desired structure will change with time as the developmental needs of it members change. More important, most desired structural goals will require for their achievement intermediate structures, each requiring some time for them to be established. Therefore, the stepfamily structure will be expected to change considerably over time, and the family must be able to tolerate intermediate stages of development which may not be as gratifying as the desired structural goal.

The recommended stages of the model, tasks for each stage, and exercises designed to assist accomplishments of the tasks are presented next. The tasks discussed should initially be implemented in the order given. Generally, each task builds on the process begun in the preceding stages, and should be continued throughout the entire initial phase of stepfamily development. One may think of the process as a spiral, or cycle, as experience gained in doing each task can cause changes in family goals, and so on.

SETTING GOALS

The parent and stepparent first need to decide on the desired long term goal for the stepfamily structure, based on the needs of all members of the family. A guided fantasy, set some years in the future, is a useful way to initiate this process. Done at the very beginning of the couples' group (or of therapy), it is a useful way to focus attention on the possible satisfactions to be gained in this stepfamily unit, rather than the almost certain dissatisfactions involving the binuclear family. The couple should focus on the stepparent-child relationships at this time, exploring fully the various possibilities of roles for the stepparent. They will want to consider drawing ideas from roles like friend, aunt or uncle, big brother or sister, coach, counselor, or even biological parent. Input from the children should be arranged for, of course, but the couple should retain the power to make the final decision.

The decision by the couple for the stepparent to attempt to achieve a role approximating that of biological parent (i.e., a role including wide nurturing and limit-setting functions) should not be taken lightly. A lot of time and effort are required for its achievement. Simple arithmetic implies that for a stepparent to achieve even half of the mutual history that the biological parent has will take a length of time equal to the child's age at the time of remarriage. That is, it will take five years to become a "parent" to a five year old. Further, the parent is not likely to give the stepparent parental authority over the children without a corresponding assumption by the stepparent of responsibility to them. A considerable amount of time spent bonding with the child is also required (to be discussed later). The couple should consider the factors which favor a parental role choice, which are: the child is young, lives with the stepfamily most of the time, the stepparent wants the experience of being a parent to this child, the child is willing, and the parent wants help. A parental choice seems generally ruled out when the child is an adolescent, or where physical custody resides in another household. The relative availability of the child's other parent (of the same sex as the stepparent) does not seem to be a strong factor for choice in either direction.

The importance of the couple making a conscious choice for the role of the stepparent cannot be emphasized enough. Most couples in stepfamilies implicitly make a "parental" choice without consideration of the alternatives or the consequences. (The difficulties this leads to have been discussed previously.) It is usually startling news to couples that there is a choice, and they frequently resist the idea. In order to experience making a choice, therefore, alternate role models must be presented to couples with substantial detail, including examples of how concrete, household problems can be handled staying within given roles. If, with this information, the couple makes a decision to work toward a parental role for the stepparent (and many do) that decision places subsequent interaction in a different context than when it is assumed that there is no choice.

Structural goals chosen for the stepfamily can (and usually should) be tentative, may require further experience to clarify, and will vary considerably from one family constellation to another. For this reason, it is impossible to provide a model for stepfamily development which is the most straightforward, economical approach for all stepfamilies. However, it is our experience that the model presented here provides a useful beginning process to achieve the desired family structures chosen by the vast majority of stepfamilies.

PARENTAL LIMIT-SETTING

The next step is to arrange that the parent is to be entirely in charge of setting and enforcing limits for that parent's biological children. When both parent and stepparent are present, the stepparent addresses any necessary requests for limits to the parent (not the child) in the form, "Would you ask your children to . . . ." When the parent is planning to be temporarily absent, he or she may ask the stepparent to act as a babysitter. This should be set up exactly as one does with a sitter — the parent gives the children explicit rules to follow and so instructs the sitter. The stepparent, in setting limits, must learn to use the form, "Your parent said you should. . . ." If, as is often the case, the stepparent is already embroiled in useless, problematic limit-setting cycles, he or she should be asked to take a vacation from the odious task of enforcing limits. If both spouses have children, the couple will need to be convinced that it is okay to have different rules for different children. One argument is of course that it is okay to have different rules for kids of different ages, or special needs, so why not different histories? In order to have different rules for different children, families often need help in disentangling the household tasks and routines. This is another example of the way stepfamilies are led to lump rules and roles together, using the nuclear family ideology, rather than taking as a functional model a more differentiated family unit.

For couples who have already been caught in problematic cycles of interaction, the initial reaction to implementing this stage is usually resistance. One idea often expressed is that "it won't feel like a family." After being persuaded to "just give it a try for a week," stepparents (and parents) often experience a great deal of relief. Now, however, conflicts which were previously expressed between stepparent and child begin to break out between parent and stepparent. The tendency for couples to detour conflicts between them to conflicts between stepparent and child will need to be discussed, and the couple will need to be encouraged to resolve their conflicts rather than slip back into the previous problematic structure. The use of executive negotiation sessions for the couple (as described in the section "Blending Family Rules") can be helpful for this purpose.

STEPPARENT BONDING

In the biological family, the first year with the infant is characterized by nurturing without limit-setting. This creates a strong initial bonding between infants and parents. As the stepparent is usually starting later in the child's life, it is necessary "artificially" to recreate a period of time for nurturing without limit-setting, to allow for bonding appropriate to the age of the child. Implementation of the previous stage (parental limit-setting) creates an opportunity for this stepparent-child bonding stage to begin. While the bonding must continue throughout the life of the relationship, the initial period usually requires the conscious cooperation of both parents. The stepparent must resist the pull to treat the child in a developmentally appropriate way as far as setting and enforcing limits, while finding developmentally appropriate ways to be nurturing to the child. For example, the stepparent will need to tie a preschooler's shoes without scolding him for misplacing them, or drive a teenager places without lecturing on dating behavior. The parent must make opportunities for the stepparent to bond without giving up the parent's nurturing role to a significant extent. Initial deliberate bonding activities should be continued a year or more, depending on those involved. It must continue until the parent is firmly convinced that the stepparent has the children's best interests at heart.

BLENDING FAMILY RULES

All stepfamilies need to develop their own new rules and traditions. The extent to which this is done depends somewhat on the goals for the stepparent-child relationship. At a minimum, comfortable rules for household functioning need to be developed, covering who should do what chores, etc. This may be accomplished through negotiation between the spouses early in the relationship. If the stepparent aspires to a role of parent in a child's life, the parent and stepparent may begin to negotiate other expectations, issues concerning the child's character, school performance, and other outside activities. (This stage of negotiations should begin only after the initial bonding phase is completed.)

Because of the unique nature of the stepfamily, if parent and stepparent cannot find agreement on a given rule, by default it must go the biological parent's way. The reason is simply that the children will not obey any rules the biological parent does not agree with. The parent will be motivated to accommodate to the stepparent in terms of rules for the children only to the extent that the stepparent makes a positive contribution to the child's life. The stepparent's "trump card" is to withdraw this support, if the parent is unwilling to negotiate.

In couples' groups (and in marital or family therapy) it is generally necessary to lead the couple through the first executive negotiation meeting, helping them stick to rules such as limiting discussion to requested behavior changes and keeping to the agenda topics. It is our experience that if couples practice a meeting in session, and also in session schedule weekly one-hour meetings at home, resistance and difficulties can be dealt with in session and results are much better. We recommend weekly meetings over several years for the couple. Couples should be cautioned at the beginning to be careful of premature or assumed agreements. The stepparent will know that the parent does not really agree to a rule when the children make an unusual protest, or say to the stepparent, "You can't tell me what to do, you're not my parent." The response in this case should be to initiate or renew negotiations between the couple rather than push harder on the children to obey.

STEP RELATIONS IN THE BINUCLEAR FAMILY

A high percentage of divorced couples fail to complete the emotional divorce and are still battling each other, even five years later (see Wallerstein & Kelly, 1980). It follows that the remarriage of one of the spouses can further stimulate these conflicts. It is our experience that stepfamilies tend to overfocus on disagreements between the binuclear households, to the detriment of the development of the stepfamily. Therefore, the model presented here focuses on deriving satisfactions from the stepfamily. A strong stepfamily unit is better able to handle outside conflicts of whatever source.

Nonetheless, some guidelines for relations with the other household seem useful. Stepparents should be encouraged to support the child's relationship with the same-sex parent in the other household, and to avoid competition with him or her. Taking the position that it is okay to have different rules in different households minimizes destructive intrusion. Stepfamilies should differentiate from, while remaining in contact with, the other household. Even if the active cooperation of the other household cannot be obtained, this process can lead to a useful differentiation between both households, similar to the differentiation triggered by individuals in family of origin therapy as described by Bowen (1978). However, the relationship between the stepparent and the child can still be limited to some extent if it is opposed by the biological parent in the other household.

The use of the couples' groups provides indirect assistance in defusing the war between the households. As the group usually consists of a variety of custodial and noncustodial stepfamily couples, the "other household" is symbolically brought into the room and seen in a more human way, as each couple's particular pain and struggle is disclosed. In more difficult cases, of course, it may be necessary to bring both households into family therapy to resolve issues (see Ahrons & Perlmutter, 1982; Sager et al., 1983).

FURTHER STEPFAMILY DEVELOPMENT

Development of the stepfamily according to the model presented here will ensure that the stepfamily avoids the difficulties that may limit many families. With a foundation established as described above, stepfamilies may go on to develop in a limitless variety of ways. With time and energy each family may develop in the idiosyncratic way which best suits the needs of its members. In this sense, the stepfamily structure has advantages in flexibility and variety over the biological nuclear family, a fact which is only recently receiving attention (Goldner, 1982; Whiteside, 1982). The model presented here provides a framework on which stepfamilies can create family structures which may better satisfy the needs of individuals in our current society.

TIME SCALES

The time required for stepfamily development beyond the initial stages described depends on the goals, the initial ages of the children, and the time, effort, and skill available to and from the parents. For example, in a custodial stepfamily with a goal of co-parenting, and reasonable effort and skill, we suggest that a stepparent may expect to achieve a role approximating (not equal to) that of a biological parent in a time scale on the order of the age of the child at the time the stepfamily forms. That is, three years for a 3-year-old, six for a 6-year-old, etc. While the actual time taken will undoubtedly depend on a number of other issues (e.g., developmental age), it seems useful when working with stepfamilies to use this simple, somewhat conservative approach to counteract unrealistic expectations.

SUMMARY DISCUSSION

The model for stepfamily development presented here provides a concrete, step-by-step process for the family for the initial phases (the first 3-5 years) of stepfamily formation. It may be usefully implemented even by stepfamilies who have been struggling for a decade or more and whose development has been arrested by problematic cycles of interaction mentioned previously, or by other causes. It is a conservative approach, intended to form a secure foundation for idiosyncratic future stepfamily development.

It is our experience that couples who are willing to try out the model presented here will find it a rewarding and successful way to help their family develop, and to avoid or stop dysfunctional interactions. Many families, however, initially cling tenaciously to those very points of view which are, in fact, the cause of their problems (principally these are beliefs that the stepfamily should operate like a biological family). Clinging to unproductive beliefs is, of course, a common problem in counseling families in general, and must be met with all the skills that the counselor generally uses to persuade or help families to try new approaches. Some particular techniques which have been found to help stepfamilies have been described in the previous sections.

In general, it appears that the majority of stepfamilies can be helped best by a short-term group of the type described here. We have found a 5-week, one and a half hour-per-week group containing 4-6 couples to be the best. These groups have both educational and group therapy functions. Information about the differences between biological families and stepfamilies is presented through lecture, discussion and printed resource materials. Participants are given in-session exercises and "homework" tasks each week designed to help them implement the successive stages of the model for their first cycle through. Typically, the first week is devoted to an assessment of the current and desired family roles. The next week the stepparent is asked to take a vacation from limit-setting and practice turning discipline over to the biological parent. Specific bonding activities, tailored to the age(s) of the child(ren) and the style of the stepparent, are practiced the next week. Parental management meetings are next practiced in the group and a meeting scheduled for home. In the last session, the process is reviewed and couples are given time to discuss their future goals for stepfamily development.

Implications and Recommendations

In this section, the implications of the model presented will be compared to other research and clinical findings, and recommendations discussed for planning intervention programs and research regarding stepfamilies.

STEPFAMILY DYSFUNCTIONS

It is generally agreed that the most frequent problem area in stepfamilies is the stepparent-child relationship, usually because of the precipitous assumption of a parental role by the stepparent. The implication is that intervention programs designed to help stepfamilies should devote a major part of the effort to improvement of the stepparent-child relationship, as does the model presented here. Programs should attempt to counteract the instant family myth, and help stepparents develop relationships with the child more naturally over time.

The idea that the eventual goal of the stepfamily need not (and in some cases should not) involve the stepparent taking on a parental role is much more controversial. In addition to arguments cited in the introduction, a common objection by professionals and family members alike is that these arrangements do not "feel like a family." The accompanying idea that the biological parent should be initially (and perhaps remain) in charge of administering limit-setting is resisted for similar reasons. It is objected that making the biological parent the "middleman" in this way will inhibit the motion of the stepparent "into the family," and result in the maintenance of two subsystems in the family, one the couple and the other the biological parent and children. It is our position that these objections result precisely from a denial of the differences between step and biological families. Stepfamilies are always composed of a number of subsystems. What is needed is not to try to make them what they are not, but to expand our notions of what it means to be a member of a family, particularly an adult member of a stepfamily.

Research on functional stepparent roles is scanty, and is needed to resolve these issues. It would be useful to know which roles stepfamily members naturally develop over time, especially over the long run, and the correlates with family satisfaction. Our clinical impression is that a significant number (but possibly less than half) of stepparents eventually adopt roles other than parental, and they and their families find satisfaction with this choice. It should be emphasized that a high proportion of those who do choose a parental role do not find it satisfactory. While waiting for definitive research, the model presented here implies that it is crucial that programs and interventions designed for stepfamilies explicitly allow for a variety of positively valued choices for the stepparent role.

BUILDING FAMILY RELATIONSHIPS

The approach suggested here is compatible with the general methods suggested by a number of authors for building stepfamily relationships. For example, Visher and Visher (1982) suggest a similar sequence of parental limit-setting and stepparental bonding, followed by negotiation between parent and stepparent of a limited number of rules for the blended household. Stern (1978) suggests that the stepparent begin by "friending" the child before moving into a "co-management" position. Both suggest a time scale of 18-24 months for the process. The model presented here recommends a more variable (and generally longer) period of time be allowed for these steps, and of course, a more variable goal for the stepfamily. There is a need for longitudinal research on the development of stepfamilies to resolve these issues. It would be useful to know the important variables in success or failure, the goals chosen implicitly or explicitly, the developmental stages and the time scales required (as functions of custody, the age(s) of the child(ren) at the time of remarriage, and other factors). Testing over a time period of at least five years from the date of remarriage is suggested by the current findings.

COUPLES' GROUPS FOR PARENTS AND STEPPARENTS

The use of the couples' groups for stepfamilies has been discussed by a number of authors, including Brady and Ambler (1982), Messinger, Walker and Freeman (1978), Pill (1981), and Visher and Visher (1979). Groups reported typically used a mixed education/discussion format. Results included a general appreciation (especially by stepparents) that problems experienced were not due to individual failure but to the complexity and role ambiguity of stepfamily life. There was a corresponding decrease in experienced isolation and an increase in respect for the difficulties in the other family positions.

Couples' groups are seen as useful to stepfamilies not only because of these substantial obvious benefits, but because such meetings help draw a boundary around the couple and cut across the pre-existing parent-child bond (Visher and Visher, 1979). The use of groups suggested here is different from those reported above primarily in the suggestion that a concrete, step-by-step model be recommended to stepfamilies, and that those wishing to implement the model be assisted in doing so as part of the process of the group.

The initial clinical success of the model described here implies that it would be fruitful to test further its short-term acceptability and long-term usefulness to stepfamilies with a rigorous research program. The ideal experimental design would be a double-blind and would involve a number of short-term groups. Both experimental and control groups could have the same educational component. The experimental groups would have as an additional component group exercises and homework to help the family implement the model for stepfamily development. Models contrasted to the model presented here could also be developed and tested in different experimental groups if desired.

REFERENCES

Ahrons, C. R., & Perlmutter, M. S. (1982). "The Relationship Between Former Spouses: A Fundamental Subsystem in the Remarriage Family." in J. C. Hansen & L. Messinger (eds.), *Therapy with Remarriage Families*. Rockville, MD: Aspen.

Bowen, M. (1978). *Family Therapy in Clinical Practice*. New York: Aronson.

Brady, C. A., & Ambler, J. (1982). "Use of Group Educational Techniques with Remarriage Couples." in J. C. Hansen & L. Messinger (eds.), *Therapy With Remarriage Families*. Rockville, MD: Aspen.

Duberman, L. (1975). *The Reconstituted Family: A Study of Remarried Couples and Their Children*. Chicago: Nelson-Hall.

Fast, I., & Cain, A. C. (1966). "The Stepparent Role: Potential for Disturbances in Family Functioning." *American Journal of Orthopsychiatry*, 36(3), 485-491.

Goetting, A. (1982). "The Six Stages of Remarriage: Developmental Tasks of Remarriage After Divorce." *Family Relations*, 31, 213-222.

Goldner, V. (1982). "Remarriage Family: Structure, System, Future." in J. C. Hansen & L. Messinger (eds.), *Therapy with Remarriage Families*, Rockville, MD: Aspen.

Kleinman, J., Rosenberg, E., & Whiteside, M. (1979). "Common Developmental Tasks in Forming Reconstituted Families." *Journal of Marital and Family Therapy*, 5(2), 79-86.

McGoldrick, M., & Carter, E. A. (1980). "Forming a Remarried Family." in E. A. Carter & M. McGoldrick (eds.), *The Family Life Cycle: A Framework for Family Therapy*, New York: Gardner.

Messinger, L., Walker, K. N., & Freeman, S. J. I. (1978). "Preparation for Remarriage Following Divorce: The Use of Group Techniques." *American Journal of Orthopsychiatry*, 48(2), 263-272.

Pasley, K., & Ihinger-Tallman, M. (1982). "Stress in Remarried Families." *Family Perspective*, 16(4), 181-190.

Pill, C. J. (1981). "A Family Life Education Group for Working with Stepparents." *Social Casework*, 62(3), 159-166.

Ransom, J. W., Schlesinger, S., & Derdeyn, A. (1979). "A Stepfamily in Formation." *American Journal of Orthopsychiatry*, 49(1), 36-43.

Sager, C. J., Brown, H. S., Crohn, H., Engel, T., Rodstein, E., & Walker, L. (1983). *Treating the Remarried Family*. New York: Brunner/Mazel.

Stern, P. N. (1978). "Stepfather Families: Integration Around Child Discipline." *Issues in Mental Health Nursing*, 1(2), 49-56.

Visher, E. B., & Visher, J. S. (1979). *Stepfamilies: A Guide to Working with Stepparents and Stepchildren*. New York: Brunner/Mazel.

Visher, E. B., & Visher, J. S. (1982). *How to Win as a Stepfamily*. New York: Dembner.

Wald, E. (1970). *The Multi-Marriage Exploratory Study*. Highland Park, IL: Family Service of South Lake County.

Wald, E. (1981). *The Remarried Family: Challenge and Promise*. New York: Family Service Association of America.

Walker, K. N. & Messinger, L. (1979). "Remarriage After Divorce: Dissolution and Reconstruction of Family Boundaries." *Family Process*, 18(2), 185-192.

Wallerstein, J. S. & Kelly, J. B. (1980). *Surviving the Breakup: How Children and Parents Cope with Divorce*. New York: Basic Books.

Whiteside, M. F., (1982). "Remarriage: A Family Developmental Process." *Journal of Marital and Family Therapy*, 8(2), 59-68.

Part

Eight

Child Care

The problems surrounding childcare for working parents have become an increasingly significant issue and represent the first of two new issues added for this edition. As mentioned in the Introduction, the major social change that has created this issue has been the phenomenal increase of women in the work force, particularly younger women who are more likely also to have young children. Among this category of women, more than 60 per cent are now working at jobs outside the home. This trend is not really as new as it might appear; women have been in the work force in considerable numbers for many years, and there have been steady increases over the past several decades. The recent differences that now make this such an important issue are, first, that working women with children now make up such a large proportion of employed people in our society, and second, the interest and involvement of the Women's Movement to focus more public attention on this problem.

Responsibility for the care and nurturing of children continues, for the most part, to be left to mothers, in spite of increased pressures upon fathers to share this load. Furthermore, a significant proportion of working women are single mothers who were brought to that condition by the high divorce rate, along with a high rate of out-of-wedlock childbirths. The childcare issue is very much a women's issue, hence the involvement of the Women's Movement in bringing it to the forefront of public attention. In fact, childcare is one of the major feminist issues, although there is certainly no clear unanimity among feminist leaders on all aspects of this problem.

Childcare is often taken for granted by those who are not faced with the dilemmas that it can present. Consider, for example, the case of a single parent who moves to a new location, away from friends and family, to take a new job. Once in the new location, she might find that there is either no childcare available due to over-crowding of existing situations, or that which is available may not be affordable—the job just might not produce enough income to pay for the care that is available. The parent is then faced with a number of choices. He or she could leave the child at home alone, could give up the job and perhaps revert to welfare support, or could find some less than suitable situation for the child. It is obvious which choice most would take; given these choices, most would choose whatever childcare arrangement could be found, no matter how undesirable. However, lacking even this choice, one of the other alternatives is usually taken.

The topic of childcare has also become a major public policy issue, concerned partly with the question of the need for care, but mainly with the question of who should bear the responsibility of providing care for children of working mothers (and fathers). Being a relatively new issue, however, the various "sides" of the issue have not come fully into focus. It may be, at this point in time, more of a problem than an issue.

Lacking boundaries that clearly define childcare as an issue, the purpose here is to take a more general approach to the topic, presenting two new articles that cover some of the more significant elements. Thus, the articles in this section deal first with the various issues of childcare in general, and second with the specific problems of children who are left to come home from school to an empty house or apartment, so-called "latch-key children." The public policy aspects of this topic will be left, to a limited extent, for the next section which is concerned specifically with family policy as an issue.

24.

Who's Minding Our Kids?

Jo Ann Miller and Gloria Norris

When it comes to childcare, you know what you don't want: a sitter who just sits there. A passive, uninvolved baby-keeper will make sure your child doesn't skip meals or walk around with soaking-wet diapers—she'll take care of basics, of course, but little else. She won't hug him or laugh with him or take an active interest in his care. "Too many people are just in it for the money," one mother says—which says it all.

Ideally, your child's caregiver would do much more than simply keep him off the streets. Your goal is to find someone who will provide a lot of individual attention, stimulate him with toys and games, and cuddle him affectionately during quiet times. In short, like all working mothers, you want quality care—only the best for your kids. How do you find it? And how do you assess the arrangement you may already have?

What Choices Does a Working Mother Have?

Close Relatives. A recent poll of *Redbook* readers revealed that many of you have chosen a relative to care for your children—and it's easy to understand why. You naturally feel that a family member will care for your child as no hired help ever could, becoming the surrogate mother you hoped for. And they are usually less expensive than any other form of childcare.

Relatives, then, can be ideal. But don't close your eyes to potential problems. For example, if your mother will be caring for your child, ask yourself whether you really *liked* her parenting style. If you remember her as over-critical when you were a child, consider the possibility that she may respond to her grandchild in the same way. Before you make any decisions, observe your mother's behavior with the child. As New Jersey psychologist Gloria Davis points out, "Grandparents are often more accepting of their grandchildren than they were of their own kids." In other words, you may be surprised to see that the same woman who never praised your good grades applauds every "B" her granddaughter brings home.

Relatives, however, may feel perfectly justified in replacing your idea of the right way to rear a child with their own. Perhaps your aunt believes that after-school TV is good relaxation for your daughter, when you'd prefer her to spend more time outdoors. While an employee might conform to your standards, a relative may insist on her own way of doing things.

Care By Older Siblings. If you leave your child in the care of his older brother or sister after school, be sure the older child knows what's expected of him. What are the house rules while he's in charge? Is he responsible for such things as preparing snacks and overseeing homework? And watch out for resentment. A 12-year-old who has to pass up soccer practice because he has to mind a little brother will probably be unhappy and may also make life miserable for everyone.

Even if the kids agree to the arrangement, realize that you may have to deal with a lot of fighting. One solution, a controversial one, is to pay the children—not merely the one in charge but also those who are expected to behave. You can pay (either in money or in privileges granted) for every afternoon the kids spend doing chores, finishing homework before dinner and not fighting. Some experts feel that paying children for good behavior sets a bad precedent—yet many parents say this method *works*. You'll have to decide who's right in your own case.

A Baby-Sitter In Your Home. There are clear benefits from a private babysitter. Your child will enjoy the attention of a person whose chief job is to care for him. Most psychologists consider this an important advantage for children less than 18 months of age. And your child will not have to adjust to a different house or to the sometimes hectic environment of day care.

On the minus side, you'll pay more for an at-home caregiver than for most day-care arrangements. Your particular baby sitter may offer your child less stimulation and companionship than you'd like. And he or she will not be supervised by any other adult, as is the case in day care.

Group Care Outside The Home. There are several kinds of group care to choose from: profit-making day-care centers, nonprofit community centers, and "family day care," in which a small group of children is cared for by a woman in her own home.

Unlike a private sitter, who may be difficult for you to find, hard to assess and even harder to keep, a center is always there. Plus, a center is more likely to have trained teachers who can provide stimulation. And day care gives children a chance to make friends—especially valuable for children older than 18 months, who, psychologists say, need the company of peers for good social development.

On the minus side: Day-care children, exposed to many people, get sick more often than home-reared ones. And getting a sitter to stay at home with your child when he's ill will add an expense to your budget. In addition, because staff members work in shifts, children may have to relate to as many as five or six caregivers in the course of a day. This is not necessarily harmful; in fact, research suggests that children can benefit from contact with a variety of caring adults.

How Do You Find the Best?

What kind of care is best for you and your family? Sally Provence, professor of pediatrics at Yale University, advises that you consider your child's age as well as his temperament. "Family day care" in the home of a woman who'll provide plenty of cuddling is especially good for infants, whereas a toddler can thrive in a more active program and can tolerate a little less personal attention. An easygoing baby who eats and sleeps at predictable times will take well to group care; a "difficult" child whose pattern changes daily may do better at home with a private sitter.

Once you've decided which kind of care appeals to you and seems most appropriate for your child, the next step is to shop around. Obviously, if you've chosen a relative as caregiver, your search is already over. But what about the other options: an at-home sitter, a day-care center, or family day care in a woman's home? Here's how to start, and what to look for.

Choosing The Right At-Home Sitter. Mary Poppins, the perfect nanny, did not place any newspaper ads; she simply appeared one day at her future employers' door. Your search for a sitter is likely to be harder than that, but following two basic rules will help.

First, cast as wide a net as possible. Post notices in the supermarket and in your pediatrician's office. Contact your state employment office and the employment offices of colleges and nursing schools. Consider exchanging room and board for the services of a live-in student. Ask all the caregivers you know to recommend friends.

Second, master the art of careful interviewing. Ask for recent references and be sure to check them. Describe the job in detail, letting her know your expectations: You want her to play with your toddler, cuddle your baby, chat with your preschooler. There's also no reason why a caregiver can't water the plants and wash the dishes, if you pay fairly—no less than the minimum wage of $3.35 an hour.

Make your interview questions very specific. Asking "What would you do if Mike hit Nicky?" will tell you more about the person's approach to behavior problems than a vague "How do you feel about discipline?" Keep your child in the room while you talk to the applicant and watch their reactions to each other. If you can, slip away for a few moments and observe how they do when you're not present.

Finding A Day-Care Center. There are eight-and-a-half million preschool children of working mothers in the United States and only two million licensed day-care places—not all of which offer quality care. To find a good one, you must be energetic, determined and coolly analytical.

Start by pursuing three approaches: asking your friends and relatives for recommendations, checking the Yellow Pages or your newspaper under "Child Care" or "Day Nurseries," and calling the agency that licenses day care in your state.

Narrow your choices by telephone. Ask about hours, costs, how many adults are on staff for each child, and how many children are in each group. For a full day (usually 8 a.m. to 6 p.m.) expect to pay from $50 to $150 a week. Generally, the younger the child, the higher the cost—all-day care for an infant of six months or less can exceed $150 a week. However, the best care isn't always the most expensive. Many dedicated and creative centers operate at reasonable cost.

Look for a center with a low adult-child ratio. Recommended ratios: one adult for every three infants or toddlers; one adult for every four two- to three-year-olds; one adult for every eight children over three. Check, too, the age range of the group your child will be in; the children should be no more than two years apart. And the group itself should be small. Twelve three-year-olds fare better with three teachers than 24 kids with six teachers (even though the ratio is the same). Recommended group sizes: no more than six children per group up to age two; no more than 12 two- to three-year-olds; 16 three- to six-year-olds.

Try to free yourself of preconceived ideas and prejudices. A nonprofit center is not necessarily better than one of the large chains. Roger Neugebauer, publisher of the magazine *Child Care Information Exchange* and an authority on infant care, says: "I've seen terrible day-care centers in churches and perfectly acceptable ones run as businesses for profit." On the other hand, don't be swayed by fancy equipment. Some chain operations invest money in that instead of in well-trained teachers.

Evaluating A Center. Once you've located a center that sounds promising, your next step is to visit the premises. Take along a written list of questions and a checklist to use as you observe. Ask the director to show you the center's license, medical release forms, weekly curriculum (it's a good sign if they have one) and a list of other parents you can contact. Question the director about the staff's qualifications and, if possible, interview a few of the teachers.

Ask whether you can visit at any time once your child is enrolled. As Susan Weissman, director of the Park Center for Preschoolers in New York City, points out, no good program will be disrupted by adults coming and going, but a center that discourages parental inspection may indeed have something to hide.

Look for clean, attractive, safe space, with a large, open area for group activities and quiet corners for individual play. Each child should have his own mat or crib (babies should not nap in strollers). There should be an outdoor play area, and equipment in good condition for each age group.

Focus on one or two children. Do they seem happy and engaged? Are they involved with the teachers and with each other? Good signs: adults getting down on their knees to talk to youngsters, displays of children's artwork around the room, toy phones on which to "call Mommy," written records of each child's social and intellectual development. Warning signs: teachers not knowing all the children's names or not moving around to give attention to each child; babies lying awake in a darkened room; children rushing over to greet visitors, which suggests they are not absorbed enough in their own activities.

Observation hints: Take along another parent or your spouse so you can compare notes later. Don't visit right after lunch, when the kids will be napping. And avoid the very end of the day, when waiting-for-Mommy may be the main activity.

Locating Good Family Day Care. Unlike most day-care centers, the majority of family day-care homes are not licensed, so it's crucial that parents evaluate them carefully. Follow the guidelines for observing a center, plus these precautions: Request at least two references from other parents. Check that there are toys and equipment appropriate to your child's age—those beautiful puzzles won't mean anything to your five-month-old. Ask what the children do each day. Although the caregiver may not be formally trained, she should still be able to put together a program of storytelling, field trips, learning games, arts and crafts and individual play. Be suspicious if the house is too neat: Children need to feel the space is their own to play in freely.

Treat the family day-care provider as a professional. Avoid misunderstandings by drawing up a written contract stipulating fees and other costs (including food, diapers, trips), as well as hours, vacations and sick days. The caregiver should give at least three weeks' notice of her own vacations and should provide for backup if she is sick.

Be Alert and Prevent Problems

You've chosen what seems to you the best arrangement for your child, but your job isn't over yet. Monitoring your childcare is an important second step; it's the only way you can learn of problems soon enough to keep them from hurting your child.

The best gauge of how your childcare arrangement is working is your child himself. Watch for changes in mood and behavior. If he suddenly becomes listless or withdrawn, if he doesn't want to go the the center in the morning, talk over the possible reasons with the caregiver. The child himself may not be able to articulate what's wrong, but he may give you a hint you can follow up. Try specific questions such as "Who do you play with?" "What did you like best today?"

Stay In Touch. Talking to the person who cares for your child is essential. Avoid the temptation to rush in and out when delivering or picking up your child. Instead, use these times to chat briefly and to report important events: that your son is cutting a tooth (which may explain things if he's cranky that day), that your daughter slept poorly the night before (she may need an extra nap). Establish a relationship with the caregiver that will help the two of you cooperate in nurturing your child.

If your day-care center allows parents to serve on an advisory board, do try to get involved. Be sure to visit often so you can sample your child's daily experience firsthand. Make friends with other parents and compare notes on your children's experiences.

If your child is being cared for by a relative, don't assume that you needn't make an effort to stay in touch. Plan a half-hour informal conference each week to discuss what's happening between relative and child. If you find yourselves disagreeing over what you consider an important issue, you might have to admit that the arrangement isn't going to work out. But before you give up, try making *one* change, one that experts say is often effective: If you aren't already paying your relative, start. Even the smallest weekly salary will make you feel more in charge, and more entitled to ask for changes. Pay in cash, not with gifts, which are too informal.

Whether you're working with family or professionals, however, psychologist Gloria Davis advises, "For your own peace of mind, don't insist on everything going your way. Pick your priorities and let other things go." For example, if the day-care center (or Grandma) likes to give the kids sweets occasionally, you may decide to overlook that as long as you both agree on nap times.

Stop Feeling Guilty. Are you afraid that your child will forget you're his real mother? Don't worry—research shows that no matter who the caregiver is, a child will invariably prefer his parents.

Don't fall into the trap of feeling so guilty about someone else caring for your child that you lose the confidence to make demands on the caregiver. And keep in mind that the baby-sitter who was wonderful when your child was an infant may not be right for an active three-year-old, who needs to be around children her own age, perhaps in group care. It's perfectly all right to change your arrangements as your children get older and have different needs.

We have found, however, that changing childcare arrangements is often easier said than done. Many women who are demons at the office suddenly find their knees turning to jelly at the thought of firing a sitter or taking a child out of a family daycare home. When a situation is clearly bad, don't procrastinate about ending the services. Unless there's been outright wrongdoing, give the caregiver fair notice and, in the case of a sitter at home, severance pay. If you're not sure what's fair, give her what you would expect if your employer fired you.

Guard Against Sexual Abuse. The abuse of children in daycare centers has received national publicity and has frightened parents enormously. But parents of children in family day care or at home with relatives should be equally concerned. Most abused children are, in fact, molested by a family member or some other adult they know well.

To guard against sexual abuse either in a day-care center or at home, teach your children the proper words for genitals, and rehearse strategies for handling a dangerous situation. A small child can learn to say, "Please do not touch me there, that's a private part of me." Tell your child to come to you immediately if anyone touches him in a way that makes him uncomfortable. Reassure him that you can always protect him. Frances Alston, assistant director of the Day Care Council of New York, points out that abusers cannot silence their young victims with threats if children believe their parents have more power than the offender does. Finally, take your child seriously if he complains of pain or discomfort. Under-fives can't always tell you where something hurts. Say, "Show me where it hurts. Tell me how that happened."

If you never asked yourself, Is my child safe and happy when he's with someone other than me? you wouldn't be the conscientious parent that you are. But researchers are optimistic about the long-range effects on children cared for by adults other than the parents. Many believe that though babies and young children do need consistent, attentive care, it needn't always come from their mothers. Sandra Scarr, professor of psychology at the University of Virginia and author of *Mother Care/Other Care* (Basic Books, 1984), concludes, on the basis of the existing research, including her own, that "babies develop as well in nonmaternal care as in maternal care, as long as the care is of good quality."

Dr. Jay Belsky, an associate professor of human development at Pennsylvania State University, who represented the American Psychological Association in testimony before a Congressional committee on day care, agrees. "We know that when the staff ratios are reasonable, when the groups of children are not too large and when the caregivers are well trained and attentive to the children, the kids do fine," Dr. Belsky said recently. "The outcome is strikingly consistent with what we know about the development of kids raised at home."

Mothers are now discovering for themselves that a child's contact with adults other than Mom can have very positive results. Says an office manager whose toddler has been in family day care since he was eight weeks old, "I have seen my child walk into a room where he has never been before, and he has absolutely no fear." "When I feel jealous," says another mother, whose child adores her at-home baby sitter, "I remind myself that love isn't a cake that has only so many pieces. Katie has already learned to love more than one person. That will help her have a wonderful life."

25.

After-School Orphans

Dean Merrill

Jeremy gets off the school bus a little after three, his bag of books, baseball cards, and gym shoes swinging at his side. He walks the block and a half to his house, stopping briefly to shoot baskets with a friend. When he reaches his door, he fishes a key out of his pocket, turns the lock, and enters the silence.

A quick foray of the refrigerator turns up a carton of ice cream, to which he helps himself. He got an A- on the science quiz today, and he'd like to tell somebody, but that will need to wait till later.

The immediate debate is homework versus a "Charlie's Angels" rerun versus MTV. What did Mom say? Homework first, always. Well, okay. The tube was boring yesterday anyway. Jeremy spreads out his math at the kitchen table.

The phone rings. He jumps to answer it. "Hi, Mom!"

"Hi, Son. You got along all right today at school?"

"Yeah."

"Good. When it gets to be five o'clock, turn the oven on to 425°, okay? We're having pizza tonight."

The call is soon over. Jeremy returns to his math, eventually getting stuck on a problem. Maybe Dad can explain it after supper. . . .

To some, the above scenario is an omen of family collapse in America; an outrage against the young, for whom adults are no longer willing to sacrifice. To others, it is merely the description of a boy growing up and learning to function independently. Whatever the opinion, it is a scene happening more and more frequently with every passing year of the 1980s. In many neighborhoods, latchkey children—a rarity no more than 15 years ago—are now the majority.

Firm figures are hard to come by, but estimates of how many U.S. schoolchildren come home to an empty house or apartment range from 2

Reprinted by permission of the author, from *Christianity Today*, August 10, 1984.

million to 6.5 million and higher. Professor Lynette Long of Loyola College, Baltimore, and coauthor with her husband of *The Handbook for Latchkey Children and Their Parents* (Arbor, 1983), thinks it is more like 10 million, which would be almost a quarter of the nation's school population.

The Department of Labor is certain of this much: 32 million children of all ages (infant through high school) have mothers who work outside the home. Thirteen million of those children are under age 14. While many of the mothers (or fathers) arrange their working hours to be home after school, many others do not, or cannot.

What is also irrefutable is that the latchkey legion is swelling steadily. Each year an additional 4 per cent of the nation's mothers take outside jobs in offices, stores, hospitals, factories—as well as churches, mission organizations, and Christian schools—so that now more than half the total are on payrolls. The parallel rise in latchkey statistics is nearly automatic.

HOW PARENTS COPE

"Telephones and televisions have made the latchkey arrangement possible," says Professor Long. "The television is the baby sitter, and the telephone is the lifeline to Mom and Dad." Most parents would not put it so bluntly; many, in fact, establish a firm list of commandments to organize their children's after-school hours: *Come straight home. No friends in the house. Do your homework. Stay away from the stove. Keep the doors locked. Don't hassle your sister.*

Older siblings are often charged with watching younger ones and, in some cases, doing housework such as laundry or dinner preparation.

The rules, however, do more to reassure parents than offspring, who say they sometimes feel like prisoners in their own homes. In one latchkey family, the younger children have dubbed the oldest brother "Adolf Hitler" for his supervisory role.

"I have nightmares a lot," says a teenager named Debbie. "They're usually about rats, but sometimes they're about people trying to get into the house." An eight-year-old named Danny in Oakland, California says, " I don't like it—especially in the winter when it gets dark and the wind blows."

Danny's mother, who has tried baby-sitters but found them too expensive or unreliable, is not happy about the situation either. "Every day I pray that nothing will happen to him while I'm gone," she says. "He's mature for his age and very responsible, but there's no getting around the fact that he's only eight years old."

On the other hand, a 12-year-old named Kevin says, "I wish my mom worked. Then I could play my radio as loud as I want without anyone yelling at me." Debbie, despite her occasional nightmares about break-ins, told a *Seventeen* magazine writer, "I'm glad my mom works. She wouldn't like staying at home, and I wouldn't want to have her home if she was unhappy.

Sometimes, when she's home a lot, we both get a little edgy with each other and don't talk to each other as much. Then we're both ready for her to go back to work."

Parental opinion, likewise, is split, depending on whom you talk to. A Los Angeles sales executive, a single mother, is proud of her ten-year-old's growing maturity. "Kim has reached the point that she doesn't want a baby-sitter. She's very responsible, and I trust her to obey my rules."

Karla Braig of Dubuque, Iowa, remembers when she first left her three children to return to school. "I had so much guilt I could fry it up and serve it for supper." But now that she is employed, she says, "There's this myth that Mommy has to be tied to the stove so the children can spill their little guts every afternoon. Eventually, they learn that gut-spilling time is from 6 to 6:30 instead of 3:30 to 4 p.m."

Others, however, are not convinced that their absence after school isn't damaging. Something about that particular hour of the day seems special, a time for the young to let down their defenses after seven hours of social combat, to relax in the protection of a grown-up who has always been their refuge. Conversation somehow flows more freely; joys and disappointments both are nearer the surface.

"You can't expect a child to go home by himself for several hours every day and not feel abandoned and frightened," says John Yunker, director of guidance services in a suburban school district outside Saint Louis. "They suffer from a lack of adult contact and a lack of security."

The hazards are not only internal—loneliness, boredom, fear—but practical as well. One out of six calls to the Newark fire department involves children alone at home. There is also the fact that surveys show the back seat of a car is no longer the prime site for teen intimacy; it is the girl's home when parents are away. That's why in one family, the 10-year-old boy may have as many friends over after school as he likes, but his 15-year-old sister may have none.

Says Vance Packard, in his 1983 book *Our Endangered Children* (Little, Brown), "Whereas parents used to worry about what their children were up to when out at night, today. . . they are more likely to worry about what the youngsters are up to in the late afternoon when so many houses are empty of adults."

A girl named Rachel is quoted in *The Gilmartin Report* (Citadel, 1978): "I have the whole house to myself when I come home from school. . . so Bob and I just make ourselves comfortable. A lot of times we just study together. Sure, we have sex a lot. But I think that is only natural."

Ultimately, the parents arrive home at day's end, but that does not necessarily signal the end of problems. Says one Florida mother, "My daughter has her rules and a list of chores to do, and mostly they get done. But when I get home and find a mess in the kitchen, I wind up screaming. Who needs that after working all day?"

THREE CAUSES

Most observers of the latchkey scene identify the same trio of reasons why the phenomenon has increased and is likely to keep growing:

More Divorce. This results in more households led by single parents— not all of whom are able to arrange substitute care while they work. The U.S. divorce rate rose from 2.2 per thousand in 1960 to 5.3 in 1981, so that one of every six children under 18 now lives in a single-parent home. (Whether the 1982-83 reprieve in the divorce rate will become a new and welcome trend remains to be seen. Perhaps the worst is over; but then again, some analysts say it was only a temporary lull due to the recession. Divorce proceedings cost money.)

Hard Times/Welfare Cutbacks. The need in some homes for two incomes has risen in recent years as inflation has sucked up more family dollars, and governments have handed out less. Fifteen per cent of all Americans are now officially classified as poor, the highest in 17 years. In a tightened market, jobs traditionally held by women have been somewhat easier to find than those held by men. Thus, more and more mothers have gone to work to ward off privation, make ends meet, or save up for kids' college bills.

Desire. The third group of mothers work outside the home not because they must but because they wish to. This group now runs as high as 67 per cent of the total, says pollster Daniel Yankelovich, who adds, "Norms affecting whether a wife should work outside the home have reversed themselves within a single generation." Three-fourths of the population in 1938 frowned on the idea if the husband was capable of supporting the household. In 1978, three-fourths approved.

"Whereas in the past it was mainly blue-collar women who worked for pay," he continues, "now it is the better educated, upper-middle-class women who increasingly work outside the home." A corollary finding is that 66 per cent of those polled feel "parents should be free to live their own lives even if it means spending less time with their children."

NEW ATTEMPTS TO HELP

Relief for latchkey distress has sprung up in recent years from several quarters. Some companies, recognizing that a worried employee is less productive, have begun offering flextime arrangements, designing jobs that can be done at home (occasionally using remote computer terminals), or running their own daycare centers on the premises. Ralston Purina in Saint Louis is one such firm that provides space for kids after school; a franchiser handles supervision. In Burbank, California, three neighboring companies—NBC, Walt Disney Studios, and Saint Joseph Medical Center— have gone in together on a joint children's center.

Schools have begun doing likewise–sometimes in self-defense–to curb after-hours vandalism. The School-Age Child Care Project at Wellesley College studied 125 programs in 33 states, some run by educators, others by parent groups, using school buildings in the late afternoons for a mix of recreation, craft projects, snacks, and music activities. Planners, they found, have to build in enough structure to maintain control but not so much that the child feels as if he is still in school. (One vital key to these programs: the good will of the school custodian!)

A Portland, Oregon, program run by the YMCA was credited with cutting vandalism at three schools from $12,000 one year to $200 the next.

In at least two regions, telephone hot lines for latchkey children have sprung up. "PhoneFriend" in State College, Pennsylvania, averages 45 calls a week between 2:30 and 5:30 p.m. from kids needing help with homework, worried about Mom being late, or feeling lonely. One troubled boy was looking in a closet for his boots when he ran across the family Christmas presents. Another wondered what to do with a sick dog. The volunteers who answer the phones–Penn State students plus some moms–say there are few emergencies, but all deserve attention. Some youngsters seem to call and then hang up, just to make sure PhoneFriend is working. (For an information kit on organizing such a service, write: PhoneFriend Committee, AAUW, State College Branch, P.O. Box 735, State College, Penn. 16801.)

"Kids Line," in a northwest white-collar suburb of Chicago, averages more than 500 calls a month. Its 140 volunteers have received intensive training from psychologists, psychiatrists, and social workers on everything from depression to drug abuse.

The one resource that often is not eager to volunteer her services is the stay-at-home neighbor–simply because her numbers are dwindling, and she can unwittingly become the unofficial "block mother" in charge of all first-aid problems and peer squabbles. In a recent "My Turn" column in *Newsweek*, Judy Paris registered her protest: "Often, during the daylight hours, mine is the only car remaining. . . . Since I am home anyway, my phone number is frequently listed on school records as a backup in emergencies. . . .

"I am not condemning mothers who work outside the home, whether through choice or need. They know and all of society must understand that a very real problem exists that needs immediate solving. . . because the lady down the street is not the answer.

"Who is this lady down the street? Probably she is the last of a tradition in transition. What she is not is lucky, lazy, or bored. Neither is she a doormat or drop-off place for your child."

FACING THE TRADEOFFS

Social psychologists and other scholars continue their study into the long-term effects of latchkey living, trying to assess its relative merits and drawbacks. A government report in *Children Today* says location makes a big difference: "In a rural area that is relatively crime-free, latchkey children are not any more or less socially and academically adjusted and fearful than children who are regularly supervised by an adult. . . . In contrast, negative experiences for latchkey children have been demonstrated in inner-city areas." In other words, the farm kid who comes home and starts his chores in the late afternoon is far different from the Phoenix child whom *U.S. News & World Report* found patrolling the house "with a baseball bat in one hand and a shoe in the other, checking the windows every 15 minutes to watch for intruders."

The National Academy of Sciences says whether the mother works outside the home has little, if any effect on children's grades. However, University of Michigan professor Selma Fraiberg, whose specialty is child psychoanalysis, is not convinced. She is especially dubious about government's involvement in what she calls "the childcare industry." In her book *Every Child's Birthright: In Defense of Mothering* (Basic, 1977), she talks about "the Looking Glass World of Day Care in which hundreds of thousand of mothers on welfare take care of the children of hundreds of thousands of working mothers and other mothers on welfare, while hundreds of thousands of women take care of the children of the mothers who are taking care of the children of mothers on welfare and other mothers."

Then she adds, "(If this sentence causes dizziness, I recommend that it be read slowly as you turn. With each full rotation, fix your eyes on a distant point. I myself use the dome of Capitol Hill.)"

A colleague of hers, Harold Shapiro, notes the economic peculiarities: "When everyone is taking care of their own children, none of this important activity is counted in the GNP. When everyone is taking care of each other's children, it is all counted. This accounting convention makes it appear as if something new, different, and better is going on when, in fact, the opposite might very well be the case."

The truth is, scholars do not know enough to draw summary conclusions based on research. James Garbarino, writing in *Vital Issues*, sums up the information so far: "No social event affects all children or youth equally. . . . Thus, we know that some children will thrive on the opportunity of being a latchkey child. Others will just manage to cope. Still others will be at risk, and still others will be harmed."

Part

Nine

Family

Policy

The second new issue to be considered in this edition deals with the controversy surrounding matters of governmental policy with respect to families. Of course, a number of the issues already covered (perhaps all of them) are related to governmental policy to one extent or another—abortion, divorce, childcare, to mention the most obvious ones. The intent of this section, however, is look more generally at the question of the extent to which society, through its various levels of government, should involve itself more directly in the development of policies that are designed and intended to have specific impacts upon the activities of families and the behaviors of individuals within family settings.

Whether a genuine issue exists regarding family policy is itself at issue. Some argue that most of these topics are matters of private individual concern, while others argue that almost everything that the government does has an impact upon families, and thus, becomes a matter of family policy. Perhaps the core issue here is where to draw the line between behaviors that are private and those that are of public concern. To put the question differently, to what extent should the society involve itself in behavior that is purely private, that is, within the family? Or, at what point does private (family) behavior impinge upon the society in such a way that it necessarily becomes of public concern? Then, at what point is the society justified in involving itself in family matters for the betterment of the general welfare? As one can see, this quickly becomes a very difficult issue with which to deal.

Beyond these very basic questions, the more visible areas of concern related to family policy may be illustrated through a series of questions that represent most of the specific issues that have emerged in recent years:

Is there a real need for family policies? Should government be concerned with behavior within families? Or, should families be left alone to solve their own problems without governmental interference?

At what point does individual behavior become family behavior? For example, is teenage pregnancy an individual problem, a family problem, or a societal problem?

What is a family? Must it consist only of an adult male married to an adult female, along with their children? Or, can a family consist of other types of arrangements? Is a homosexual couple a family?

To what extent should family policy reflect the various feminist agendas? What direction should policies take in the many areas where these agendas conflict?

How much responsibility should the government take for childcare? Should help be provided only for poor women, or should women in higher paying jobs also receive help with childcare?

To what extent should tax policy be used to influence family decisions and behavior? Should tax policy encourage women to work outside the home? Should it encourage people to marry or to stay single?

Should welfare policies be used to encourage or discourage certain kinds of family behaviors?

What role should policy play in the problems of violence and abuse in families?

To what extent should policy affecting the aged be coordinated with family policy?

Are family problems in our society really caused by situations external to the family? Are many family problems really caused by poverty, unemployment, and by other changes in the structure of the economy?

Looking into the issue of family policy, one is immediately plunged into a veritable maze of conflicting needs, desires, and priorities. The articles in this section will not even come close to solving the questions raised above. Rather, they offer a broad perspective on the matter of family policy. The first article places the issue in recent historical perspective by describing how the last few Federal administrations, beginning with that of John F. Kennedy, have concerned themselves with family policy. The article briefly reviews some of the programs of the past and present, how those programs were brought about, and some of the positive and negative aspects of the programs.

The stage then is set for the next two articles that present the "liberal" view, on the one hand, and the "conservative" view, on the other. They illustrate very well the extent to which this issue has become politicized into a liberal vs. conservative debate, involving much more than just the family. The first of the two articles, "Family Fever," aims to reject both the liberal and conservative views, but succeeds in summarizing much of the more liberal point-of-view. It states that government should see to all of its other responsibilities, and in so doing, the family would prosper if simply left alone to take care of itself.

The second article, "Families, Sex and the Liberal Agenda," presents a conservative view by "lambasting" what it calls the liberal agenda. It implies that many of the family's problems today are direct outgrowths of the misdirected programs of past liberal administrations. Neither of these articles represent definitive statements of either position, but they are both informative as well as provocative.

26.

Family Policy

Lawrence Grossman

Family policy, or the impact of government actions on the family, has become the focus of wide-ranging debate in American society over the past two decades. Bringing together the most public of our institutions—government—with the most private—family—this debate underscores profound differences over such crucial issues as the responsibilities of a society toward its members, the proper boundaries between the public and private spheres, the competence of "experts" in solving family problems—in fact, over the definition of "family" itself.

GOVERNMENT AND FAMILIES

In the broadest sense, virtually everything government does affects families in some way. This is most evident on the state and local levels, which have traditionally maintained jurisdiction over marriage and divorce laws, child custody and adoption procedures, welfare, education, housing and sanitation.

On the national level, too, policy decisions often have implications for the family. Foreign policy can trigger or avert war, with momentous consequences for families. Government regulation of the economy and of the money supply, which has increased dramatically in the 20th century, affects the material well-being of families, and the Internal Revenue code, with its complicated system of exemptions and deductions, can help or hinder family formation and stability.

Through most of our history the family implications of public policy were rarely given explicit recognition on the assumption that families were primarily responsible for their own welfare, and if they could not cope,

Reprinted by permission from the *Newsletter* of the William Petschek National Jewish Family Center, Spring and Fall issues, 1985.

private philanthropy would step in. Even with the dramatic shifts in American life at the turn of the 20th century, critics and reformers talked about the special problems of workers, of women, and of children in an urban, industrialized society, without addressing the broader question of what was happening to the family as an institution. In the 1930s, the New Deal initiated numerous Federal programs to help those hardest hit by the Depression. Indeed, Aid to Families with Dependent Children (AFDC) began at this time, its primary purpose to provide for widows with young children. But the New Deal's focus was on aiding people in crisis, not to get government involved on an ongoing basis with the routine of American family life.

It was John F. Kennedy who, in 1962, became the first President to articulate a Federal responsibility vis-a-vis the family. Moved by the discovery of widespread poverty in the midst of America's overall prosperity, Kennedy asked Congress to reform the welfare system in a way that would enhance the preservation of the family unit. His successor, Lyndon Johnson, incorporated this perspective into his Great Society programs, adding a special emphasis on the needs of poor black families. The Nixon Administration attempted to alleviate the burdens of poor families by imposing a "negative income tax"—a subsidy to raise family income above the poverty level—but Congress failed to go along.

By the 1970s public concern about the state of the family had broadened beyond the specific problems of the underprivileged to encompass the stresses and strains of American families in general. A widespread consensus emerged that shifting patterns of attitudes and behavior were altering the family almost beyond recognition, and that government, especially on the national level, should do something about it.

Family pathology seemed to be on the rise in the 1970s. The number of illegitimate children increased, as did the incidence of runaway youths, teenage alcoholism, drug abuse, criminality and suicide. Physical and mental abuse of spouses and children, previously seen as problems of the poor, emerged as middle-class phenomena as well.

Demographers provided data about changing family patterns that many people thought were related to the symptoms of pathology. Throughout the 1970s divorces increased far more than marriages, so that by 1980 the number of divorces granted was 50 per cent of the total of marriages performed. While the number of married couples rose only 6.6 per cent in the decade, the number of adults living alone rose 58.5 per cent, and the number of unmarried couples living together skyrocketed by 157.4 per cent. As average household size dropped from 3.3 to 2.8 persons, the number of children living with only one parent rose over 40 per cent, while the total of those in two-parent families actually declined by 18 per cent. Complicating the picture further, many children living with two adults were actually part of "blended" families, the results of previous divorces by one or both parents.

The 1970s witnessed a jump in the number of working mothers—indeed, for the first time in 1978, a majority of American mothers were in the workforce. Impelled both by economic considerations and career aspirations, most of them were working full-time. Who was minding the children? In two-parent families, despite considerable optimism about fathers sharing child-rearing responsibilities, reality lagged far behind the rhetoric. Such families, as well as the growing number of single working parents, bemoaned the lack of adequate childcare facilities, and looked to the Federal Government to help provide them.

THE EVOLUTION OF FAMILY POLICY

Walter Mondale was the first prominent politician to put the problems of ordinary American families on the public agenda. In 1973, the Democratic Senator from Minnesota had his Subcommittee on Children and Youth conduct hearings on "American Families: Trends and Pressures." Convinced by these hearings that government was insufficiently attentive to the needs of families, Mondale urged that before government undertook any plan, it should ask: "What is this going to do to the average family?"

The idea caught on. A Family Impact Seminar, supported by private funds and affiliated with George Washington University, was set up in 1976 to seek ways to measure the specific effects of policy decisions on families. Then, two prestigious foundations—the National Research Council and the Carnegie Council on Children—called on the Federal Government to coordinate its various family programs into one clear and coherent family policy, eliminating those that worked to families' disadvantage and strengthening those that helped them.

It was this climate of opinion that led Presidential candidate Jimmy Carter to use the alleged breakdown of the family as a campaign theme in 1976. Telling voters that "the American family is in trouble," Carter nevertheless vowed to "restore what was lost." With Mondale, now his running mate, he pledged that, if elected, he would see to it that "every decision our government makes is designed to support and strengthen the American family." Once elected, he announced plans for a White House Conference on the Family to be held in 1979 that would "examine the impact of our institutions, public policies and laws, the media, and voluntary organizations on the capability of families to meet basic needs and respond to changes and increased pressures produced by our society."

Subsequent developments, however, showed that it was not easy to translate pro-family sentiments into government policy. From beginning to end, the Carter Administration's family initiatives were frustrated by persistent ideological disputes; for, while virtually everyone could agree that government actions should help the family, this consensus masked significant differences over what was wrong with the status quo, let alone what should be done to set it right.

For many Americans, the traditional two-parent family with children was the desired norm. As far as they were concerned, the increase in deviations from that norm was tantamount to the decay of the family. A national family policy, therefore, should try to reverse the trends of the 1970s by encouraging marriage and child-bearing, preventing family breakup, and generally fostering traditional values. On the whole reluctant to encourage government intervention into the lives of families, these traditionalists hoped that a White House Conference would focus on the emendation or elimination of policies that undermined family stability.

There was also a highly organized network on the extreme right of the political spectrum that showed far greater zeal in defense of what it considered to be the traditional family. Identified with the Moral Majority and fundamentalist protestantism, this element at first looked with great suspicion on a White House Conference, viewing it as one more step toward government regulation of private family relations. Once plans for the Conference were finalized, however, they exerted considerable energy in having it reflect their priorities: anti-feminism, anti-abortion, and an insistence that values be taught at home, not in public schools.

Many Americans assumed that the White House Conference would perform yet a different function. Not at all enamored of the traditional family model, they looked favorably on the recent demographic shifts, recognizing in them some liberating new options.

Feminists, for example, many of whom classified the traditional family as a remnant of patriarchy, applauded the large-scale entrance of women into the workforce. From their perspective, female dependence on males should be further discouraged by a family policy that rooted out sexism in the workplace, ensured women's reproductive freedom, and provided quality day care.

Similarly, people with non-traditional lifestyles, such as unmarried couples living together, the voluntarily childless, and gays, were hopeful that the decline of the traditional family would hasten public legitimization of their alternatives to it. Organizations representing such groups saw a White House Conference as a means of modifying Federal policy in the direction of greater recognition of diverse family forms.

Yet another constituency interested in a White House Conference were the sociologists, psychologists, social workers and counselors who were professionally involved in studying families and helping them deal with their problems. As a rule, the training these professionals receive encourages a value-free approach and a hesitation to make normative judgments about the respective merits of different lifestyles. From their standpoint, a White House Conference should neither approve nor disapprove of changes in the family structure. Rather, following the path of many European countries, it should develop a comprehensive plan of government support for all families through universal and free health care for mothers and children, direct payments to families based on how many children they have, and high-quality, tax-supported day care.

THE WHITE HOUSE CONFERENCE

The conflicting aims and assumptions of those involved in planning the Conference surfaced as soon as the Administration tried to devise a definition for "family." The Census Bureau's definition, "a group of two persons or more related by birth, marriage or adoption and residing together," was too restrictive to encompass the new family forms, while the alternative offered by the Family Service Association of America, a "person-to-person mutual aid system" providing "emotional support. . .and the assurance of economic and physical survival of the total constellation" would, one traditionalist noted, include "a pair of winos sharing a boxcar and a bottle." Here, in what seemed a dispute over words, was a confrontation over basic values. The problem was circumvented, temporarily, by avoiding any definition and by calling the project a White House Conference "on Families," instead of "on the Family."

But the same ideological clash plagued the planning of the Conference. A complicated system of delegate selection was designed to produce a mix of people, some chosen at the grassroots by peer groups, others appointed by state governors, and another "at-large" category picked by the President. Although this formula was meant to assure the broadest possible spectrum of participation, ethnic and racial minorities claimed that they were underrepresented, and conservatives complained that the President had used his appointment powers to pack the Conference with liberals and feminists. Two conservative governors, from Indiana and Alabama, flatly refused to have their states participate.

Predictably, discussion of substantive issues at planning meetings, state conferences, and three regional gatherings in Baltimore, Minneapolis and Los Angeles evoked fireworks. A number of right-wing groups, intent on combatting abortion, the Equal Rights Amendment, sex education and gay rights, because of their alleged harm to family preservation, formed a National Pro-Family Coalition. In response, some of the mainstream liberal groups joined with organizations favoring a plurality of lifestyles in a National Coalition for the White House Conference. There were demonstrations or walkouts at all three regional meetings, as well as a host of minority reports dissenting, for one reason or another, from the consensus of the meetings.

These ideological confrontations combined with some annoying bureaucratic bottlenecks to delay and finally alter President Carter's original plan: Instead of a White House Conference in 1979, there was just a meeting at the White House in August 1980, which approved a report summarizing what occurred at the regional meetings, and recommending those proposals that enjoyed broadest support.

This report, entitled *Listening to America's Families*, downplayed the importance of the ideological polarization and announced that its recommendations would "disappoint those on both political extremes who use 'family' as a codeword." The most popular proposal at the regional conferences turned out to be relatively uncontroversial suggestions for more childcare facilities, flexible hours for working parents, changes in the tax code and Social Security System to benefit full-time homemakers, and more effective action against drug and alcohol abuse. Although the report contained an ambitious plan to implement its recommendations, Jimmy Carter and the Democrats were voted out of power three months later. There seemed little likelihood that the new Republican Administration of Ronald Reagan, committed to reducing government's role in domestic affairs, would formulate a family policy of its own.

THE REAGAN ADMINISTRATION

Ironically, some of President Reagan's closest allies in Congress, abandoning their old distrust of Federal involvement in family matters, proposed a Family Protection Act in 1981. It combined in one package some recommendations emerging from the White House Conference together with elements of the agenda advocated by the "New Right."

The Act's provisions for tax incentives to encourage corporate day care and home care for the elderly and the handicapped aroused little opposition. Moreover, considerable support was forthcoming for its alteration of the law to allow homemakers to put the same sum of money into an Individual Retirement Account as working spouses.

In contrast, certain elements of the Family Protection Act either had nothing to do with families, or else seemed designed to intrude, in an unprecedented way, on the lives of individuals, families, and communities. Contraception or abortion services funded by government would not be available to minors without parental consent; Federal authority over cases of family violence would be weakened; Federal funding for educational materials that reflect the influence of the feminist movement would be denied; voluntary prayer would be allowed in the public schools; and religiously affiliated institutions would be exempt from affirmative-action regulations.

The extreme elements of the Family Protection Act never stood a chance of passage, since Democrats controlled the House of Representatives. The only family legislation adopted during the first Reagan term was acceptable to both liberals and conservatives: partial elimination of the "marriage penalty" in the income tax code, more tax benefits for the care of dependents, renewed funding of the Office of Adolescent Pregnancy Programs, and a more vigorous Federal role in the enforcement of child support payments. Democrats did complain that the Reagan cuts in the domestic budget were hurting families, but the Administration responded that its triumph over inflation, promotion of economic growth, transfer of responsibility to states and localities, and maintenance of a safety net for the "truly needy" constituted a true pro-family policy.

Senator Daniel Patrick Moynihan (D.N.Y.) delivered the prestigious Godkin Lectures at Harvard University on April 8-9, 1985, speaking on the subject of "Family and Nation." The morning after the first lecture, *The New York Times*, in a lead editorial entitled "Senator Moynihan and the Children," called his talk "an act of intellectual and political leadership," and urged that its message "be heard right and left, far and wide."

Why so much excitement about a lecture on an issue that has been extensively debated for more than a decade? Underlying the *Times*' enthusiasm was the hope that Moynihan's voice would help overcome the widespread skepticism about whether government can do anything to help families. Indeed, ever since the 1980 White House Conference on Families failed to live up to expectations, the notion of a national family policy has been in eclipse, and proponents of such a position have been very much on the defensive.

CAN GOVERNMENT HELP FAMILIES?

An early indication of this trend came in 1981, in a book by Gilbert Y. Steiner entitled *The Futility of Family Policy*. Steiner, a senior policy analyst at the Brookings Institution, which published the book, detailed the steps that had led to the White House Conference and concluded that the effort to develop a coherent family policy was doomed to fail because "our intangible sentiments that are the foundation of strong family relations can neither be legislated nor set forth in executive order or court decree."

Reviewing issue after issue, Steiner showed that individual policy options could be seen as pro- or anti-family, depending on the observer's own values. Does making contraceptives available to adolescents without parental knowledge strengthen the family by preventing teenage pregnancy, or weaken it by breaking down communications between the generations? Does government-supported day care benefit parents and children or discourage parental concern and responsibility for their offspring? Does barring welfare to children unless the father is absent from the home encourage men to work, or to abandon their families?

Family policy, Steiner argued, can be "whatever the particular discussant wants it to be," and therefore does not exist. Government, he suggested, should set itself a more modest goal—"to protect or compensate as best it can troubled members of dysfunctional, unhappy families."

The next important attack on government involvement in family life came from sociologists Brigitte Berger of Wellesley College and Peter Berger of Boston University, whose book, *The War Over the Family* (Anchor/Doubleday) appeared in 1983. Convinced that the great majority of families are

quite capable of coping on their own, the Bergers charged that family
professionals—social workers, psychologists, counselors—"have an interest
in defining situations in such a way that their services appear necessary.
Not surprisingly. . .the family [was] increasingly held to be incompetent
to deal with its own problems." For families that do need help, the Bergers
urged the involvement of churches, neighborhood organizations, and other
voluntary groups, rather than government.

HELPING OR HURTING?

The most controversial critique of government attempts to help families
appears in Charles Murray's *Losing Ground: American Social Policy,
1950-1980* (Basic Books, 1984)—a wide-ranging attack on virtually all the
social programs legislated over the last generation.

Murray, a fellow at the Manhattan Institute for Policy Research, makes
his argument by pointing to the sharp rise in illegitimate births and single-
parent families since the 1960s, precisely when government "job programs,
education programs, health programs, income maintenance programs" were
supposed to strengthen the family.

These programs, he contends, not only did no good, but actually caused
family breakdown by "changing the rules of the game." With federal support so easily available, the poor quite rationally made use of that support
instead of struggling to earn a living on their own. The shortrun benefit
for the poor turned into a long-term tragedy for society because it led to
the development of a welfare-dependent underclass.

Since trying to "provide more for the poor. . .produced more poor instead,"
Murray urges the elimination of all government social programs for
working-age people (except unemployment insurance), in order to restore
the incentive to work.

Murray's damning diagnosis and extreme remedy unleashed a bitter controversy. Those eager to cut the federal deficit by reducing domestic spending have seized upon this thesis to argue that social programs not only
waste money but also hurt the intended beneficiaries. *Losing Ground*, said
The New York Times, "is this year's budget-cutters' bible."

The book has also attracted its share of critics. Some cite data that seem
to refute Murray. Since, for example, there is no correlation between the
level of state welfare payments and the incidence of illegitimacy in that
state, his opponents argue, how can Murray claim that public aid promotes
out-of-wedlock births? Others insist that the high inflation rate and rising
unemployment of the 1970s bear more responsibility for family breakdown
than government programs, which were being cut back, not expanded, during that time.

Whatever the merits of their case, Murray, Steiner, the Bergers and others
who feel as they do have forced liberals to rethink old assumptions about
the automatic beneficence of government programs. As Andrew Cherlin

of Johns Hopkins University, a leading mainstream sociologist of the family, recently reported, there is "a retrenchment in the professional camp from the heady days of the 1970s when the creation of a vaguely-thought-out national family policy seemed imminent."

Writing in the *Journal of Family Issues* (June 1984), Cherlin agreed with Gilbert Steiner that a comprehensive family policy is impossible, and with Brigitte and Peter Berger that families are more capable of handling their own problems than previously assumed. And Christopher Jencks, the eminent sociologist at Northwestern University, conceded at the end of an otherwise critical review of *Losing Ground* (*New York Review of Books*, May 9, 1985), that Federal social policy has "often rewarded folly and vice" and "never had enough confidence in its own norms of behavior to assert that those who violated these norms deserved whatever sorrows followed."

THE ROLE OF TAX POLICY

Senator Moynihan, who has considerable family policy credentials, has sought to overcome the inertia of the sociologists and the policy analysts with a call for new Federal initiatives in support of the family that he hopes will be acceptable to both liberals and conservatives.

In his Godkin Lectures, Moynihan noted that government programs, whatever they might have achieved for other groups, have not helped children. The poverty rate among Americans under the age of 18 jumped from 14 per cent to 22.2 per cent between 1973 and 1983, and these youngsters now constitute 40 per cent of all poor people. Fully half of these children live in female-headed households, and since family breakup is on the increase, the number of poor children is likely to rise even further.

Moynihan thinks that alterations in the income tax code might reverse the trend. In 1948, personal and dependent exemptions ensured that over three-quarters of median family income was not taxable. He comments: "Was this not in effect a powerful national family policy? It takes money to raise a family, and the federal government chose not to tax most of the income so required." But the value of these exemptions lagged behind the rising median income and the cost of living, pushing a growing number of poor families onto the tax rolls. Moynihan seeks to remedy the problem and ease the financial burdens of childrearing by increasing the exemptions.

The Senator's hope for bipartisan tax reform has been partially fulfilled by President Reagan's tax plan which, as initially drafted, would double the personal and dependent exemptions to $2,000 and index them to inflation, reduce rates for most taxpayers, and exempt virtually all of the poor from paying income tax.

But other features of the plan have revived some familiar ideological conflicts. Allowing full-time homemakers to put $2,000 into an Individual Retirement Account, just like women who work outside the home, changing the childcare expense credit to a deduction, and eliminating the special "marriage penalty" deduction for two-paycheck families are clearly meant to reward the wife who stays home. For traditionalists, this is pro-family; but others would echo Colorado Representative Patricia Schroeder's charge that it denigrates "the more than 50 per cent of U.S. families where the female spouse works outside the home."

For families so poor that a tax break would not help them, Moynihan is co-sponsoring a bill that mandates a national minimum standard for welfare benefits indexed to inflation, an end to the requirement in many states that children get welfare only if the father is absent from the home, job training for teenage mothers, and more effective initiatives to prevent adolescent pregnancy. Since this proposal flies in the face of current skepticism about government programs, its passage is far from assured.

27.

Family Fever

Jeff Riggenbach

"The family is a hot issue," writes Letty Cottin Pogrebin, long-time feminist and one of the founding editors of *Ms.* magazine, in her book *Family Politics*, published last year. "Judging by the proliferation of magazine cover stories, television features, talk show discussions, academic research, and public policy discourse being devoted to the state of the American family, it seems safe to say that what civil rights and Vietnam were to the Sixties, and women's rights and the environment were to the Seventies, family issues have become to the Eighties."

Pogrebin may be overstating the case somewhat, but not by much. The evidence in support of her contention is to be found not only in the magazine articles, academic publications, and TV shows to which she alludes, but also in the pages of the many books on marriage and family matters that have been published over the past few years.

In one of these books, *What's Happening to the American Family?* (1981), sociologists Sar Levitan and Richard Belous write, "Marriage and family appear to have fallen on hard times," and the resulting "sense of something falling apart has even reached the White House. . . . Both Democratic and Republican Presidents have foreseen disturbing omens in current family trends. The Carter Administration launched a nationwide White House Conference on Families in an effort to cope with these problems. Not to be outdone, Ronald Reagan proclaimed, upon accepting the Republican nomination, that his administration would be a crusade to revitalize American institutions. The first institution on his list was the family."

Nor is this official concern for the vitality of the family confined to the White House. Over on Capitol Hill, a group of Republican lawmakers has also been anguishing over the plight of the family. And in every session of Congress since 1979, these congressmen have been proposing a Family Protection Act to set things right again. For the moment, the act is dead. But odds are it will resurface in the fall. Those who have been backing it for the past five years are unlikely to give up so easily on their desire (in the language of the act) "to preserve the integrity of the American family, to foster and protect the viability of American family life. . .and to promote the virtues of the family."

The problem is that what the Moral Majoritarians and hidebound traditionalists behind the Family Protection Act really mean when they talk about "the family" is the so-called traditional family: a breadwinning father, a full-time housewife mother, and one or more children. But fewer than one American household in five these days is inhabited by such a family. In fact, even if you consider families like mine to be "traditional"–families in which both parents work, both parents are on their second marriages, and the children have different fathers and different surnames–even then the traditional family is in a minority. More than half of all American households are now occupied by untraditional families or by single individuals living alone.

According to the partisans of the Family Protection Act, what lies at the heart of the current crisis of the American family is precisely the fact that the traditional family–the household type that (they contend) has always been the norm in America–has lately begun eroding away, mostly in response to certain meddlesome policies of the Federal government. It is true, of course, that certain recent Federal programs have created incentives to break up traditional families–the welfare rules, for example, that reward an unemployed father for deserting his family. Yet in point of fact, the decline of the traditional family did not begin a mere few decades ago with the birth of Federal meddling. It began long, long before.

"The family, in its old sense," wrote a contributor to the *Boston Quarterly Review* of October 1859, "is disappearing from our land, and not only our free institutions are threatened but the very existence of our society is endangered." Jonathan Gathorne-Hardy reports in his book *Marriage, Love, Sex and Divorce* (1981) that the same state of affairs existed 300 years ago in Stuart England, where many of the original American colonists came from. "So far from stable," writes Gathorne-Hardy, the family in 17th-century Britain "was in a state of 'collapse' which it has not yet reached even in America. At Clayworth (one of the parishes where evidence over time exists) in 1688, 39 per cent of marriages were with a partner married before; 13 per cent were second marriages, 3 per cent were third marriages, 4 per cent were fourth and one person had had five previous partners. From other sources one can gauge that approximately one-third of all marriages in Stuart England were second marriages or more."

Of course, the reasons for marital termination were different in those days. "Death played the part then that divorce does now," Gathorne-Hardy notes. And "one can speculate that, if the same conditions existed today and if death struck by chance as often, then one-third of the marriages which today solve their difficulties by divorce would have solved them by death.

"The idea that the instability of modern Western marriage, all the divorcing and splitting and affairs, somehow means that society is actually less stable, is not true," Gathorne-Hardy concludes. "The institutions in the old world were expedients to provide an illusion of permanence in a world which was impermanent and insecure. They were therefore talked and written about as permanent to such an extent that we have come to believe it. The evidence, however, is that they were not." All in all, "we are just as stable as the past."

Is more evidence needed? Very well. "In the 1860s," Richard Sennett wrote eight years ago in *The Fall of Public Man*, "social workers in both London and Paris were. . .worrying about the demoralization of the poor, and linking that demoralization to the family conditions in which the poor lived. In the 1860s, as in the 1960s, a 'broken home' was usually taken to be the specific culprit, again with a female as the usual head of the household." Levitan and Belous, in *What's Happening to the American Family?*, sum the matter up: "Marital disruption was also a problem in the 'good old days,' even though its causes have shifted. With vast improvements in health, plunging death rates for all ages counterbalanced increases in the divorce rate during this century to such a degree that the rate of marital disruption for all causes was fairly stable until 1970."

Levitan and Belous remind us also that 19th-century America "was full of experimental communities that explored new family forms," communities like John Humphrey Noyes's Oneida, which did away with traditional marriage altogether on the grounds that it was contrary to human nature. But, Levitan and Belous comment, even when it has been "granted that alternative family structures have always existed, it has been argued that a growing number of individuals are availing themselves of these opportunities. Even this point is highly debatable. For example, while there has been a vast increase in the reported number of couples living together without the blessings of state or church, it is quite difficult to know how much of this shift is really a new trend. With diminished social pressures to follow any one pattern, a good portion of the reported increase in this behavior may represent only the increased willingness of people to be open about what has always taken place. 'Swinging' is probably one of the oldest indoor sports known to humanity, as even a casual reader of the Bible would easily find, and not all of the participants were villains. What may be new is the willingness on the part of the players to publicly extol its virtues to the multitudes."

Johns Hopkins University sociologist Andrew Cherlin, author of *Marriage, Divorce, Remarriage* (1981), carries this line of thinking to its obvious conclusion by arguing that what we see around us today, what the Moral Majoritarians decry as the crisis of the family, is in fact the norm in American life, the norm from which our national experience during the hallowed 1950s was a unique deviation. "The birthrate has been declining since the 1820s," Cherlin writes, "the divorce rate has been climbing since at least the Civil War, and over the last half century a growing number of married women have taken paying jobs. Thus, many of the changes we witnessed in family life in the 1960s and 1970s were a continuation of long-term trends that have been with us for generations.

"The only exception occurred during the late 1940s and the 1950s," Cherlin continues. "After World War II, Americans raised during the austerity of the Depression and the war entered adulthood at a time of sustained prosperity. The sudden turnabout in their fortunes led them to marry earlier and have more children than any generation before or since in this century. Because many of us were either parents or children in the baby-boom years following the war, we tend to think nostalgically that the 1950s typify the way 20th century families used to be. But the patterns of marriage and childbearing in the 1950s were a historical aberration: the patterns of the 1960s and 1970s better fit the long-term trends."

What is the meaning of these long-term trends? What is their cause? If they have been with us since the last century it would seem obvious that they can hardly be attributed to the interventions of big government and the welfare state. In fact, there is evidence to suggest that even in recent years government interventions have been only a minor factor in accelerating these trends. It is common knowledge, for example, that the Federal welfare program known as Aid to Families with Dependent Children (AFDC) encourages the formation of single-parent households, commonly consisting of unmarried, unskilled, unemployed women and their children. Yet Levitan and Belous report that "most of the increase in the number of female headed households is accounted for by childless women who are ineligible for public assistance benefits."

These childless women are forming their own self-headed households, not because of some action of some government, but *because that is how they choose to live their lives*. Cherlin refers to "the growing likelihood that unmarried individuals will choose to maintain their own households rather than live with kin" as perhaps the most important change [that has] affected the composition of households." He writes: "It used to be common . . . for a woman to move back to her parents' home after she separated from her husband, but today separated and divorced women are much more likely to set up their own households. Nevermarried young adults, whose numbers have been increasing, are less likely to remain at home until they marry than they were twenty years ago. Similarly, more older, widowed people are living by themselves rather than moving in with their children. It may be that the preferences of unmarried adults concerning living arrangements have changed. I suspect, however, that most unmarried adults always have preferred to live independently, only today they are more likely to have the financial resources to do so."

It might also be argued, of course, that most married adults always have preferred to remain married only when they found their marriages personally satisfying, but are more likely today to have the financial resources to exercise such a preference. "Many of the traditional reasons why people got married and stayed married are less compelling today," Cherlin writes. "The greater economic independence of women means that marriage is less necessary as an economic partnership, as a common enterprise that creates a joint product neither partner could produce alone. And as the success of the economic enterprise becomes less crucial to husbands and wives, their personal satisfaction with their marriage becomes relatively more important. Consequently, it seems to me, husbands and wives are more likely today than in the past to evaluate their marriage primarily according to how well it satisfies their individual emotional needs. If their evaluation on these terms is unfavorable, they are likely to turn to divorce and then, perhaps, to another marriage."

The conclusion seems inescapable: people used to have children because they had to. They used to get married and stay married because they had to. And once they had become old and feeble they used to live with their children and rely upon them for their support because they had to. Once they no longer had to do these things, they stopped doing them.

This is, says Andrew Cherlin, "the way in which the United States—and, indeed, every advanced industrial society—has developed. As we moved from a rural, agricultural society to an urban, industrial one, the economic value of children declined and people had fewer of them. As the production of goods and services shifted from the home to the factory or the office, women were drawn into the labor market, thereby becoming more independent of men. And as the school, the hospital and the old-age home took over many of the functions family members used to perform for each other, men and women found it progressively easier to live nontraditional family lives."

Should it surprise anyone that people took advantage of their newfound opportunity? Does it really come as a surprise even to the prating Bible thumpers of the Moral Majority to learn that the "traditional" nuclear family is not the best of all possible worlds for everyone?

"When I can no longer bear to think of the victims of broken homes," says humorist Peter De Vries, "I begin to think of the victims of intact ones." And the latter are legion. "A high incidence of violence within the family has come to light in recent years," write Levitan and Belous. "Almost 1 million children may be neglected or abused each year, and as many as 2 million women may experience violence in the home.... The Office of Domestic Violence in the Department of Health and Human Services estimated that about one of four couples will undergo serious family violence during the course of a marriage or relationship. Roughly 25 per cent of all homicides involve spouses, and 20 per cent of all police deaths and 40 per cent of police injuries occur when an officer responds to a 'family violence' call." Moreover, they report, "automobile accident cases still make up the majority of suits in court, but family-related cases are currently running a close second."

Karen Lindsey, the avowedly leftist and feminist author of the 1981 book *Friends as Family*, paints an even grimmer picture. "As many as 60 per cent of all married women are beaten at least once by their husbands," she writes. "And between 500,000 and one million elderly parents are abused each year by the adult offspring they live with." The National Campaign for the Prevention of Child Abuse and Neglect estimates that "in up to 20 per cent of American families, children are subjected to physical abuse, sexual abuse and neglect." And then there's the runaway problem. "An estimated 2 million youngsters run away from home every year," the *Los Angeles Times* reported in late November 1981, "and that rate is steadily increasing. While 15- and 16-year-olds account for nearly half the runaways, they range in age from 10 and 11 on up, and the national Runaway Switchboard reports serving children as young as 8 and 9."

If these kids run away, if their mothers seek divorces, if their grandparents choose to live by themselves, can anybody realistically contend that they have made these choices because an unholy alliance of secular humanists and godless communists has conspired against the traditional family? These people leave the family because in their homes familiarity has bred contempt—and worse than contempt. "The family is the American fascism," said Paul Goodman. And for many in our society, that is precisely what it is.

Of course, for many others, myself included, the family is something else entirely. It is a way of life, and one which we feel we have freely chosen because of the various satisfactions it offers us. Why do we do it? Why do people form families? What are families for, anyway?

There are those—fundamentalist Christians, for example—who argue that such questions are pointless. We live in families because that's the way God set things up in the beginning, with Adam and Eve and Cain and Abel. That's all we know and all we need to know. Trying to figure out why God set it up that way is as foolish as trying to figure out the significance of the fact that the very first nuclear family in all of human history exploded into an act of violence that left one of its members dead at the hand of another of its members, even though violence on TV, rock music, secular humanism, and the Federal government of the United States were not problems in the Garden of Eden.

But set these true believers aside for the moment; we'll be coming back to them soon enough. The conventional wisdom among most other students of the family as a social institution is that its purpose is economic and broadly cultural. On the one hand, it offers its members the easiest or most efficient way of getting a decent living. On the other, it provides its members, especially its child members, with practical training in the skills one needs to deal with other people in the outside world.

When life was mainly agricultural and the home was the workplace, families were large and typically included several generations. This assured an adequate number of able bodies to do the work, and it assured that those who had become too old and feeble to do any hard work would be available to look after those children who were still too small to do any hard work. And everyone benefited from the arrangement. The children and the old folks were obviously able to get a better living for themselves by living in a family than they could have got by themselves. And the able-bodied adults in their prime who might have done all right on their own also gained certain economic advantages by living in the family. Perhaps most important among these was the knowledge that in time of illness or temporary disability, there would be people to care for them and absorb the cost of their daily lives until they could work again. In this sense, the family was a source of security, an insurance policy.

But as the Industrial Revolution simultaneously raised per capita income and moved the population into cities, this kind of security became increasingly irrelevant. The home was no longer the workplace, so it was not advantageous to add members to the household, whether in the form of new children or aged relatives. Now that the work of the family was done outside the home, new additions were no longer added hands; they were added *costs*—parasites, if you will. On top of that, while space for additional people was cheap in the country, it was very expensive in the city. So people began living in smaller families, and the norm became parents and their children, but neither the parents' parents nor the children's children. The extended family had given way to the nuclear family.

Since that time, per capita income has continued to climb, and various institutions, some of them voluntary, some of them governmental (which is to say compulsory), have begun taking over many of the old functions of the family. You don't have to live in a family any longer to assure yourself of income during time of illness or temporary disability—all you have to do is buy an insurance policy. You no longer need your aged parent at home to watch the kids while you work—you can send the kids to a day-care center or a public school, and you can send the aged parent to an old-folks' home. If your income is high enough, you can pay strangers to do all the things for you that you used to get from family members. And if your income isn't high enough, you can probably get some extra money from the government to make it high enough.

For people who don't like the members of their biological families (and such people have been quite common ever since the days of Cain and Abel), the temptation to hire strangers and live alone is apparently great. Others who don't like the members of their biological families seem to feel a different temptation, however. They leave their biological families, but they don't hire strangers. Instead, they move in with other individuals and form surrogate families of various kinds.

These surrogate families have become quite controversial of late, particularly among those who feel that since God has decreed what sorts of groups we are to live in, that settles the matter and anyone who chooses to live in a group of any other sort is tantamount to a sinner. "The public continues to receive a steady parade of examples 'proving' that divorced, never-married, homosexual, bisexual, transsexual, communal, and living-together units form the bulk of today's 'families,' " writes Jeane Westin, author of *The Coming Parent Revolution* (1981). "The most noted 'family experts' huddled together for a four-day conference in the late 1970s to answer the question, Who can define 'family' in a way everyone would accept? No one pointed out that 'family' has always been defined as parents plus children and that family experimenters can jolly well come up with their own concepts rather than asking the traditional family to move over." Westin asserts, "The continual extension of the concept of family to include every social fad and sexual fancy has resulted in the trivialization of the family."

"If you recall," Sen. Roger Jepsen (R-Iowa) told his fellow members of the upper house of Congress in June 1981 when he introduced the then-current version of the Family Protection Act, "after the 1970 White House Conference on Children and Youth, the Forum 14 report redefined the family as a group of individuals in interaction.

"The American Home Economics Association has determined that the family is a unit of two or more persons who share values and have a commitment to one another over time. Unfortunately, such all-encompassing definitions, which at first glance may appear bland and academically accurate, actually extend the meaning of family to include anyone and anything from group marriages to homosexual and lesbian couples who want to adopt children."

The question is, Why is this "unfortunate"? If the purpose of the family is economic—if, that is, the family is an institution that is entered into by its members in order to improve their overall standard of living and provide themselves with a measure of security during hard times—why isn't any group of individuals who live together for these purposes properly considered a family? If another function of family life is to provide moral and emotional support for family members when they are demoralized, disgraced, or defeated, why isn't any group of individuals who live together and support each other in this way properly considered a family? If still another function of the family is to provide education in living skills for children, why isn't any group of adults and children who live together properly considered a family? If it weren't possible for biologically unrelated individuals to interact satisfactorily as family members, conventional marriage—that is, marriage to nonrelatives—would be impossible, as would adoption. The old adage that you can choose your friends but not your relatives is universally acknowledged to be untrue when it comes to husbands, wives, and adopted children. Why then is it true of parents, grandparents, aunts, uncles, cousins, and siblings?

In fact, people *have* been exercising choice with respect to their family members for hundreds of years, albeit in a more informal manner than the one that typifies legal marriage or adoption. All of us have heard people remark of unusually close friends that "I love him like a brother," or "I love her like a sister," or "She's been like a second mother to me," or "He's like the father (or son or daughter) I never had." Many of us have known people who have informally adopted other unrelated adults into their families, shared holidays with them, and named them "honorary" aunts or uncles of their children. Many of us have friends who are looked upon by all the members of our biological families as loved ones and who are entitled, in our minds, to the same treatment we would extend to our own brothers or sisters. We tell these friends to feel free to visit any time, even on an unannounced basis. We tell them to "make themselves at home." We lend them our money and our cars and our irreplaceable treasures—things we make a policy of never lending to anyone else. We give them keys to our homes, trust them with our children, turn to them for moral and emotional support. And we feel able to call upon them in any emergency, just as they feel able to call on us. What are these special friends but adopted family members, people we have adopted without the usual bureaucratic rigamarole that ordinarily accompanies adoption, but adopted nonetheless?

Social observers Karen Lindsey and Jonathan Gathorne-Hardy see this phenomenon of "friends as family" as the wave of the future. But as we have seen, it might equally be regarded as the wave of the past re-establishing itself after a brief apparent absence during the 1950s. For most of the past two centuries, with the exception of that brief but crucial period of slightly more than a decade, the "traditional" family has been merely one of a number of possible household units, all of which have been common. It may be useful at this point to repeat the admonition of Levitan and Belous that "with diminished social pressures to follow any one pattern, a good portion of the reported increase in this behavior [unconventional family types] may represent only the increased willingness of people to be open about what has always taken place."

But of course such increased openness can only serve to encourage those who waver between following established social practice despite the fact that they find it unrewarding and doing their own things, unconventional though those things may be. Inevitably, some of the apparent increase in unconventional family life that we seem to see all around us *is* new, *is* a real increase. It is the natural tendency of market economies to gradually increase the personal wealth of almost all who participate in their operation. And increased personal wealth means wider personal choice—in the current vernacular, more options. So it is that as per capita income has grown in our country, it has become increasingly possible for more and more people to live in untraditional households. The expanding market for goods and services has led to the establishment of an expanded market for types of families. And the majority of Americans have voted with their feet and their pocketbooks and their hearts for untraditional family lives.

And what should be the role of government in all this? There is widespread consensus that it should be an active one. Letty Cottin Pogrebin speaks for the political left, but no right-wing defender of the family would disagree with her when she writes, "Families might be less sophisticated political activists than the farm or tobacco lobby. . . but who's to claim families are not more entitled to Federal supports and subsidies?" No, the only real argument between the liberals and the conservatives when it comes to government family policy is over which kind of family should be singled out for benefit—traditional families or untraditional families. The reactionary right would have government set up incentives so that Americans who opted for traditional family life would be rewarded, often at the expense of those who prefer untraditional family life. The liberal left would have government subsidize untraditional family life, often at the expense of those who prefer traditional family life.

I say a pox on both their houses. To each his or her own. Let government adopt a family policy of laissez-faire. Let each man and woman, and to the extent that it is feasible, each child, do what he or she wants. They have, all of them, the inestimable advantage of knowing much better than any government bureaucrat exactly what they want, and what price they are willing to pay to get it.

28.

Families, Sex, and the Liberal Agenda

Allan C. Carlson

The concept of "family policy" has attracted unprecedented attention within liberal political circles over the past four years. This attention, in turn, has generated numerous proposals aimed at strengthening American family life through government action.

The arguments of family-policy advocates follow a fairly standard analytical line. They begin by calling for a new emphasis, which Kenneth Keniston described for the Carnegie Council on Children as "abandoning the tendency to deal with children in isolation from their families or the society they live in. . . ." This change, advocates continue, involves a whole new perspective on public policy. The 1978 report by the National Commission on Families and Public Policies of the National Conference on Social Welfare (NCSW) suggests that the family-policy concept "may well provide fresh insight into social welfare, new perceptions of the individual's relationship to society, [and] a new formulation of the role of government in human affairs. . . ." The analysis then commonly turns to a presentation of statistics reflecting family stress, break-up, or change—such as a rise in the number of single-parent families, the growing percentage of working mothers, the swelling divorce rate, illegitimacy figures, rising welfare dependency, figures on teenage pregnancies, suicides, and runaways, and the number of unmarried, cohabiting couples.

Assessments of cause for this evident stress in American family life usually follow. The Carnegie Council's report faults in part the "American myths" of family independence, personal responsibility, technological advance, economic growth, and *laissez faire*. In addition, the report points to "the broad ecological pressure on children and their parents," chemicals in food, nuclear power, the unplanned nature of broadcasting, and "the economic drain of children" on parents, as forces undermining families' "capability to perform." The NCSW group cites the rigidification of the nineteenth-century American family ideal around a work-devoured, paycheck-oriented male tied to an economically and socially dependent woman and a brood of children, who are isolated from traditional sustaining institutions such as the extended family, neighborhood, and community. The Advisory Committee on Child Development of the Assembly of Behavioral and Social Sciences of the National Research Council (NRC), in its 1976 report *Toward a National Policy for Children and Families*, sees family difficulties related in significant degree to poverty, racial and sexual inequality, the decline of cities, poor housing, unemployment, inadequate health care, lack of transportation, the deterioration of the environment, and poor education. Every source agrees that existing governmental programs supporting children and families are totally inadequate and often destructive of family life.

In developing their family-policy proposals, advocates posit two principles: comprehensiveness and pluralism. Concerning the first, the carnegie group argues for a United States family policy "as comprehensive as its defense policy," involving "coherent" social and economic planning, a multitude of services, and a multifaceted approach to the issues. As for "pluralism," advocates all agree that it requires recognition of "the many lifestyle choices that may produce a wide range of family forms." "Lifestyle" choices with some legitimate claim to family status are said by some to include "child free" couples, unmarried couples, single-parent families, "single persons" families, homosexual pairings, communal arrangements, and—to fill in the gaps—assorted "minority lifestyles."

While varying in emphasis, specific family-policy proposals tend to include the following:

Income Security. All family-policy proponents agree that family income in the United States remains significantly maldistributed. They support establishment of a guaranteed annual family income, or "decency standard," representing half of the U.S's median income. Means to that "family stabilizing" goal vary. The NCSW group advocates a taxable federal family allowance of $750 per dependent (to replace the personal income-tax deduction), at a cost of approximately $70 billion. The Carnegie group proposes a comprehensive "credit income tax" scheme, granting households a refundable $1500 tax credit for each family member, tied to an adult work requirement (no work, no credit) and a straight 50 per cent tax on all income above the credit line. The NRC report leans toward an unspecified "negative income tax."

Full Employment. Joseph Califano stated in his widely praised September 1976 memo to Presidential candidate Jimmy Carter on American families:

"[T] he most severe threat to family life stems from unemployment and lack of an adequate income." Most other advocates agree, and call for legally guaranteed jobs to all heads of households, tied to more and better central economic planning.

Affirmative Action. Given particular emphasis by the Carnegie report is the belief that current efforts at eliminating racial, sexual, and other forms of discrimination are moving with intolerable slowness. Equality of opportunity, many contend, is not enough to insure a stable basis for family life among minorities, women, and the handicapped. Greater affirmative-action effort is needed.

Health Care. Citing the American preoccupation with individuals, the relatively high infant mortality rate among minorities, and the lack of pre- and post-natal maternity care for the poor, family-policy advocates call for a national health policy emphasizing preventive health care for all children. Their means to better health include "integration" of the health-care delivery system with other family services, public accountability, more research, and national record keeping and monitoring of children's health.

Social Services. Finding the existing 280 federal programs aiding families and children to be "inadequate, uncoordinated and patchwork," the NCSW, and the NRC and Carnegie groups as well, support the creation of integrated family-support services funded at appreciably higher levels.

Day Care. All family-policy advocates agree that the government has a responsibility to ensure that families needing child care during working hours have available a wide range of substitute choices.

Sexual Law. While avoiding most references to sex, family-policy advocates do tend to cite the need for more sex education and wider availability of contraceptives to reduce teenage pregnancy. Many support widening access to abortion.

Family Law. While emphasis varies, family-policy supporters tend to argue for stronger legal supports for families (including guaranteed due process in child-removal situations), greater legal autonomy for children, and reform of such abuse-prone areas of government involvement as foster care.

Work Law. All advocates support changes in work laws and new government incentives to accommodate the childcare needs of working parents.

Government. All sources agree that the government should be more aware of its impact on families. Most advocates support the idea of requiring that "family impact statements" be attached to proposed legislation and regulations.

In sum, family-policy advocates offer, as the way to reinvigorate American family life, virtually the entire liberal agenda: greater income redistribution, guaranteed minimum incomes, full employment policies, more social and economic planning, more and better integrated social services, reorganization and public funding of health care, more affirmative-action programs, better sex education, increased availability of contraceptives and abortion, government-funded day care, an emphasis on legal rights, work-law reforms, and a more sensitive, activist, and reorganized government.[1] They are focusing their attention on the scheduled 1980 (formerly 1979) White House Conference on Families. A "Coalition for the White House Conference" was organized in 1978 with a membership list "representing dramatically different family life styles and values" and including—together with more traditional family advocates such as the U.S. Catholic Conference and the YWCA—such reform oriented groups as the American Association of Sex Educators, Counselors, and Therapists, the Child Welfare League of America, the National Council of Churches, the National Gay Task Force, the National Organization of Non-Parents, Women's Action Alliance, and Zero Population Growth.

Family-policy advocates are certainly correct in their perception of stress and basic change. For though several recent studies—notably Mary Jo Bane's *Here To Stay*—have argued that American families are adjusting well to current social pressures, statistical evidence reflects fundamental alterations in the nation's family life. The divorce rate, for example, rose 150 per cent between 1958 and 1974, with the annual number of divorces climbing to nearly 1 million. The number of children affected by divorce each year rose from 379,000 in 1957 to 1.1 million in 1974. The fertility rate (births per 1,000 women aged 15-44) has fallen from 122.7 in 1957 to 66.7 in 1975, reflecting a major retreat from child-bearing. The illegitimacy ratio (illegitimate births per 1,000 live births) has tripled in less than two decades, reaching 142.5 in 1975. The percentage of single-parent families, relative to all families with children under age six, rose from 8 per cent in 1960 to 17 per cent in 1974. In 1977, nearly 18 million U.S. children lived with only one parent—a 100 per cent rise since 1960. Yet despite their appropriate emphasis on such changes, family-policy advocates have stumbled into definitional, attitudinal, and analytical errors that compromise their proposed policy response.

First, while paying deference to a "pluralism of family forms" may appear to reflect a sound liberal principle, the refusal of most family-policy advocates to set any identifiable norms at all leaves critical policy-related issues begging the question: What exactly is a "family"? If there can be no definition that excludes any form of human cohabitation, then what is a family policy trying to save, or restore, or strengthen, or help? And if all forms of human cohabitation are essentially equal, why have an expensive policy aimed at no particular goal? Inflation alone will ultimately compel most people to live with others. The "pluralism" school of family sociology, when translated into public policy, flounders on the hollowness of its basic concept.

Second, many family-policy advocates appear to be ambivalent toward birth and children. All Western European family policies developed in the 1930s and 1940s were predicated on pro-natalist sympathies. The state enthusiastically welcomed babies and encouraged parents to bear larger families. This gave some logical coherence to efforts to socialize child-rearing costs and justified the clearly stated policy preference for traditional nuclear families. However, many American liberals are now committed to a version of neoMalthusianism that emphasizes over-population as a national threat and a relatively high birthrate as a cause of continuing poverty and ecological distress. Births—especially of third or later children, or among teenagers or the welfare population—are not particularly welcomed. In line with their ideological commitment, family-policy advocates usually buttress support for family allowances and the like with evidence that such measures will have no pro-natalist effect. Rhetorical support for infants and children, it would seem, has a somewhat airy core.

Third, family-policy activists have built their reform proposals on misinterpreted statistical evidence. The most significant and startling change—revealed by virtually every measure of family stability (divorce rate, number of children affected by divorce, illegitimacy ratio, fertility rate, juvenile-delinquency rate, or percentage of single-parent families)—is from a remarkable health and vitality for the American "nuclear" family in the 1946-60 period, followed by a striking shift toward marked instability *after* 1960. This historical shift of bewildering proportions has been ignored by most family-policy advocates, because their analysis of the causes behind contemporary family problems cannot explain the extraordinary change from evident family vitality in the late 1940s and 1950s to accelerating instability after 1960.

Examine, for instance, the "poverty argument": that poverty and low incomes create family stress and instability. Personal income, in fact, was everywhere rising and poverty progressively declining throughout the 1960s, and at rates far more rapid than during the 1950s. The percentage of children below the poverty line actually fell from 27 per cent in 1959 to 15 per cent in 1968. Yet at the same time, families clearly began to fragment.

Or take the "jobs argument": that unemployment is a chief cause of troubled families. During the 1960s unemployment rates for white and black workers progressively declined to levels equal to or below those achieved during the 1950s. Yet family disintegration in the post-1945 era began to accelerate only after 1960.

All other explanations similarly fall short. The 1960s experienced unprecedented advances in incomes, jobs, and status by racial minorities and women. Inflation remained at tolerably low levels from the early 1950s through the late 1960s. The movement of women into the post-World War II labor market began during the late 1940s, not the 1960s. Medicare and Medicaid extended health coverage in the 1960s to many of the aged and poor, part of an extraordinary nationwide expansion of quality health care. Social services grew dramatically during the 1960s under the auspices of hundreds of new federal and state programs. The number of social workers tripled in that decade alone. The presumed pressures of technology— television, nuclear power, processed foods—had their counterparts in the 1950s without appreciable results. The "myths" of technological advance, economic growth, family independence, personal responsibility, and *laissez faire*, all existed with equal or greater virulence in the late 1940s and 1950s without apparent effect on families. In fact, under the causal analysis and policy recommendations advanced by recent family-policy advocates, the 1950s should have been marked by family turmoil and instability, while the 1960s should have evidenced a new blossoming of family life. But exactly the opposite happened. Why?

THREE DEVELOPMENTS

The instability characterizing American family life since 1960 results from the interplay of three developments: one demographic, one physiological and attitudinal, and one broadly ideological. None is amenable to intervention by a democratic state.

1. *The Demographic Bulge.* The very success of family life in the 1940s and 1950s generated the occasion of subsequent turmoil—a vast age cohort that began reaching adolescence in the early 1960s.

The most unstable stage of an individual's life, adolescence is characterized by confused emotions, rebellion against parental and other authority, and the questioning of values and ethical constraints. To deal with adolescents, parents and other responsible adults require confidence in their own values, personal strength, and willingness to administer discipline tempered by understanding and love. Yet, apparently overwhelmed by the surging numbers of youth during the 1960s, American adults and the institutions they controlled collectively showed few such qualities. Only now is the last of the "baby boom" generation passing into the more stable young-adult years. In a complex manner, this demographic bulge certainly conditioned, and to some degree caused, the other two developments.

2. *The "Second" Sex Revolution.* Historian Edward Shorter argues for the existence of two sex revolutions in Western history: The first occurred in Europe between 1750 and 1850 (the United States, he suggests, was "born modern"), and was marked by the initial incursion of premarital sexual intercourse into the lives of the unmarried. The second, says Shorter, began

between 1955 and 1965, and saw the generalization of intercourse among the majority of unmarried.

In the United States, the evidence reflecting major discontinuities after 1960 in the erotic life of the average young, white, unmarried woman seems conclusive. Among unmarried white women, ages 15 to 19, the illegitimacy rate was relatively stable through the 1950s—rising from 5.1 per 1,000 in 1950 to only 6.5 in 1962. Thereafter—and despite the spread of "the pill" and the widening availability of abortion—it climbed steadily, and reached 12.1 in 1975. A series of surveys from the 1960s shows as well startling increases in American "nonvirginity rates." Within a typical group of adolescent women questioned in 1971, nearly half had experienced intercourse by age 19, compared to only 17 per cent in Alfred Kinsey's study during the 1940s. And the pace of this change is accelerating: A recent study found a 54 per cent jump between 1971 and 1976 in the number of 16-year-olds having had intercourse at least once. Interestingly, the illegitimacy rate among non-white females rose through the 1950s in conjunction with the surge of marital fertility, but began to *fall* in 1961. In many respects, the "second" sex revolution was a white, middle-class phenomenon.

It soon spread from youth to other parts of the population. In a major 1972 statistical study commissioned by the Playboy Foundation, Morton Hunt discovered that all Americans in the early 1970s—young and old alike—were having more sex, doing it in different ways, with a greater variety of partners, and feeling less guilty about it afterwards, than did their Kinsey-survey counterparts. Whereas 41 per cent of married females ages 35 to 44 had experienced premarital sex, 81 per cent of married females ages 18 to 24 had. While only 14 per cent of Kinsey's "adolescent to age 25" group of white males had used cunnilingus in premarital foreplay, 69 per cent of the same age cohort in 1972 said they had. Kinsey reported a median weekly marital coitus figure of 2.45 for persons ages 16 to 25; Hunt found a median of 3.25 for the 18 to 24 age group, with similar increases for all older cohorts.

Even more striking are the shifts in sexual attitudes evident in the period after 1960. Opinion surveys among college students show that virginity was still a mythically prized virtue in the late 1950s; a poll in 1970 found that three out of four students thought it unimportant whether or not they married a virgin. Whereas legal and easy abortion had been unthinkable in the United States in 1963, by 1972 it was legal, subject to certain limitations, in half a dozen states and was to be legally available everywhere only one year later. In the 1973 "Sorenson Report," researchers described the growing predominance of situation ethics in the sexual liaisons of young people. Rejecting laws or religious dogma as irrelevant to the problems of sexual partners, distrusting lifelong monogamy, suspicious of the restraints of fidelity, and believing "family" to interfere with sexual fulfillment, a growing number of youth placed sexual satisfaction at the center of their personal relationships.

What caused this upheaval in American sexual actions and attitudes after 1960? Among background factors were advances by the biological sciences, such as oral contraceptives; physiological changes such as earlier menstruation and later menopause; the dramatic growth in higher education, which drew together large numbers of unmarried youth; and changes in the national mood, including the decline in religious values and a new emphasis on "rights" which led to an obsession with self. Sexual researchers, from Freud through Kinsey to Masters and Johnson, moved emphasis ever further away from the idea of the sex act as an expression of human love toward preoccupation with the nature of the physiological release and "health" of the sex organs.

Perhaps more critical was what Vance Packard calls "the crumbling of traditional controls" over youth sexuality. The decline in parental authority over the awakening process, the decrease in community scrutiny, and the rise of a youth subculture, made it vastly more difficult to assure female virginity until marriage. Surveys from the 1940 to 1960 period show a clear correlation between religious devoutness and abstinence from premarital coitus. Yet with the apparent American retreat from religious belief starting in the late 1950s, church leaders grew pliable and non-judgmental in matters of personal morality. In addition, the spread of "the pill" and waning concern about social stigmatization led to a decline in the fear that sexual activity might lead to premarital pregnancy.

Allan Sherman—in his episodic, rude, but nonetheless insightful *The Rape of the A*P*E* (*American *Puritan *Ethic)*—offers a "conspiracy" theory of the sexual revolution. Sherman traces the sexual revolution's origins to the social upheaval of World War II, follows it through an underground existence in the 1950s, to its fullblown emergence after 1963 and final victory in the 1973 Supreme Court abortion decisions. Led by scattered members of the generation reaching adulthood in the 1940s who were bent on the "obscening of America," the attack centered on the sexual restraints imposed by nineteenth-century bourgeois culture—such as the repression of obscenity, pornography, indecent exposure, nudity, premarital sex, extramarital sex, abortion, divorce, desertion, perversion—and on the whole "incredibly clean-cut and impossibly wholesome" American world of Disney, church socials, Shirley Temple, the YMCA, Blondie and Dagwood, *The Saturday Evening Post*, Motherhood, miniature golf, Coca-Cola, Apple Pie, and Hot Dogs. By the late 1960s, writes Sherman, "Legions of Lolitas joined the battle with battalions of Babbits and platoons of Portnoys. Manners and morals and great institutions bit the dust. Waterbeds splashed and vibrators jiggled. And when the air was cleared . . . the world was never going to be the same again. No one knew exactly how, but Western Civilization had been caught with its pants down."

And the impact of the sex revolution? Sherman suggests that it "removed America's backbone and revealed our awful secret: Stripped of the Puritan ethic, we have no morals at all." He adds that "nothing was reduced

to less recognizable rubble than the revered... Institution of Marriage."
Edward Shorter, a less euphoric coroner, considers the nuclear family of
the 1970s wracked by some form of final tubercular spasm.

The institution of monogamous marriage is clearly in trouble, for the
sexual revolution has made it vastly more difficult to retain monogamy's
monopoly on sex. Marriages predicated mostly on sexual capability and
erotic arousal prove fragile. Parents abandon and adolescents reject all sense
of lineage, which monogamy alone can provide. The latter turn instead to
peer groups and their own subculture in search of values and sexual
gratification. As Pitirim Sorokin once observed: "A sex revolution drastically
affects the lives of millions, deeply disturbs the community, and decisively
influences the future of society." Families, simply put, were major casualties
of the Western world's "second" sex revolution.

FROM "FATHER KNOWS BEST"...

3. *Collapse of the Nuclear Family Norm.* The emergence of industrial
capitalism and bourgeois society in the period from 1750 to 1850, according to Shorter, was tied to a dual revolution in "sentiments": heightened
sexuality and gushing maternal love. The former change, rising among men
and women of the European industrial class who were newly liberated from
the sexual restraints of traditional agrarian communities, produced the
"first" sex revolution referred to above. The latter change in sentiment well-
ed up among the bourgeoisie, for economic growth had liberated women
from other labor and allowed them to devote more time to better mothering and infant care.

Family life took shape about the home. The vital center of this new
domesticity was the infant. An emotional web was spun around mother
and baby, predicated on a new sense of the preciousness of infant life. Lloyd
de Mause has compiled a large body of evidence showing the sweeping improvement in childcare practice that accompanied the rise of the
bourgeoisie. Shockingly widespread practices of swaddling, child beating,
infanticide, wet nursing (virtually an institutionalized form of infanticide),
abandonment, sexual abuse, and even the sale of children, gave way to a
surge of parental affection, as demonstrated by the rising popularity of
maternal nursing, dramatic drops in infant mortality rates, a new popular
emphasis on the joys of domesticity and family life, and recognition of the
priceless importance of infants and children. This valuation spread even
to prenatal life. Nineteenth-century campaigns against abortion were largely a bourgeois phenomenon.

Girded by this value structure, the bourgeois nuclear family emerged as
the Western family norm. Its characteristics were a stable heterosexual
coupling based on love, the exclusiveness of the male-female sexual bond
in marriage, the primacy of family attachments, the expectation of children,
economic security for women and children, the obligation among family

members for mutual support in crises, the acceptance of sex-determined roles within the family, and the prolongation of childhood. There was as well a linkage to bourgeois values of hard work, delayed gratification, and self-imposed restraints on personal behavior. The bourgeois nuclear family certainly never extended to a majority of American households. But like any social or cultural norm, it stood into the twentieth century as the ideal form of American family life, as the measure of normality or deviance, and as the mark of responsibility and respectability. It drew support from most other American social institutions – including law, government, organized religion, neighborhood, the media (such as it was) and the educated elite.

The American nuclear family first ran into trouble during the late nineteenth century, as evidenced in rapidly rising (although still relatively low) divorce figures and falling fertility. A retreat from parenthood grew more evident in the interwar period, primarily in the form of a significant rise in childless marriages. This apparent decline of family life led to the pessimistic sociological formulations of the 1930s which described the family's loss of function and approaching demise.

The post-1945 era, however, witnessed a remarkable and totally unexpected surge of familism and re-emergence of the belief that a family was incomplete without children. Fueled by the flood of GIs returning home to build normal lives, the period was marked by a dramatic rise in the marriage rate, a downward movement in average marriage age, swelling fertility among the married, increasing remarriage, and even higher fertility among the remarried. Sociologists now gave optimistic, supportive assessments of American family life. Capping this genre was William Goode's *World Revolution and Family Patterns*, which argued (with a heady dose of New Frontierism) that the "conjugal family" found in the industrial West – and linked to an ideology first shaped by Protestant asceticism – was the emerging norm among virtually all developing peoples.

...TO "THREE'S COMPANY"

In the mid-1960s, however, the nuclear family came under sustained ideological attack. The New Left revived the Marxist critique of the bourgeois family, viewing it as predicated on property relations, male supremacy, and the boredom of domestic bliss. Bourgeois marriage represented the crassest prostitution of both men and women and the domestic slavery of wives. Inspired by Friedrich Engels, the left stressed the relationship between heightened sexuality and the approaching demise of bourgeois family values. Unrestrained sexual intercourse and "true" sexual love demanded the dissolution of the "home," the transformation of housekeeping into a social industry, the collectivization of child care and education, and elimination of the concept of "illegitimacy."

For their part, radical minority spokesmen derided the "racist cultural imperialism" of the white middle class in imposing its family norms and supposedly alien morality on blacks, Hispanics, Native Americans, and other ethnic groups. Feminists drew on the Marxist analysis, arguing that the purpose of the family had been to secure men's ownership of women and children and to sustain male domination over women deprived of any life other than a restraining and debilitating motherhood. "Populationists" resurrected the Malthusian fear of resource shortages and economic decline arising from overpopulation, and opened their assault on the reproductive energies of the nuclear family. Casting parenthood in a negative or, at best, ambivalent role, they argued for "micro" or "childfree" families to save the world from disaster.

In face of this onslaught, institutions once sustaining the nuclear-family norm either proved crippled themselves, or deserted to the other side. Remnant white ethnic groups, which once served a supportive function for families in European immigrant communities, came under regular government and media attack during the 1960s as racist and reactionary. Minority groups found their destinies tied to federal power and the schemes of intellectuals. Neighborhood communities were broken apart by federal urban-renewal and housing programs, and by court-ordered busing.

Many churches, once supportive centers of nuclear family life, shifted ground. By the early 1970s, liberal Protestant and Jewish groups had abandoned many traditional moral and social precepts, including normative support for the nuclear family. For instance, a panel representing one large Protestant body affirmed in 1976 that "there is a diversity of types or forms of family existing in modern American society." Defining family as "a relationship community of more than one person," its list of variant forms includes two-parent, one-parent, childless, parentless, and "single persons" families. The traditional family norm found occasional support and sustenance only among culturally-derided Roman Catholic, Mormon, and scattered evangelical Protestant and orthodox Jewish groups.

The media, attracted to protest and evidence of unsettling change, wandered from the nuclear-family norm it had supported in the 1950s. Documentaries probed the failings and pathologies of the American family. Newscasts riveted attention on the New Left, youth culture, minority protests, and the dissolution of old values. *Father Knows Best, Leave It to Beaver*, and *I Love Lucy* gave way to *One Day At a Time, Three's Company*, and *Miss Winslow and Son*.

The corporate world followed the lure of money and struck its Faustian bargain with the anti-nuclear-family cause. Large corporations proceeded to publish books and magazines, press records, produce motion pictures, and sponsor television shows that struck at the heart of middle-class family values.

Legal institutions began to be reshaped. Research showed that most state marriage laws presumed lifelong commitment, a first marriage, procreation as an essential element of marriage, some division of labor in the family, middle-class status, and the Judeo-Christian ideal of a monogamous, heterosexual union. Stripped of their normative character—and portrayed as elements of bourgeois cultural imperialism—these family laws came under challenge; many have already been changed. In its 1973 *Roe* and *Doe* decisions, the U.S. Supreme Court struck down existing state abortion statutes that sustained the bourgeois belief in the sanctity of prenatal infant life. The Court's 1976 *Danforth* decision denied that abortion was in any sense a "family issue" and prohibited interference by a husband, or by a parent of a minor, with the absolute right of a woman to undergo an abortion during the initial three months of pregnancy.

THE DESERTION BY THE PROFESSIONALS

The abandonment of the nuclear-family norm was most dramatic among family counselors, social workers, and sociologists. Articles appearing in the mid-1960s exposed and critically dissected the nuclear-family mythology encrusting family sociology and family counseling. Authors termed this mythology dangerous, arguing that because it served as the standard used by marriage and family counselors in judging family health it led to culturally biased advice. Starting in the late 1960s, a veritable flood of sociological books and essays attacked all aspects of middle-class family life. One searches in vain during this period for an authoritative voice defending the rapidly collapsing nuclear-family norm.

Revealing evidence of desertion from the old normative family concept comes from a comparison of successive editions of family-sociology textbooks. Those published before 1972 continue to view the middle-class nuclear family as the American norm. Those appearing after 1972 abandon normative concepts altogether.

For instance, Ira Reiss's 1971 text, *The Family System in America*, stresses the continuity and stability of the nuclear-family model, which he terms a system undergoing only "moderate change," not radical transition. The nuclear-family norm forms the book's ordering principle, and is used to identify deviant behavior such as premarital pregnancy and homosexuality. Reiss then saw the rest of the world as moving toward the American model.

In his 1976 edition (revealingly pluralized as *Family Systems in America*), however, Reiss emphasizes that "choices in all stages of the family are now legitimate far beyond what they were just five or ten years ago." The nuclear family no longer serves as the ordering principle of his text. In fact, there are no longer any family norms: "We are now involved in a society with a variety of life styles that necessitates that people be able to feel that their life style is proper to them, even though it may not be a proper life style for other people."

Bert Adams, in his 1971 text, *The American Family: A Sociological Interpretation*, essentially describes an American nuclear-family norm that, "[b]arring a major historical upheaval . . . is likely to persist over the next generation." Such an upheaval apparently occurred, for his 1976 edition,

The Family: A Sociological Interpretation, stresses alternatives to the old nuclear family and the need for personal choice of an appropriate family life style.

Gerald Leslie, in his 1967 edition of *The Family in Social Context*, clearly states that the "white, Anglo-Saxon, Protestant, middle-class family is a kind of prototype for the larger society. . . . Its patterns are "ideal" patters for much of the non-white, non-Anglo, non-Protestant, non-middle-class segment of the population. . . . In twentieth-century America, however, *an increasing proportion of the population is achieving the ideal*" (emphasis added). Among the values found in this ideal family are: marriage as the dominant life goal for men and women; marriage based on love and free choice; the expectation that marriage should produce happiness for both partners; the belief that life has much to offer the young; the idea that childhood should be protected and prolonged; the confinement of sexual relations to marriage; the belief that husbands and wives have some traditional roles to play; and the idea that individual fulfillment should be sought in family living. This family model is clearly the classic bourgeois family.

Yet Leslie's 1976 edition not only discards the "middle class" family as the cultural norm (he finds it rejected by, among others, blacks, Chicanos, Indians, and Jews who are fighting "forced cultural homogenization"), but even attributes new values to the middle-class family that are radically different from those in his 1967 list. These are: equality of the sexes, including a flexible division of tasks between men and women; democracy in all status and power roles among and between parents and children; permissive, person-centered mate selection, including free sexual experimentation for youth and the right of men and women to enjoy sex, including premarital liaisons; a strong emphasis on sexual and conjugal companionship, tied to continuing functions such as child bearing, socialization, and economic cooperation; the professionalization of marriage and parental roles, including counseling and classes on marriage, childbirth, and parenthood; and a turn to divorce if counseling and classes fail.

Given the startling changes to be found in sociology textbooks, one might assume that the number of nuclear families fell dramatically in this period. But the proportion of nuclear families relative to all households in fact remained relatively steady through 1970. Prevailing family structures were not radically altered; but *the normative concept of the nuclear family*—attacked from many sides in the 1960s and abandoned by most theretofore supporting institutions—effectively collapsed in the early 1970s.

Cultural and social norms provide a civilization with its ordering principles, its measures of morality and deviance, and its legacy to subsequent generations. They define for individuals the nature of responsibility, the ultimate purposes of social life, and the proper basis for human relationships. Nuclear families, now deprived of such a normative nature and the support thereby entailed, have fallen progressively into disarray.

In place of the nuclear family, the dominant voices in sociology and family-counseling professional journals are now describing the emergence of new normative concepts to define acceptable family life in the post-bourgeois era. While varying their emphases, such professionals cite certain values with regularity:

1. *Mutability.* There are no constants in moral questions nor in personal relationships.

2. *Choice.* There should be no bias toward marriage and children. Everything is open. All habitual and cultural attitudes may be question-ed. All values are on trial.

3. *Experimentation.* Since there are no family or sexual norms, no tradi-tions worthy of universal emulation, and no restraints, persons must be free to experiment with a variety of sexual partners and practice to find the sexual and family life styles appropriate for themselves.

4. *Self-fulfillment.* Morality demands freedom for people to realize their own potentials—and their own needs, desires, and taste—with a minimum of social rules and regulations. Relationships should last only so long as they are mutually self-fulfilling.

5. *Uninhibited Sexuality.* Sexual gratification represents one of life's ultimate values. Access to regular sexual satisfaction should be viewed as a basic human right. There is no true humanness devoid of sexuality.

6. *The Problem of Children.* Sexuality used be viewed as totally separated from procreation. Parenthood should be undertaken only after a careful weighing of social, cultural, and economic costs. The burden of social proof is shifted away from the right of persons to remain "childfree" to question-ing the right of persons to procreate. Given the problem of overpopulation, reproduction may have to be viewed as a privilege granted by a govern-ment working towards the goals of decreasing the quantity while increas-ing the quality of humankind. unwanted pregnancies should be aborted.

In sum, any human relationship involving cohabitation that produces self-gratification and sexual fulfillment has some claim to valid family status. "Human actualizing" contracts, progressive monogamy, group mar-riage, polyandry, polygyny, communal arrangements, homosexual pairings, open marriage (involving group sex, swinging, or revolving mates), heterosexual and nonmonogamous cohabitation, "singlehood," *and* the old nuclear family, are all legitimate family "life styles." "Immorality" in sex-ual matters or "deviance" in family structure have become empty concepts.

Such new values are supported by and particularly evident among elements of the college-educated upper-middle class. While reassuring voices are correct in arguing that most Americans still live in traditional nuclear families, post-bourgeois family norms are starting to make a statistical dent. In 1970, for instance, there were 1,046,000 unmarried adults sharing living quarters with one person of the opposite sex; by 1977, the figure had swelled to 1.9 million. While such households still form only 2 per cent of all "couple households," the 12 per cent figure now found in Sweden may suggest the immediate American future.

THE HELPING HAND THAT HARMS

American family life is being fundamentally altered by two forces: from within, by the impact of the "second" sex revolution on male-female ties and on the linkage of generations; and from without, by the cultural abandonment of the nuclear-family norm and the normative embrace of amoral family and sexual ethics by elements of the educated upper-middle class. Even if a majority of Americans thought it desirable, a democratic government could not check or reverse these trends. On the one hand, the state cannot undo the sex revolution. It might as easily try to reverse the Industrial Revolution or any other nexus of social change that has substantially altered our national evolution. On the other hand, while the government of a free people may reflect a social norm and give it legal recognition and support, it cannot create such a standard, nor long sustain a normative concept devoid of cultural recognition.

Nor will state intervention on behalf of families succeed. Full-employment policies might achieve sound economic goals, and a national health-insurance program could democratize the provision of health care. Daycare subsidies would certainly ease the financial costs of single-parent or two-earner families and free more women for paid labor. Family allowances might help many children, and legal reforms could secure more legally enforceable rights for families and children. *But these measures will not strengthen families.*

The results, in fact, would probably be the opposite. In his review of Soviet attempts to strengthen family life in the Stalinist era, Lewis A. Coser was led to the conclusion that the state, by its very interference in the lives of citizens, must necessarily undermine the parental authority it seeks to restore. Recent research on the effects of Sweden's 1937 marriage-loan act— which was intended to encourage earlier marriage and more children per family—shows that the couples participating had *fewer* children than the unbenefited control population. And while defensive explanations abound, the fact remains that U.S. Department of Health, Education and Welfare experiments with income-maintenance programs have seen divorce, separation, and desertion figures significantly higher among families receiving a guaranteed federal income than among control families receiving no

benefits. *The disconcerting reality appears to be that state social intervention on behalf of families actually weakens or destroys families.*

Harvard sociologist Carle Zimmerman concluded his massive 1947 study
on the relationship of family and civilization by predicting that the final
collapse of the traditional Western family would occur before the end of
this century. "The results," he added, "will be much more drastic in the
United States because being the most extreme and inexperienced of the
aggregates of Western civilization, it will take its first real 'sickness' most
violently."

Can this reckoning be avoided? Viable family life may somehow survive
in a normative vacuum. Or, echoing the experience of the 1950s, certain
bourgeois family values—now enjoying something of an underground existence in little-noticed movements such as La Leche League
International—might re-emerge as normative guides. Or, a new legitimate
ordering principle for family life could evolve. The one certainty, though,
is that the liberal family-policy agenda cannot overcome—for in some ways
it actually reflects—the shallowness and confusion of prevailing cultural
norms and the personal hedonism dominating American life.

FOOTNOTE

[1] The political strategy being followed by American family-policy advocates
has historical precedents. European social democrats have regularly used "family policy" as a potent argument, attracting conservative backing for a variety
of welfare-policy proposals designed to save the family from dissolution or sterility.
Swayed by the pro-natalist arguments of the 1942 Beveridge report, a number
of British Conservatives lent their support to social-welfare policies such as
children's allowances and creation of a national health service. They hoped such
measures would stabilize family life, raise the United Kingdom's birth rate, and
continue to people the Commonwealth with British stock. When Alva and Gun-
nar Myrdal advanced a sweeping pro-natalist family policy in 1934 that involved the socialist reconstruction of Swedish society, even the veteran conservative
economist Gustav Cassel had to acknowledge the strength of their arguments
and the need for some state intervention to support families.

Part

Ten

The Future

Outlook

Each of the preceding segments of this book has dealt with a specific family-related issue that is to one degree or another a point of contention in our society. This final section departs somewhat from the format of the preceding parts in that considerations concerning the future are not really issues confronting the family. However, there are a few ways in which the future of the family might be considered a social issue. First, it might be an issue because of the fact that often there are heard, from various sources of public comment, statements to the effect that the family is disintegrating or disappearing. The source of these types of comments most often is the political stump or the pastoral pulpit, but because such statements usually either are ignored or go unanswered, no real social issue is created on this topic. Another way in which the future of the family might be seen as an issue is within what broadly might be called the field of family studies. Among that group of sociologists, psychologists, lawyers, and doctors who refer to themselves as family specialists, there has been a continuing debate over the types of organization and structure families might assume in the future. However, because this debate is very cool and academic in nature, it could hardly be seen as a full-blown issue, even within the family field. Furthermore,

there is very little argument over the various views that are expressed; rather, experts simply present their own speculations without
a great deal of agreement or disagreement from other professionals
in the field.

But as to the future of the family, there rarely are any significant
political, legislative, or moral confrontations relating specifically to
the subject. Thus, there will be no attempt to present this topic as
an issue, but instead two articles will be presented that speak of the
future of the family in light of some of the issues dealt with earlier.
However, because the concern of this section is the future, it might
be appropriate to summarize a few speculations about the outcome
of each of these previously discussed issues.

On the issue of marriage versus nonmarriage, it appears likely that
marriages will continue at a pace approximating the current high
rate. Although the marriage rate declined steadily for several years
through 1976, it again increased into the 1980s, and has remained
stable to the present time. Not only will most young people continue
to marry, the rate of remarriage among the older widowed and divorced probably will continue to be high, although this rate also has
shown some recent fluctuations. The preferred form of marriage will
continue to be monogamy for almost everyone, both legally and otherwise. Experiments with communes and group marriages have essentially disappeared. There will, however, be some reinstitution of the
common-law marriage as some of the states attempt to register and
regulate informal living-together arrangements. With the failure
of most attempts to change the structure of marriage, experimentation probably will be more along the lines of developing informal,
less structured types of variations of intimate relationships and
developing family networks that approximate the earlier extended
family.

It is hard to predict whether or not the issues surrounding cohabitation will be clarified or resolved quickly. Both behavior and attitudes
in this matter still are in a state of flux and could remain so for
several years. However, present indications are that cohabitation will
continue to be viewed with disdain by the older generations, while
being accepted increasingly by the younger ones. On the other hand,
as the picture clarifies, there also could be a sort of backlash against

this behavior by young people, especially if it comes to be seen as a type of exploitation on the part of one sex by the other.

There is little doubt that significant shifts have occurred in the definitions of men's and women's roles, not only within the family, but in the larger society as well. And more changes likely will occur. What began as "women's liberation" soon broadened its concern to sexual equality in a more general sense, with the involvement of men in the movement. We seem to be now in the midst of a society-wide effort to clarify the definitions of the roles of both men and women in all spheres of life. Men's involvement in sexual equality, however, is somewhat bifurcated. That is, some male activities oriented toward the enhancement of male roles are an outgrowth of and an integral part of the women's movement. On the other hand, there is increasing evidence of a sort of backlash by some men against the gains women have made through such programs as affirmative action, which are seen by some as giving women, as well as other minority groups, an unfair advantage. These differing orientations to the issues of sexual equality have produced some conflict, and could produce more in the future, but it is difficult to know for sure just what will develop.

Predictions concerning parenthood and nonparenthood were made in the commentary beginning Part Four, but to summarize, it appears that at least for those young couples who marry in the next decade, families will be smaller by one or two children than families in the previous two decades. The average family will have two children, whereas many will have only one and some will have none. In this regard, the status of nonparenthood will be further legitimized as more young couples follow that course.

In the area of childbearing alternatives, the issues have not yet been defined clearly. It even could develop that no real division will occur in the feelings and attitudes of the public on the ethical and other problems related to some of these possibilities. However, given the rather unusual nature of some of these alternatives, as well as the possibility of even more bizarre technological advances in the near future, it seems highly likely that some controversies will emerge.

Given the Supreme Court's 1973 decision and subsequent lower court decisions on the right to abortion, it had been expected that those individuals and organizations opposed to freedom of choice in abortion would cease to clamor over this issue. However, this has not occurred; they simply have broadened the battlefront. They have begun to work in the lower Federal and state courts and the state legislatures, as well as in the Congress. To this point, however, the victories of the anti-abortion forces have been few and far between, and the increasing public opinion in favor of freedom of choice likely will make their path an even harder one to pursue.

Almost every state now has passed some kind of divorce reform legislation, although in many cases the reforms are piecemeal, not really dealing with the significant issues related to the adversary system and to sex discrimination, particularly in the areas of property settlements and child custody. Attention has now turned to the problems that people encounter after divorce, problems of the single-parent family and the reconstituted family. There is a good possibility that many of the problems these types of families have will be alleviated, at least partly, as we begin to know more about their situations.

Because there is such tremendous pressure, coming especially from working women, to do something about the childcare problem, it is likely that the immediate future will see significant experiments designed to provide relief for this need. Nevertheless, concern will continue as to what is best for children—being placed in daycare or having their mothers stay home to care for them. This question could become the center of future debate.

The childcare issue is often dealt with as a separate issue in its own right, but it is also a significant part of the larger family-policy debate. It is likely that not only childcare, but many of the other issues will increasingly be brought under the umbrella of family policy, because our society is becoming more sensitive to the needs and problems of families as they are affected by various policies and programs. Disputes in this area could become bitter, but I feel that such disputes could ultimately be very healthy for the family.

The first of the two articles in this section, "The American Family in the Year 2000," was written by two outstanding specialists in the study of the American family. Their predictions about the nature of marriage and family life at the beginning of the next century center around ideas of diversity. They see continued high divorce rates, with more single-parent and reconstituted families. Otherwise, they predict no radical departures from present marital and family norms and practices.

The final article closes out the book with a survey report. In 1973, *Better Homes and Gardens* reported on a survey of over 300,000 of its readers concerning the state of the American family. A few years later, the magazine conducted another survey that repeated many of the questions raised in the earlier one, but that was considerably more comprehensive. The second report, presented here, deals with the attitudes and opinions of what might be considered a "middle-class" sample of the population. However, because it is such a large sample, it certainly should be considered as somewhat representative of the bulk of the population. In spite of the fact that the data for this report is almost ten years old, recent similar studies continue to come to the same conclusions.

One of the general findings of the survey is that things really might not be as bad as many in our society think they are. Large numbers think the family is in trouble, but when asked about their own situation, the large majority believe they themselves are in pretty good shape. The article might be summarized as saying that the greatest thing wrong with the American family today is that everyone thinks there is a great deal wrong with the American family today. That the family is in trouble is perhaps just one more of the many myths that plague our society. In fact, one of the purposes guiding the selection of all articles for this book, along with the commentary accompanying each section, has been to demonstrate that there is good reason to be optimistic about the future of marriage and the family in American society.

29.

The American Family in the Year 2000

Andrew Cherlin and Frank F. Furstenberg, Jr.

• At current rates, half of all American marriages begun in the early 1980s will end in divorce.

• The number of unmarried couples living together has more than tripled since 1970.

• One out of four children is not living with both parents.

The list could go on and on. Teen-age pregnancies: up. Adolescent suicides: up. The birthrate: down. Over the past decade, popular and scholarly commentators have cited a seemingly endless wave of grim statistics about the shape of the American family. The trends have caused a number of concerned Americans to wonder if the family, as we know it, will survive the twentieth century.

And yet, other observers ask us to consider more positive developments:

• Seventy-eight per cent of all adults in a recent national survey said they get "a great deal" of satisfaction from their family lives; only 3 per cent said "a little" or "none."

• Two-thirds of the married adults in the same survey said they were "very happy" with their marriages; only 3 per cent said "not too happy."

• In another recent survey of parents of children in their middle years, 88 per cent said that if they had to do it over, they would choose to have children again.

• The vast majority of the children (71 per cent) characterized their family life as "close and intimate."

Reprinted, with permission, from *The Futurist*, published by the World Future Society, 4916 St. Elmo Ave., Bethesda, Maryland, 20814.

Family ties are still important and strong, the optimists argue, and the predictions of the demise of the family are greatly exaggerated.

Neither the dire pessimists who believe that the family is falling apart nor the unbridled optimists who claim that the family has never been in better shape provide an accurate picture of family life in the near future. But these trends indicate that what we have come to view as the "traditional" family will no longer predominate.

DIVERSE FAMILY FORMS

In the future, we should expect to see a growing amount of diversity in family forms, with fewer Americans spending most of their life in a simple "nuclear" family consisting of husband, wife, and children. By the year 2000, three kinds of families will dominate the personal lives of most Americans: families of first marriages, single-parent families, and families of remarriages.

In first-marriage families, both spouses will be in a first marriage, frequently begun after living alone for a time or following a period of cohabitation. Most of these couples will have one, two, or, less frequently, three children.

A sizable minority, however, will remain childless. Demographer Charles F. Westoff predicts that about one-fourth of all women currently in their childbearing years will never bear children, a greater number of childless women than at any time in U.S. history.

One other important shift: in a large majority of these families, both the husband and the wife will be employed outside the home. In 1940, only about one out of seven married women worked outside the home; today the proportion is one out of two. We expect this proportion to continue to rise, although not as fast as it did in the past decade or two.

SINGLE-PARENT FAMILIES

The second major type of family can be formed in two ways. Most are formed by a marital separation, and the rest by births to unmarried women. About half of all marriages will end in divorce at current rates, and we doubt that the rates will fall substantially in the near future.

When the couple is childless, the formerly married partners are likely to set up independent households and resume life as singles. The high rate of divorce is one of the reasons why more men and women are living in single-person households than ever before.

But three-fifths of all divorces involve couples with children living at home. In at least nine out of ten cases, the wife retains custody of the children after a separation.

Although joint custody has received a lot of attention in the press and in legal circles, national data show that it is still uncommon. Moreover, it is likely to remain the exception rather than the rule because most ex-spouses can't get along well enough to manage raising their children together. In fact, a national survey of children aged 11 to 16 conducted by one of the authors demonstrated that fathers have little contact with their children after a divorce. About half of the children whose parents had divorced hadn't seen their father in the last year; only one out of six had managed to see their father an average of once a week. If the current rate of divorce persists, about half of all children will spend some time in a single-parent family before they reach 18.

Much has been written about the psychological effects on children of living with one parent, but the literature has not yet proven that any lasting negative effects occur. One effect, however, does occur with regularity: women who head single-parent families typically experience a sharp decline in their income relative to before their divorce. Husbands usually do not experience a decline. Many divorced women have difficulty re-entering the job market after a long absence; others find that their low-paying clerical or service-worker jobs aren't adequate to support a family.

Of course, absent fathers are supposed to make child-support payments, but only a minority do. In a 1979 U.S. Bureau of the Census survey, 43 per cent of all divorced and separated women with children present reported receiving child-support payments during the previous year, and the average annual payment was about $1,900. Thus, the most detrimental effect for children living in a single-parent family is not the lack of a male presence but the lack of a male income.

FAMILIES OF REMARRIAGES

The experience of living as a single parent is temporary for many divorced women, especially in the middle class. Three out of four divorced people remarry, and about half of these marriages occur within three years of the divorce.

Remarriage does much to solve the economic problems that many single-parent families face because it typically adds a male income. Remarriage also relieves a single parent of the multiple burdens of running and supporting a household by herself.

But remarriage also frequently involves blending together two families into one, a difficult process that is complicated by the absence of clear-cut ground rules for how to accomplish the merger. Families formed by remarriages can become quite complex, with children from either spouse's previous marriage or from the new marriage and with numerous sets of grandparents, stepgrandparents, and other kin and quasi-kin.

The divorce rate for remarriage is modestly higher than for first marriages, but many couples and their children adjust successfully to the remarriage and, when asked, consider their new marriage to be a big improvement over their previous one.

THE LIFE COURSE: A SCENARIO

FOR THE NEXT TWO DECADES

Because of the recent sharp changes in marriage and family life, the life course of children and young adults today is likely to be far different from what a person growing up earlier in this century experienced. It will not be uncommon, for instance, for children born in the 1980s to follow this sequence of living arrangements: live with both parents for several years, live with their mothers after their parents divorce, live with their mothers and stepfathers, live alone for a time when in their early twenties, live with someone of the opposite sex without marrying, get married, get divorced, live alone again, get remarried, and end up living alone once more following the death of the spouses.

Not everyone will have a family history this complex, but it is likely that a substantial minority of the population will. And many more will have family histories only slightly less complex.

Overall, we estimate that about half of the young children alive today will spend some time in a single-parent family before they reach 18; about nine out of ten will eventually marry; about one out of two will marry and then divorce; and about one out of three will marry, divorce, and then remarry. In contrast, only about one out of six women born in the period 1910 to 1914 married and divorced and only about one in eight married, divorced, and remarried.

Without doubt, Americans today are living in a much larger number of family settings during their lives than was the case a few generations ago.

The life-course changes have been even greater for women than for men because of the far greater likelihood of employment during the childbearing years for middle-class women today compared with their mothers and grandmothers. Moreover, the increase in life expectancy has increased the difference between men's and women's family lives. Women now tend to outlive men by a wide margin, a development that is new in this century. Consequently, many more women face a long period of living without a spouse at the end of their lives, either as a widow or as a divorced person who never remarried.

Long-lived men, in contrast, often find that their position in the marriage market is excellent, and they are much more likely to remain married (or remarried) until they die.

CONVERGENCE AND DIVERGENCE

The family lives of Americans vary according to such factors as class, ethnicity, religion, and region. But recent evidence suggests a convergence among these groups in many features of family life. The clearest example is in childbearing, where the differences between Catholics and non-

Catholics or between Southerners and Northerners are much smaller than they were twenty years ago. We expect this process of convergence to continue, although it will fall far short of eliminating all social class and subcultural differences.

The experiences of blacks and whites also have converged in many respects, such as in fertility and in patterns of premarital sexual behavior, over the past few decades. But with respect to marriage, blacks and whites have diverged markedly since about 1960.

Black families in the United States always have had strong ties to a large network of extended kin. But in addition, blacks, like whites, relied on a relatively stable bond between husbands and wives. But over the past several decades—and especially since 1960—the proportion of black families maintained by a woman has increased sharply; currently, the proportion exceeds four in ten. In addition, more young black women are having children out of wedlock; in the late 1970s, about two out of three black women who gave birth to a first child were unmarried.

These trends mean that we must qualify our previously stated conclusion that marriage will remain central to family life. This conclusion holds for Americans in general. For many low-income blacks, however, marriage is likely to be less important than the continuing ties to a larger network of kin.

Marriage is simply less attractive to a young black woman from a low-income family because of the poor prospects many young black men have for steady employment and because of the availability of alternative sources of support from public-assistance payments and kin. Even though most black women eventually marry, their marriages have a very high probability of ending in separation or divorce. Moreover, they have lower likelihood of remarrying.

Black single-parent families sometimes have been criticized as being "disorganized" or even "pathological." What the critics fail to note is that black single mothers usually are embedded in stable, functioning kin networks. These networks tend to center around female kin—mothers, grandmothers, aunts—but brothers, fathers, and other male kin also may be active. The members of these networks share and exchange goods and services, thus helping to share the burdens of poverty. The lower-class black extended family, then, is characterized by strong ties among a network of kin but fragile ties between husband and wife. The negative aspects of this family system have been exaggerated greatly; yet it need not be romanticized, either. It can be difficult and risky for individuals to leave the network in order to try to make it on their own; thus, it may be hard for individuals to raise themselves out of poverty until the whole network is raised.

THE DISINTEGRATING FAMILY?

By now, predictions of the demise of the family are familiar to everyone. Yet the family is a resilient institution that still retains more strength than its harshest critics maintain. There is, for example, no evidence of a large-scale rejection of marriage among Americans. To be sure, many young adults are living together outside of marriage, but the evidence we have about cohabitation suggests that it is not a lifelong alternative to marriage; rather, it appears to be either another stage in the process of courtship and marriage or a transition between first and second marriages.

The so-called "alternative lifestyles" that received so much attention in the late 1960s, such as communes and lifelong singlehood, are still very uncommon when we look at the nation as a whole.

Young adults today do marry at a somewhat older age, on average, than their parents did. But the average age at marriage today is very similar to what it was throughout the period from 1890 to 1940.

To be sure, many of these marriages will end in divorce, but three out of four people who divorce eventually remarry. Americans still seem to desire the intimacy and security that a marital relationship provides.

Much of the alarm about the family comes from reactions to the sheer speed at which the institution changed in the last two decades. Between the early 1960s and the mid-1970s, the divorce rate doubled, the marriage rate plunged, the birthrate dropped from a twentieth-century high to an all-time low, premarital sex became accepted, and married women poured into the labor force. But since the mid-1970s, the pace of change has slowed. The divorce rate has risen modestly and the birthrate even has increased a bit. We may have entered a period in which American families can adjust to the sharp changes that occurred in the 1960s and early 1970s. We think that, by and large, accommodations will be made as expectations change and institutions are redesigned to take account of changing family practices.

Despite the recent difficulties, family ties remain a central part of American life. Many of the changes in family life in the 1960s and 1970s were simply a continuation of long-term trends that have been with us for generations.

The birthrate has been declining since the 1820s, the divorce rate has been climbing since at least the Civil War, and over the last half century a growing number of married women have taken paying jobs. Employment outside the home has been gradually eroding the patriarchal system of values that was a part of our early history, replacing it with a more egalitarian set of values.

The only exception occurred during the late 1940s and the 1950s. After World War II, Americans raised during the austerity of depression and war entered adulthood at a time of sustained prosperity. The sudden turnabout in their fortunes led them to marry earlier and have more children than any generation before or since in this century. Because many of us were either parents or children in the baby-boom years following the war, we tend to think that the 1950s typify the way twentieth-century families used to be. But the patterns of marriage and childbearing in the 1950s were an aberration resulting from special historical circumstances; the patterns of the 1960s and 1970s better fit the long-term trends. Barring unforeseen major disruptions, small families, working wives, and impermanent marital ties are likely to remain with us indefinitely.

A range of possible developments could throw our forecasts off the mark. We do not know, for example, how the economy will behave over the next twenty years, or how the family will be affected by technological innovations still at the conception stage. But, we do not envision any dramatic changes in family life resulting solely from technological innovations in the next two decades.

Having sketched our view of the most probable future, we will consider three of the most important implications of the kind of future we see.

GROWING UP IN CHANGING FAMILIES

Children growing up in the past two decades have faced a maelstrom of social change. As we have pointed out, family life is likely to become even more complex, diverse, unpredictable, and uncertain in the next two decades.

Even children who grow up in stable family environments will probably have to get along with a lot less care from parents (mothers in particular) than children received early in this century. Ever since the 1950s, there has been a marked and continuous increase in the proportion of working mothers whose preschool children are cared for outside the home, rising from 31 per cent in 1958 to 62 per cent in 1977. The upward trend is likely to continue until it becomes standard practice for very young children to receive care either in someone else's home or in a group setting. There has been a distinct drop in the care of children by relatives, as fewer aunts, grandmothers, or adult children are available to supplement the care provided by parents. Increasingly, the government at all levels will be pressured to provide more support for out-of-home daycare.

How are children responding to the shifting circumstances of family life today? Are we raising a generation of young people who, by virtue of their own family experiences, lack the desire and skill to raise the next generation? As we indicated earlier, existing evidence has not demonstrated that marital disruption creates lasting personality damage or instills a distinctly different set of values about family life.

Similarly, a recent review on children of working mothers conducted by the National Research Council of the National Academy of Sciences concludes:

> If there is only one message that emerges from this study, it is that parental employment in and of itself—mothers' employment or fathers' or both parents'—is not necessarily good or bad for children.

The fact that both parents work *per se* does not adversely affect the well-being of children.

Currently, most fathers whose wives are employed do little childcare. Today, most working mothers have two jobs: they work for pay and then come home to do most of the childcare and housework. Pressure from a growing number of harried working wives could prod fathers to watch less television and change more diapers. But this change in fathers' roles is proceeding much more slowly than the recent spate of articles about the "new father" would lead one to expect. The strain that working while raising a family places on working couples, and especially on working mothers, will likely make childcare and a more equitable sharing of housework prominent issues in the 1980s and 1990s.

FAMILY OBLIGATIONS

Many of the one out of three Americans who, we estimate, will enter a second marriage will do so after having children in a first marriage. Others may enter into a first marriage with a partner who has a family from a previous marriage. It is not clear in these families what obligations remain after divorce or are created after remarriage. For one thing, no clear set of norms exists specifying how people in remarriages are supposed to act toward each other. Stepfathers don't know how much to discipline their stepchildren; second wives don't know what they're supposed to say when they meet their husbands' first wives; stepchildren don't know what to call their absent father's new wife.

The ambiguity about family relations after divorce and remarriage also extends to economic support. There are no clear-cut guidelines to tell adults how to balance the claims of children from previous marriages versus children from their current marriages. Suppose a divorced man who has been making regular payments to support his two small children from a previous marriage marries a woman with children from her previous marriage. Suppose her husband isn't paying any child support. Suppose further that the remarried couple have a child of their own. Which children should have first claim on the husband's income? Legally, he is obligated to pay child support to his ex-wife, but in practice he is likely to feel that his primary obligation is to his stepchildren, whose father isn't helping, and to his own children from his remarriage.

Our guess, supported by some preliminary evidence from national studies, is that remarriage will tend to further reduce the amount of child support that a man pays, particularly if the man's new family includes children from his new wife's previous marriage or from the current marriage. What appears to be occurring in many cases is a form of "childswapping," with men exchanging an old set of children from a prior marriage for a new set from their new wife's prior marriage and from the remarriage.

Sociologist Lenore J. Weitzman provides a related example in her book *The Marriage Contract.* Suppose, she writes, a 58-year-old corporate vice president with two grown children divorces his wife to marry his young secretary. He agrees to adopt the secretary's two young children. If he dies of a heart attack the following year:

> In most states, a third to half of his estate would go to his new wife, with the remainder divided among the four children (two from his last marriage, and his new wife's two children). His first wife will receive nothing—neither survivors' insurance nor a survivors' pension nor a share of the estate—and both she and his natural children are likely to feel that they have been treated unjustly.

Since the rate of mid-life divorce has been increasing nearly as rapidly as that of divorce at younger ages, this type of financial problem will become increasingly common. It would seem likely that there will be substantial pressure for changes in family law and in income security systems to provide more to the ex-wife and natural children in such circumstances.

INTERGENERATIONAL RELATIONS

A similar lack of clarity about who should support whom may affect an increasing number of elderly persons. Let us consider the case of an elderly man who long ago divorced his first wife and, as is fairly typical, retained only sporadic contact with his children. If his health deteriorates in old age and he needs help, will his children provide it? In many cases, the relationship would seem so distant that the children would not be willing to provide major assistance. To be sure, in most instances the elderly man would have remarried, possibly acquiring stepchildren, and it may be these stepchildren who feel the responsibility to provide assistance. Possibly the two sets of children may be called upon to cooperate in lending support, even when they have had little or no contact while growing up. Currently, there are no clear guidelines for assigning kinship responsibilities in this new type of extended family.

Even without considering divorce, the issue of support to the elderly is likely to bring problems that are new and widespread. As is well known, the low fertility in the United States, which we think will continue to be low, means that the population is becoming older. The difficulties that this change in age structure poses for the Social Security system are so well known that we need not discuss them here. Let us merely note that any substantial weakening of the Social Security system would put the elderly at a great disadvantage with regard to their families, for older Americans increasingly rely on Social Security and other pensions and insurance plans to provide support. A collapse of Social Security would result in a large decrease in the standard of living among older Americans and a return to the situation prevailing a few decades ago in which the elderly were disproportionately poor.

The relations between older people and their children and grandchildren are typically close, intimate, and warm. Most people live apart from their children, but they generally live close by one or more of them. Both generations prefer the autonomy that the increased affluence of the older generation has recently made possible. Older people see family members quite often, and they report that family members are their major source of support. A survey by Louis Harris of older Americans revealed that more than half of those with children had seen them in the past day, and close to half had seen a grandchild. We expect close family ties between the elderly and their kin to continue to be widespread. If, however, the economic autonomy of the elderly is weakened, say, by a drop in Social Security, the kind of friendly equality that now characterizes intergenerational relations could be threatened.

One additional comment about the elderly: Almost everyone is aware that the declining birthrate means that the elderly will have fewer children in the future on whom they can rely for support. But although this is true in the long run, it will not be true in the next few decades. In fact, beginning soon, the elderly will have more children, on average, than they do today. The reason is the postwar baby boom of the late 1940s and 1950s. As the parents of these large families begin to reach retirement age near the end of this century, more children will be available to help their elderly parents. Once the next generation—the baby-boom children—begins to reach retirement age after about 2010, the long-term trend toward fewer available children will sharply reassert itself.

Were we to be transported suddenly to the year 2000, the families we would see would look very recognizable. There would be few unfamiliar forms—not many communes or group marriages, and probably not a large proportion of lifelong singles. Instead, families by and large would continue to center around the bonds between husbands and wives and between parents and children. One could say the same about today's families relative to the 1960s: the forms are not new. What is quite different, comparing the 1960s with the 1980s, or the 1980s with a hypothetical 2000, is the distribution of these forms.

In the early 1960s, there were far fewer single-parent families and families formed by remarriages after divorce than is the case today; and in the year 2000 there are likely to be far more single-parent families and families of remarriage than we see now. Moreover, in the early 1960s both spouses were employed in a much smaller percentage of two-parent families; in the year 2000, the percentage with two earners will be greater still. Cohabitation before marriage existed in the 1960s, but it was a frowned-upon, bohemian style of life. Today, it has become widely accepted; it will likely become more common in the future. Yet we have argued that cohabitation is less an alternative to marriage than a precursor to marriage, though we expect to see a modest rise in the number of people who never marry.

30.

What's Happening to the American Family?

Gordon G. Greer and Kate Keating

HOW'RE WE DOING? NOT SO HOT

It's obvious in the answers to our very first question that most readers are disturbed by the present state of the family.

Do you feel that family life in America is in trouble?
Yes: 76 per cent   No: 22 per cent*

We wondered what readers viewed as the greatest threats to family life. In descending order, 37 per cent said inattentive parents ("Parents don't want to be bothered anymore"); 36 per cent said the absence of religious and spiritual foundation ("Living contrary to God's laws can only lead to great unhappiness"); 21 per cent said materialism ("Necessities are confused with luxuries"); 18 per cent said financial pressure ("It drives the mother and father out of the home to work, thus leaving the raising of children to other people and turning the home into no more than a motel for an overnight stay"); and 18 per cent said divorce ("Obviously, the greatest threat to a family is having it broken up").

In their comments, many readers seemed especially distressed by the "me first" attitude they observed all around them (" 'Doing your own thing' is irresponsible and selfish"), the decline they perceive in adherence to

* Throughout this report, you might notice that the answers don't always add up to 100 per cent. This is caused in some cases by multiple answers and in others by rounding off decimal points or by omitting those respondents who "don't know" or didn't answer.

religious credos ("Man has made a mess of his life without God"), and a
widespread malaise and purposelessness they blame on a lack of worthwhile
goals ("In our family we don't really know where we're at or where we're
headed").

"People don't care enough" was a common lament. "They aren't willing
to extend themselves for one another. We don't feel deeply enough about
things—the family, the community, the inner cities, whatever—to give up
our material comforts or our security to improve them."

Or as a reader from Connecticut expressed it, "Every person who marries for any reason other than to love and to share; any person who has
a child without committing twenty years or more to the nurturing and support of that child; any teacher who does not teach; any lawyer who is incompetent; any seamstress whose seams rip; any doctor who is too busy
to heal; any clerk who is rude—all assault the community and its ability
to exist."

HOW'RE YOU DOING? I'M O.K.

In their own pursuit of happiness and satisfaction, most readers say they
put greater value on intangibles—raising kids, staying healthy, continuing to grow in mind and spirit—than on materialistic achievements, career
success, or social status. When we asked what they considered "very important" to them personally, 86 per cent said physical well-being, 77 per
cent said raising children, 65 per cent said intellectual growth, and 55 per
cent said spiritual growth. Ranked lowest of the eleven items on our list
were recognition by others (13 per cent), influence over others (9 per cent),
and social status (5 per cent). Sharing the middle ground were house and
property (37 per cent), financial achievement and salary (35 per cent), job
status and career (26 per cent), and sexual attractiveness (22 per cent).

And how are they doing? Quite well, on the whole. In only one of the
eleven areas did even a third of our respondents report dissatisfaction with
the progress they're making—39 per cent listed themselves as "not satisfied"
in the realm of intellectual growth.

Are you better off materially than your parents were? Are you happier?
Better off: Yes, better off, 71 per cent; About the same, 20 per cent; No,
worse off, 7 per cent.
Happier: Yes, happier, 48 per cent; About the same, 42 per cent; No, less
happy, 6 per cent.

Some readers said they didn't feel as happy as they should: "I love my
husband, we're very good friends, we love our son. But still there is
something missing in my life. I just don't know anymore." Others seemed
almost to purr with contentment: "After twenty-six years, if we had it to
do over, we'd do it—hopes, fears, heartaches, joys, hardships, and all. I'm
a very happy woman today. Life has been good to me. I'm thankful for what
I have."

KIDS: ARE THEY WORTH IT?

These are hard times for parents, our readers reported, but the rewards outweigh the difficulties in more than nine homes out of ten.

If you had it to do over, would you have children?
Yes: 91 per cent   No: 9 per cent

For many readers, their children are their greatest satisfaction: "They are people I like and enjoy as well as love." For a less lucky few, they seem a shattering disappointment: "Child-rearing has to be the hardest, most demanding, most worrisome task there is—I don't know what happened to joyous, fulfilling, rewarding." Some parents say that if they were starting all over again, they'd have children but perhaps fewer of them: "We have three and find each well worth the effort—but the costs of feeding, clothing, lessons, camps, and so forth, are so high that two children are the most I'd consider if we had it to do over."

When we asked what they considered the ideal number of children for their own family, 47 per cent said two; 23 per cent said three; 11 per cent said four; 8 per cent said one; 5 per cent said five or more; and 5 per cent said none.

Arguments for childlessness often were well presented: "My husband and I have tried to analyze our relationship to discover why it only improves continually (into our thirteenth year) while others are failing. One conclusion is the fact that we are childless by choice."

How do readers feel about other married couples deciding not to have children? Only 15 per cent disapprove. Another 43 per cent checked "Not my concern," and 40 per cent checked "Approve."

Asked if working parents spend enough time with their children, readers gave low marks to both sides of the family. Fathers drew a response of 86 per cent "No." Working mothers did slightly better: 72 percent "No." "I'm glad you included fathers," wrote one woman, a doctor. "I'm often asked, 'Do you think you can be a good mother and wife and be a doctor, too?' My answer is usually, 'Are you a good father, husband, and doctor, too?' "

The issue of working mothers drew trenchant comments from all sides. "In my job as an adult counselor at our community college," said one letter from Illinois, "I encounter many working mothers and student mothers. They agree that the changes made in their families because of their working status have been good. Many report that their children's schoolwork has improved because of the example they set. Many become better organized and more efficient in housekeeping because they have less time to spend on it. Their children become more independent and resourceful because they are not always under the watchful eye. The children take their house responsibilities more seriously because they learn that Mom won't be there to pick up the slack. The mothers become more aware of the quality of time they spend with their children. In general, the families seem to take each other less for granted." Equally compelling comments expressed an entirely different view: "Some of my fondest childhood memories are when I would run in the house and tell my mother all about my day. I always have been thankful that she didn't work outside the home. It has made a real difference in my life."

The importance of the mother's remaining at home depends, our readers told us, on the age of their kids. For preschool children, 88 per cent said it was important for the mother to stay home; for grade school kids, the figure dropped to 56 per cent; for junior high students, 36 per cent; and for high school youngsters, 24 per cent.

GROWING UP: THE IMPRESSIONABLE YEARS

Second only to parents themselves, television emerges in our survey as the greatest influence on the general development of children under age twelve – and by no means are all readers happy about it. ("Television is one of the worst things that ever has happened to family life. Next to that is interfering relatives.") After parents (84 per cent) and TV (48 per cent), readers see other important childhood influences as friends (40 per cent), teachers (33 per cent), church (19 per cent), organized activities – scouting, sports and so on (14 per cent), books (8 per cent), and other relatives (6 per cent). The overall effect of these forces disturbs them.

Is America a better or worse place to raise children than it was ten or fifteen years ago?

Better: 15 percent   Same: 26 percent   Worse: 58 per cent

Not that parents got particularly high marks either. Nearly two thirds of our readers (66 per cent) said parents put too much pressure on their kids to achieve, and a whopping 87 per cent think most parents are too permissive with their children – although only 26 per cent of the parents answering recognized that fault in themselves. A higher number – 33 per cent – admitted to overindulging their kids' material requests. "Doesn't everybody?" one reader remarked.

Are readers having trouble communicating with their children? Only 3 per cent of our parents said, yes, a great deal of trouble; 31 per cent said some; 49 per cent said very little; and 17 per cent said none. Many suggested that our questionnaire had helped them find out. "I thought it might interest you to know," wrote a reader from California, "that my two teenagers and I filled this out together using the majority rule law. It was surprising to us to find out how we differed on some subjects and never even had discussed them. We enjoyed doing it, and it did bring us closer to understanding one another."

THE TEEN YEARS: TRYING TIMES

"My psyche has holes in it from seeing our kids through their teens" is typical of the troubled comments this subject elicited. But, all in all, America's youngsters are judged as coping pretty well – maybe even upgrading the art of adolescence.

In your opinion, are teenagers today more qualified or less qualified to make independent value judgments than was true ten years ago?

More qualified: 37 per cent
Less qualified: 19 per cent
No change: 42 per cent

Which better prepares youngsters for the future, a strict home environment or a permissive one? No contest: strict 73 per cent, permissive only 20 per cent. But many readers touted a combination: "Too much permissiveness leaves a child so confused and undisciplined that he is not desirable in an orderly society. Too much strictness can inhibit him so that his creativity is stifled and he is afraid to show initiative – thereby limiting his potential as a contributing member of the community."

Lack of communication is a widely felt concern. Asked if teenagers share their personal problems with either parent, a sobering 42 per cent of our readers said no. Only 10 per cent said yes, with both parents; 44 per cent said mostly with the mother; and just 1 per cent said mostly with the father. "Kids who come to see me," a social worker told us, "say there is no guidance in their life and that they're making decisions they're fearful of making alone. Parents in turn tell me they're afraid to offer advice, fearful that it will be wrong or turn their kids off. The parents' values are in turmoil, so they're having a hard time advising their kids. It's a dilemma – one generation seeking advice, the other afraid and unwilling to give it."

LOVE AND MARRIAGE: WHAT IT'S ALL ABOUT

We asked a lot of questions concerning marriage in our survey, and the answers showed respondents to be more satisfied than not.

Do you and your spouse share enough interests and activities? Among all married readers, 70 per cent said "Yes."

Do you share an understanding about what you want from marriage? "Yes" said even more marrieds: 85 per cent.

Do you share personal problems? "Yes" said nine out of ten.

Do you and your spouse talk to each other enough? "Yes" said 63 per cent – and even some of the "No's" made it clear they weren't complaining: "We *never* could talk enough. There's too much to say for just one lifetime."

(There were curves on the other side, too: "Yes, we talk to each other enough. It's just that we sometimes don't listen enough.")

Do you and your spouse have enough time together? "Yes" answered 60 per cent.

Within the marriage relationship, do you have enough time to yourself? "Yes" beat "No" by four to one.

Are most of your expectations of happiness in marriage being fulfilled?
Yes: 85 per cent   No: 15 per cent

When we asked for the strongest reasons why couples stay married, love triumphed over all with a score of 43 per cent. Second came children (34 per cent), then companionship (27 per cent), security (24 per cent) and the sharing of mutual goals (20 per cent). Readers gave less importance in this regard to religion (12 per cent), the comforts of home (11 per cent), psychological dependency (11 per cent), money (6 per cent), material possessions (5 per cent), and last of all those listed, sex (4 per cent).

How important is it that a husband and wife have separate interests and activities? "Very important" said 42 per cent; "some importance" said 50 per cent; "not important" said 8 per cent. "After seven years of marriage," one reader told us, "I'm just now branching out on my own and doing things I want to do. It took me a long time to learn that you don't have to be together twenty-four hours a day." Another said, "I know of many husbands who seem to resent the fact that their wives cling to them so. It's not that they are not happy being married—just that they feel guilty if they continue with their own interests while the wife is left without anything to do. I do not believe it was intended for two people to come together in a unifying relationship of marriage just to be made exactly alike. Instead, they should complement each other."

Do you think an occasional big argument to "clear the air" helps the husband-wife relationship? "Yes" said 67 per cent.

Would you consider a decline in the husband's dominance to be beneficial or harmful to family life? "Beneficial" said 45 per cent; "harmful" said 52 per cent. But many readers gently chided us for asking such a question: "A family is a unit; there should be no dominant partner."

THE NEW WOMAN: WHO IS SHE?

If we heard it once, we must have heard it from at least one thousand women: "I'm a full-time homemaker and I'm proud of it! I love it!" And among all of our respondents 76 per cent agree that the traditional role of wife and mother as a full-time homemaker can lead to a fulfilling life.

Does this mean that readers reject the women's movement? Not at all.

**All in all, do you feel that the movement for women's rights
is a force for the better?**
Yes: 60 per cent   No: 37 per cent

The good thing, readers told us, is that women now have choices. And no stigma should attach to whatever choice they make. "Some women can fulfill their lives better by being full-time homemakers; others find working outside the home helps satisfy their own needs, so they're better able to deal with the role of wife and mother, if they choose it. Women are individuals, too."

Most objections to the movement seem to center on its tactics ("too divisive for the overall good"), particularly the tendency among some of its leaders to belittle traditional points of view: "The women's movement has some good goals, such as equal pay for equal work, but I feel the bad effect of it all has been to downgrade the role of homemaker and mother. *There is no more important job!*"

In general, we asked, has the new awareness of women's rights altered the husband-wife relationship significantly? "Yes" answered 66 per cent. For better or for worse, among the marriages you know? By nearly two to one, "good effect" beat "bad effect."

"I'm for equal rights and equal pay," one woman said, "but I still like to be treated like a lady by a gentleman."

The "new" American woman who emerges from our survey is no fiery-eyed radical set on making men knuckle under. Instead, she turns out to be the familiar "traditional" woman blessed with previously unheard-of opportunities and choices.

MONEY: WHERE DOES IT ALL GO?

As economic forecasters, the majority of respondents are cautious and sober, if not downright glum. For example, 77 per cent think the rate of inflation over the next five years will increase (only 1 per cent say it will decrease); 59 per cent consider it likely that we'll have a major economic depression in the next decade; only 2 per cent believe Social Security will provide enough money to live on when they retire; 87 per cent think the single-family home will be priced out of reach of the average American family; and as a threat to the future of family life, they rank inflation second only to moral decay.

Yet in their own financial affairs they seem to be doing all right.

**After meeting essential monthly obligations, is it possible
for your family to make regular deposits in a savings
program?**
Yes: 64 per cent   No: 35 per cent

They think it's sound financial planning to put money in a savings account (by a margin of 87 per cent to 12 per cent), but they recognize (by 55 per cent to 43 per cent) that the importance of having a large amount of money stashed away has declined for most families in recent years.

What do they consider the best hedge against inflation? The majority (69 per cent) said owning real estate. And they practice what they preach; 82 per cent own their homes.

In the way they use credit, most respondents seem prudent. Only 11 per cent regard the use of credit cards as essential (20 per cent don't use them at all), and 66 per cent believe that the ease of obtaining credit has not caused overspending problems for their family. Only 10 per cent say having credit cards and charge accounts frequently causes them to make unnecessary purchases.

Departures from this conservatism were mostly among the young: "My generation wasn't scared by the Depression the way our parents were, so a big savings account isn't as important to us. We're accustomed to traveling and spending money."

THE ELDERLY: SANS EVERYTHING

Nowhere did respondents show more sadness or guilt than when describing what they saw as the neglect of America's elderly and their underutilization as a vital human resource. "Do you think it's important for a child's development that he or she have contact with the elderly?" The answer was a resounding 96 per cent "Yes." But *do* most children have enough contact with the elderly? This time it was a resounding 87 per cent "No."

Do you think the elderly are generally forgotten by their families?
Yes: 72 per cent   No: 27 per cent

A common observation was nicely phrased in a letter from Utica: "The elderly are not forgotten in thought, but the time actually spent with them is short."

Older people themselves did little complaining. Indeed, of those age sixty-five and over, only 64 per cent answered the above question "Yes"–a significantly lower figure than that of any other age group. Sometimes the problems of aging appear more fearful from a distance. "It scares me to see myself lonely and forgotten," wrote a woman who gave her age as between eighteen and twenty-four. "That's why I volunteer at the psychiatric hospital and visit with the older patients. I just hope someone will reciprocate when I grow old."

One question on this subject split right in half: Where is the best place for aging parents no longer capable of living alone? Half the respondents said "Retirement or nursing home"; the other 50 per cent said "With their children."

The comments on this question were particularly poignant, obviously inspired by intense inner conflicts and the weight of emotional debts too enormous to repay. "I've worked in a nursing home and vowed I never would see my parents in a home like that," one young woman told us. "Even the good ones can't supply the love and care that a family can. My parents cared for my needs as a child, so I should do the same for them if they need it. I realize that saying and doing are two different things. I only hope to be able to live up to my ideals."

Not everyone of good intent is successful, of course: "I think it's wonderful when three or more generations can share the same household. However, my husband's grandmother lived with us for ten months and it didn't work."

Even apparent success can exact an extremely high toll: "My husband's ninety-one-year-old father has lived with us for the past five years at our invitation, and we wouldn't have it any other way. But when we no longer are able to maintain a home for ourselves, we are going to try at almost any cost to avoid living with our children."

In any case, the agony of decision is acute, the choice among the toughest a son or daughter ever faces. "The question can't be answered until a person has been through it. The reversal of roles—now I make the decision for Mom and Dad, when all my life it was the other way around—is terrible!"

SEX: TOO MUCH, TOO SOON?

A comparison with the results of our first family survey, which was published in 1972, shows that attitudes toward sex have relaxed since that time. For example, when we asked readers six years ago if they would approve or disapprove of two people living together for a while before making the commitment of marriage, 26 per cent said "Approve." That figure has now risen to 41 per cent.

But this is no wild embrace of the sexual revolution, no headlong rejection of responsible behavior. On the question of living together, only 22 per cent approve when the arrangement is a substitute for marriage rather than a prelude to it, and even those who approve often insist on a mature relationship: "Living together is a cheap cop-out when it's simply 'playing house.' "

"I don't like the idea of my children living with someone," another reader said, "but neither would I approve of their rushing blindly into a marriage. To say it is not my concern is dodging the issue. Perhaps the best answer is that it depends on the maturity of the individuals."

Premarital sex also was viewed realistically. Although a majority of readers (57 per cent) disapprove of premarital intercourse, 80 per cent believe that birth control methods and information nevertheless should be available to anyone—including unmarried teenagers. "I don't condone promiscuity," reasons one reader, "but withholding information on birth control doesn't help. And there are already too many unwed parents and unwanted kids.".

Is there too much emphasis on sex in all aspects of our society today?
Yes: 84 per cent   No: 15 per cent

Some readers told us sex isn't all that important: "If couples would spend more time in conversation and less in bed before marriage, they would make more rational choices in their selection of a person to spend their life with."

Others are offended by the tasteless distortions of sex: "I'm not a prude, but I'm sick and tired of being hit in the face with pornographic material in drugstores, shopping malls, bookstores, theaters, and on TV and record albums. How can children be expected to maintain high standards in a world cluttered by trash?"

DIVORCE: FIGHT OR FLEE?

Nobody feels very good about divorce, but most respondents accept it as sometimes the lesser of two evils. "Take it from me," one reader remarked, "it's better to come from a broken home than to live in one."

Do you think it's right or wrong for a couple who simply can't get along to get a divorce?
When no children are involved:
Right: 84 per cent   Wrong: 12 per cent
When children are involved:
Right: 75 per cent   Wrong: 22 per cent

Most readers who added comments lined up on two sides: "better to get divorced than to live together in misery" versus "quitting never solves anything." Of course, there were many less adamant remarks, too: "Sometimes the most loving solution to an unhappy marriage that has disintegrated because the lines of communication have been cut off is to divorce and give each other a chance to find a more fulfilling relationship. But this should not be done without much soul-searching and honest evaluation of the marriage."

We asked what readers considered the main reasons for failed marriages. Immaturity finished highest, checked by 61 per cent. Next came selfishness (51 per cent), followed by changes in or lack of mutual interests and goals (44 per cent), financial problems (41 per cent), third-party entanglements (24 per cent), personality conflicts (22 per cent), poor sexual adjustment (16 per cent), job pressures (14 per cent), and the burden of children (10 per cent).

Whatever the particular problem, the prospect of divorce always is wrenching. "Truthfully," one reader confided, "having to raise my family without my husband, having to work to meet the financial burdens, and most of all, not to have him with us, scares the life out of me."

ABORTION: NO EASY ANSWERS

Most readers find the thought of abortion abhorrent. Yet the majority condone it under special circumstances—90 per cent if the mother's health is in danger, 84 per cent to abort a malformed fetus, 84 per cent to end a pregnancy caused by rape. For an otherwise normal unplanned pregnancy, however, only 39 per cent approve abortion for married women, 50 per cent if the woman is unmarried. Readers were nearly unanimous in their strong disapproval of abortion as a means of birth control: "The use of abortion in 'family planning' is abominable—married or unmarried."

When we made the question personal, we got somewhat different answers.

Would you consider an abortion for an unplanned pregnancy?
Yes: 34 per cent   No: 65 per cent

Many comments we received were as personal as the question. "I fully support abortion in any case," said one reader. "I was an unwanted child and it's a hell of a life." A Michigan woman had a different perspective: "To consider abortion is one thing—to go through with it is another. I have considered it but didn't go through with it. An unwanted pregnancy can and usually does turn out to be a very wanted baby." A letter from Hawaii viewed the problem from another angle: "I have worked in both a state health department and a university hospital emergency room, where I encountered many tragic cases of child abuse and neglect from parents who did not want the children or who were too young to accept the responsibility of a child. If these unspeakable crimes can be eliminated or lessened by allowing abortions, then even though the thought is repugnant to me, abortions must have a real purpose in our society." Then, too, a cry we heard often is: "Abortion is murder!"

Assume a woman chooses to have an abortion. Should her husband have the right to prevent it? The majority of women readers (51 per cent) said yes. On the other hand, the same percentage of men said no.

WORKING: JUST A GRIND?

The majority of our respondents (58 per cent) think that most other people are unhappy in their jobs. They don't show much unhappiness themselves, however.

Do you like your job?   Yes: 83 per cent   No: 12 per cent

Nor do they appear overeager to quit work at sixty-five. Only 15 per cent favor mandatory retirement at that age, and just 9 per cent think forced retirement affects family life for the better. They also reject the idea of a shorter work week (by 66 per cent to 31 per cent) if it entails a reduction in family income.

On the other hand many readers endorse split jobs: "For instance, two men could semiretire and share a single position; or two women could share a job to have time for home responsibilities as well as a career."

"Fifteen years ago," another reader told us, "my husband and I would have been delighted to each have a half-time job. He was great with kids and enjoyed being with them. I was overwhelmed by the whole business of childcare and total family responsibility and would have appreciated a chance to get out to a job and think about other things. But that kind of arrangement was an idea before its time, and so I was a full-time homemaker and my husband was a full-time breadwinner. As retirement approaches, we hope half-time positions will be available. Perhaps we could share a job with a new parent."

What about the time not spent on the job? Nearly two thirds of our respondents (65 per cent) say they spend most of their evenings and weekends doing what they want to do, as opposed to the 32 per cent who spend them on what they *have* to do. Only 18 per cent say their life is "frequently" a rat race; 67 per cent say "sometimes" and 14 per cent say "never."

THE FUTURE: WHAT NEXT?

The naive romanticism of American folklore apparently has yielded to a more realistic outlook that nonetheless is strongly laced with personal optimism. When we asked readers for their assessment of the American family's next ten years, only 18 per cent checked "Things will be better"; 33 per cent thought "Things will be worse," and the others said "Things will remain about the same"—not a particularly starry-eyed view. Yet when asked to predict their own fortunes in that decade, 53 per cent said "My life will be better," and only 3 per cent allowed as how "My life will be worse." ("My life will be the pits!" was one comment, but it was most unusual.)

Older people, of course, confront the fear of age and loneliness, and many readers added thoughtful comments on those subjects. "I don't dread growing old," a Wisconsin reader told us, "but I do worry about the financial hardships associated with old age in our country. The escalation of inflation, the devaluation of the dollar, and the meagerness of Social Security present a bleak retirement picture. The only encouraging aspect is that, by the time I reach old age, senior citizens will have a majority vote, and together, they can be a beneficial influence on the way our country is managed."

Statistically, however, other fears ranked much higher.

Are you seriously worried or fearful about any of the following?
Possible harm to or death of a loved one: 46 per cent
Debilitating disease: 32 per cent

Financial hardship: 26 per cent
Being a victim of crime: 21 per cent
Loneliness: 19 per cent
Old age: 17 per cent
Failing to reach personal goals: 16 per cent
Failing to find a meaningful purpose in life: 13 per cent
Losing your youth: 10 per cent
None of the above: 23 per cent

Other woes were seen as serious threats to family life in general: moral decay (53 per cent), inflation (41 per cent), energy shortage (41 per cent), crime (28 per cent), pollution (28 per cent), recession/depression (19 per cent), food shortage (14 per cent), changing weather patterns (10 per cent), war (9 per cent).

But even as they brooded on such ominous problems, most readers resisted the temptation to despair. Why? Because, for one thing, they have faith in the young ("There are so many outstanding young people around, the future surely has to be brighter"). For another, they show similar faith in themselves ("Our family will cope, no matter what happens"). Also as a reader from Washington put it, "There always will be a family—just as long as there is love."

Date Due